THE POLITICS OF AMERICAN FOREIGN POLICY

James Dull

University of New Haven

Prentice-Hall, Inc., Englewood Cliffs, New Jersey 07632

Library of Congress Cataloging in Publication Data

Dull, James W., (date)
  The politics of American foreign policy.

  Bibliography: p. 307
  Includes index.
  1. United States—Foreign relations—1945-
2. United States—Foreign relations administration.
I. Title.
JX1417.D85 1985   327.73   84-18207
ISBN 0-13-684291-7

Editorial/production supervision:
  Virginia McCarthy
Cover design: Wanda Lubelska Design
Manufacturing buyer: Barbara Kelly Kittle

Printed in the United States of America

10 9 8 7 6 5 4 3 2 1

ISBN 0-13-684291-7 01

Prentice-Hall International, Inc., *London*
Prentice-Hall of Australia Pty. Limited, *Sydney*
Editora Prentice-Hall do Brasil, Ltda., *Rio de Janeiro*
Prentice-Hall Canada Inc., *Toronto*
Prentice-Hall of India Private Limited, *New Delhi*
Prentice-Hall Hispanoamericana, S.A., *Mexico*
Prentice-Hall of Japan, Inc., *Tokyo*
Prentice-Hall of Southeast Asia Pte. Ltd., *Singapore*
Whitehall Books Limited, *Wellington, New Zealand*

CONTENTS

PREFACE

The threat of human extinction that has hovered over the world since the onset of the nuclear age in 1945 continues to pose the most serious challenge in history to the makers of American foreign policy and to people everywhere affected by their decisions. The needs and desires of other national states, the thrust of peoples everywhere for a better life, and the new realities created by science and technology provide Americans and their leaders with immense opportunities and awesome burdens in an epoch when the United States is the richest, most powerful, and most influential country on earth.

In view of the immense stakes involved in America's actions in the world, the need for citizens to know and to understand what is involved in shaping American foreign policy and the consequences that may result from it is greater than ever before in the nation's history. This book is an effort to acquaint Americans with many of the basic elements of foreign policy: the people who make it, the ways in which it is made, the forces affecting policy decisions, and the problems of reconciling it to the foreign policies of other countries. The book provides an eclectic and comprehensive introduction to the actors, structures, processes, beliefs, issues, and choices involved in foreign policy and foreign relations. Under the assumption that policy is most often the result of the interactions of rational and practical individuals seeking satisfaction of their goals, I have set the study of foreign policy in a political framework—as a process of political accommodation both within the American political system and between the United States and other actors in the global political system. The conflicting ambitions, pressures, demands, convictions, and solutions faced by decision makers; the wide variety of tools available to them in pursuit of national goals; and the perplexing diversity of issues in every part of the globe are matters that citizens must recognize if they are to play the responsible role in the democracy envisioned by Thomas Jefferson. Inevitably, a comprehensive treatment of so vast a subject limits the discussion of many of the subtleties and nuances of policy making and the issues confronted by policy makers. In the belief, however, that awareness of the broad panoply of American behavior in the world is necessary, we have embarked on the effort to examine as wide a range of elements as possible in the space alloted.

In part I a broad framework is sketched for the study of foreign policy and of how it functions in and responds to the global system and a world of rapid and unpredictable change.

Part II is an introduction to the actors, structures, practices, and processes involved in the formulation and implementation of foreign policy by the United States.

Part III reviews some of the major ideas, theories, philosophies, and images that are part of the belief systems of leaders, and it also looks at the personalities of leaders, the effects of decision-making groups, the distribution of power within the nation, and the nature of the state itself.

Conceiving of foreign policy in four separate tracks, I examine in some detail in part IV the impact of goals and means in the political, economic, military, and cultural realms.

Finally, in part V, I present an overview of the key issues facing American foreign policy throughout the world and make some observations about the American political process, the levels of choice facing policy makers, and the vision that Americans may wish to present to the rest of the world for pursuit of a peaceful future.

Implicit in the book is the optimism that humanity possesses the rationality and the mechanisms by which national interests can be satisfied and reconciled if all states recognize their universal community of interests.

ACKNOWLEDGMENTS

It is with considerable gratitude that I note the contributions of many people to the production of this work. First, I should like to acknowledge the University of New Haven whose support of research and unencumbered time contributed to the content and writing of the text. Every effort of this kind inevitably derives in large measure from the data, the brilliant insights, and the knowledge and experience of thousands of teachers who have provided a basis of thought. I especially want to note the support and encouragement of Roger Hilsman—teacher, scholar, statesman, and friend. Also of incalculable assistance were the efforts of those who read the text in whole or in part and provided invaluable insights and corrections. They include Bruce Cummings of the University of Washington; Caroline A. Dinegar of the University of New Haven; Lloyd Jensen of Temple University; Charles W. Kegley of the University of South Carolina; Roy E. Licklider of Douglas College; Curtis H. Martin of Merrrimack College; Harold Molineu of Ohio University; John H. Petersen of Western Kentucky University; and Stephen A. Snyder of the University of Wisconsin. Their insightful comments have strengthened the analysis, and those errors which remain are wholly the responsibility of the author.

I am deeply grateful to Stan Wakefield at Prentice-Hall for his confidence and support and to Virginia McCarthy, whose efforts at every step of production have made the job a joy.

To Frances Tomczyk and Elizabeth Allard, my appreciation for their efforts in typing the manuscript under difficult time pressures is unbounded.

Finally, the sacrifices, devotion, and love of my wife, Marguerite, are interwoven into each page and into the years of effort and the skills that went into producing this book.

CHAPTER ONE
THE PUZZLING PROCESS

The final seconds ticked off the clock—four, three, two, one—and with the sound of the final buzzer, millions of Americans, in the arena and watching television around the country, went into a frenzy of delight. It was February 1980, and the American hockey team had just defeated the Soviet Union in the winter Olympics in Lake Placid, New York, by a score of 4–3. The team went on to capture the Gold Medal. Later in the year, Americans would not participate in the summer Olympics in Moscow because President Jimmy Carter had ordered a boycott of the games in protest of the Soviet Union's military intervention in Afghanistan. In 1984 the Soviet Union responded by boycotting the summer Olympics scheduled in the United States.

In the spring of 1981 the Japanese government, responding to requests from the American government and the American automobile industry, voluntarily agreed to reduce their exports of automobiles to the United States in order to help sales in the lagging American auto industry.

In early 1981 an American pianist again won the first prize in the Tschaikowsky competition in Moscow, and Metropolitan opera star Roberta Peters returned from China, where she had conducted classes in opera singing among promising young Chinese performers.

The assassination of Egyptian president Anwar Sadat in October 1981 was the occasion for three former American presidents to travel to Egypt for the state funeral of the slain leader, and Americans began talking of increased security measures in the Sudan, which was seemingly threatened by Libya.

Earthquakes in several parts of the world in 1980 produced sizeable governmental and private efforts within the United States to provide aid to the stricken people of the devastated areas.

What do all of these events have in common? They are all part of the foreign relations and the foreign policy of Americans and their government, and they are a partial indication of the scope, variety, and importance of the role of the United States and its citizens in the world today. They sharply contradict an impression held by many Americans that foreign relations and foreign policy consist mainly of summit conferences among leaders, military threats among adversaries, or expressions of anger by governments. Foreign policy and foreign relations encompass tens of thousands of peaceful and cooperative daily transactions among governments as well as a vast volume of contacts among people of all nations that occur because it is the foreign policy of states to permit them, require them, or respond to peoples' desire for them. At the same time policy adopted by governments may create countless new opportunities for contacts among people. In short, foreign relations and foreign policy include not only the formal, legal, and informal contacts among governments but also the contacts of private citizens, businesses, clergy, professionals, artists, athletes, and many other groups whose interests operate within the international or transnational community.

Formally and legally, foreign relations and foreign policy are a matter of state. For example, one constitutional scholar, Louis Henkin, has written:

> Foreign affairs are national affairs. The United States is a single nation-state and it is the United States (not the States of the Union, singly or together) that has relations with other nations, and the United States government that conducts these relations and makes foreign policy.[1]

The state is regarded as the basic sovereign unit within the international system, and thus all of the relations in which its people engage are reflections of the policy of the state. However, there is an international life of people, which, though made possible by the state and its policy, often seems to be independent of that policy. The deep and intense impulse among people to travel, to do business, and to join in social activity exists whether the state permits it or not.

Indeed, this profound human impulse to explore, to trade, to interact with others may often induce the state to formulate or to change policy toward other states.

The reciprocal effect between American behavior, either governmental or nongovernmental, and that of other countries and people is made even more important by the fact that the United States has become the most powerful nation-state in the global system and has interests in virtually every part of the world. What happens elsewhere is often of considerable importance to Americans, and what Americans do often has a profound effect on the rest of the world.

This was not always so. Just a century ago, the United States was effectively separated from much of the world by the huge oceans, on which travel by clipper ship required several weeks. Contacts among people were largely limited to those between governments, the activities of a few businessmen, and the travels of missionaries and other clergy and a few rare tourists. Increasingly, large emigrations to the New World multiplied contacts. In the past century the telephone has made conversation possible within minutes, even seconds, anywhere in the world; travel between Europe and North America has been reduced to a little more than two hours on the Concorde; businesses based in America now operate all over the world; and 159 independent nation-states have joined the United Nations. In addition, great numbers of people have accumulated sufficient resources to visit all of the wondrous foreign places they have heard about from history books, the movies, or television.

Since 1945 changes in the patterns of social, economic, and political life resulting from developments in science, technology, industrialism, and other forces have created a more complex world than the one that existed before World War II. These changes would have occurred even if the world's two superpowers had not found themselves in the global competition called the Cold War. Vast changes, occurring with startling speed, produced not only "future shock" in the United States but also powerful new forces of human activity for which policy had to be made. Understanding how American foreign policy is made in this environment can be a mind-boggling task for statespeople or other citizens, yet the effort is necessary if we are to avoid catastrophe.

The number of actors, ideas, institutions, objectives, and tools involved in the process may confuse the student about the making of policy, but there are a number of additional complexities that must be considered. Differences between foreign policy and foreign relations have already been mentioned.

Foreign policy is the formal, legal, and authoritative expression of national interests by the government through the constitutional process of the state. *Foreign relations* are the formal and informal interactions by both governmental and nongovernmental actors with foreign states, people, and institutions. Occasionally foreign policy and private foreign relations may conflict. For example, the behavior of American corporations abroad may run counter to the policy intentions of the government of the United States, or such behavior might involve the government in matters it would rather avoid. In a world of increasing complexity and interdependence this distinction between policy and relations is not an insignificant element in studying America's role in the world.

The process includes a further distinction of which the student must be aware—the *making of policy* is not the same as the *implementation of policy*. Different parts of the system may be involved in formulating policy and in implementing it, and the wisest policy cannot possibly succeed if it is carried out poorly or not at all.

A number of additional distinctions requiring attention involve the number, scope, and types of foreign policies in which the United States is engaged. First of all, there is not *one* American foreign policy, but *many,* each designed for particular circumstances and for achieving broad national goals. Whether these varied policies contribute to achievement of these goals or serve any "grand plan," if any such plan exists, will be assessed elsewhere. Second, policies differ in importance and in the levels at which they are decided and implemented. Many issues must be decided by the president, while others can be made at a low level of the bureaucracy or by a minor official in an overseas embassy. These levels have been classified in a number of ways—high, middle, and low policy; crisis decisions and routine program-policy decisions; or on a scale including minor, routine, significant, fundamental, and critical decisions. Third, there are distinctions between foreign policy and domestic policy, although on some issues they have been rapidly disappearing in recent decades. Many domestic issues have foreign implications, and many foreign policies can have profound effects on domestic life in the United States. Fourth, the policy process operates both internally, within American government, and externally, in international affairs. Policy derives from the internal political processes in Washington, but once decided it must then be accommodated to, and integrated with, the policies of other states through the processes of diplomacy. Finally, although all foreign policies and foreign relations are political in the broadest sense, at least four different tracks or types of policies can be identified: political, economic, military, and cultural, each with its own unique impact on the achievement of the international goals of the United States. Some elaboration of this point will help clarify the distinctions.

The Political Track. Among the political relations pursued by the United States are the formal, informal, legal, and practical arrangements made by government. These may be bilateral, that is, relations between two governments, or multilateral, those among several governments acting together in alliances, treaties, blocs, markets, cartels, or international organizations with the objectives of peace or war, security or trade, or the facilitation of other contacts among people.

Customary political goals include the acquisition of statehood and independence (sovereignty), legal recognition by others, security and survival, and peace, power, and influence; some countries, including the United States, have sought in different periods such goals as hegemony or spheres of influence in which prevailing influence over other nations may be established, and some states have sought empire, i.e., the conquest, control, and political domination of other countries by force. Still other countries, among them the United States at some periods, have sought isolation and/or neutrality, the desire to avoid participation in the affairs of other countries.

The Economic Track. Economic relations include, among other things, agreements among governments on such matters as trade, aid, loans, investments, money, balances of payments and trade, and other forms of economic activity. Also found on this track are the economic objectives and activities of private citizens, corporations, and international organizations; for example, tourism, multinational corporations, and the International Monetary Fund.

The subsistence of a people is the primary economic goal of governments, and the American experience has provided satisfaction of this goal for the great majority of citizens. Internal economic development beyond mere subsistence then becomes a primary goal, and for the United States it remains an objective with the highest priority. Favorable trade with other countries; the development of stable money; and the need for raw materials, technology, and a skilled labor force are some of the major goals essential for the economic well-being of a nation. In some cases nations seek autarky, that is, a reliance of their own internal resources and a minimum dependence on relations with other states, while other states seek to follow a path of exploitation of other nations in order to acquire the most favorable terms of trade.

Military Goals. Although military goals are part of the larger political strategy of the United States, they are considered separately because of their distinctive effects on society, values, and policies; on the allocation of national resources; and on the definition of the global environment.

Military capability sufficient to assure security and defense has been a major goal of the United States from the War of Independence to the present day. The acquisition of military power and the means to exercise power are among the primary goals of government, although power consists of many factors other than military capability. Forming or joining alliances is one way of enhancing power and of deterring potential aggressors.

While alliances may emphasize defense, they may also be essential if a state adopts a goal of conquest. The major goals of American military policy today, however, are deterrence and defense—deterrence of war and successful defenses if war should occur.

Cultural Goals. Cultural relations take place not only as a result of direct and conscious policies formulated by government but also because people wish to interact with each other in a number of ways. Private citizens, businesses, and governments relate to each other within a transnational community, and in the process they expand people's awareness of the existence of that broader community. Among the mutual communications among people and states are the ideological, behavioral, ethical, and value patterns transmitted by international contact through governmental programs; cross-cultural relations among those in the arts, the humanities, science, sports, business, and religion; and tourism. Also involved are functional contacts developed in international organizations, both governmental and nongovernmental.

Clearly, among the cultural goals of the United States and of most other countries are mutual friendship, understanding, status, prestige, and emulation.

Hard Lines and Soft Lines. As if all of this weren't confusing enough, policies toward other countries may reflect a wide range of postures: friendship and cooperation, competition and conflict, or some combination of all of these.

At the base of these postures is the view that as an independent nation-state the United States must serve its national interest even as other states are also seeking to do the same thing. An extreme view of this fact is that the service of the national interest is a zero-sum game, that is, winner take all, and this leads to the perception that relations with other countries require a sense that it is "us" against "them," a necessary conflict or competition with others. Another view, of course, is that the satisfaction of national interests may be pursued in a positive-sum game, that is, all participants can share interests and benefits equitably. This view leads to the perception of a "one for all, and all for one" posture that is the basis for friendship and cooperation.

America's foreign policy and its foreign relations have always reflected a combination of these views, and thus a mixture of hard lines and soft lines in differing circumstances can be observed.

In the contemporary world, hard lines seem to rest on three types of differences among states: ideology, national interests, and the search for preeminence in the global system. For the United States the primary adversary or antagonist in recent decades has been the Soviet Union, each side engaged in the Cold War.

One of the major foundations of this relationship has been the ideological competition inherent in the contrasting claims of communism against capitalism and democracy. These are differing views of the ways human beings should live, work, and govern themselves.

Intense differences among states also emerge in pursuit of what they regard as national interests. The history of the last four hundred years has been a chronicle of wars, disputes, and battles over land, boundaries, resources, and people. Not every state has all that it needs to achieve such basic goals as security, prosperity, and dignity, and occasionally states try to compensate for these problems by taking what they need from others. When they do, war is one result. No matter how friendly the relations between countries may be, differences of opinion may arise over national interests. For example, an American-Canadian clash over fishing rights a few years ago saw each government banning fishermen from the other country from using national waters. The point is that even best friends sometimes disagree. When the disagreement is among enemies and is bitter, war need not necessarily result. Despite intense conflict over specific national interests since 1945, the United States and the Soviet Union have not gone to war.

Another conflictual element to the relationship that is more difficult to define is based on the desire for preeminence in the global system. In most of the systems of states in history there has existed a competition between and among dominant members of the system for supremacy, or preeminence. In some cases the competition has been primarily psychological. In others creation of an empire has been the motivation. The competition between Athens and Sparta in ancient Greece, between Rome and Carthage, between England and Spain, between England and France, and between France and Germany are examples of the drive of powerful competing members of an existing system to dominate it politically, psychologically, militarily, or economically. In the contemporary world the United States prefers to retain the position of preeminent power that it attained during and after World War II, and the Soviet Union seeks to surpass the United States. Leaders in both countries have repeatedly said so.

So there is a strong tendency for many Americans to perceive the relationship with some of the rest of the world in an "us" versus "them" perspective. Still the world includes many countries that are regarded as friends of the U.S., and the "us-them" perspective is not as sharply dominant, although it is never entirely absent. In addition there are many countries that are neither adversaries nor allies. The United States, given its position in the modern world, must deal with all of them, and the "us" versus "them" approach and the hard policy line that stems from it may not only be a mistake but may even be destructive of American purposes.

Of course governments and their leaders may take the "us" versus "them" perspective because they believe that the people do, or they may take it even when they know that the people do not share that view. This disparity may produce a contradiction between the country's foreign policy and its foreign relations. Maintaining perspectives that are sufficiently subtle and flexible to adapt policy to varied conditions is far more difficult for governments than maintaining a simple "us" versus "them" image. All of this suggests the relationship between domestic politics and foreign policy. An analysis of this subject will be pursued later in the book, but a word or two is necessary to suggest the importance of domestic opinion on shaping the "us" versus "them" image or on other images of foreign relations and foreign policy. American opinion is the product of many influences, but once set, it will shape the selection of presidents, the limit of policy, and basic choices. It is not immutable, as the public acceptance of "détente" with the Soviet Union in the 1970s suggests. Since 1945, however, it has fluctuated between the friendship/cooperation and the conflict/competition choice, and this has had much to do with the development of hard lines or soft lines of policy to friends and adversaries alike.

A final word: There *are* enemies, and there *are* dangers. Real, determined, unchangeable enemies exist, and it is essential for successful foreign relations and foreign policy to be able to perceive the differences between them and those with whom there are just important differences of opinion. Nazi Germany, ruled by Adolph Hitler, was a real enemy, who carried out threats to conquer Europe and to destroy Jews and Slavs. In the present day there are real enemies of freedom, of justice, and of truth, who imprison, torture, and exterminate those who disagree with them, who purge large parts of their populations, or who seek to dominate others.

For the most part, however, an awareness of the necessity to orchestrate hard lines and soft lines and to apply each in appropriate circumstances is essential for the most fruitful foreign relations among people and the most effective foreign policies by their governments. The recognition that there are no single causes or single solutions is the beginning of wisdom.

Beyond the fact that there are many levels of policy lies the question of who actually decides what the foreign policy of the United States will be. Does a small, secret "power elite" run the country and dominate the president's decisions in foreign policy? Do the large corporations control policy as some critics allege? Or is the president of the United States really in charge? As we grapple with these questions, we will find it necessary to draw the distinction between those who have the *power* to make the decisions and those who have the opportunity to *influence* them. The countless governmental and nongovernmental actors engaged in foreign relations, in the debate of foreign-policy issues, or with specific special interests in the policy of the United States create considerable confusion in the search for the locus of actual decision making. Both power and influence are exceedingly important subjects, but they need not be the same thing. Influence may or may not be transformed into the power to decide or to affect a decision on policy.

Still another complicating factor in trying to understand policy formation is the body of theories, ideas, philosophies, models, and hypotheses that either seek to explain political reality or that serve as guides to reality for policy makers. The ones that are held by specific presidents, advisers, and the American people at a given time in history can be a key to understanding why leaders think and behave as they do and why they create the policies they do.

How can we ever hope to integrate all of these factors into a clear understanding of policy, and policy making? Perhaps we can't. At least so far we haven't, despite intense work by both traditional and modern scholars. Although this book will present a somewhat eclectic approach to the understanding of how all of these pieces fit together, it will proceed on the assumption that a useful framework for studying the complexities of foreign policy, foreign relations, and the processes by which they evolve is the "politics" framework. Essentially it is through politics as it will be defined here that policy is initiated, debated, decided, accommodated to other countries, and implemented.

The "politics" framework has been clearly outlined in the work of Roger Hilsman.[2] In its broadest sense, says Hilsman, politics concerns the activities and relationships of groups of people acting as groups. Therefore the political process is a device for making group decisions; it is a set of procedures for people to decide what they should do as a group, the goals they should seek, the means for achieving their goals, and the ways in which benefits should be allocated.

Politics comes to the fore, says Hilsman, when there is disagreement about (1) the goals the group should seek as a group, (2) values and the kind of society the group wants to be, (3) the effects of alternative policy means for achieving the goals or values the society seeks, (4) the sacrifices required from different segments of society, (5) the allocation of benefits among different segments of society, and (6) the rules governing competition between individuals and subgroups within the society.

A second characteristic of the political process is that while there is disagreement, there is also a strain toward agreement, toward consensus, and toward accommodation and compromise in order to preserve the system.

Third, it is essential that competing clusters of people exist within the society to be identified with each of the alternative goals and policies.

Finally, power is a characteristic of politics. The relative power of different people and groups is most relevant to the final outcome or policy decision. The presence of countervailing powers affects the result.

In Hilsman's framework of politics what is required is a vigorous interplay of competing voices and demands from many different sources. In parts II and III we shall examine many of these sources: the president and his advisers, other elements within the executive branch, key leaders in Congress, bureaucrats, the courts, special-interest groups, the mass media, research institutions, foreign governments, and differing ideas and concepts of global reality and how foreign policy works.

When we have examined the great array of actors, institutions, and groups involved in the process and some of the many explanations of how it works, the process may seem more confusing than ever.

It may look cumbersome, petty, combative, uncertain, chaotic, clumsy, and ineffective. As we examine American foreign policy, however, we may be surprised to find how often the process has exhibited more of a pattern, more continuity, and more consistency than we could imagine and that it has often produced policies that are successful, productive, and even noble. As commentator David Brinkley once said, "Somehow it works."

Indeed, the politics framework is a most useful one for understanding the links, the interactions, and the search for consensus among all of the actors: between the president and Congress; between the president and public opinion; among departments, bureaus, and agencies and among their leaders; between all of them and the mass media. Politics is a string that ties them all together, and while it may not explain everything we need to know about policy, it is a key to understanding one way in which the elements all relate to each other. For policy is often not the product of some "grand concept." More often it is the product of intense bargaining, manipulation, persuasion—in short, politics. It may evolve from the piecemeal responses to immediate problems that add up to a policy in the end.

Furthermore policy is hewn from uncertainty in a world of startling change brought on by many forces outside the control of governments, change that must be understood and integrated into the process in some way. Politics serves that function. In the next chapter some of these forces for change will be examined.

Part II includes examination of many of the actors involved in the formation and implementation of foreign policy, including both those in government and those outside government who play special roles in exercising influence in the process.

In part III we will examine some of the concepts, theories, and models of foreign-policy behavior that influence the judgment and perceptions of those involved in foreign policy.

Part IV includes an examination of the formation, execution, and effects of policies in the four tracks: political, economic, military, and cultural.

Finally, in part V, we will explore the most urgent policy choices facing the United States in the 1980s, and some of the global issues facing all countries as the twentieth century approaches its end.

At the conclusion the student of foreign policy should have a clear idea of the major factors involved in the foreign-policy process, a somewhat better understanding of contemporary policies, and some insight into what lies ahead.

NOTES

[1] Louis Henkin, *Foreign Affairs and the Constitution* (Minneola, N.Y.: Foundation Press, 1972), p. 15.

[2] Roger Hilsman, *The Politics of Policy Making in Defense and Foreign Affairs.* (New York: Harper and Row Publishers, Inc., 1971), pp. 117–50; and *To Govern America* (New York: Harper & Row Publishers, Inc., 1979), pp. 3–19.

CHAPTER TWO
ENVIRONMENT
AND OBJECTIVES
OF FOREIGN POLICY

The evolution of the foreign policy of the United States and of the foreign relations of Americans has occurred within a context of a broad global environment characterized by rapid and complex change wrought by powerful, impersonal forces often beyond the direct control of governments.

Among the most important of these forces are science and technology, population growth and mobility, the emergence of a system that is truly global in many significant ways, the imperatives of history, the norms and demands of industrialism, the desire to change the status quo, and the power of ideas and ideologies.

It is not fully known precisely how each of these factors interacts on nation-states, on their people, and on their governments, but it is believed that the effects are real and profound. It is necessary for the student of foreign policy to recognize their existence and to consider their role.

SCIENCE AND TECHNOLOGY

One major scholar and policy maker has written:

> The impact of science and technology on man and his society, especially in the more advanced countries of the world, is becoming the major source of contemporary change.[1]

Characterizing these conditions in America as a "technetronic" society, Zbigniew Brzezinski defines this as "a society that is shaped culturally, psychologically, socially, and economically by the impact of technology and electronics, particularly in the area of computers and communications."[2]

Although, in practice, it is not easy to find the dividing line between science and technology, it is useful to consider them separately for a number of reasons.

Science is a method of inquiry and of discovery requiring the formulation and testing of hypotheses concerning objective phenomena through experimentation, observation, and verification. It requires intense questioning of existing beliefs, open criticism of claims to truth, refinement and reevaluation of facts and hypotheses, and a redefinition of truth. In the United States science and democracy evolved simultaneously as the power of ideas and their right to be heard led to the belief that Americans could solve almost any problem. It was a view that led to enormous self-confidence, some would say overconfidence, that America's way is the best one for all of the peoples of the world. Science as a way of thinking contributed to American attitudes toward policy and toward other people, leading to the cultural openness that produced one of the most mixed societies in history. It was also one of the primary sources of new products so diverse in their variety and effects that it is difficult to catalog them all. New medicines, foods, machinery, therapies, fuels, and techniques poured out of laboratories, creating a larger, healthier, longer-living, stronger population than the Founding Fathers had ever dreamed. Science, functioning in a country rich in natural resources, led to the growth and expansion of American power and to an open-mindedness that was to break down many historic barriers to human interaction and would include all citizens within the national community. In the process science became the partner of technology.

Oversimplified, technology is applied science. It is the method by which scientific knowledge is transformed into applicable methods of production, growth, and further discovery. As part of the industrial revolution that spread over the western world in the last two centuries, technology became one of the bases of American wealth, power, and progress. The products of technology have led to new social patterns, new hopes, new fears, and new capabilities in the United States. The new technologies have not only created the instruments of increased economic and social comfort but have also produced the most awesome means of power and war in history. It is no coincidence that as the world leader in science and technology for the past century, the United States has also become the most powerful country in the world. Many of the instruments of modern power—the nuclear bomb, the intercontinental missile, the spy satellites, to name just a few—are the products of science and technology, just as many of the instruments of a more humane life—penicillin, the CAT scanner, and the automobile, among many others—are also the results of science and technology.

A final point: From the perspective of American foreign policy the effects of science and technology on the way people think in other countries all over the world and on the things they want to share have produced new ideas, expectations, movements, and demands that affect American behavior in the world and the American position among nations. Since the end of the Second World War more than one hundred new nation-states have come into existence, and we have seen changes in ancient cultures as these states adapted to their new political roles. American foreign policy clearly must recognize and understand these changes and indeed respond to them, for science and technology will continue to affect American strength and America's relationships with all states.

POPULATION

The increase in the population of the United States and of most other nation-states in the world is one of the most inexorable and important forces working within the global system today and one of the most relevant to American foreign policy.[3]

Since the size, character, and distribution of a country's population is one of the primary elements of its power, the rapid growth of the American population in the last two hundred years has been a notable factor in the expansion of American power. Immigration and high birth rates have contributed to the increase of the American population from some 4 million in 1776 to more than 230 million at present. While rapid population growth creates intense pressures on a country's supply of food, water, energy, raw materials, and space, the richness of the United States in materials and in the capacity to produce food in abundance not only have met the demand of existing populations but have been powerful inducements to producing larger families and to increased immigration. Meanwhile, science and technology have evolved methods to reduce infant mortality, prolong life, and produce healthy survivors. Although birth rates have been stable in the United States for some years, new immigration from Latin America and Southeast Asia has provided an expansionist thrust.

From the perspective of American foreign policy, the growth of the world's population poses some important challenges in the decades ahead. As the world's major exporter of food, the United States is faced with the need to evolve foreign policies that are responsive to the world's demand for food. It is notable that in the past decade the sale of food to the Soviet Union has increased substantially and has come to play a major role in the relationship between the two superpowers.

The growth of population, however, will also affect the ways in which many states respond to the United States and to the rest of the world. It is one of the factors behind the call by many of the less developed countries in the world for a New International Economic Order, which will make it possible for governments to deal with problems arising from expanding populations.

In addition to the growth of population and to the new political pressures it creates, the mobility of populations is also a force of some importance and unpredictability. Economic necessity, political oppression, and the attraction of other cultures have always produced mass migrations of people from one place to another. Migrations of large groups of people have been one of the primary foundations of the growth of the American population and of American power. From the original settlers in the early seventeenth century to the Hispanics fleeing to the United States from Cuba and elsewhere in the 1980s, immigrants have enriched the American experience. The involuntary immigration of African slaves provided the basis of the economy of the South for many decades, and their descendants, as free citizens, are a vital force in American life today.

Contemporary evidence suggests that there is no end in sight for the emigrations of people from one place to another. Whether it be East Germans seeking a place in West Germany, Soviet Jews seeking emigration to Israel, or Cubans and Mexicans seeking entry into the United States, the large movements of people present problems for American foreign policy. For example, on September 29, 1981, President Ronald Reagan ordered that the Coast Guard turn away boatloads of Latin Americans heading for refuge in the United States.[4] While such decisions may be painful for many Americans who wish to maintain an open-door policy, other policy considerations may also come into play.

In any event, population growth and mobility are forces that policymakers cannot ignore, for they affect policy in innumerable direct and indirect ways.

THE EVOLVING GLOBAL SYSTEM

In the contemporary world the United States is at one of the centers of what has become a truly global system, a system in which the majority of states directly and indirectly interact with each other politically, economically, and culturally. In matters of security, trade, money, investment, and political leadership the United States is enmeshed in a number of treaties, alliances, markets, and global organizations that have emerged since the end of World War II. Although the United States did not invent the system, it has assumed one of the leadership roles in relating the capabilities of technology with the demands of most other states to participate in the world system. The United States took the leadership role in creating the United Nations, an organization with 159 members in 1984, representing nearly universal membership. Within the Bretton Woods system, the United States took the leadership in creating a global monetary system with the dollar as a base, and in the General Agreement on Tariffs and Trade the United States took the leadership in establishing a world trading system in which the American market would be opened to those countries that opened their markets to America. Militarily, American foreign policy was designed to create a balance of power against the Soviet Union and to provide security for nations in all parts of the globe.

Although American foreign policy since 1945 has facilitated the evolution of the present global system, the United States did not invent the forces and the tendencies toward the formation of the system that had long existed. Peoples and states have always displayed the inclination to explore, to forage, to trade, and sometimes to conquer. Centuries before the birth of Christ, people were sailing their small vessels to the limit of endurance and finding new lands. Tribes and caravans were hacking out and crossing trade routes, and leaders were organizing military forces to exploit the resources of their neighbors. At the very least, the fragments of a global system were visible by the sixteenth century, and modern technology has made time and distance shrink to the point where communication is nearly instantaneously possible anywhere in the world, and travel to any point on earth is possible in less than twelve hours.

Today networks of formal and informal contacts exist in abundance among people, organizations, and governments, including, for example, the United Nations, the International Monetary Fund, the Red Cross, the International Olympic Committee, the Roman Catholic Church, and General Motors. Tourists from many countries constantly visit other countries.

On September 28, 1981, a warning by an American stock analyst that a market crash would occur on that day sent the prices of stocks sharply downward in London, Hong Kong, and Australia, among other places.[5] It was an example of the existence of an interconnected global system and of the impact of the parts of that system on one another.

In addition there are now perceptions throughout the system of common threats, such as nuclear war, pollution, starvation, and a lack of energy, and the system, through its individual members and its common institutions, creates pressures and constraints on those responsible. Mere recognition of the existence of interdependence among states for their security, prosperity, health, and happiness creates a normative and ethical pressure on the actions of states, a sense of responsibility that may exist even in the absence of direct pressures from the system, its members, or their common institutions. The realization that the policy that a state adopts may affect so many other parts of the system is not without its place in the consideration of policy makers.

Contemporary American foreign policy must accommodate both the restraints and the opportunities that the existence of this global system creates. The system itself is a reflection of the deeper sense of human community sought by many citizens of the twentieth century. Nation-states can still go it alone and reject the norms evolving within the system, but with scores of new states demanding to have their interests considered when the great powers act, it is likely to be more and more difficult, even for superpowers, to be indifferent to the imperatives of the system or to the interests of smaller states.

HISTORY

If these preceding forces require policy makers to confront change and to adapt to the future, the imperatives of history and of national experience confront them with the forces of the past. The American experience has produced nearly four centuries of values, roles, objectives, and systems which each new generation is expected to absorb, accept, and transmit. History provides the foundation for national identification, for an American nationalism that brings to its citizens a sense of worth, of purpose, and of justification for present behavior. While history has the virtue of providing the basis for national stability and order, it also has the capacity to freeze peoples and their leaders into rigid values and behavior that may have become outmoded, unproductive, and even destructive.

Whatever the moral and practical values represented by a country's experience, its history has made it what it is—its territory, its laws, its self-perceptions, and self-images.

For the United States the historical experience was one of expansion—from a small group of colonies along the eastern seaboard into one large, populous, highly developed, and powerful nation-state on the North American continent. The experience of World War II left the United States as the richest and most powerful country on earth, and although the process had been a gradual one spanning almost two hundred years of national experience, Americans reluctantly accepted the massive political, social, and economic opportunities and defined a new set of values, a new internationalism to blend with a strengthened sense of nationalism.

Historical experience shapes other countries and their values, too, and these considerations are essential elements in the formulation of American foreign policy and in the conduct of foreign relations.

INDUSTRIALISM

The impulse of states to develop industrial economies in the past two centuries has been almost as powerful a force as nationalism. Based in the belief that it is the most rapid and assured path to prosperity, industrialism remains one of the cherished goals of virtually every new nation-state created in the past thirty years. Closely linked to the evolution of science and technology, industrialism has evolved its own imperatives—profit, efficiency, productivity, cost effectiveness. It has required the development of national surpluses of capital and the investment of that capital to create additional wealth. It has also required the development of managerial leadership adequately skilled in utilizing available resources. The success of industrialism in the United States has been achieved with the help of American pragmatism—a trial and error method of experimentation and work that discovers those methods that work most profitably and most productively. In the combination of pragmatism with such mechanisms as the free market and material incentives, the United States found the means to produce immense wealth.

Industrialism and the pragmatism that sustains it are not without their drawbacks. Large social costs, such as depleted resources, a polluted environment, and dehumanization of work and community create tensions within the social cohesion of the nation. Nonetheless industrialism has been the primary instrument used in producing the wealth to create and sustain American power. The financing of the military establishment has grown dramatically in the past two centuries at the same time that personal wealth, consumption, and massive new investment resources have also increased.

In any event, the ethics of industrialism as well as its fruits are, directly and indirectly, elements of American foreign policy, providing the means of American power and the models that many other countries and peoples wish to emulate. The imperatives of industrialism—efficiency and productivity—are causing profound changes in many societies, just as they did within the United States in the nineteenth century, and are creating new forces, which challenge the ingenuity of American foreign-policy makers and which will continue to alter the patterns of American foreign relations.

IMPULSE TO CHANGE
THE STATUS QUO

In his insightful analysis of politics among nations, Hans Morgenthau drew the distinction between what he called status quo countries and revolutionary countries.[6] His view was that developed states create conditions in an existing global system that they regard as stable, orderly, and highly satisfactory for the achievement of their purposes and goals. Other countries, unhappy with the status of things for any number of reasons, set out to change the system in ways that will create more advantages for themselves. Underlying these "revolutionary" movements designed to change the world order as it exists may be such powerful forces as universal religions and ideologies. In other cases, it is what Raymond Aron calls glory or prestige.[7]

Thus history shows that countries or groups of countries that feel disadvantaged in the existing system usually seek to reconstruct the system in ways that will benefit them. This impulse to change the staus quo may arise in states whose governments adopt a universalist posture, that is, the wish to extend their influence, their beliefs, and their system to the rest of the world. It may also arise in states that merely seek an adjustment of existing borders with another state or other states. Or it may arise in states that wish to be regarded with "glory" or prestige equal to that of other states.

All of this applies more or less to the United States. The impulse to change the status quo led to the American Revolution, to the creation of a new nation, and to its expansion across the American continent to become a new world power, establishing the American way—democracy, free enterprise, individualism, a sense of manifest destiny, and what later came to be called an "arrogance of power."[8] In the process the United States has been accused of changing from a revolutionary power to a status quo power, more interested in maintaining the existing order than in promoting change beneficial to all humanity.

From the perspective of American foreign policy, it is important to recognize that the world is filled with other states, both large and small, that are eager to change the status quo, in which they have been mired in poverty, domination, and exploitation by others. Although there are many who would deny that the United States has become a status quo power, the agenda of American foreign policy must respond to the forces of change created by America's own example and by the desire of billions of people throughout the world for a better life.

POWER OF IDEAS, IDEOLOGIES

Much of human behavior and the behavior of nation-states can be explained in the effort to obtain the necessities of life—land, food, water, shelter. Beyond the necessities people have also been motivated by a number of powerful ideas, some of which are inescapably intertwined with obtaining necessities, but others of which are linked to such human qualities as faith, glory, justice, pride, God, or truth. Such intense human forces as nationalism, religion, science, freedom, and equality have arisen from these kinds of human qualities with their bases in needs and desires.

The values and beliefs that people develop from these sources create the foundation on which their hopes, desires, visions, goals, ambitions, and wants are evolved, shaping their desires to become a nation, then to become a nation-state, and then to acquire other things characteristic of that status.

The powerful ideas embodied by religions and theologies are among the earliest systematic formations of values, ethics, and purposes, and they remain passionately important to people in the twentieth century, as the resurgence of Islam in many countries at the present time suggests. That religious ideas have played a role of great importance in the American experience and in the development and use of American power in the world is clear. Escape from religious persecution was one of the primary reasons for the first settlers to come to the New World, and the new nation was established on Christian principles and on the claimed sanction of God, since "man was endowed by his Creator with certain unalienable rights. . . ." the Constitution provides for freedom of religion.

Apart from the powerful religious ideas that have saturated history and the American experience, other impressive ideas have emerged from secular philosophies and ideologies. Democracy, free enterprise, capitalism, and the dignity of the individual emerged from sources as diverse as Athens, Rome, Locke, Montesquieu, Rousseau, and Adam Smith. More detailed systems of ideas, called ideologies, have also evolved in the modern era—Marxism-Leninism, Maoism, capitalism, colonialism—and have shaped the thinking and behavior of peoples throughout the world. Of particular interest from the perspective of future American foreign policy is the mixture of ideas forming in many countries composed of ancient cultural values, ideas from the West and from the Orient, and ideologies from the Soviet Union and other socialist states. In addition, some observers have found in the late twentieth century the slow formation of a common set of global values and ideas shared by most countries and peoples. For example, one noted scholar has found striking similarities in the legal systems of many otherwise different countries and cultures.[9] In addition, virtually all existing nation-states subscribe to the principles of the United Nations Charter, the Universal Declaration of Human Rights, and the conventions on economic and political rights. Still, American foreign policy confronts the contradictions between capitalism and socialism, between the United States and the Soviet Union, between democracy and authoritarianism, between Islam and Judaism, to name just a few of the conflicts of ideas that exist in the modern world.

Indeed, policy makers also face the challenge of understanding the forces of change wrought by new ideas within America itself, ideas that could affect the views of Americans toward themselves and toward their role in the world. One such challenge is the rise of popular sentiment against the further development or use of nuclear weapons in any form. If foreign policy is to be responsive and successful, and if foreign relations among peoples are to be facilitated, the power of ideas must be appreciated and accommodated.

SUMMARY

No one can know with certainty how the forces for change discussed above will affect the United States or other countries or whether they will eventually make all traditional styles and methods of conducting foreign policy outmoded and irrelevant. Some would argue that the more things change, the more they stay the same. Despite the immense changes of the past two centuries, many patterns in the relations among nations have remained the same. What is essential is that future policy makers and citizens recognize that American foreign policy and foreign relations exist amid these turbulent forces. This awareness should embody policy with humility and with a sense of the possible, and if politics is the art of the possible, it is an ideal instrument to adapt and to adjust American interests to a changing world.

NOTES

[1] Zbigniew Brzezinski, *Between Two Ages: America's Role in the Technetronic Era* (New York: Penguin Books, 1970), p. 9.

[2] Ibid.

[3] "World's People Total 4.7 Billion," *New York Times*, September 4, 1983, p. 9. The most populous states include the following: China (1 billion plus), India (730 million), the Soviet Union (272 million), the United States (234 million), and Indonesia (161 million). These five states account for more than half the world's population. The American population increased by over 2 million between June 1982 and June 1983.

[4] "Reagan Orders Refugees Halted on the High Seas," *New York Times*, September 30, 1981, p. 1.

[5] Robert A. Bennett, "Stock Prices Fall Sharply Abroad, But New York Shows Strong Rally," *New York Times*, September 29, 1981, p. 1. Analyst Joseph Granville had predicted a sharp drop in prices late in the preceding week.

[6] Hans Morgenthau, *Politics Among Nations*, 4th ed. (New York, Alfred A. Knopf, 1967), pp. 41–82.

[7] Raymond Aron, *Peace and War*. (New York: Praeger Publishers, 1967), pp. 71–93.

[8] J. William Fulbright, *Arrogance of Power* (New York: Random House, 1966), pp. 3–22.

[9] Wolfgang Friedmann, *The Changing Structure of International Law* (New York: Columbia University Press, 1964), pp. 297–316.

CHAPTER THREE
THE PRESIDENT
AND THE PRESIDENCY

Asked how many people control foreign policy, former president Richard Nixon told a writer, "Very few. Two thousand? Three thousand? I'd put the number around there. That's how many people a president would find it worth talking to."[1] Foreign-policy expert Stanley Hoffmann of Harvard University agreed: "I think that the group has expanded over the years. But it could be two thousand, three thousand. . . ."[2] According to Richard Reeves, "It is the closest thing to a governing aristocracy that has survived in American democracy. . . . a self-selected aristocracy [made up of] Americans who studied, spoke, sold, bought, or went to anything or everywhere foreign. . . . They cared about foreign policy so they made foreign policy."[3]

However, Nixon's former special assistant for national security affairs and secretary of state, Henry Kissinger, has indicated that during the Nixon administration, the range of control was much more narrow, resting primarily in the White House. This occurred, according to Kissinger, because of "Nixon's insistence, with my help, on White House control of foreign policy. In 1971 we took over not simply the planning but also the execution of major initiatives."[4] Citing what he considered to be some of the obstacles to policy making posed by the bureaucracies involved in foreign policy, Kissinger notes: "That Nixon chose to circumvent the process rather than discipline it reflected his personality."[5]

For many Americans the president of the United States is seen as the single source, the symbol, and the spokesman of American foreign policy.

At most, there may be a vague awareness that a secretary of state or a flamboyant national security adviser also plays a part in foreign policy. Occasionally a secretary of defense may even be recognized as a commentator on foreign policy. Beyond these few individuals, however, there is often little or no citizen awareness of the numerous individuals and structures in government who play an important role in the formulation and execution of foreign policy and in the participation in foreign relations.

Governmental participants in foreign policy and foreign relations include a wide range of groups and individuals—the presidency, many other segments of the executive branch of government, several relevant parts of Congress, occasionally the judiciary, on some occasions state and local governments, and finally, international intergovernmental organizations to which the United States belongs. In addition, as we shall see, there are numerous nongovernmental actors who participate in foreign relations and in the foreign-policy process.

Yet despite the participation of all of these groups, the impression that the president is the center of policy is not wrong. Although he is subject to the views of advisers, of Congress, of public opinion, of special-interest groups, and of other governments and international organizations, the president possesses the final decision-making authority. In this context, we begin an examination of the president and the presidency.

THE PRESIDENT

There is an enormous impulse in the United States to equate the president with the presidency. Nothing could be more misleading. The president is certainly the central part of the presidency, but the presidency is a structure with many parts, many of which may play a decisive role in foreign policy.

In addition to the president, the institution of the presidency may include the first lady and the rest of the first family, the vice-president and some members of his family, the White House staff, the National Security Council, the national security adviser, the secretaries of state and defense, the cabinet, the chairman of the Joint Chiefs of Staff, the director of the Central Intelligence Agency, and a variety of other governmental officials who may be consulted on specific policy issues. The presidency may also include those friends, advisers, former officials, or cronies that a president may consult from time to time, whether they are in government or in private life.

Different presidents have used these components of the presidency differently, and the role and influence of any of them may vary from president to president and, sometimes, even during the term or terms of the same president. In one period the secretary of state might be the dominant force with the president. In another it could be the secretary of defense or the national security adviser.

In any event, few modern presidents have been only passive or uninformed receptors, dependent upon others for their ideas, their values, and their decisions. In more than one sense, the president orchestrates the process and remains in control of the final decision. It is fundamental, then, to understand his powers, his relations with his associates, his perceptions of the world, and the ways in which he gets things done.

In foreign policy the president has more power and freedom of action than he has in domestic affairs, a fact of considerable interest and importance to students of foreign policy and foreign relations. In order to understand this power, it is necessary to examine its sources and the means with which a president exercises it. It will also be helpful to look at the ways in which particular presidents in the modern era have dominated the foreign-policy process.

1. ***Formal powers.***[6] In order to understand the formal powers possessed by the president, it is important to understand the Constitution and the ways in which its meanings have evolved. In the long, tedious Constitutional Convention of 1787, the framers concluded that they needed to create a national executive, even though having overthrown royal rule from England, they were suspicious of executive power and intended the legislative branch to be dominant. Not very clear about what they wanted the executive to be and to do, with time running out after completion of several major and bitter battles, they agreed to a relatively short article giving the executive a few major powers. On the foundations of those few powers presidential authority has grown, not only in foreign policy but in domestic affairs also.

Among the foreign-policy powers granted to the executive by the Constitution are the following:

1. The general executive power, including the directive to "take care that the Laws be faithfully executed."
2. The right to receive ambassadors.
3. The right to appoint ministers and consuls (with the advice and consent of the Senate).
4. The right to negotiate treaties (with the advice and consent of the Senate).
5. The role of commander-in-chief of the armed forces.
6. The right to propose legislation.
7. The right to demand accountability of officers of the government.

Perceiving the extensive authority of the president in the contemporary world, we are aware that it is built upon these few but important constitutional grants of specific power. One of the reasons the president's power has expanded is that it is possible to construe these specific grants broadly, and historically presidents and the Supreme Court have done so. In a long and substantial history of the interpretation of foreign-policy powers, probably no decision states the national and the presidential powers in foreign policy as clearly as does the decision in the case of the *United States* v. *Curtiss-Wright Export Corporation* (1936). It affirmed that "the powers of the national government in foreign affairs did not depend upon the affirmative grants of the Constitution."[7] The Court reasoned that as a sovereign state, the United States possessed a body of powers in foreign affairs that were common to those possessed by all sovereign states. In addition, the Court decided that the president was the "sole organ" of the United States in its relations with other countries: "In this vast, external realm, with its important, complicated, delicate and manifold problems, the President alone has the power to speak or listen as a representative of the nation."[8]

In addition to the powers formally granted to the president by the Constitution and by the Court, there are numerous occasions when the Congress through legislative act gives the president specific authority in areas in which it may share power. For example, in the areas of international trade, the Congress has frequently authorized the president to negotiate matters of economic and commercial importance, areas in which Congress has constitutional authority to regulate commerce among nations.[9]

Thus the formal powers of a president are not inconsiderable in the foreign-policy field. However, the president possesses other formal powers that may be linked to foreign policy. The veto power, for example, may be threatened or used by a president to defer or deny foreign-policy legislation to which he is opposed.[10] Further, foreign policy and domestic policy are often inextricably linked. Foreign policy has many effects on domestic society, and domestic policy may have an impact on foreign policy and foreign relations. The political bargaining in one area can and often does involve the other. Thus presidential powers that are usually regarded as applicable primarily in domestic affairs may well strengthen the president's power in foreign policy as well.

Looking at the formal powers of the president, one can perceive how the general grants of authority have gradually been expanded since 1789. The general executive power has been used by presidents from the beginning to carry out a responsibility for the overall security and welfare of the country.[11]

Article 2 of the Constitution states that "the executive power shall be vested in a President of the United States of America." In addition to the authority to carry out laws passed by Congress, the article also lists many other independent powers intended to safeguard the interests of the country. The responsibility to see that the laws are faithfully executed imposes on the president the obligation to put laws passed by Congress relating to American foreign policy into effect. This gives the president the power to interpret international law and to assure that its obligations are carried out by the government, by other Americans, and by foreign countries— by force, if necessary.

The right to appoint and receive ambassadors provides the basis for communication with other countries, for legal recognition of other countries, and for a worldwide foreign policy; and the right to negotiate treaties includes the right to seek informal agreements, to form alliances, and to negotiate with other states.[12] The commander-in-chief role has been expanded to support presidential decisions to commit American forces abroad in a variety of circumstances and to support the development of policies designed to protect the security of the United States.[13] The right to demand accountability of government officials has given the president the authority to make the entire executive branch and its leading officials in foreign policy subject to his control. The right to propose legislation has meant that the president may place any agenda of his choice before the Congress and before the people.

Despite what appears to be an awesome array of formal, legal powers in the hands of the president, there are those who have raised serious doubts about the view that the president has much usable power. Richard Neustadt has argued that, aside from the power to command the armed forces, the president has few powers to command anyone to do anything.[14] To be sure, within the civilian part of the government, the president can appoint and remove, and therefore command, top officials of the major foreign-policy structures. However, he has more difficulty in commanding the professional bureaucracies of these structures. He cannot command Congress or the people at all. Thus in order to create policy and move the nation, he must rely on persuasion, politics, and personality.[15] His powers to negotiate treaties and to make war are limited by congressional power and authority in these areas.[16] His power to recognize and to negotiate with states may be limited by public opinion. His power to use the armed forces is limited by law and custom.

Therefore, in order to define a problem and to design and implement a policy, the president must rely primarily on a number of informal powers.

2. *Informal powers.* Most of the informal powers of the president can be organized under the general heading of persuasion. What he cannot command others to do, he must be able to persuade them to do. The techniques by which this is done may be divided between politics and communication, although in reality there may be little difference.

By the time a person reaches the presidency, he will have acquired a number of political skills that have been successful. Some of these have to do with the president's own personality—the dynamism, vitality, conviction, and credibility with which he has related to people whether they are professionals or the public. The individual's charisma can be used to create a receptivity in the minds of others for the thoughts of a leader. Beyond that, the skills required to create consensus among those whose support is needed, to motivate others, and to facilitate their capacity to work together for a common purpose must be developed, or the president must quickly find someone who can do these things for the administration.

Certainly one effective way of persuading others to support a president's policies is through the use of rational, logical, factual argument so that a person will change position on policy. However, a president has many instruments other than reason that can increase persuasiveness. One of these is patronage. Although there are fewer jobs now available to a president to dispense than there once were, a president is not without resources in this regard. Positions in the executive branch; appointments to regulatory agencies, governmental boards, and commissions; ambassadorships; and judgeships are just a few of the types of positions subject to presidential authority.

Another persuasive instrument is the pork barrel, that package of governmental expenditures that can include defense contracts, military bases, new highways, sewer projects, bloc grants for urban development, and countless other items on which the government spends money and presidential acquiescence is a necessity.

Besides pork barrel, the promise of White House support for proposed legislation dear to a congressional representative's heart and needed in the representative's district can be a pretty effective way to convince that representative that support of the president is reasonable.

Another inducement a president can offer is the willingness to campaign on behalf of a representative or senator or to give a fund-raising speech in his or her district to buttress the campaign kitty.

The other side of the coin of what a president can offer is what he can withhold. He can threaten to oppose or to delay patronage, pork barrel legislative support, and campaign help. He can also threaten to criticize, castigate, and characterize unfavorably those who refuse to support him. He can even threaten to use his influence to remove an office holder from the party ticket in the next election, or to delay or decline to reappoint someone of interest to the representative or senator.

In short, the president has access to a wide assortment of threats, promises, and arguments to achieve his goals.

The president also has available to him the instruments of mass communication.[17] Although much less is really known about the effects of the complex interactions among the government, the media, and the public on the formation of policy than is supposed, there is a widespread assumption among many Americans that the media, especially television, have become vital instruments of policy. These assumptions and the relations among the major forces involved in the policy process will be reviewed in greater detail in chapter 9. Accepting for a moment that mass-communication facilities can be effective instruments of policy in the hands of a skillful president, we can acknowledge that they provide a method by which a president can take his case directly to the public to gain their support and to induce their pressure upon Congress. A recent study of the media, power, and politics offered this conclusion about the relationships:

When events cooperate, a President who skillfully uses his considerable power assets to manipulate coverage obtains potent power resources. Journalists purvey images that enhance his control.[18]

Of course the media can prove to be a most serious liability to a president, too. Criticism of Lyndon Johnson's Vietnam policies and the criticism of Richard Nixon in the Watergate crisis are just two examples of what may occur when the media become almost uniformly opposed to a president. In any event, the media may have changed much less about the policy process than is sometimes claimed. Indeed it was reported that Secretary of State George Shultz rarely read the morning papers or watched the evening television news.[19] Thus it would appear that any claimed effect of the media is not universally shared by all key policy holders.

Still the president has many means to utilize information for his own advantage.

First of all, the president has access to information unavailable to Congress or to the public, and there are many ways in which this can be used to build public support. Basing his decision on this information, he can declare that a crisis exists requiring congressional and public support, hoping not only to convince them but also to induce the public to exert pressure on Congress in support of the president. Another option in the handling of information is the utilization of news leaks, the release of certain information to selected news media without direct attribution. Also the use of "backgrounders" may be expanded, involving lengthy background briefings of reporters by unidentified administration officials, sometimes by the president himself.

Of course, for most presidents the most effective means of communication for building broad public support is television. The road to the White House has usually provided enough experience to presidents so that they can effectively communicate on television. The presidential speech from the Oval Office, the presidential news conference, and the personal interview in the White House are effective ways for a president to say something in exactly the manner he chooses. Coverage by television of formal speeches outside the White House for use on newscasts, though not subject to the direct control of the president, provides massive exposure. Combined, these forums give a president the attention of the public that no other official can remotely match.

Then, too, a president can arrange tours and speeches throughout the country and visits throughout the world, which permit him to articulate his views and the position of his administration. Coverage by the news media of such events is massive and may be effective in building support.

Few state events are as filled with gravity as are presidential speeches to a joint session of the Congress. Normally, except in extraordinary crisis, the president appears in such a forum only once a year in the annual State of the Union address. In late April 1983 President Ronald Reagan called a joint session to discuss what he regarded as a major Communist threat to the Western Hemisphere. In the large chamber of the House of Representatives, facing the assembled Congress, the Supreme Court, the foreign diplomatic corps stationed in Washington, Reagan had access to the television networks and the press and the attention of the public. Democrats accepted the opportunity to respond and Senator Christopher Dodd of Connecticut, speaking on behalf of the party, labeled the president's proposals a "formula for failure." The event increased congressional and public support for the president's programs in Central America and highlighted a president's ability to command a massive worldwide hearing for his policies among the widest possible audience.

There are less dramatic, but sometimes no less effective, means of personal communications. White House breakfasts or dinners, arranged for selected groups of representatives and senators, are more intimate and personalized contacts designed to flatter and appeal to supporters and opponents alike. Telephone calls from the president involving direct appeals for support, appeals to patriotism or party and personal loyalty, personal letters, and even presidential visits to Capitol Hill have been known to be effective in some tough policy battles.

All recent presidents have attempted to use all of these techniques at one time or another to build support for their policies. Franklin Roosevelt was highly effective with his radio "fireside chats" and in the use of threats and promises. Harry Truman and Lyndon Johnson were most effective in behind-the-scenes negotiation with opposing members of Congress. John F. Kennedy was most persuasive on television, especially in presidential news conferences, a format in which Lyndon Johnson was ineffective. Richard Nixon was a superb speech maker and user of the drama of foreign travel and summit conferences. Jimmy Carter had trouble on all fronts in using the informal powers of persuasion, and most recently, Ronald Reagan used most techniques effectively.

What should be obvious is that a president has a great number of powers, both formal and informal, and a wide variety of techniques available to him to facilitate formulation of foreign policy. The capacity to manipulate information, opinion, and support, however, is a function of his own intelligence, experience, and personality, for it requires skill and judgment to know how and in what combinations to use the tools at hand.

PRESIDENTIAL FUNCTIONS

Having examined the powers of the president, we may proceed to discuss what a president does in the process of defining foreign-policy problems, choices, and decisions.

First of all, long before a person becomes president, he develops beliefs, values, knowledge, and public positions on the role of the United States in the world, on previous American policies, on the state of foreign relations, and on the challenges that face the United States in the world. Although the study of such matters may be a lifelong enterprise, ideally the potential president will have developed informed perspectives before becoming a candidate. As the campaign begins, the candidate must offer to the people a comprehensive and clear-cut analysis of world affairs and a general framework for policies to be pursued if elected. More than one candidate in the past has reached the stage of active candidacy without a broad and clear-cut view of foreign policy.

Once elected, the president must select a team, the leading members of his administration in both the domestic and the foreign-policy field. Frequently these appointments are made from among those who have been key advisers in the campaign. A number of major criteria are usually involved: the confidence of the president-elect, political recognition and acceptance, expertise, and views similar to those of the president.

Early in an administration a president must set out some general statements of the administration's interpretations of the global political environment, of its goals, and of its priorities. This step is essential to clarify the administration's purposes for its own members, for the Congress, for the people, and for other countries.

In the process the president must meet with those agencies involved in foreign policy, develop good relationships with the leadership, make contacts with Congress, especially with key leaders in the major foreign policy committees, and receive as many views from special interests as possible.

Even as the president assigns specific responsibilities and absorbs the advice of associates, the chief executive must receive masses of new information while taking care to obtain as much background, history, and theory as possible. Since most presidents have had experience in positions of great responsibility—in the Senate, in governorships, or in the military—the capability to absorb knowledge and new information should be highly developed.

The president, through subordinates, then must organize the discussion and debate over both immediate and long-range problems. Access to the president by key subordinates must be assured, and the administration must gear itself for crisis management, that is, dealing with unexpected problems and issues in a limited time.

In many cases immediate decisions may be required, while in others decision may be deferred. The president must find time in a busy schedule for private study of the decisions and then find the determination to make the decision. The choices may include maintaining a policy, changing it, delaying it, or creating an entirely new policy.

Once the decision is made within the administration, it must be "sold" to Congress, to the people, and to allies, and this process may require some of the techniques identified above. Indeed it must also be sold to those within the administration and in the bureaucracy who must carry it out.

Once the policy is adopted, the President must take care to monitor its implementation, to check carefully with subordinates to assure that the policy is being carried out so that it will achieve its intended goals. This also involves monitoring the reaction of foreign governments, of public opinion, and of Congress, as well as of potentially divergent views within the administration itself.

Concurrently the president must take part in formal state visits to other countries and from leaders of other states. He may plan and participate in formal meetings with leaders in summit conferences, at regional organizations, and at the United Nations.

In addition the president must set the priorities of the administration in the national budget, considering such matters as the size and composition of the defense budget, the types and amounts of foreign assistance, and support for other programs associated with foreign relations.

During the process the president must become aware of the changes underway within the world community and with the ways in which these might affect the interests of the United States. This may entail detailed studies of new policy approaches the administration has to develop.

Of course, the president's use of the communications media affords the opportunity to do more than merely promote specific policies. It provides the forum by which a president can educate the American public to world realities and to the role of the United States in the world. It is a broad educational function, which is essential for the development of support in the United States and abroad for American goals and objectives. Ironically, at least four recent presidents are regaded as failures in this function. Henry Kissinger has written:

To be sure, Nixon had failed in the task of education. He had been too unsure of himself to inspire his society not only by technical virtuosity but by nobility of purpose. He had not met the moral challenge.[20]

Kissinger's successor as special assistant to the president for national security affairs, Zbigniew Brzezinski, commenting on Jimmy Carter's role in the process, said:

> Given the centrality of the Presidential office in foreign affairs, the President needs to be an effective mobilizer of public support, a persuasive educator who simultaneously enlightens the public about global complexities and generates support for his policies.—Surprisingly, for a political leader who scored such an unexpected and meteoric electoral success, Carter was a much less effective speaker.—On balance, Carter was not good at public relations, he did not fire enthusiasm in the public or inspire fear in his adversaries.[21]

Lyndon Johnson was unable both to develop an inspiring model and to communicate effectively his Vietnam policies, and Gerald Ford in his short presidency was also unable to develop an inspirational vision.

More recently most analysts regard Ronald Reagan as a superb communicator, whose efforts in the media were instrumental in the passage of much of his foreign policy program.

Finally, the president must make a determination of whether the foreign policies of the administration are achieving their objectives and whether they are promoting the security and the interests of the United States.

Since foreign policy is only one part of the president's job, this brief review of the requirements and functions of the task indicates how awesome are the responsiblities of the chief executive. Yet in our system the president has the primary political responsibility, the basic constitutional authority, and access to the means to conduct foreign policy. How well or how poorly America's presidents have done the job is a matter for some disagreement, but an examination of some of the successes, failures, and mixtures of both will be useful.

PRESIDENTIAL INITIATIVE

From 1789 onward all American presidents have been actively engaged in relations with foreign countries and with the evolution of American foreign policy.[22] The efforts under George Washington to maintain American independence and at the same time to find foreign support and foreign investors, the bold action of Thomas Jefferson to acquire the Louisiana Territory from France, and the successful waging of the War of 1812 under James Madison were early examples of presidential leadership in foreign affairs. By 1898 President William McKinley was ready to take on and to defeat Spain and in the process acquire Cuba, Puerto Rico, the Philippines, Guam, and Hawaii. As the United States moved into the twentieth century, President Woodrow Wilson led the country into World War I and into prominence as a world power and then set the tone for the anticolonial movements later in the century with his call for "self-determination." Wilson also proposed the foundations of a new world order under an international organization, the League of Nations, although he failed to persuade the Congress to approve it.

It was Franklin Delano Roosevelt, however, who presided over the rise of the United States to world leadership. Drawn into World War II against the Axis powers—Germany, Italy, and Japan—the United States built the most powerful military force in history, and although Roosevelt died before the war ended, he had been the architect not only of massive American power, but also of a new international organization designed to maintain peace, the United Nations.

When the wartime alliance with the Soviet Union collapsed and when the British were unable to resume their position of global leadership, President Harry S. Truman assumed the responsibility. In such actions as the Bretton Woods monetary system, the Truman Doctrine proclaiming American intentions to defend freedom, the Marshall Plan with its billions of dollars in aid to Western Europe, and the North Atlantic Treaty provisions for the joint military defense of Western Europe, the United States under Truman's leadership established supremacy in the non-Communist world. In addition, convinced of the need to punish aggressors under the concept of collective security, Truman committed American forces to the defense of South Korea against the invasion by North Korea in 1950.

Truman's successor, Dwight D. Eisenhower, maintained American leadership of the Western Alliance and threatened massive retaliation with nuclear power against any Soviet attack on Europe. In his Eisenhower Doctrine, the president proposed exclusion of foreign intervention in the countries of the Middle East. Having decided not to intervene in the Hungarian uprising against Soviet domination in 1956, and having demanded that a joint British-French-Israeli invasion of Egypt be abandoned, the Eisenhower administration decided toward the end of its term to plan an overthrow of a new Cuban government led by Fidel Castro.

The Cuban-intervention plan was continued by the new administration of John F. Kennedy in 1961, and it led to the first major American foreign-policy fiasco of the postwar period, the Bay of Pigs. Despite this early failure, Kennedy recouped, and his administration gained a number of successes in the remaining years of Kennedy's term, tragically ended by assassination of the president in Dallas November 22, 1963. Among the Kennedy initiatives were the Alliance for Progress, a program of aid and social reform for Latin America; a nuclear-test-ban treaty; and the hot line with the Soviet government. Kennedy's greatest triumph was the Cuban missile crisis in which the Soviet Union agreed to remove offensive missiles from Cuba in 1962. More questionable was the decision by Kennedy to send 16,000 military advisers to South Vietnam, and although it is reported that he planned to withdraw gradually from Vietnam by the fall of 1963, the American commitment was still in place when Lyndon B. Johnson became president.

Vietnam was the major element of Johnson's foreign policy, and it is a policy that remains highly controversial two decades later. It provoked massive internal American protest, and it led to Johnson's decision not to seek reelection in 1968.

Johnson's successor, Richard M. Nixon came into office claiming that he had a secret plan to end the war in Vietnam, and eventually his administration sought to "Vietnamize" the war, to withdraw American forces, and to negotiate a settlement that would preserve the independence of South Vietnam. At the same time Nixon embarked on a policy of détente with the Soviet Union in an effort to relax tensions between the superpowers and to increase trade with the Soviet Union. Simultaneously, Nixon moved to establish friendly contacts with the People's Republic of China. In addition, he proclaimed the Nixon Doctrine, which advocated the settlement of disputes in Asia by Asians themselves without the intervention of foreign troops.

Forced to resign by the scandal of Watergate, Nixon was succeeded by Gerald Ford.

In his brief tenure in the White House Ford sought to build upon the Strategic Arms Limitation Treaty (SALT I) negotiated by Nixon and met with Soviet leader Leonid Brezhnev to initiate a general understanding of the goals for SALT II limiting the number of nuclear delivery systems permissible to both countries. It was during Ford's first year that the government of South Vietnam collapsed when the armies of the North overran South Vietnamese forces. To recoup American prestige Ford ordered a Marine rescue mission to free crew members when Cambodians seized the containership Mayaguez and held its crew captive. Forty-one Marines died in the effort, even as reports circulated that the diplomatic efforts of the Chinese had secured the release of the captured crew.

In any event, Ford was defeated in the 1976 election by Jimmy Carter, who brought with him to the White House a dedication to human rights as an essential element of American foreign policy. In addition, the Carter administration established formal diplomatic relations with the People's Republic of China, negotiated a new Panama Canal Treaty to eventually restore sovereignty over the Canal Zone to Panama, and concluded a SALT II Treaty with the Soviet Union. The Soviet intervention into Afghanistan, however, made Senate ratification of the treaty impossible, and Carter initiated a grain embargo against the Soviets and withdrew American participation from the 1980 summer Olympic games in Moscow. But Carter's major foreign-policy crisis was the seizure of the American Embassy and American hostages in Iran in the wake of the Iranian overthrow of the shah and his subsequent admission to the United States for medical treatment. The long and painful negotiations for the release of the hostages, interrupted by an abortive military rescue mission in which eight Americans died, did not end until one hour after the inauguration of Ronald Reagan, Carter's successor. The hostages were safe at last, but the crisis had been major factor in Carter's defeat by Reagan in the 1980 election.

Many observers consider Carter's greatest triumph in foreign policy the achievement of peace between Israel and Egypt in the Camp David agreement. In intense efforts Carter personally negotiated with Egyptian President Anwar Sadat and Israeli Prime Minister Menachem Begin an agreement that led to peaceful relations between the two countries, the return of Egyptian lands conquered by the Israelis, and the establishment of normal diplomatic relations between Israel and Egypt.

In 1981 the new president was immediately confronted by events in Central America—political unrest in El Salvador, Nicaragua, and other states. Claiming that the unrest was promoted by Cuba and the Soviet Union, the president announced a new economic-development plan for the Caribbean Basin to provide economic help to the countries of the region. Determined to expand the military to close what he termed a window of vulnerability to the Soviets, Reagan proposed large increases in the nation's defense budget and the construction of such new weapons systems as the B-1 bomber, the MX missile system, and cruise missiles. In addition, he condemned the imposition of marital law in Poland to suppress the increasingly influential Solidarity movement, critcized the Soviets, and imposed trade restraints on both Poland and the Soviet Union. In 1982 Reagan, primarily through his secretary of state, Alexander Haig, attempted to mediate a dispute between Argentina and Great Britain over the Falkland Islands and to prevent war between two nations considered friendly to the United States. Mediation failed, and during a short war Britain drove the Argentinians from the Falklands with help from United States bases in the Atlantic.

This brief sketch of presidential involvement in the foreign policy of the government and of the foreign relations of the American people can only suggest the broadest of outlines of the importance of the president in the process. Nor does it purport to be more than identification of some of the issues and the problems that have confronted the nation in its history.

It is meant to suggest, however, that some presidents have had broad visions of goals and policies and an intense understanding of how to achieve them. These visions have come to shape the lives of Americans and the lives of people all over the world. Wilson, Roosevelt, Kennedy, Nixon, Carter, and Reagan all brought with them to the White House comprehensive concepts of how the world should be organized and how the United States should act in leading the process. Indeed by the time of Wilson there was little doubt among many presidents and many other Americans as well that the United States should *lead* in the creation of policies and systems that would promote American ideals and American interests. A few presidents had less activist or less clear visions about the role of the United States in the world. Many of Truman's views came from his closest advisers, but his convictions developed with force and clarity. Eisenhower was committed to maintenance of existing arrangements rather than to dramatic new departures in policy. Ford seemed to have no overarching concept, but under the guidance of Secretary of State Henry Kissinger might well have developed one. Johnson's views were shaped by the Vietnam experience, and no broader vision emerged during his presidency. The American presidents of the 1920s, Warren G. Harding, Calvin Coolidge, and Herbert Hoover, were more dedicated to internal developments and to an absence of presidential activism than to a vigorous American role in foreign affairs.

American presidents have been at the center of the growth of American power and the expansion of American involvement in world affairs.

Their ideas, their beliefs, and their decisions have shaped much of the history of the twentieth century. In important ways presidents seek to reflect the moods and the desires of the American people, and they play a powerful role in shaping the moods, expectations, hopes, and perspectives that the people come to hold. In some ways the people and the president both inspire and constrain each other simultaneously. Still, at present there can be little doubt that the people look to the president to define our problems, identify the issues, and propose our policies. On the other hand, no president can be indifferent to the wishes of the people to trade with, visit, and talk to other peoples in peace. Few presidents can fail to respond to these impulses in the contemporary world. This sensitive relationship between people and president is fundamentally political, and the politics of foreign policy suggest the possibilities and the limits of what the United States can do.

Of course no President designs or executes foreign policy alone. Whatever the clarity of his own vision, he requires and is subject to the ideas, pressures, and recommendations of many other individuals, groups, organizations, and structures both within government and from private sources. Among the most important of these are those closest to him in the presidency and in the rest of the executive branch.

NOTES

[1] Richard Reeves, *American Journey* (New York: Simon and Schuster, 1982), p. 349.

[2] Ibid., p. 348.

[3] Ibid., p. 349.

[4] Henry Kissinger, *White House Years* (Boston: Little Brown & Company, 1979), p. 840.

[5] Ibid., p. 841.

[6] Cecil Crabb Jr., *American Foreign Policy in the Nuclear Age,* 4th ed. (New York: Harper & Row Publishers, Inc., 1983), pp. 60–72; Gerald Gunther, *Cases and Materials on Constitutional Law* (Mineola, N.Y.: Foundation Press, 1980); Louis Henkin, *Foreign Affairs and the Constitution* (Mineola, N.Y.: Foundation Press, 1972), pp. 37–65.

[7] Gunther, *Cases and Materials,* pp. 402–3.

[8] Ibid., p. 403.

[9] Charles W. Kegley and Eugene R. Wittkopf, *American Foreign Policy: Pattern and Process,* 2nd ed. (New York: St. Martin's Press, 1982), p. 320.

[10] Henkin, *Foreign Affairs,* pp. 32–33.

[11] Ibid., pp. 42–43.

[12] Ibid., pp. 48-49.

[13] Ibid., pp. 50–54.

[14] Richard Neustadt, *Presidential Power* (New York: John Wiley and Sons, 1980), pp. 26–44.

[15] Ibid., passim.

[16] The president's powers to commit armed forces and the limitations imposed on that power by Congress under the War Powers Act will be discussed further in chapter 7. The issue arose in September 1983 during the crisis in Lebanon in which American forces, as members of an international peacekeeping force, came under fire in Beirut. A compromise solution between the president and Congress permitted the president to keep the force there for eighteen months after which Congress would reconsider the matter. Steven V. Roberts, "Congress Adopts Measures Allowing Marines in Beirut," *New York Times,* September 30, 1983, p. 1.

[17] Thomas R. Dye and L. Harmon Zeigler, *American Politics in the Media Age* (Monterey, Calif.: Brooks/Cole Publishing Co., 1983), pp. 300–309; and David L. Paletz and Robert M. Entman, *Media Power Politics* (New York: Free Press, 1981), pp. 54–78.

[18] Paletz and Entman, *Media Power Politics,* pp. 77–78.

[19] Bernard Gwertzman, "Under Shultz, A Shift to a Less Personalized Role," *New York Times,* October 28, 1982, p. B12.

[20] Henry Kissinger, *Years of Upheaval* (Boston: Little Brown, & Company, 1982), p. 1209.

[21] Zbigniew Brzezinski, *Power and Principle* (New York: Farrar, Straus & Giroux, 1983), pp. 524–25.

[22] Lloyd C. Gardner, *American Foreign Policy: Present to Past* (New York: Free Press, 1977); James A. Nathan and James K. Oliver, *United States Foreign Policy and World Order* (Boston: Little, Brown & Company, 1976); Thomas G. Paterson, J. Garry Clifford, and Kenneth L. Hagen, *American Foreign Policy, A History* (Lexington, Mass.: D.C. Heath and Co., 1977); John Spanier, *American Foreign Policy Since World War II,* 8th ed. (New York: Holt, Rinehart, & Winston, 1980).

CHAPTER FOUR
THE FIRST TEAM

THE VICE-PRESIDENT

Harry Truman was about to have an afternoon bourbon with Sam Rayburn, the speaker of the house, in Rayburn's office on April 12, 1945, when he received a call to come to the White House. There he learned from Eleanor Roosevelt, Franklin D. Roosevelt's wife, that FDR was dead and that he, Harry Truman, was president of the United States. Stunned, the new president held himself together, prepared to be sworn in, and called a cabinet meeting for later. It was after that meeting, just a few hours after Roosevelt's death, that Truman was informed of the Manhattan Project—the atomic bomb—which he had known nothing about.[1] When Truman finally had a vice-president after the 1948 election he was determined that the vice-president would be included in the inner circle of policy makers, and Truman insisted on the inclusion of the vice-president in the National Security Council. Biographer Robert Donovan writes:

> Truman's own unhappy experience as vice-president caused him to bring about a broadening of the role that now devolved upon (Vice-President Alben) Barkley. When Truman was vice-president, Roosevelt largely ignored him and excluded him from the innermost discussions of strategy and diplomacy as the Second World War was nearing a climax.[2]

Since the Truman administration vice-presidents have been included in the policy-making bodies, but their role in foreign policy has remained inconsistent, subject to the wishes of a given president.

Vice-President Richard Nixon, although not personally close to President Eisenhower, traveled abroad occasionally as spokesman for the administration, and his travels resulted in two major events—an attack by demonstrators in Venezuela and the famous "kitchen debate" with Soviet Premier Nikita Khrushchev in which the two differed heatedly on the two different systems they represented. The exchange took place in a model kitchen being displayed at an American trade fair in Moscow.

In the Kennedy administration Vice-President Lyndon Johnson was kept at a distance in terms of policy making, but he too was permitted to make trips abroad representing the United States. On one notable trip to the Middle East he extended to a camel driver an invitation to visit the United States, an invitation that was accepted once Johnson had become president and given wide coverage by the press and TV.

Presidents usually set the limits of a vice-president's role and influence in the policy process. President Jimmy Carter, for example, repeatedly emphasized the importance of his vice-president, Walter Mondale. Carter reports:

> . . . we agreed that he would truly be a second in command, involved in every aspect of governing. As a result he received the same security briefings I got, was automatically invited to participate in all my official meetings, and helped to plan strategy for domestic programs, diplomacy, and defense.[3]

The relationship extended to inclusion of Mondale in learning the procedures for response to a nuclear attack, a process in which vice-presidents had never previously been involved, according to Carter.[4] From the beginning of the Carter administrtion, the vice-president was among those included in Friday morning foreign-policy breakfast meetings, along with Secretary of State Cyrus Vance and National Security Adviser Zbigniew Brzezinski, and thereafter was involved in most major foreign-policy discussions and decisions.[5]

Vice-President Spiro Agnew did not fare nearly so well in the Nixon administraton. Kissinger writes:

> He (Nixon) started out thinking of Agnew as a political bungler; always sensitive to being overshadowed, he may well have picked him (Agnew) for that reason. Later, he came to see Agnew's utility as a hired gun, attacking targets not suitable for Presidential assault or venting emotions that Nixon secretly shared but did not dare to articulate. He never considered Agnew up to succeeding him. He once said, partly facetiously, that Agnew was his insurance policy against assassination.[6]

Although Agnew took part in major foreign-policy discussions, there is little evidence that his views were consistently taken seriously by the president.

Clearly, two more different relationships between a president and a vice-president are not easy to find in recent years. Yet whatever the relationship, the vice-president must be prepared to assume the presidency instantly. In the last four decades alone vice-presidents have either succeeded to the presidency or have been prepared to do so no less than six times. Truman succeeded Roosevelt in 1945; Johnson succeeded Kennedy in 1963; and Ford succeeded Nixon in 1974. Nixon was in readiness during two critical illnesses of President Eisenhower in 1956, and George Bush hurriedly returned to Washington on the day in March 1981 that President Reagan was shot. In addition, two assassination attempts on Gerald Ford emphasized the important role of (then) Vice-President Nelson Rockefeller.

In late January and early February 1983 Vice-President George Bush traveled to seven European nations to emphasize the Reagan administration's commitment to arms reduction. The trip was also designed to strengthen the position of West German chancellor Helmut Kohl in upcoming elections. Bush also met with the new Soviet leader, Yuri Andropov, in late 1982 after the death of Leonid Brezhnev and in 1984 with Konstantin Chernenko, who succeeded to the leadership after Andropov's death.

In general, with some exceptions, vice-presidents have had more responsibility in foreign policy since the 1950s, and in many instances they have played a very active role.

THE WHITE HOUSE STAFF

The television lights go on in the White House, crews sharpen the focus of their cameras, and reporters are alerted to the approach of the person moving into the room. It is the *press secretary*. Whether it be Jim Hagerty, Pierre Salinger, George Reedy, Ron Ziegler, Jody Powell, Jim Brady, or Larry Speakes, the daily briefings of reporters at the White House have become a major link between the president and the news media and thus a link to the people.[7] The position of press secretary is one of the many White House staff positions that have developed in importance in recent years. News coverage of the presidency has grown, and television has created the demand for live, talking figures. Relations with the news media have expanded considerably since the days when Franklin Roosevelt met occasionally with the relatively few newspaper and radio reporters who covered the White House. With the onset of the television age, the press secretary required not only journalistic experience but also some sense of how television could be utilized to serve the presidency. Eventually the press secretary became a public figure himself as television carried his face and voice into millions of homes. However, like other officials in the White House, the press secretary may or may not be directly involved in the policy process, depending upon his relationship with the president and the president's assessment of his competence in the field. In recent years, for example, Jody Powell, President Jimmy Carter's press secretary, was in the inner circles of Carter's advisers on all matters,[8] while in the Nixon administration, Ron Ziegler was not as close an adviser to Nixon.[9] In any event, the press secretary may be expected to contribute to decisions concerning the manner and techniques by which information should be communicated to the press and the public. Thus even when he does not influence the substance of policy, he may well affect the style in which it is presented and consequently the public perception of the policy. This perception, in turn, may be highly relevant to the success or failure of the policy.

Another White House staff position of considerable importance is that of *chief of staff*. Although this job is often regarded as one that relates to the administrative and organizational aspects of the presidency, some chiefs of staff have been more policy oriented than others. The chief of staff in the Nixon administration, H.R. Haldeman, rarely became involved in policy, especially foreign-policy issues,[10] according to Henry Kissinger. In the Carter administration Chief of Staff Hamilton Jordan, largely because of his long and close relationship with Jimmy Carter, participated in policy discussions, played an active role in the negotiations with Panama over a new canal treaty, and later played a large role in the Iranian hostage crisis.[11] On December 11, 1979, the president asked Jordan to make a secret trip to Panama to meet with Omar Torrijos to determine whether Panama would admit the shah of Iran. For the next several months Jordan was involved in some of the negotiations to obtain release of the hostages. It was a different role for the chief of staff—for any chief of staff—but the style of the president and his relationship with Jordan had this chief of staff directly involved in foreign policy.

In the Reagan administration, Chief of Staff James Baker returned to more conventional assignments. However, Reagan created a new position, *policy counselor,* answerable directly to the president and responsible for overall policy, although foreign policy remained primarily with the assistant for national security affairs. On occasion the policy counselor, Edwin Meese, acted as administration spokesman on a wide range of matters, including foreign policy. In past administrations certain special presidential advisers have also played major roles in the policy process. Colonel Edward House was a key figure in the administration of Woodrow Wilson, and Franklin Roosevelt utilized Harry Hopkins as adviser on both foreign and domestic policy. In the Kennedy administration Theodore Sorenson played an important role in policy formation.

To be sure, other White House staffers may be welcomed into the inner policy circle from time to time, and their entry may contribute to promotion and to increased influence. General Alexander Haig, at first a national security assistant to Henry Kissinger in the Nixon administration, went on to become chief of staff, succeeding Haldeman and becoming in one sense Kissinger's superior officer. Later, in the Reagan administration, Haig became secretary of state.

It is apparent that White House staff aides, under particular presidents and circumstances, may play important roles in the foreign-policy process.

THE NATIONAL SECURITY ADVISER

Henry Kissinger. Zbigniew Brezezinski. Very few Americans alive in the last fifteen years could have missed these names on the nightly television news or on the front pages of the nation's newspapers. Few Americans have ever had more influence on American foreign policy, and yet neither was elected by the American people or was directly responsible to Congress while holding the position of special assistant to the president for national security affairs, or as it is usually called, the national security adviser. Although the National Security Council was created by Congress in 1947 in the National Security Act, the position of special assistant was not established until the early years of the Eisenhower administration. Since then the position, like that of the council itself, has greatly expanded in functions and importance as well as in prominence. In the early years of the National Security Council system, the position of special assistant developed gradually. President Truman at first relied on cabinet officers or uniformed military officers until the period just prior to the Korean War when Averell Harriman was placed in the job. When General Eisenhower became president in 1953 he relied for security assistance in part on General Andrew Goodpaster, who was an assistant to the Chairman of the Joint Chiefs of Staff, and on other assistants brought in for special tasks. However, Robert Cutler became the first Special Assistant to the President for National Security Affairs and was succeeded by Gordon Grey. All three played a minimal public role in an administration where the public spokesmanship for foreign policy was concentrated in the secretary of state, John Foster Dulles. McGeorge Bundy became the special assistant to John F. Kennedy, and a number of factors converged in 1961 to provide Bundy with more responsibility and influence than his predecessors had had in the job.[12] Bundy continued in the position for a time in the administration of Lyndon Johnson but was eventually replaced by Walt W. Rostow, whose relationship with the president and whose influence on policy reached an even more intense level than his predecessors.

With the beginning of the Nixon administration, Henry Kissinger came into national prominence as special assistant to a president who had deep and knowledgeable convictions of his own. Kissinger succeeded in making his own role central to the White House in the president's leadership policy, and he remained a central figure after Nixon's resignation and replacement by Gerald Ford. In the process Kissinger also became secretary of state in late 1973 and held both positions simultaneously until 1975, when he was replaced as special assistant by General Brent Scowcroft.

The election of Jimmy Carter in 1976 brought Zbigniew Brzezinski to the position, and although he never matched the public prominence of Kissinger, he played an influential and vital role in developing Carter's foreign-policy views.

Convinced that the inevitable competition between the adviser and the secretary of state was inadvisable, President Ronald Reagan decided to lower the public profile of the adviser and to reinforce the power and position of the secretary of state. Yet inevitable conflicts arose. Reagan's special assistant, Richard Allen, was regarded as the symbol of administration differences with Secretary Alexander Haig, and Allen subsequently resigned over other matters. He was replaced by William Clark, a Reagan confidant, whose influence increased steadily. In the fall of 1983 Clark was replaced by Robert McFarlane.

Haig, however, had major differences of views with others within the

administration and resigned in mid-1982 to be succeeded by George
Shultz.

Whatever the differences in the personalities of the occupants and the
differing relationships with those in any administration with whom they
share power, the position of special assistant is immensely influential for
several reasons. First, he may be regarded as a personal adviser, mentor,
confidant, and friend to the president. Second, he has regular, immediate,
and undeniable access to the president. Third, he organizes and assigns the
work of the staff of the council, and finally, he chairs and supervises the
work of several major interdepartmental committees of the council. In this
role he is perceived as having the confidence of the president and the
delegation of presidential authority. As a public spokesperson for the
administration's policy, he also is regarded as a symbol of that policy. He
also has the forum from which to help shape the attitudes and the ideas of
the news media. Kissinger, using lengthy "backgrounders," both with and
without attribution, had extensive opportunity to persuade opinion makers
to see the world his way.

In any case the role of the national security adviser and his staff has
varied not only because of the personality and style of different presidents
but because there is inherent conflict over the desirable and appropriate
roles for the major actors. Kissinger offers his views of the boundary lines
of activity:

> I have become convinced that the running of interdepartmental machinery
> ought to be preeminently the responsibility of the security adviser (except
> perhaps in a crisis). A determined Secretary of State cannot fail to have his
> views heard whoever chairs the committees. The security adviser's contact
> with the media and with foreign diplomats should be reduced to a minimum;
> the articulation and conduct of foreign policy should be left in the main to the
> President and the Secretary of State (and of course their designees). The
> preparation of options, which is in the main what interdepartmental machin-
> ery does, should be the province of the security adviser chosen for fairness,
> conceptual grasp, bureaucratic savvy, and a willingness to labor anony-
> mously.[13]

It must be noted that these views were written after Kissinger had
achieved, with the support of President Nixon, more centralization of foreign-policy control within the White House than at any time since World
War II.

Arguing that the coordination of foreign and domestic policies
should remain with the president and with the White House, Brzezinski
says that "the central role of the Assistant for National Security Affairs
should be openly acknowledged and institutionalized."[14] He proposes
making the appointment subject to Senate confirmation and permitting the
adviser to appear before congressional committees. He further suggests
that the title be changed to director of national security affairs.[15]
Brzezinski writes:

> Today foreign affairs, diplomacy, and global security need above all to be
> coordinated. They cannot be made subject to decisions by a single depart-

ment. Rather, someone close to the President has to make certain that the President does not become a prisoner of departmental briefs.[16]

Further, such central direction makes it possible to better manage the interconnection between domestic policy and foreign affairs.[17]

Whatever the theoretical arguments about the best division of labor among the president's top advisers, each president will undoubtedly continue to shape the foreign policy machinery in the executive branch to his or her own purposes. And even when a president chooses to deemphasize the role of the national security adviser, the person who occupies the job will still have far more influence on policy than all but a few others.

THE NATIONAL SECURITY COUNCIL

The council, established in 1947, includes the very people who, individually are the president's key advisers. In addition to the president, the council formally includes the vice-president, the secretary of state, and the secretary of defense. The director of the CIA and the chairman of the Joint Chiefs of Staff are, by law, formal advisers. Other participants may include other officials at the pleasure of the president or those whose areas of operations are relevant to particular policies. Of course, the special assistant is also a part of the organization.

From the early days when President Truman barely used the council to the present, it has undergone several transformations, additions, and reorganizations to suit particular presidents. The result, however, has been that today the council is one major body in which policies are raised, considered, and decided. Ironically, it was Truman who began the enhancement of the role of the council, its staff, and its committees once the Korean War had begun.[18] President Eisenhower, experienced in the military staff system, transformed the council and its staff into a complex staff system, adding, as we have noted, the position of special assistant. For a number of reasons John Kennedy turned to the council and to McGeorge Bundy for personal advice and brought increased centralization of policy making into the White House. During the Cuban missile crisis of October 1962 Kennedy devised what he called the ExCom, an executive committee of the council formed to deal with the issue. It included not only the usual members of the committee but also the attorney general and a former secretary of state, Dean Acheson. The attorney general happened to be the president's brother, Robert Kennedy.

In Lyndon Johnson's administration the council was used less formally and less importantly. Johnson concentrated on a type of ExCom, a more informal gathering of the top officials at the "Tuesday Lunch." It was a system that concentrated decisions in the hands of the president during the Vietnam War.

When Richard Nixon became president, he reorganized the council under the leadership of Kissinger, and it again reflected a complex system of interdepartmental groups and committees, this time with Kissinger at the center of many of them. The system was designed to bring policy choices to the president, but as Kissinger's personal role grew, the importance of the committees receded. In Gerald Ford's short term following the resignation of Nixon, a reorganization of the council occurred, with control of the committees dispersed and distributed.

President Jimmy Carter again reorganized the council and simplified its committee system; control was divided between Brzezinski and other cabinet members affected by a given issue. Carter had hoped to coordinate more closely than his predecessors with formal executive departments, but Brzezinski's committee gained influence, as did the special assistant himself. In general, however, Carter attempted to deemphasize the role of the council, utilizing informal "foreign-policy breakfasts" and a four-man group including the special assistant, the secretaries of state and defense, and Vice-President Walter Mondale. It may be ironic that despite all the efforts to deemphasize the council, it was the secretary of state who eventually resigned over policy choices—especially the decision to send a military rescue mission to Iran in 1980.[19]

The National Security Council has been used extensively in the Reagan administration for deliberations of foreign policy problems and policies. Although its three directors, Richard Allen, William Clark, and Robert McFarlane, have kept a lower public profile than their predecessors, their influence on presidential decisions continues to be substantial, according to former Secretary of State Alexander Haig, who regards the NSC system as "incoherent."[20]

Like many other elements in the system, the council may be used in any way that a president determines, but it is clearly in an advantageous position to influence policy.

THE CABINET

Few presidents in the last fifty years have utilized the cabinet as a decision-making body, especially in foreign affairs. Composed basically of the president and the secretaries of all the major executive departments, the Cabinet may also include other officials designated by the president. Since Franklin Roosevelt, only Presidents Eisenhower and Reagan have seemed to place any major emphasis on policy making within the cabinet. Most presidents have utilized individual members of the cabinet on policies affecting their areas of activity. In some cases, however, presidents may have reservations about their cabinets. Henry Kissinger reports:

> Nixon's distrust of his Cabinet members exaggerated their already strong self-will. Partly through ignorance, partly because they felt no commitment to policies they had not shaped, they consistently cut across our initiatives or challenged our strategies that had been clearly articulated.[21]

Although Kissinger blames this situation on the secretive methods used by the president and himself in pursuing certain foreign policies and now regards this secrecy as unwise,[22] the pattern during the Nixon administration has been the customary one. The decision-making circle in foreign policy rarely includes most members of the cabinet.

Brzezinski, too, regards the cabinet with little enthusiasm:

> I should add that the Cabinet meetings never dealt with foreign-policy issues. Moreover, they were almost useless. The discussions were desultory, there was no coherent theme to them, and after a while, they were held less and less frequently.[23]

Even in the case of President Reagan, who announced his intention to utilize the cabinet more fully, decision making seemed to become more concentrated on a few key members and on the White House staff.

Before dismissing the cabinet as a serious instrument in the policy process, we must make two points. First, the cabinet is a useful body in which the president may articulate policies, in which expert advisers can explain it, and in which the president can seek the consensus needed to promote and support any policy. The second point is more long-range. In today's changing world the boundary line between foreign policy and domestic policy is becoming increasingly blurred, and many issues that previously would have been regarded as domestic now have complex foreign implications, and many foreign policies have domestic effects that must be integrated into domestic policies of an administration. One has to think only of farmers adversely affected by the grain embargoes imposed on the Soviet Union or of auto workers unemployed because of the increased import of foreign cars. Foreign policies deeply touch their lives, and their protests may inevitably affect foreign policy.

Thus it is not impossible to conceive that in the not-too-distant future the cabinet could return to the vital role it played in policy formation up to the time of the Franklin Roosevelt administration. Most departments of government, whose secretaries sit in the cabinet, have occasional stakes in foreign policy and foreign relations. The growing circle of issues and problems that constitute foreign policy may require the use of a broader consultative body to consider foreign poliy, and that body could well be the cabinet.

In any case there are at least three major cabinet departments whose involvement in foreign-policy formulation is already extensive: State, Defense, and Treasury, and their secretaries are among the president's most important advisers.

THE SECRETARY OF STATE

Historically the secretary of state has been seen as the president's chief adviser on foreign policy, and from the time of Thomas Jefferson's service as the first secretary of state to the present, the secretaries have tried vigorously to play that role. Although we shall discuss the State Department and its role in policy later, in this section our concentration is upon the individuals who have served in the office of secretary and of the unique position of the secretary, for some occupants of the position have had a personal influence on policy almost wholly independent from that of the department.

Since the Kennedy administration, secretaries have often had to compete to achieve or to hold their supposedly preeminent position as foreign-policy adviser and spokesperson for the president. Sometimes they have lost the competition, as the resignations of Vance and Haig in the last two administrations indicate. One of the reasons for the competition is the rise of new, relevant, and important structures involved in foreign policy. The growing importance of the National Security Council and the national security adviser has been noted. Elsewhere the scope and influence of Defense Department and the Treasury Department will be discussed. Another reason for the competition is the personality of presidential appointees and the capacity of some individuals to achieve influence equal to or greater than that of the secretary of state. Finally, another reason for the competition secretaries of state must endure is the president himself. As we have seen, presidents may rely upon different officials and different structures over time, and the secretary of state may or may not be favored. A president may simply prefer to be, in essence, his own secretary of state, or he may come to trust someone other than the secretary.

Henry Kissinger cites numerous instances during the Nixon administration in which Secretary of State William Rogers was not even informed of some secret foreign policy initiatives, such as Kissinger's secret trip to China to arrange for Nixon's later trip.[24] Kissinger's own appointment as secretary of state to succeed Rogers in 1973 came because Nixon was at that point in deep trouble over Watergate.[25]

There was never any doubt that Cyrus Vance would play a major role in the Carter administration as secretary of state. Regarded by Carter as "cool under pressure" and "very knowledgeable in both military matters and foreign affairs," Vance had served in a number of high positions in the Defense Department and in diplomacy.[26] Carter wanted the secretary to assume the role of educating the American public about foreign policy. However, Carter writes, "Secretary Vance was not particularly inclined to assume this task on a sustained basis: it is time consuming and not always pleasant."[27] On the other hand, National Security Adviser Zbigniew Brzezinski "was always ready and willing to explain our position on international matters, analyze a basic strategic relationship, or comment on a current event."[28] Although the former president said he appreciated the differences between the two men, their different views added to the inherent conflicts between the national security staff and the State Department. Still, until his resignation, Vance was a key participant in the formation of foreign policy in the Carter administration. Vance, however, opposed the military rescue mission to Iran and after warning against it, he resigned when the president ordered it. The resignation was painful for both men. As Carter described it:

> We discussed the fact that my general views and political philosophy were very close to his, and that there was no serious difference between us on major issues of American foreign policy. We agreed that I would speak with him later about whether he should leave, but I said I would not try to talk him

out of it. We both knew he had made an irrevocable decision—the only decision possible.[29]

Soon afterward Carter appointed Senator Edmund Muskie as secretary. In his book he comments on the change:

> He [Muskie] enjoyed the role of public spokesman and had an easier relationship with Zbig [Brzezinski] and the staff around the Oval Office. Not as knowledgeable as Cy [Vance] about the details of diplomacy, Ed nevertheless brought to the Secretary's office a broad and mature understanding of our nation itself and its international role. . . .[30]

The tenure of Alexander Haig Jr. as secretary of state in the Reagan administration was unexpectedly short. According to Haig, "lack of communication, aggravated by staff mischief, was the root problem".[31] In the book on his experiences in the administration, *Caveat*, and in numerous interviews in the media, Haig reported that when President Reagan asked him to take the job, Haig understood that the president wanted him to be the "vicar" of foreign policy, that is, the primary administration architect and spokesman of foreign policy. Haig argued that a National Security Council memo establishing the structure of control of the administration's foreign policy was never signed.[32] Haig contends that his access to the president was limited by the White House staff and that it was rarely private.[33] In general, Haig believes that a president must have a clearly designated deputy in charge of foreign policy:

> . . . It does not really matter whether the Secretary of State or the National Security Adviser or some other official carries out the president's foreign policy and speaks for the administration on these questions. What does matter is that the person chosen by the President must be seen to have his total confidence and that he be his sole spokesman, since policy has been decided through the free but unbreakably confidential discussion of advice within the National Security Council.[34]

When the president fired Haig in June 1982, he turned to George Shultz as a replacement. Although Shultz subsequently faced some of the same internal problems as Haig had, he brought to the job a less intense public profile. *New York Times* reporter Bernard Gwertzman wrote:

> There is a discernible shift in emphasis at the State Department these days, away from the personal role of the Secretary of State in the management of foreign policy.[35]

But as time went on, Shultz' travel schedule and his public appearances, like those of his predecessors, increased considerably. Nonetheless, Shultz managed to remain less controversial than his predecessor and was thought to have won the battle for influence within the administration. It was reported in November 1983 that Shultz and his top aides had emerged "as the paramount voice in the Reagan administration's foreign policy."[36]

Of course, whatever the impact of a secretary on a given president or on history, the making and articulation of high policy and the advising of the president are not the only duties of the secretary.[37] In a constitutional and political sense, he is also responsible for the *execution* of that policy throughout the world, and that means responsibility for administration and management of the entire State Department, with its embassies, consulates, offices, and related agencies scattered in scores of countries. He must either exercise direct supervision or take care that it is well done by key subordinates. At the same time, he must direct the study, analysis, and formulation of positions by the many regional and functional parts of the department. Finally, whether it is wise or not, the secretary is sometimes expected to personally conduct high-level diplomacy with representatives of other nations and to occasionally engage in "shuttle diplomacy" to settle some impending crisis or another.

Former Secretary of State Cyrus Vance has noted:

> All sorts of demands impinge on the life of the secretary of state and restrict his ability to set his own agenda; the exigency of events overseas, over which he may have little, if any, control; time spent with the president and the Congress; weeks of foreign travel; and meetings with the press.[38]

Vance states that meetings with the president take precedence, and he estimates that at least one-quarter of his time was spent on congressional matters. For every hour of congressional testimony, Vance reports, five to six hours of preparation were necessary. "Even working 12–14 hours a day, secretaries are hard pressed to discharge their responsibilities effectively."[39] In an effort to deal with these time pressures, Vance relied heavily upon his deputy, Warren Christopher; assigned greater responsibility and authority to senior subordinates in Washington and ambassadors in the field; and drew increasingly on the career foreign-service personnel for advice on major issues. However, Vance notes that sharing authority was "to prove an extremely difficult matter, perhaps indicating an underlying institutional problem requiring major structural reforms."[40]

Certainly these difficulties and time pressures were not unique to Secretary Vance, and they raise serious questions about how the secretary and the department are to be most effectively utilized in any administration for maximum productivity and efficiency.

That all of these simultaneous responsibilities are excessive for any secretary of state seems to be overlooked most of the time. Given their number and scope, however, it is little wonder that the opportunity, perhaps even the need, exists for others to assume major responsibilities as advisers to the president on foreign policy. Still, with all of it, a surprising number of secretaries in recent years have been able to establish and maintain the traditional role of the secretary of state as the primary adviser to the president when and if the president wants it that way.

THE SECRETARY OF DEFENSE

An occasional rival to the secretary of state within the president's cabinet has been the secretary of defense.[41] His power stems not only from the fact that he is the head of the largest single department of government and that the department is responsible for guaranteeing the nation's security but also from the implicit fact that a nation's foreign policy is to a considerable extent based on the effectiveness of its military capability. When a country has worldwide political and military interests, defense policy is necessarily foreign policy, and foreign policy must often take military matters into consideration. In view of this, surprisingly few secretaries of defense have become challengers in the public mind for eminence in the foreign-policy process, but this does not mean that they do not participate vigorously in the process. As formal members of the National Security Council, secretaries are well informed, intensely interested, and frequently involved when foreign policy is considered. Since military operations overseas require social and political accommodation to host governments, secretaries of defense are necessarily sensitive to political relations with those governments.

Like other department secretaries, the secretary of defense is responsible for the management and administration of a huge and complex organization as well as for articulating to the president and to the public his and the department's views on sound foreign and military policy. The administrative job is made even more awesome by the necessity for, and the responsibility of, the secretary to assert civilian control over the professional military. This control includes three separate military departments, two of which have existed since the beginning of the Republic—the Department of the Army and the Department of the Navy. The Department of the Air Force was created in 1947.

Still some defense secretaries have sought to play a prominent role in broad foreign-policy questions.

The rivalry that developed in the Ford administration between Kissinger and James Schlesinger has been noted in Kissinger's memoirs:

> At any rate, the differences between Schlesinger and me, though partly rooted in the different perceptions and missions of the departments we headed, were more personal than intellectual. . . . Schlesinger saw no intellectual reason for conceding my preeminence as Presidential counselor. . . . After a while, Schlesinger missed few opportunities to score points against me, even though our strategic assessments were substantially similar.[42]

More recently in the Reagan administration, Defense Secretary Caspar Weinberger publicly and also, according to some reports, privately, expressed differences of policy with Secretary of State Haig.[43] That, however, as noted above, was part of the deeper internal conflicts of personalities and policies that existed during the first two years of the Reagan administration.

During the Carter years Harold Brown assumed an expanded role as spokesperson for Carter policy for two reasons: First, Secretary of State Cyrus Vance was not always dominant within the administration on foreign policy; and second, Vance virtually ignored the role of public spokesperson. Indeed it was during this period that Vance's press secretary, Hodding Carter, became more familiar to the public as the voice of foreign policy than either his boss, Vance, or the president. The result was that Brown's influence in private councils as well as in the public was enhanced.[44]

What is clear, however, is that the potential exists for secretaries of defense to become major figures and major influences in making foreign policy and also as foreign-policy spokespersons.

THE FIRST FAMILY

In 1961 Jacqueline Kennedy, who speaks fluent French, accompanied her husband on a state visit to France designed to improve American relations with French president Charles DeGaulle. In the glitter of state dinners in Paris Mrs. Kennedy charmed DeGaulle, impressed the French people, and contributed to a warming of relations between the two governments. Upon the return of the Kennedys from France, the president noted, "I am known as the man who accompanied Jacqueline Kennedy to France."[45]

To be sure, there is no evidence that Mrs. Kennedy ever attempted to make any contribution to her husband's views or policies or even had the remotest interest in doing so. Yet her presence on the Paris trip underscored the fact that members of a president's family may, indeed, play an important foreign-policy role on occasion. For John Kennedy's brother Robert the role was much more direct. Appointed attorney general in his brother's administration, Robert Kennedy was a close personal confidant and adviser on all policy, and his participation in the ExCom decision-making group in the Cuban missile crisis is well documented.[46] In 1968 Robert Kennedy himself was a candidate for the Democratic nomination for president before his assassination in June of that year.

As a daughter in a former first family, Margaret Truman concludes: "There is no doubt that, as First Lady, Mrs. Roosevelt had the greatest impact on our country."[47] While FDR was alive, Mrs. Roosevelt's influence was largely confined to domestic concerns. It was only after his death that Mrs. Roosevelt became a major figure in the creation and passage of the United Nations Universal Declaration of Human Rights.[48]

A more intensive and complex role in policy marked Rosalynn Carter's years as first lady. Carter wrote in his memoirs: "All of us turned to her for sound advice on issues and political strategy."[49] In Washington she participated in activities involving mental health, the aged, and community improvement. Her role was much broader, however, as Carter describes it:

> She and I continued to discuss the full range of important issues and, aside from a few highly secret and sensitive security matters, she knew all that was going on. When necessary, she received detailed briefings from members of my domestic and national security staff; it was most helpful for me to discuss questions of importance with her as I formed my opinions.—Rosalynn has strong opinions of her own and never gave up on one of her ideas as long as there was any hope of being accepted.[50]

During Carter's term his wife traveled abroad frequently on official trips, and during the Iranian hostage crisis, "she felt strongly that we should stop buying Iranian oil and announce this decision as soon as possible.[51] Carter discussed the idea with the cabinet and two days later ordered the move.

Of course, not all first ladies or first families become involved in the policy process, and very few are known to have contributed to foreign policy.

In the Reagan administration the first lady, Nancy Reagan, confined her public activity in foreign policy to accompanying the president on trips abroad. Her domestic interests included work with the handicapped and drug addicts. There were some reports, however, that she played a part in Reagan's decision to accept the resignation of National Security Adviser Richard Allen after revelations that he had accepted gifts from Japanese businessmen. It was reported that she felt Allen's actions had embarrassed her husband and his administration.[52]

Occasionally, of course, family members other than the first lady may become involved in the public image of an administration, and the involvement may not always be welcome. During the last days of the Carter administration, for example, the president's brother, Billy, received considerable notoriety for accepting a fee as a lobbyist for Libya, a country regarded as not very friendly to the United States.[53] The president declined to be critical publicly, but many commentators regarded the matter as highly embarrassing to him.

SUMMARY

These people, and many more, constitute a presidency. Their importance and their influence on policy obviously vary considerably. In this section we have tried to identify some of the major factors that affect the variance. Of course there are also other individuals in key jobs who might have been included. Many of those key jobs will be discussed in the next chapter, for their involvement is usually based more on institutional factors than on personal ones.

The officials discussed in this chapter are more likely to play the public roles and the roles primarily designated for foreign-policy responsibilities under the Constitution and the laws of the United States. They tend to be elected or selected for their perceived views on foreign policy; for their experience and expertise in dealing with matters of negotiation, administration, and management; and/or for their symbolic representation of various constituencies.

There is another important consideration. Just as it is their duty to communicate their advice upward to the president, these officials, in turn, are the recipients in their own departments of pressures from subordinates directed upward to them. Both the president and his immediate advisers are also subject to demands, pressures, and influence from numerous outside, private sources.

This brief review of key decision makers, their actions, and the interplay among them clearly underscores the importance of the "politics" framework. The selection of the president results from the operations of competitive politics in regular elections. His choice of key assistants is, in part, based upon his political considerations of their constituencies, their political capabilities, and their political experience as well as their expertise, and in some cases expertise is the least important factor. Then in addition to certain inevitable conflicts within an administration that derive from the very structure of the presidency and of the executive branch as a whole, strong personalities with strongly held views inevitable engage in political conflict in order to prevail in the policy process. Furthermore, the major advisers must also engage in political bargaining within their departments before they can stand before the president with a solid and unified position.

It is from the interplay of all these forces, and many others, that policy emerges. Beyond the key figures already discussed, there are many other vital actors in the process, and the next chapter includes an identification of other parts of the executive branch with major involvement in foreign policy.

NOTES

[1] Margaret Truman, *Harry S. Truman* (New York: Pocket Books, 1974), pp. 226–32.

[2] Robert J. Donovan, *Tumultuous Years: The Presidency of Harry S. Truman, 1949–53* (New York: W. W. Norton & Company, 1982), p. 20.

[3] Jimmy Carter, *Keeping Faith* (New York: Bantam Books, 1982), p. 39.

[4] Ibid., p. 40.

[5] Ibid., pp. 55–56.

[6] Henry Kissinger, *Years of Upheaval* (Boston: Little, Brown & Company, 1982), p. 92.

[7] William C. Spragens with Carole Ann Terwoord, *From Spokesman to Press Secretary: White House Media Operations* (Lanham, Md.: University Press of America, 1980), pp. 1–90; Kenneth W. Thompson, ed., *Ten Presidents and the Press* (Washington, D.C.: University Press of America, 1983), passim.

[8] Carter, *Keeping Faith*, p. 44.

[9] Kissinger, *White House Years*, (Boston: Little, Brown & Company, 1979) passim; and Kissinger, *Years of Upheaval*, passim. I find no citations in either book of Zeigler's involvement in the decision process.

[10] Kissinger, *Years of Upheaval*, p. 437.

[11] Hamilton Jordan, *Crisis: The Last Year of the Carter Presidency* (New York: G. P. Putnam's Sons, 1982), pp. 48, 74–75.

[12] I. M. Destler, "The Rise of the National Security Assistant 1961–81," in Charles W. Kegley and Eugene R. Wittkopf, *Perspectives on American Foreign Policy* (New York: St. Martin's Press, 1983), pp. 260–81.

[13] Kissinger, *Years of Upheaval*, p. 437.

[14] Zbigniew Brzezinski, *Power and Principle* (New York: Farrar, Straus & Giroux, 1983), p. 536.

[15] Brzezinski, *Power and Principle*, pp. 536–37; and "Deciding Who Makes Foreign Policy," *New York Times Magazine*, September 18, 1983, pp. 56–74.

[16] Brzezinski, *Power and Principle*, p. 527.

[17] Ibid., p. 537.

[18] Charles W. Kegley and Eugene R. Wittkopf, *American Foreign Policy: Pattern and Process*, 2nd ed. (New York: St. Martin's Press, 1982) p. 329.

[19] Carter, *Keeping Faith*, p. 513.

[20] Alexander M. Haig, Jr., *Caveat: Realism, Reagan, and Foreign Policy*, (New York: Macmillan Publishing Company, 1984), p. 147.

[21] Kissinger, *White House Years*, p. 448.

[22] Ibid.

[23] Brzezinski, *Power and Principle*, p. 67.

[24] Kissinger, *White House Years*, p. 28.

[25] Kissinger, *Years of Upheaval*, p. 4.

[26] Carter, *Keeping Faith,* p. 50.

[27] Ibid., p. 54.

[28] Ibid.

[29] Ibid., p. 513.

[30] Ibid., p. 521.

[31] Haig, *Caveat:* p. 147.

[32] Ibid., p. 355.

[33] Ibid., p. 141.

[34] Ibid., p. 356.

[35] Bernard Gwertzman, "Under Shultz, A Shift to a Less Personalized Role," *New York Times,* October 28, 1982, p. B12.

[36] Leslie Gelb, "Shultz, Pushing a Hard Line, Becomes Key Voice in Crises," *New York Times,* November 7, 1983, p. 1.

[37] John H. Esterline and Robert B. Black, *Inside Foreign Policy* (Palo Alto, Calif: Mayfield Publishing Co., 1975), pp.45–46; Kissinger, *White House Years,* pp. 27–28.

[38] Cyrus Vance, *Hard Choices: Critical Years in America's Foreign Policy* (New York: Simon and Schuster, 1982), p. 14.

[39] Ibid.

[40] Ibid., p. 41.

[41] Esterline and Black, *Inside Foreign Policy,* pp. 26–30.

[42] Kissinger, *Years of Upheaval,* pp. 1154–55.

[43] James A. Nathan and James K. Oliver, *Foreign Policy Making and the American Political System,* 2nd ed. (Boston: Little, Brown and Company, 1983), pp. 76–79.

[44] Carter, *Keeping Faith,* p. 55; Kegley and Wittkopf, *American Foreign Policy,* pp. 366–67; Brzezinski, *Power and Principle,* pp. 44–47.

[45] Arthur M. Schlesinger, Jr., *A Thousand Days* (Greenwich, Conn.: Fawcett Publications, 1965), pp. 331–32.

[46] Schlesinger, *A Thousand Days,* pp. 733–49; Theodore Sorenson, *Kennedy* (New York: Harper & Row, Publishers, 1965), pp. 674–76.

[47] Margaret Truman, "The Second Toughest Job," *Parade,* August 15, 1982, p. 4.

[48] Joseph Lash, *Eleanor, The Years Alone* (New York: W. W. Norton & Company, 1972), pp. 55–81.

[49] Carter, *Keeping Faith,* p. 31.

[50] Ibid., pp. 32–33.

[51] Ibid., pp. 461–62.

[52] Jack Nelson, "Washington Week in Review," Public Broadcasting System, January 28, 1983, 8:00–8:30 P.M. EST.

[53] Carter, *Keeping Faith,* pp. 545–50.

CHAPTER FIVE
DOING THE JOB:
STATE AND DEFENSE

> The complexity of modern government makes large bureaucracies essential; but the need for innovation also creates the imperative to define purposes that go beyond administrative norms. Ultimately, there is no purely organizational answer; it is above all a problem of leadership.
>
> Henry Kissinger

Few analysts or decision makers have been more critical of the role of bureaucracies in the foreign-policy process than Henry Kissinger. Bureaucracies differ in size and complexity, but in general they are structured divisions of labor, performing specific tasks, composed largely of career professionals operating under specific rules and norms. In the foreign-policy field, they include a surprising number of government departments, agencies, and functions, including the State, Defense, and Treasury Departments; the Central Intelligence Agency and other parts of the intelligence system; the Office of Management and Budget and the Federal Reserve Board; partially autonomous structures such as the Agency for International Development, the U.S. Information Agency, and the Peace Corps; parts of such other government departments as Labor, Agriculture, Commerce, and Justice; and a number of other participants.

In the past few decades substantial scholarly attention has been devoted to the study of bureaucracies and of their effects on the formulation and implementation of policy. In each new presidency speculation emerges about how the chief executive will finally take control of the bureaucracies or whether he will attempt it at all. In the foreign-policy field presidents have frequently turned to the smaller bureaucracy of the National Security Council staff and to the National Security adviser to explore policy initiatives, policy options, and implementation.

Consideration of the role of the bureaucracies in the process is important because (1) they play a role in determining policy; (2) they are usually indispensable in the implementation of policy; and (3) they have their own internal political battles over development of their institutional positions on issues.

Two students of bureaucracies have described the situation:

> The individuals involved in decision-making do not see the problem in the same way, nor do they have the same interests. Each participant, because of his background and his particular role in the government, has access to different information and different concerns. Each sees a different *face* of the issue.[1]

Each will have different stakes and will take different stands on issues.

The bureaucracies often recognize and raise issues that are brought to the attention of the president, requiring a decision. First, the bureaucracies must each decide on a position to present, and that can lead to intense internal debates over what position to take. Once positions are developed, each bureaucracy involved in an issue may engage in a debate with other departments and agencies promoting their own proposals, each seeking to prevail in the policy preferences of the president.

Then, as Halperin and Kanter put it:

> Despite the enormous time and effort which goes into the struggle over the decisions the President will make, in most cases the decisions which emerge are in no sense definitive. Often, they are very general. They may be only statements of aspiration—vague policy decisions—or they may be somewhat more specific in that they assign a general action to a particular organization or individual. Even then, they are likely to leave considerable leeway as to who should act, what precisely they should do, and when they should do it.[2]

Thus "complete and faithful implementation of a presidential decision remains the exception rather than the rule."[3] Compliance may depend on "whether the executors favor implementation."[4]

In addition, some decisions may be made in the field without any decision or direction. "Instead of sending an issue to Washington for a decision, they may act without instructions."[5]

The problem is complicated by the growing number of departments and agencies involved in the foreign-policy process. A president must take their recommendations into consideration, must listen to their arguments, and must be sensitive to their insights because he will need their cooperation if he is to make the administration's policy work.

In formulating policy presidents and some of their top advisers have often disregarded the contributions of the bureaucracies and have relied on the White House staff, the national security adviser, and their own judgment.

Nonetheless, the bureaucracies are the source of important information and expertise on which policy decisions are often made. It is useful, therefore, to identify and assess the roles of some of the key departments and agencies.

THE STATE DEPARTMENT

No department of government has been more subject to debate, criticism, reorganization, and scholarly analysis than the State Department. Arguments persist up to the present moment about the role that the department should ideally play in the policy process, the effectiveness or lack of it with which the department has historically played its role, and the capacity of any large bureaucratic structure to play an effective role at all in the affairs of the modern global environment where rapid change is the rule rather than the exception. In the last fifty years presidents have alternately tried to control it, circumvent it, ignore it, or reorganize it and have often distrusted it. During the 1950s the very loyalty of its personnel was attacked and its confidence badly shaken. Yet it is "an organization staffed by probably the ablest and most professional group of men and women in public service. They are intelligent, competent, loyal, and hardworking."[6] They constitute a repository of experience and expertise in dealing with foreign affairs largely unmatched by any other institution in the country.

Despite all of this, the State Department's role in the formulation of policy, its participation in the politics of the policy process, and its success in developing and advocating specific positions and having them adopted are more modest than many department professionals desire. Indeed, the internal political process by which the department arrives at a position is cumbersome and contributes to the problem.

In one study of the department it is contended that the role of the department may be considered on a continuum of five levels of decision making: minor, routine, significant, fundamental, and critical.[7] Most of the department deals only with minor and routine decisions; only a few significant decisions are made by officials other than the secretary and his major subordinates; and the bulk of significant decisions are made in consequence of interactions with the White House and other agencies. All fundamental and critical decisions involve the White House. The authors of the study conclude that the basic relevance of the department to policy is through implementation, not formulation, of policy.[8]

There are other views about the future role of the department in the policy process. Stanley Hoffmann suggests:

> The real mission of State ought to be to provide what functional departments rarely possess: skill in *political* analysis and *synthetic* ability—the capacity to study in depth the political conditions abroad (a very different task from reporting the latest public news and the latest private chit-chat), and the capacity to show to the President, to the public, and, of course, to the Congress (with which the State Department has to deal) how the functional pieces of the puzzle fit or conflict.[9]

This process, according to Hoffmann, would provide directly to the president the possible policy alternatives on a steadier and broader basis than the National Security Councils have. However, Hoffmann notes another inherent obstacle in the path of State Department management of foreign policy, namely, the fact that policy encompasses so many aspects of the global system and that "almost every domestic function has an international component."[10] At the very least, this would also involve strengthening the department's capability in the economic field.

In any event, the debate over the appropriate role of the department in the policy process is certain to continue, and each new president and each new secretary will continue to mold the system to personal predispositions of how policy should be made.

Whatever its role, the department will continue to be involved in the process and in making policy decisions work.

The challenge to the department's preeminence in foreign policy is hardly new.

The colonies conducted foreign relations before they formally became the United States of America.[11] Between 1775 and 1789, the Continental Congress exercised authority in the name of the United States. Between 1775 and 1777 Congress maintained a Committee of Secret Correspondence, which preceded creation of a Committee of Foreign Affairs. When, under the Articles of Confederation, Congress created a Department of Foreign Affairs with Robert Livingston as secretary, the Congress retained authority. Later, in 1784 John Jay was given the responsibility, and during the period Jay, Benjamin Franklin, and John Adams, among others, conducted diplomatic relations abroad in search of financial, military, and political support for the new nation-state.

With the ratification of the new Constitution in 1789, the First Congress moved quickly to create the first executive department—the State Department—on July 27, 1789. At first, it was called the Department of Foreign Affairs, and Thomas Jefferson was named as the first secretary of state.

The next year, 1790, Congress moved to formalize the establishment of a diplomatic service, adding the consular service in 1792; the two services were combined in 1924, and later, in 1954–57, they were made an integrated part of the State Department.

Personal and departmental competition for dominance in foreign policy developed early between the State Department under Thomas Jefferson and the Treasury Department under Alexander Hamilton. The two personal and political rivals carried their differences into foreign policy. The competition still exists and now the adversaries are not just State and Treasury but also State and the White House staff or State and Defense.

When Jefferson became the first secretary of state under the new Constitution, the department was made up of the secretary and five assistants: a chief clerk, three ordinary clerks, and a translator.[12] By 1980 the department had some twenty-one thousand employees (still one of the smallest of the departments), operating in 234 posts around the world in 133 countries, including 143 embassies, 12 missions, 67 consulates general, 42 consulates, 3 branch offices, and 14 consular agencies.[13]

The department is located in a section of Washington known as Foggy Bottom in an eight-story building. The secretary has a deputy secretary;

undersecretaries for political, economic, and security affairs; a counselor; and a deputy undersecretary for management.[14]

Customarily the undersecretary for political affairs is the major subordinate to the secretary in developing overall policy positions. Ideally the relationship should be a close personal and professional one, but occasionally sharp differences develop, causing internal department conflict. One such case involved Secretary of State Dean Rusk and his undersecretary, Chester Bowles. Bowles believed that President John F. Kennedy wanted the department to take charge of foreign policy and to develop new ideas to cope with new developments as many new nation-states emerged in the 1960s. As Bowles tells it, "Rusk was far more comfortable with the traditional State Department approach than I was, or I believed the President to be."[15]

According to Bowles, Rusk's view seemed to be that "the primary task of the State Department was not to think up 'new ideas,' "[16] while Bowles felt that "in the conduct of foreign policy the United States government was urgently in need of new ideas."[17] The differences in perspective eventually led to Bowles's reassignment as ambassador to India.

Apart from his direct responsibilities to a president, the secretary spends most of his time carrying out his major responsibilities within the department, including going to daily staff conferences, appointments, and social and protocol functions, reading cables and other communications, dealing with the news media, monitoring the administrative operations of the department, conducting personal diplomacy abroad, and testifying before Congress.[18]

The deputy secretary and undersecretaries must respond to the demands of the secretary and operate their own functional areas as well. However, very often the process that leads to departmental decisions begins at the level of the assistant secretaries, especially those responsible for the various geographic regions of the world: African affairs, European affairs, East Asian and Pacific affairs, Inter-American affairs, and Near Eastern and South Asian affairs.[19] In addition, there is an assistant secretary for international organization affairs, and given the expansion of American participation in international organizations, this is a post of increasing importance.

The role of the regional assistant secretary has been summarized as follows:

> The ultimate decision-makers—whether they be on the seventh floor, in the White House, the military, the intelligence community, or even in Congress—need the informational input of the assistant secretary as well as his assessment and judgment. But the regional assistant secretary cannot move toward basic problem resolution without the input, assessment, and sanction of his own principals and those of other agencies. He may propose, but he may not dispose.[20]

Once decisions are made, it is often left to the assistant secretary to write them, explain their rationale, and argue for support, and the policy direction the assistant secretary receives may be vague, ambiguous, or uncommunicated.[21]

One study suggests that "a degree of week-to-week decision-making about shifts in policy emphasis and policy recommendation does take place at the level of regional assistant secretary."[22] Any policy decisions at this level, however, must be reviewed by department superiors, and often final concurrence must occur at the White House or elsewhere.

The level at which the most direct contact occurs between the department and operations abroad is the country director, whose assignment is to coordinate daily activity with a particular country or countries.[23] The country director is the principal point of contact not only for the American mission abroad but also for the foreign country's ambassador in Washington. Although the views of country directors may be well informed and may occasionally impress their superiors, the directors' contribution to decision making is limited.

In addition to the levels just described, there are numerous special functions within the department: operation and administration of the Foreign Service Institute; the policy planning staff; the Bureau of Intelligence and Research; press relations; public affairs; educational and cultural affairs; economic and business affairs; legal adviser; congressional relations; politico-military affairs; security and consular affairs; the inspector general; administration; and oceans and international environment and scientific affairs.[24]

In July 1982, when George Shultz succeeded Alexander Haig as secretary of state, some apparent changes in emphasis were expected, including a less personalized and public role in policy by the new secretary. As one report indicated in October 1982, Shultz remained "something of a mystery not only to the press but to most of the State Department."[25] Although Shultz reportedly felt that the diplomats in the field should carry the primary responsibility for dealing with crises under the overall direction from the State Department hierarchy, it was reported that a number of Foreign Service officers had said he had "not yet passed on a clear idea of where he wants to change policies, if at all."[26]

The final level of organization in the department consists of those who operate American diplomatic missions abroad. Although the missions are by no means the exclusive province of the State Department, the ambassador and the officers of the foreign service remain formally in charge.

The Overseas Establishment

Almost anywhere in the world where you might travel you will find an official representative of the United States government. American embassies, military bases, consulates, missions, and volunteers abound throughout the world, and more than forty governmental departments, agencies, and organizations operate in some of the larger countries abroad. This vast network of American influence and enterprise is the framework of American global activity. Although it is impossible to generalize about its effect on the formation of American policy, some members of this foreign establishment may occasionally play an important role in the policy process when they provide new and crucial information or when their recommendations are sought. The primary impact of these agents of American policy, however, stems from their implementation of policy already established in Washington. Second, the effectiveness of their communication, associations, and cooperation with the leaders and peoples of other countries contributes to the formation of attitudes in those countries toward the United States and its purposes. This foreign establishment is by no means monolithic, however. It is composed of many parts with different and sometimes conflicting missions, but in theory in each country all of these groups and activities come under the general supervision of the ambassador.

Ambassadors

As representative of the president of the United States with full power to act in his behalf, the ambassador is the chief executive of all American operatives in a given country. In the past, when transportation and communication facilities were comparatively slow, the ambassador was empowered to act with the full authority of the United States within the country to which he was assigned. But in this era of instantaneous communication and jet travel the ambassador is subject to constant direction from superiors in Washington. Nonetheless, the ambassador remains a central figure in the foreign relations of the United States. However, there have been numerous cases in which representatives of other agencies—the military, the CIA, or AID—have either circumvented the authority of the ambassador or actually exceeded it, making control of foreign policy and foreign relations less complete than it was intended to be.

Like so many other presidential appointments, ambassadors vary in skill, background, experience, and training. They may be past political supporters of a president, career diplomats, or experts with experience in universities, foundations, or corporations. In one case in the Reagan administration, the president appointed an actor-colleague, John Gavin, as ambassador to Mexico. Unlike some political appointees, Gavin spoke the language and was knowledgeable about Mexican-American affairs.

Whether or not the ambassador is experienced in foreign policy, he or she will have access to the expertise of the professional career embassy staff.

Embassy Staff

Although some of the components of an embassy staff may consist of members of departments other than the State Department, the highest ranking members of the staff are members of the Foreign Service in a number of ranks: minister, counselor, first secretary, second secretary, third secretary, attaché, and Foreign Service officer class. Of somewhat lesser status are Foreign Service information officers, Foreign Service reserve officers, and Foreign Service staff officers.[27]

Military embassy staff with the rank of general or admiral rank with the senior Foreign Service officers.

In general the diplomatic mission includes a chief of mission (the ambassador in most cases); a deputy chief of mission and staff aides; and subdivisions in political, economic/commercial, consular, administrative, and science and technology affairs. There are other agencies attached to the misison at various levels: ICA, AID, defense attachés, treasury, and so on.[28]

The number of functional units attached to the mission has increased rapidly in the expanded specialization that has developed since World War II, and the number of people working in the embassy under the jurisdiction of the ambassador has also increased substantially. In some places where the United States has extensive interests the staff may be in the hundreds.

Although the diplomatic mission is the source of intense internal political competition and the interplay of conflicting views, its role in the formulation of policy is, with rare exceptions, quite indirect. During the Vietnam War, for example, Ambassadors Henry Cabot Lodge or Ellsworth Bunker acquired a notable influence on high policy in Washington. For the most part, however, the policy views of a particular embassy, by whatever internal means a position was reached on a given question, necessarily must be processed through the State Department hierarchy back in Washington, and top department officials are free to utilize the ambassador's recommendation in any way that they decide is most prudent. If the embassy recommendation is accepted by the secretary and his key aides and is adopted as the policy of the department, it may then be supported in discussions with the president and in the National Security Council. Thus the embassy's role in the policy process may be indirect at best.

The Foreign Service

America's diplomatic representation abroad began in 1776, although informal contacts operated prior to independence. Notably, Benjamin Franklin's efforts to obtain French assistance for the Revolution highlighted successful American diplomacy during this critical period of history.[29] Once the Constitution was ratified in 1789 and the new government established, Congress moved quickly to establish the diplomatic service in a more formal way, and in 1792 it also established the consular service. The two services were combined in 1924, and the Foreign Service has been integrated into the State Department since the period of 1954–57.[30] This service has become the basic professional structure of diplomacy. In 1968 Congress created the category of Foreign Service information officer to integrate professionals working in the United States Information Agency.[31] However, the FSIO does not share equal status in the embassy with the FSOs. Two additional categories of Foreign Service officers, the Foreign Service reserve officers, and Foreign Service staff officers, also have lower official status.[32]

With the exception of the top positions open to presidential appointment, most of the key positions within the State Department are occupied by career Foreign Service officers. They are chosen from an intense selection process, and their experience includes alternating tours of duty between Washington and foreign assignments, the purpose of which is to develop both specific and general knowledge and experience in the diplomatic process.[33] Experience and expertise are supplemented by additional training in the Foreign Service Institute, which provides background in foreign languages, politics, management, and other diplomatic skills.

In short, the Foreign Service provides the pool of highly trained and experienced personnel to serve in the nation's most sensitive foreign-policy posts.

This brief description of the structure and operation of the State Department suggests at least four broad levels at which the processes of politics are at work as the department seeks to participate in the formulation of policy: the political struggle within the mission, the relations between the missions and the department, the internal argument within the department as a policy position evolves, and the attempt by the department to have its views prevail against other structures—the White House staff, the Defense Department, the National Security Council staff, among others.

It is a very clear political process, and the outcome is never certain.

Agency for International Development

In 1961 the foreign-aid component of the United States government became known as the Agency for International Development (AID). It evolved from a number of other agencies that had existed during the immediate post-World War II period, and in many ways it has reflected over the years the changing American attitudes toward foreign aid to other countries.[34] As many Americans came to view foreign aid as a giveaway, new forms were sought to package aid in ways that would be effective and acceptable.

In the process AID came to dispense loans, grants, and Security Supporting Assistance (designed to support internal security efforts of recipient governments).[35] Among the types of assistance offered by the agency are advice in population planning, the largest technical-aid sector of the AID program; loan or credit authority for the purchase of goods or services in the United States; training of foreign personnel in the United States or elsewhere; and provision of technical assistance personnel in such areas as farming techniques, weather forecasting, or organizational management.[36] In addition, AID may contract with universities, private groups or companies or church groups to provide services.

Arms Control and Disarmament Agency

Like AID, the Arms Control and Disarmament Agency was created in 1961 as an autonomous agency but has been placed under the direction of the State Department.[37] Its major responsibilities include the continuing research into the development of arms-control policy and the negotiation of agreements with other countries. It participated in the negotiation of SALT I and SALT II agreements with the Soviet Union, and in the Reagan administration, the agency has played a major role in two sets of negotiations—the Strategic Arms Limitation Talks (START) and the Intermediate Nuclear Force (INF) discussions. Both sets of talks were suspended in 1984 when the Soviet Uion left the bargaining sessions in protest over the introduction of Pershing II and cruise missiles by the United States into Western Europe.

United States Information Agency

In an era when modern communications media have become an increasingly important part of the foreign-policy process, the USIA is the formal propaganda agency of the United States government. It is charged with conducting informational and cultural activities directed at the leaders and peoples of other countries to promote the goals of American foreign policy and to disseminate abroad an accurate portrait of American society.[38] The USIA administers the Voice of America radio network, cultural-exchange programs involving numerous groups and individuals, libraries, publications, exhibits, motion pictures, television programs, and the like.

Predated by a number of propaganda agencies beginning with the Committee on Public Information during World War I, the United States Information Agency (USIA) was gradually brought under the operational jurisdiction of the State Department, and information officers have been given special status as Foreign Service information officers.[39]

The role of the agency has varied over time from one of independent speaker for American policy to one of service office for other governmental agencies and leaders. Its activities will be more fully examined in chapter 17.

The Peace Corps

Established by the Kennedy administration in 1961, the Peace Corps consists largely of volunteers who serve as teachers and as workers in community projects abroad. The Peace Corps was integrated into a new agency in 1971, ACTION, and gradually the number of volunteers has declined.[40] Peace Corps workers have had the opportunity to work with host-country people in a variety of grassroots projects outside of the formal diplomatic mission.

The Military

The role of military personnel overseas may vary widely from country to country, depending upon the military relationship between the United States and the host country and whether the United States has military bases on the soil of the host country.

As part of the normal structure of the diplomatic mission, there are Defense Department military attachés as well as attachés representing each of the military services. In addition, there is a military advisory group.[41] In

European missions military liaison offices operate to maintain contact and communications with the military leadership of the host country.

In many cases the military leaders oversee the provision of training and supplies to the host national government.

Where American military bases and personnel are stationed, the presence of thousands of Americans creates a foreign and sometimes frictional set of relationships with nationals.

Within the mission internal conflict may occur between military and civilian sectors, and strong ambassadorial leadership is required to maintain the political perspective of the mission.[42] In any event, the military perspective is represented in high policy councils by the individual service chief of staff, by the Joint Chiefs of Staff, and by the degree to which the viewpoints of the military leaders can motivate the top civilian leaders of the Defense Department to make their case with the president and within the National Security Council.

THE DEFENSE DEPARTMENT

In the glare of bright lights and television cameras, Defense Secretary Caspar Weinberger appeared before the Senate Armed Services Committee the week of February 1, 1983, in support of the Reagan administration's proposed record budget for the Department of Defense.[43] In many ways the modern congressional committee hearing is a trial by combat when matters of crucial national importance are being examined. The witness is seated at a table facing the examiners, who are on a slightly elevated level, some of them glaring with hostility as they wait their chance to dissect the witness' arguments.

Weinberger defended the record spending of $365 billion, arguing that serious cuts in the budget proposal would endanger the security of the United States. Many of the senators remained unconvinced.

This incident underscores one of the many duties—one of the many political duties—of the secretary in behalf of the department he represents. However, relations with Congress and advocacy of the budget are only one level of the department's involvement in the politics of making foreign policy.

In the broadest sense, defense policy *is* foreign policy, and a large portion of the foreign policy of the United States is based on, or derives its substance from, its military power. Henry Kissinger has written:

> Throughout history the political influence of nations has been roughly correlative to their military power. While states may differ in the moral worth and prestige of their institutions, diplomatic skill could augment but never substitute for military strength. . . . [However,] a calculus of power . . . is only the beginning of policy; it cannot be its sole purpose. The fact remains that without strength even the most elevated purpose risks being overwhelmed by the dictates of others.[44]

Thus while not all foreign policy is either dependent upon or requires military strength in order to function, the foreign policy of a great power is more likely to be made credible and fulfillable when that great power possesses the military capability to maintain its own security and the maximum latitude in relating to other countries. Foreign policy must be realistically based on military capabilities. Clearly the United States, given its position in the world in the second half of the twentieth century, has required military strength, and the availability of military strength has played a significant role in developing many of the foreign policies followed in the period. Further, diplomatic skills have been required to carry out military and foreign policies, and inevitably in today's interdependent global system, the choices of military policy are political in a broad sense and are often, therefore, aspects of foreign policy. For example, the foreign policy of containment, adopted by the Truman administration toward the Soviet Union in 1946, was political in nature but contained a military element in substance. The military element, symbolized in NATO, was designed to demonstrate the political objective of a maintenance of balance of power with the Soviet Union and deterrence of Soviet military action to change the political map of the world.

There are four distinct levels at which the Defense Department is involved in the politics of the foreign-policy process: in the formulation of high policy; in the definition of military policy, strategy, and expenditure levels; in the resolution of internal differences within the military establishment; and in direct relations with the governments and peoples of foreign countries.

High Policy

Enough has been said to indicate the close, and sometimes inseparable, connection between foreign policy and defense policy. It is a connection that gives to the Defense Department a major voice in the foreign-policy process, in the determination of long-term goals and strategies, and in the implementation of policies. The views of the department are represented in the National Security Council, in the cabinet, and in relations with Congress, and as observed in chapter 3, the secretary of defense has, on some occasions, become a dominant voice with the president in the policy process.

The most clear-cut demonstration of the predominance of the military in the shaping of the overall foreign-policy priorities of the United States has occurred during periods of war. Although President Franklin D. Roosevelt held on tightly to the final decision-making power during World War II, the top military advisers of the time, men such as Army Chief of Staff George C. Marshall and Admiral William Leahy, exercised an influence on policy that would be unheard of in peacetime.[45] Winning the war became America's number one policy priority, and consideration of the postwar global politico-economic system was relegated to a less urgent status until very late in the war.

The Korean and Vietnam Wars, on the other hand, were clearly examples of civilian control of policy. In June 1950 President Harry Truman's decision to use American forces to thwart the North Korean invasion of South Korea arose from Truman's personal conviction that miltiary force was necessary to stop the expansion of communism.[46] Thirteen years later President Lyndon Johnson was personally persuaded that South Vietnam could not be permitted to fall under the control of the North.[47] In neither case is there much evidence that a president succumbed to sudden undue pressure or influence from a military establishment eager to plunge the nation into war. However, once the commitments were made in both cases, the war became the primary foreign-policy question confronting the government, temporarily pushing other political-economic issues into the background. Once committed to war, however, the incumbent presidents came to rely more heavily upon advice from the Defense Department than they would otherwise have done.

Aside from periods of war, given the almost uninterrupted tensions of the cold war, much of American foreign policy has been based upon the military aspects of the American-Soviet relationship, with the result that the views of the Defense Department were necessarily directly involved in policy decisions. Since 1945 the political-military doctrines of the United States have included the maintenance of a balance of power, deterrence, and defense. Balance of power, i.e., the availability of countervailing force sufficient to prevent an aggressor from acting, has often been interpreted to mean the availability of force superior to that of an enemy, although American policy in the 1970s seemed to accept a principle of parity. Deterrence of an aggressor from action is one of the purposes of a balance of power and of the "balance of terror" that has arisen from the existence of the nuclear weapons and delivery systems available to the United States and the Soviet Union.

The concept of defense encompasses the commitment to be able to successfully defend the United States and its allies in case deterrence fails.

Since these concepts contain both political and military aspects, they provide the Defense Department with the opportunity and, indeed, the right to offer policy options, thereby increasing its influence and its role. One of the great fears expressed by critics of the role and influence of the military on foreign policy is that in reviewing the many options available in a wide variety of issues and problems, policy makers will be subject to undue pressure to choose the military option rather than an economic or political one.[48] This fear considerably predated the Vietnam War, although the debate over the war often focused on the wisdom of the choice of the military option rather than a political-diplomatic one. Much earlier, in 1960, President Eisenhower had warned about what he considered to be undue influence by a so-called military-industrial complex.[49] Since that time the evidence is less than persuasive either that the influence of the Defense Department is overwhelming or that decision makers will inevitably choose military policy options. One report in 1971, for example, indicated that Defense Department views in that year were rejected as often as they were accepted.[50] While this does not prove the lack of Defense Department influence nor the absence of strength of military-type thinking on the part of decision makers, it does suggest that the views of the military and military policy options usually receive attention and consideration at the top.

The Domestic Level

Aside from its role in the creation of high-level foreign policy, the department plays a political role in the budget process, in the determination of how national resources will be spent, and in the advocacy of a larger role for the military component of national life. Indeed, this element of the department's role in policy is described in relation to the efforts of Weinberger to promote the defense budget "through a recalcitrant Congress, a divided White House, a hostile press, and a major depression."[51] Because of the demand on national resources for other purposes, the budget fight also has profound effects upon domestic politics and policies. It includes quite explicit questions about military judgments concerning correct military strategies, new weapons systems, and the nature of the balance among the military components of the defense establishment. Some of these issues are, in fact, debated within the highest councils dealing with foreign policy, and tentative decisions are made. However, strong disagreements may persist within the Congress, within the administration, within the scientific and academic communities, and among the general public. One widely debated issue in the last five years has been the proposed new MX intercontinental ballistic missile system and the ways in which it should be deployed and utilized. In late 1982 Congress rejected the Defense Department proposal for the so-called dense-pack system, and the department was forced to go back to the drawing boards.[52] A deeper question implicit in the MX issue was the continuing utility of the concept of the strategic triad: long-range land-based missiles, long-range manned bombers, and submarine-launched missile systems. On such questions the Defense Department must contend with, and satisfy, those who have strongly differing views concerning long-range political and military strategy. Thus the budget battle involved questions not only of money but also about concepts, weapons, and policies.

On this level some consideration must be given to the so-called military-industrial complex and its influence on both domestic and foreign policy. Some observers have argued that if such a complex is real at all, then it is much more inclusive than the term *military-industrial* would imply, since there are so many elements of the society with high stakes in military spending. Labor unions, state and local governments, colleges and universities, local businesses—they all have considerable economic interests in the presence of military bases in their areas or of large firms in the defense-contracting business. In a small state such as Connecticut, for example, a significant portion of the state's economy is associated with such firms as United Technologies, which includes Pratt and Whitney engines and Sikorsky helicopters, and General Dynamics, which produces Trident submarines. In addition, the New London-Groton area of eastern Connecticut includes a submarine base and the Coast Guard Academy. When the budget for the Department of Defense is considered in the Congress, senators and representatives from such a state find it difficult to oppose expenditures that will strengthen their state economically. Yet military expenditures are distributed throughout all fifty states. In the 1983 budget fight

Senator John Tower, chairman of the Senate Armed Services Committee, sent a letter to all ninety-nine other senators requesting that they list the military expenditures in their states they felt could be cut from the budget. There was little response.[53] Whatever the final result of the annual budget battle there is little doubt that the Defense Department budget will dwarf those of other departments involved in the foreign-policy process.

Far more complex and difficult domestic arguments arise from the choices made and recommended by the Defense Department over such matters as defense strategy, tactics, technology, and weapons. Here the issue is not strictly a budgetary one, although the military choices are usually immensely costly. The deeper questions involve (a) assessments of the intentions and capabilities of the Soviet Union, (b) planning for "worst case" possibilities in case of war, (c) the utility and implications of new technology, (d) the selection of new systems and the "best" mixture of these systems, and (e) the integration of all services and systems into a coherent and effective defense establishment.

Questions such as these often seem esoteric and incomprehensible to the general public and produce deep disagreements among the military professionals, scientific experts, and security analysts both inside and outside government. The question of "how much is enough" has been raised not only in relation to the budget but also in relation to the numbers, types, and mixtures of various weapons systems.[54] Beyond this are questions about the policy and about the political implications new systems may have. For example, in the early 1980s discussion had reached the public about proposed new antiballistic missile systems to be deployed in space. Based on research on laser and nuclear particle beam capabilities and on other techniques, the proposals would essentially shift nuclear missile strategies from basically offensive ones to defensive ones.[55] Is this good or bad? At this point the answer depends upon the subjective views of the person answering. A seemingly less mysterious debate has taken place over the usefulness and the cost of the proposed B-1 bomber. Although the Reagan administration proceeded with the project, once canceled by the Carter administration, questions persist concerning not only the capabilities of the B-1 bomber but the continued utility of manned bombers in the missile age. Similar debates have occurred over proposals to continue to build aircraft carriers, to recommission battleships, and to produce the new M-1 tanks.

In short, the arguments rage over military doctrine and not just money, and they are not strictly confined to the internal processes of the Defense Department because the department must "sell" its doctrine to the country, and that process is deeply involved in politics.

Interestingly, with all of the concern among many Americans that through the massive influence of military thinking the public will come to believe in military solutions, a public-opinion survey taken in January 1983 by the New York Times-CBS Poll indicated that the "weight of public opinion favors less rather than more spending on military programs." The poll further indicated that those surveyed "no longer feared that the United States is lagging behind the Soviet Union in military prowess and feel that the Reagan administration is spending too much money on sophisticated new weapons systems."[56]

In the process of politics it would appear that the influence of the Defense Department is not unlimited, even though during the Reagan administration, the president has fully supported and shared the views of the department. The 1980 election of Ronald Reagan was based in part on Reagan's claim that the United States had fallen behind the Soviet Union militarily and his promise that he was committed to redress the unfavorable balance. There can be little doubt that public opinion and much of informed opinion continues to support the concept of a military establishment strong enough to deter the Soviets.[57] Further, notwithstanding the Vietnam experience, public opinion has not been unwilling to have American forces used in Lebanon for peace-keeping operations or in Central America.

In summary, the voice of the Defense Department is rarely ignored in matters affecting foreign policy and military policy. It has a broad base of support, and its recommendations are often accepted. Still, its influence is not universal or unlimited.

The Internal Department Level

A third major level at which politics plays a large role in determining policy is found within the department itself. Indeed, one can identify two levels at which internal politics operates within the department. Under the Constitution of the United States, the president is the commander-in-chief of the armed forces, thereby establishing the principle of civilian control of the military. The president's authority is customarily expressed through the civilian leaders of the department: the secretary, numerous other civilian subordinates, and civilian secretaries of the individual services. Not infrequently, sharp differences of opinion over policy emerge between the military leadership and the civilian leadership, but in most administrations the military leaders exercise considerable influence on the thinking and the policy decisions of their civilian chiefs. A second type of political warfare that operates within the department is the competition between and among the services for their share of the budget, for their concepts of appropriate military strategy, and for control of new systems. A recent example of the first type of internal disagreement involved the MX missile "dense-pack" basing mode. Of the five commanders who make up the Joint Chiefs of Staff, the top level leadership of the professional military, three opposed the idea and even the chairman, General John Vessey, opposed it, although he came to support the secretary's advocacy of it.[58]

Despite the conflicts inherent in civilian control of the military, there are surprisingly few high-level resignations from the military service in protest over civilian policy that have become public disputes. Theoretically officers are expected to confine their disagreements over policy to the inner circles of the government and to support the policy in public when it is announced. Most do, and many of those who do not support policy decisions may resign or retire without public discussion. There are occasional exceptions, such as retired Admiral Elmo Zumwalt, who resigned in protest and subsequently ran for public office in protest of administration policies. He lost the election.

A most conspicuous example of the clash between civilian and military authority was the firing of General Douglas MacArthur in 1952 over MacArthur's public dispute of government policy during the Korean War. In the wake of the immense public controversy that the dispute touched off in the United States, MacArthur made himself available for the Republican nomination for president in 1952, but the Republicans turned to another general instead—Dwight D. Eisenhower.

It would be too much to conclude that Americans politically mistrust military professionals who challenge civilian policy, but the deep beliefs among Americans and, indeed, among most military professionals concerning the separation between civilian and the military in politics seem to remain operative in the 1980s.

On the second level, internally, arguments among the services over such issues as manned bombers, aircraft carriers, or missile submarines have provoked considerable interservice rivalry, as each service campaigns for a larger share of the budget and for a more important mission than the others. The disputes are often no less intense within each service. Intraservice rivalries for prestige, resources, and preference may affect the modernization of each service and its capability to perform the mission assigned to it.

In his autobiography General Omar Bradley, army chief of staff in the late 1940s, details the bitter interservice rivalries over missions, weapons, and budgets.[59] Battles over the building of a super aircraft carrier for the navy, expansion of the number of air force wings and of their strategic role, pressures for an increase in army manpower—all faced the intense budget restrictions imposed by President Truman prior to the Korean War. Facing a Truman directive in 1948 for a defense budget of no more than $14.4 billion, the service chiefs fought out the allocation of those funds, in what Bradley calls "bloody committee combat."[60] After Truman rejected one set of proposals, Defense Secretary James Forrestal directed the chiefs to return a unanimous budget of $14.4 billion. Bradley writes: "On November 8 we complied, splitting the money as follows: $5 billion to the Air Force, 4.8 billion to the Army, and 4.6 billion to the Navy."[61] In the process the navy and the air force waged intensive and competitive public campaigns for citizen support for pet projects. When NSC/68, the National Security Council paper recommending sizeable increases in defense spending was approved, and when the Korean War broke out, defense expenditures did, in fact, increase substantially.[62] However, the fact that determination of the defense budget resulted from intense politicking by the services among themselves, with Congress, and with the president may strike the student as less than an ideal way to determine strategic capabilities.

Inter- and intraservice rivalries not only make coordination of military operations difficult, but they make the formulation of a single Defense Department position a matter of politics, of compromises, and of positions that may be less sharply defined than desirable. The internal process may produce delays and accommodations that weaken the department's arguments in the interdepartmental policy committees and in the councils of policy makers.

In any case, given the pluralist nature of the organization of the department, disagreements and rivalries are probably inevitable.

The Foreign Level

Finally, the Department of Defense, in carrying out its basic responsibility to guarantee the security of the United States and to implement policy, maintains troops, bases, and formal representation in countries all over the world. Large contingents of American forces remain in Europe, South Korea, and the Philippines; smaller units are stationed in many other countries. American bases are located in many places. In addition, military representatives are assigned to duty in embassies all over the world and with military allies. In these situations not only are American military personnel formal, legal representatives of the United States government and its policies, but they all perform both a diplomatic and social/cultural function in foreign societies, creating and disseminating impressions of the United States among many peoples and cultures. Under some circumstances the military representatives may supersede the diplomatic staff in practical authority, even though the ambassador is legally the senior official of the foreign mission.

To the extent that the military professionals abroad take part in explaining American policy and in providing information to policy makers back in Washington, their political role may be considerable.

Organization

Since its creation in 1947, the Department of Defense has been subject to several reorganizations that have strengthened the position of secretary and the civilian administration of the institution. The secretary is supported by a deputy secretary, a number of assistant secretaries, several functional units, the Joint Chiefs of Staff, and the three military departments.[63]

The Joint Chiefs of Staff is composed of the chiefs of staff of the army, navy, air force, and marines plus a chairman selected by the president from one of the services. Each service is also directed by a civilian secretary and his staff. The basic level of the department includes the various geographic-area military commands.

The power, influence, and authority of the secretary of defense and of various component units varies over time, and the relationship between the staff and the professional military leadership has also varied. Unquestioned authority by the seretary was clearly established under the administration of Robert McNamara, whose "whiz kids," using modern management techniques and computers, brought a sharp break with traditional decision making to defense.[64] Since that time, a series of secretaries, including Clark Clifford, Melvin Laird, James Schlesinger, Donald Rumsfeld, Harold Brown, and Caspar Weinberger, have maintained civilian control with more or less influence from the military leadership.

In the Reagan administration Weinberger has embraced and advocated the views of professional military leaders enthusiastically,[65] and one writer suggests that as a result Weinberger has not managed the department effectively. Theodore White notes that

> "the Pentagon has been his client; the public the jury, and, in defending his client, he has been overwhelmed."[66]

When the argument over the MX missile dense-pack basing mode proposal arose in 1982, Weinberger faced Congress. White writes: "It did not want to hear a lawyer's brief; it wanted to hear the decision of a judge who stood between what domestic politics required and the thrust of the Pentagon."[67] Thus in leading the department, Weinberger absorbed the views of the military leadership and unwaveringly supported them rather than forcing the military to tailor their requests to the political and economic reality of the possible.[68] In addition to the pressures of the military professionals from below, any secretary is also caught under the pressures from above, when a president insists upon a particular defense policy and posture, as has been the case in the Reagan administration.

In the previous administration of Jimmy Carter, Defense Secretary Harold Brown often "appeared not to advocate the military's views, or to defend them, at the White House."[69]

Whether Weinberger or Brown's approach to the professional military is preferable is subject to debate, of course. Perhaps all that can be said is that while civilian control of military policy must remain in force, no secretary can or should disregard the recommendations of the military all of the time. What he must do is what McNamara and Brown apparently did—subject military policy recommendations to the most intense analysis and scrutiny and place them in a broader context of national foreign, domestic, and security policy.

Of special interest when considering the Department of Defense role in foreign policy is the department's Office of International Security Affairs (ISA). Sometimes called a little State Department, the ISA, according to one study, became under Presidents Kennedy and Johnson "the major source for major foreign policy initiatives. Under other administrations, however, ISA has wielded little influence as a policy development staff, reduced almost entirely to its line function."[70]

During the Vietnam War, the staff of ISA numbered some three hundred people, and its views were believed to have influenced policy during the periods of escalation and deescalation.[71]

In the final analysis, the influence of the military on the formulation of foreign policy depends not only upon the personality and convictions of the secretary of defense but also upon the secretary's relationship with the president.

NOTES

[1] Morton Halperin and Arnold Kanter, *Readings in American Foreign Policy: A Bureaucratic Perspective* (Boston: Little, Brown & Company, 1973), p. 6.

[2] Ibid., p. 31.

[3] Ibid., p. 33.

[4] Ibib., p. 35.

[5] Ibid., p. 37.

[6] Henry Kissinger, *White House Years* (Boston: Little, Brown & Company, 1979), p. 27.

[7] John H. Esterline and Robert B. Black, *Inside Foreign Policy* (Palo Alto, Calif.: Mayfield Publishing Co., 1975), p. 63.

[8] Ibid.

[9] Stanley Hoffman, *Primacy or World Order* (New York: McGraw-Hill Book Company, 1978), p. 237.

[10] Ibid., p. 236.

[11] Julius W. Pratt, *A History of United States Foreign Policy*, 2nd ed. (Englewood Cliffs, N.J.: Prentice-Hall, 1965), pp. 5–8.

[12] Ibid., p. 6.

[13] B. Drummond Ayres, Jr., "A New Breed of Diplomat," *New York Times Magazine*, September 18, 1983, p. 74; Charles W. Kegley and Eugene R. Wittkopf, *American Foreign Policy: Pattern and Process*, 2nd ed. (New York: St. Martin's Press, 1982), p. 355, fn.

[14] Esterline and Black, *Inside Foreign Policy*, pp. 40–43.

[15] Chester Bowles, *Promises to Keep* (New York: Harper & Row, Publishers, 1971), pp. 361–62; Roger Hilsman, *The Politics of Policy Making in Defense and Foreign Affairs* (New York: Harper & Row, Publishers, 1977), pp. 168–70.

[16] Bowles, *Promises to Keep*, pp. 361–62.

[17] Ibid.

[18] Esterline and Black, *Inside Foreign Policy*, p. 45.

[19] Ibid., pp. 46–50.

[20] Ibid., p. 49.

[21] Ibid.

[22] Ibid., p. 59.

[23] Ibid., pp. 59–63.

[24] Ibid., pp. 42–44.

[25] Bernard Gwertzman, "Under Shultz, A Shift to a Less Personalized Role," *New York Times*, October 28, 1982, B12.

[26] Ibid.

[27] Esterline and Black, *Inside Foreign Policy*, pp. 73–74.

[28] Ibid.

[29] Thomas G. Paterson, J. Garry Clifford, and Kenneth J. Hagan, *American Foreign Policy: A History* (Lexington, Mass.: D. C. Heath & Company, 1977), pp. 3–30.

[30] Pratt, *A History of United States Foreign Policy*, p. 8.

[31] Esterline and Black, *Inside Foreign Policy*, p. 74.

[32] Ibid.

[33] U.S. Department of State, "Foreign Service Careers," Department and Foreign Services Series 249, Rev. July 1982, p. 2.

[34] Esterline and Black, *Inside Foreign Policy*, pp. 207–12; Kegley and Wittkopf, *American Foreign Policy*, pp. 128–29.

[35] Kegley and Wittkopf, *American Foreign Policy*, p. 129.

[36] Esterline and Black, *Inside Foreign Policy*, pp. 189–98.

[37] Ibid., p. 104.

[38] Ibid., pp. 121–22.

[39] Ibid., pp. 135–36.

[40] Ibid., p. 101.

[41] Ibid., pp. 85–88.

[42] Ibid., pp. 77–79.

[43] Theodore H. White, "Weinberger on the Ramparts," *New York Times Magazine*, February 6, 1983, p. 20.

[44] Kissinger, *White House Years*, p. 195.

[45] Leonard Mosley, *Marshall: Hero for Our Times* (New York: Hearst Books, 1982), chaps. 12–18.

[46] Robert J, Donovan, *Tumultuous Years: The Presidency of Harry S. Truman, 1949–53* (New York: W. W. Norton & Company, 1982), p. 202.

[47] Lyndon B. Johnson, *From the Vantage Point: Perspectives of the Presidency 1963–1969* (New York: Holt, Rhinehart and Winston, 1971), pp. 147–52.

[48] Henry T. Nash, *American Foreign Policy: Changing Perspectives on National Security*, rev. ed., (Homewood, Ill.: Dorsey Press, 1978), p. 61; Kegley and Wittkopf, *American Foreign Policy*, pp. 367–68.

49 Cecil V. Crabb, Jr., *American Foreign Policy in the Nuclear Age,* 4th ed. (New York: Harper & Row, Publishers, 1983), p. 244.

50 William Beecher, "Foreign Policy: Pentagon Also Encounters Rebuffs," *New York Times,* January 21, 1971), p. 1.

51 White, "Weinberger on the Ramparts," p. 14.

52 Ibid., p. 24.

53 Senator John Tower, Senate Armed Services Committee, "Sunday Morning," CBS News, April 10, 1983.

54 Alain Enthoven and K. Wayne Smith, *How Much Is Enough?* (New York: Harper & Row, Publishers, 1971), pp. 13, 325; Bruce M. Russett, *What Price Vigilance?* (New Haven: Yale University Press, 1970), pp. 181–83.

55 "President's Speech on Military Spending and a New Defense," *New York Times,* March 24, 1983, p. 20; Hedrick Smith, "Would a Space-Age Defense Ease Tensions or Create Them?" *New York Times,* March 27, 1983, sect. 4, p. 1. Also see footnotes #9 and #10 in chapter 16.

56 William E. Schmidt, "Poll Shows Lessening of Fear That U.S. Military Is Lagging," *New York Times,* February 6, 1983, p. 1.

57 Leslie Gelb, "Poll Finds Doubt on U.S. Strategy on the Russians," *New York Times,* April 15, 1983, p. 1.

58 White, "Weinberger on the Ramparts," p. 64.

59 Omar N. Bradley and Clay Blair, *A General's Life: An Autobiography* (New York: Simon & Schuster, 1983), pp. 487–519.

60 Ibid., p. 496.

61 Ibid., p. 497.

62 Ibid., pp. 518–19.

63 Esterline and Black, *Inside Foreign Policy,* pp. 26–32; Nash, *American Foreign Policy,* pp. 73–80.

64 Kegley and Wittkopf, *American Foreign Policy,* p. 279.

65 White, "Weinberger on the Ramparts," p. 22.

66 Ibid., p. 24.

67 Ibid.

68 Ibid., pp. 22, 24.

69 Kegley and Wittkopf, *American Foreign Policy,* p. 367.

70 Geoffrey Piller, "DOD's Office of International Security Affairs: The Brief Ascendancy of an Advisory System," *Political Science Quarterly,* spring 1983, p. 60.

71 Esterline and Black, *Inside Foreign Policy,* pp. 31, 32.

CHAPTER SIX
DOING THE JOB:
TREASURY,
INTELLIGENCE,
AND OTHER ACTORS

The preeminence of the bureaucracies of the National Security Council, the State Department, and the Defense Department in the policy process is shared in some important ways with other parts of the executive branch. In the sphere of economic policy several departments and agencies contribute to the formulation and implementation of policy. In the intelligence process a community of agencies plays an important role in providing information and analysis to policy makers. In areas of energy, communications, and transportation a number of regulatory and coordinating agencies contribute to the development of national and international policy.

In this chapter we will examine some of the key structures whose activities constitute a significant part of the policy process, keeping in mind that many others could also be included.

TREASURY DEPARTMENT

In mid-1970 a new force emerged from the Nixon administration—John Connolly. The attractive, brash, self-confident Democrat had been named secretary of the treasury, and the world economic system would never be quite the same as the result of a blend of the Connolly bravado and the Nixon toughness.

Broad changes in the non-Communist economies of the world since 1945 had brought new pressures on the American dollar, on the American balance of payments, and on the sales of American products abroad. To many experts some basic structural changes in the system of monetary exchange rates, trading practices, and economic relations with Europe and Japan had been needed for several years. In August of 1970 the value of the dollar declined sharply. After challenging the Europeans and the Japanese in May to accept greater economic responsibility, Connolly proposed to the president in August a number of sweeping measures that would, in effect, revolutionize the system, measures that Nixon accepted without fully discussing them within the administration.

Henry Kissinger writes:

> The fact was that a decision of major foreign policy importance had been taken about which neither the Secretary of State nor the National Security Adviser had been consulted. . . . Since Nixon had already made the decision, there was no point in debating it.[1]

On August 15 Nixon announced the policy changes in a television address. As Kissinger notes, the effects abroad were profound:

> The industrial democracies, especially Japan, were in a state of shock because of the suddenness of the announcement, the unilateral nature of some of the measures, and the necessity they imposed to consider a formal restructuring of the entire international economic system.[2]

Many points could be made about this story: First, economic policy is often foreign policy, or at the very least, has political effects. Second, a powerful and dynamic secretary of the treasury galvanized comprehensive action on sweeping reforms with effects the foreign-policy apparatus would have to reconcile with many countries. Third, a president was perfectly willing to accept the recommendations of a cabinet member with little or no discussion. Finally, in many respects the State Department and the national security adviser had to pick up the pieces through "negotiations, conflict, and confrontation."[3]

Although most treasury secretaries are not so visible or persuasive as Connolly, the story also suggests the fact that the Treasury Department is an important element in the foreign-policy process in the 1980s, and indeed has been since the beginning of the new Republic.

Early in the Washington administration, the newly created Treasury Department, established on September 2, 1789, under its first secretary, Alexander Hamilton, dominated diplomacy because Hamilton's fiscal program had important foreign-policy and foreign-trade implications.

Hamilton sought to establish credit in international markets and developed an ambitious fund-raising program, which required tariffs on imports and taxes on shipping tonnage.[4] The new navigation laws were designed also to stimulate American shipping, and Hamilton pursued preferences with England. Consequently, much of his work involved international diplomacy.

By the middle of the twentieth century the Treasury Department had returned to a major position in the foreign-policy process and in the foreign relations of the United States.

In general the Treasury Department has responsibility for a wide range of activities in the international economic system. Since the end of World War II, when the dollar became the central currency of the non-Communist world, the management of monetary policy has been critical not only to American domestic affairs but also to American foreign policy and to the interests of nations all over the world. Such matters as taxation, tariffs, balance of payments, balance of trade, and the public debt are under the jurisdiction of the Treasury Department, and the secretary serves on a number of major international monetary agencies, such as the IMF, the IBRD, the IDB, and the Regional Development Banks.[5] Further, under the global monetary system established in 1971, the managed float, in which the value of currencies is determined on a daily basis in world money markets, the Treasury Department plays an active role in the valuation process.

The role of the secretary and of the department in the global environment of the 1980s has been a major one in view of the economic problems of many countries. Secretary Donald Regan has represented the United States at important meetings of the International Monetary Fund (IMF), the 146-member organization that acts as a type of international bank.[6] In late 1982 Regan announced an agreement to increase the American contribution to the IMF to help the agency increase its resources and thus have more funds available to lend to countries with troubled economies or balance-of-payments deficits. Playing a large role in the meetings of the IMF was Beryl Sprinkel, the undersecretary of the treasury for monetary affairs.[7] Another departmental official, the assistant secretary for international affairs, oversees issues dealing with monetary affairs, developing countries, trade and investment policy, commodities, and natural resources.

The increasing role of the Treasury Department in the foreign-policy process stems, in part, from the leadership of the international economic system that the United States assumed at the time of the Bretton Woods Conference in 1944. The development of a postwar monetary system at Bretton Woods, the promotion of a free-trade policy committed to a reduction or elimination of all tariffs, the extensive support for the recovery of European and Japanese economies, the expansion of American multinational corporations abroad, participation in numerous international organizations dealing with economic affairs—all reflect a mixture of foreign-policy goals and economic necessities. In contributing to the evolution of an international economic system, the United States has helped to create new conditions in which economic competition has increased. New problems have emerged among the U.S., the European Economic Community (EEC)—more commonly known as the Common Market—Japan, and the nations of the Third and Fourth Worlds. By the 1980s the debt of many of the less developed countries approached the $700 billion mark, threatening the stability of the international monetary and banking systems and imposing new challenges to creative foreign economic policy.[8] In this environment the Treasury Department has had the major responsibility for developing policy, although the State Department has also strengthened its capability in economic affairs and given new importance to the position of undersecretary for economic affairs. Foreign Service officers in overseas missions increasingly are involved in economic matters, and some rivalry has developed between Treasury and State over the distribution of foreign economic assistance.[9] The Agency for International Development (AID), which is under the direction of the State Department, is the government agency traditionally responsible for providing assistance, especially to less developed countries. However, Treasury also has the responsibility for channeling aid funds through many multilateral agencies.

Additional subdivisions of the Treasury Department touch upon such international problems as drug traffic (the Bureau of Alcohol, Tobacco, and Firearms), immigration (Customs), and intelligence (the Secret Service, Internal Revenue Service).[10]

The dangers of lack of coherence and coordination of political, economic, and security policy are fairly obvious, especially if the government is to pursue a global policy of linkages, i.e., linking agreements in one field to those in another, as in the détente period with the Soviet Union.

As economic issues tend to dominate the attention of most countries, the relationship between economic policy and foreign policy tends to merge, but in the process the Treasury Department will continue to exercise considerable influence to the formulation of overall policy.

COMMERCE, AGRICULTURE, AND LABOR

In an international economy in which vast trade linkages exist and multinational corporations operate in almost every part of the world, three departments have acquired increased relevance in foreign policy in the last four decades.

The Commerce Department is directly interested in promoting the sale of American products and the expansion of American companies throughout the world. Through its Domestic and International Business Administration, its Bureau of International Commerce, and Bureau of East-West Trade, the department does what it can to facilitate trade not only with American allies but with the Soviet bloc and China as well.[11]

Since American grain constitutes about half of the world grain trade, the *Agriculture Department* is also involved in the promotion of American sales and in the administration of such programs as P.L. 480, the Food for Peace Program. It is also involved in the development of import quotas and in negotiations through the General Agreement on Tariffs and Trade involving agricultural products.[12]

Structurally, much of this work is handled through the Foreign Agricultural Service, which maintains attachés overseas dealing with more than one hundred countries and works with GATT, OECD, and FAO.

The interests of the *Labor Department* in foreign policy relate to questions of the immigration of foreign labor, such as the influx of Mexican workers into the United States. In addition, the department may provide technical assistance in labor questions overseas.[13]

A NEW AGENCY

In late 1982 and early 1983 the Reagan administration began to promote the restructuring of the federal agencies responsible for international trade.[14]

On June 1, 1983, the president proposed abolishing the Commerce Department and creating a new cabinet agency just for trade. Proposing to merge the trade duties of the Commerce Department and the cabinet-level office of U.S. trade representative, the president wants to call the new structure the Department of International Trade and Industry. The non-trade functions of the Commerce Department would be assigned to other agencies. The sale of farm products would remain under the jurisdiction of the Agriculture Department. The proposed new agency is designed to place greater emphasis on promoting the sale of American products abroad.

THE ECONOMIC SUMMIT

In early June 1984 President Ronald Reagan met in London with the leaders of America's six most important trading partners in the tenth in a series of annual summit conferences begun in 1975. Also attending were the leaders of West Germany, Japan, Great Britain, France, Canada, and Italy.

In Williamsburg, Virginia in 1983 and in London in 1984, the primary subject was American interest rates. The six other leaders pressured Reagan to lower American interest rates, and Reagan promised that the rates would soon fall.[15]

Originally started as a means to coordinate economic policy, the annual sessions have turned into opportunities for wide-ranging discussions of common political and economic problems in the world. Among the topics on the 1984 agenda, for example, were the large global debt, American budget deficits, the war in the Persian Gulf, terrorism, arms control, and relations with the Soviet Union.

Although few major agreements emerge from these talks, and very few are ever expected, the summit meetings provide leaders the means to explore common problems.

THE INTELLIGENCE SYSTEM

Americans have often had conflicting views about operating an organized intelligence system. On the whole, they have accepted the idea that a modern superpower must have an effective intelligence-gathering capability.

But they have often been disturbed by covert activities carried on by parts of the system. Senate hearings in the 1970s revealed a number of activities by the Central Intelligence Agency to which there was an unfavorable public reaction.[16] These activities included assassination plots against foreign leaders, and the revelations produced a loss of confidence by the public and a loss of morale in the intelligence system. Although many writers refer to the machinery of intelligence as a community, the term *system* is more accurate. It is argued that the agencies working in the intelligence field are a hodgepodge of assorted and distinct groups that are often in conflict with each other and that they constitute neither a community nor a system. The perspective adopted here is that those working in intelligence are part of a system that, conceptually and structurally, is designed to be organized, coordinated, interacting, and cohesive. That the system doesn't always work perfectly doesn't prevent us from thinking of it as a system.

"Intelligence" is sometimes conceived of in the public mind as a process of spies, secret agents, moles, and other infiltration of foreign societies. The covert side of the intelligence system is often seen as a web of sabotage, subversion, and subterfuge. In general, however, "intelligence" largely means the gathering and analysis of information related to the American national interest and essential to the formulation of American foreign policy.[17] It includes all information that may be gathered through public informational media, through legal and public channels, and through direct observation. To be sure, some information is obtained through covert means, through electronic surveillance, or through agencies of friendly foreign governments. Beyond mere acquisition of information, "intelligence" also provides analysis and evaluation of the massive amounts of raw data available to policy makers. Ideally, the intelligence system provides leaders with needed knowledge.

However, reservations about the operations of the intelligence system have arisen in the past four decades not so much from the gathering and analysis of information as from the various forms of covert activities employed or considered by some elements of the system. Covert operations will be considered in more detail in part IV.

Since the bulk of public and press discussion of intelligence activities focuses on the Central Intelligence Agency, it is not difficult to understand the public misconception that the CIA is the only structure involved in the process. Actually, the governmental intelligence system includes other vital components: the Defense Intelligence Agency (DIA) and the separate military intelligence units of the army, navy, and air force; the National Security Agency (NSA); the State Department's Bureau of Intelligence and Research (INR); operations within the Departments of Energy, Treasury, and Justice, such as the Drug Enforcement Agency, the Federal Bureau of Investigation, and the Bureau of Alcohol, Tobacco, and Firearms.[18]

According to one estimate, the intelligence system operates on a budget of at least $15 billion and has nearly 150,000 employees.[19] With a work force of about 18,000, the CIA constitutes less than 15 percent of the total intelligence-system work force.[20]

Before proceeding with an examination of the issues surrounding intelligence activities, it is necessary to examine the key parts of the system.

THE CENTRAL
INTELLIGENCE AGENCY

Prior to World War II, the United States had only the barest capabilities for gathering information, and furthermore, many at high levels of government didn't believe the United States needed an intelligence service. As high an official as Secretary of State Henry L. Stimson believed it to be unseemly. "Gentlemen don't read other people's mail," he said.[21] Much of the country shared this view if they thought about it at all. World War II changed all of that, and by 1945 the United States had developed one of the world's most effective intelligence and espionage services, the Office of Strategic Services (OSS). Postwar conditions confirmed for American leaders the necessity for such a service in the postwar world. In 1947 the National Security Act created a Central Intelligence Agency to provide the National Security Council with necessary information.[22] Originally conceived as a central coordinating agency through which information from other intelligence units would be processed, the agency gradually was assigned various covert activities beyond the range of intelligence gathering. The budget for clandestine activities of the CIA continued into the 1970s at nearly 40 percent of the agency's budget.[23]

The CIA was created to coordinate all American intelligence and counter-intelligence activities in the system and to perform services for the National Security Council. It is responsible for the gathering and evaluation of information and the preparation of a formal national intelligence estimate of affairs concerning the council.[24] It has been estimated that about half of the information available to the agency comes from open public sources; about one-third comes from the electronic monitoring by satellites and other means; and only about 10 to 15 percent from secret agents.[25] In 1982 Congress passed a law prohibiting the disclosure of the names of agents and otherwise tightened access to information about the intelligence system.[26]

The Defense Intelligence Agency. In 1961 the Defense Intelligence Agency was established to coordinate the intelligence activities of each of the units of the military services, namely, *army intelligence, naval intelligence,* and *air force intelligence.* The National Reconnaissance Office is also part of the DIA.[27] In practice, it is believed that the separate service units continue to play a predominant role in the military intelligence system, although DIA is designed to provide coordinated intelligence advice to the secretary of defense.

The National Security Agency. Of increasng importance in an era of developing technology in electronics and in space, the NSA has long been one of the most secret parts of the intelligence system.[28] Created in secret in 1952 by President Truman, the NSA has received considerable study and attention in a recent book by James Bamford.[29] The NSA is located at Fort Meade, Maryland, and, according to Bamford, maintains American listening posts throughout the world through new highly sensitive and precise listening devices and cameras. [30]

State Department Bureau of Intelligence and Research.   Although not primarily a gatherer of secret intelligence, the bureau evaluates and analyzes all of the normal information reported by American embassies throughout the world, advises the secretary of state, and distributes overt intelligence reports to the intelligence system abroad.[31] The role of the embassy staff in reporting raw data and in distributing intelligence may be considerable, since the embassy is an important locus of most American operations abroad. Technically the local CIA officials abroad are under the jurisdiction of the ambassador. In any case, the bureau has immediate access to, and the job of evaluating, the bulk of information obtained through normal diplomatic procedures.

The Treasury Department.   A number of agencies under the jurisdiction of Treasury are engaged in obtaining a wide range of information. The Secret Service, charged with protecting the president and other officials, obtains all necessary data relating to security during the president's travels abroad.[32] The Bureau of Alcohol, Tobacco, and Firearms conducts wide-ranging international operations in the areas under its jurisdiction, and the U.S. Customs Service is involved in obtaining information concerning immigration, imports, and terrorist threats at transportation facilities.[33] The Internal Revenue Service often seeks foreign information relating to the collection of taxes.

The Justice Department.   As a a part of the Justice Department, the Federal Bureau of Investigation concentrates on domestic intelligence, but frequently, this may cross over into investigation of foreign events and individuals. In addition, internal security against foreign threats provides an area in which the FBI and the CIA may operate simultaneously.[34] Of increased importance in the past two decades has been the effort to police illegal drug traffic involving foreign sources.

The Energy Department.   Monitoring the behavior of other states in the nuclear field has come to be a most important activity in the post-World War II world. The department is required not only to monitor nuclear agreements but also to gather information on the activities of foreign states in the nuclear field.[35]

Other Government Sources.   In one sense any and every governmental agency operating abroad is a source of information, although few may engage in secret operations. Among those agencies are the *Agency for International Development*, which provides economic and technical assistance in many countries, the *United States Information Agency*, which conducts American propaganda efforts in foreign countries, and the *Peace Corps*.

Nongovernmental Sources. Although not technically or formally a part of the intelligence system, there are many private, civilian sources of information about foreign countries.[36] The *news media*, always insistent on their independence from the government, are excellent sources of public information. *American multinational corporations*, whether or not they openly cooperate with the government intelligence system, are important sources of data about the countries in which they operate. Clearly, the news media and the corporations often have access to a wide range of foreign government officials and leading private citizens whose information may be useful. Such other sources as *scholars*, *scientists*, or ordinary *tourists* may be able to provide information, impressions, and experiences that could be useful to skilled intelligence analysts.

Thus there are massive amounts of information available to the intelligence system. Yet speedy and accurate evaluation of this raw data may be an even more challenging task for those responsible for making formal estimates of impending dangers, immediate crises, and long-term policies. After the revolution in Iran, an event that seemed to surprise the Carter administration, the American people, and the intelligence agencies, the CIA director at the time, Admiral Stansfield Turner, in an interview on "Meet the Press" acknowledged that while the agency was aware of the existence of a multiplicity of angry revolutionary groups, it had not foreseen the coalescence of those groups into a massive, successful, revolution. In essence, a failure of evaluation rather than a lack of accurate information caused the surprise with which the revolution was received.

Other factors that can affect the ability of the system to produce accurate estimates for policy makers include a certain amount of bureaucratic inertia, competition among elements of the system, legitimate and sincere disagreement among expert analysts about which data is important and which is not, different interpretations of the meaning of the information, and refusal to share all data. They may all contribute to a breakdown of the process. Each part of the system is a bureaucracy with its own internal factions, and the system as a whole is an even larger bureaucracy with its own divisions, perspectives, and interests.

Clearly, the major obstacles to a productive intelligence system may not lie at all with the gathering of information, even the most secret information. They may lie predominantly with the ways in which the data is handled when it is available.

Rational policy requires the most accurate information and the most deft utilization of that information. The information itself and those who provide it may, therefore, shape the perceptions that policy makers acquire about global reality. It is believed that those who provide the information have long since gone beyond the mere providing of information and have become participants in the policy process. The policy views of the CIA directors and other key intelligence sources may be not only offered but eagerly sought in the councils of government. Perhaps the classic case in recent history was the Bay of Pigs operation in which CIA officials actively advocated a policy and helped to persuade President John F. Kennedy to proceed with their plan. Further, many of the directors of the CIA have been close personal or political associates of the presidents they have served. From Allan Dulles, who was director when his brother was secretary of state, to William Casey, President Reagan's CIA director, many of the directors have been in a position not just to advance policy recommendations but to enjoy considerable confidence from the president, giving weight to the views of the intelligence community as reflected by the director of the CIA.

However, there are exceptions. Zbigniew Brzezinski, national security adviser under President Jimmy Carter, notes that Admiral Stansfield Turner, director of the CIA in the Carter administration, was not usually invited to the Friday morning foreign-policy breakfasts the president held with his top advisers.[37]

According to Brzezinski: "He had throughout the four years practically no one-on-one meetings with the President, and all CIA reporting was funneled to the President through me."[38]

In any case, whatever the relative influence of the director of the CIA and of the intelligence system in any given administration, both are likely to be in a position to have considerable impact on policy.

OTHER AGENCIES

Many other parts of the government may also have a direct or indirect role in the foreign-policy process, and some of them may not be recognized as customary actors in the process.

Within the last decade, the effect on American foreign policy of the *Federal Reserve Board* and of its chairman has been substantial. Originally created in 1911 as a type of central bank for the United States, the Federal Reserve System has considerable authority to affect the supply of money in circulation, interest rates, and other key elements of the American banking system.[39] With the rise of the dollar as a central currency in world affairs during the twentieth century, the board of governors of the Federal Reserve System has found itself with the power to profoundly affect the global economy. In the severe inflation of the 1960s and 1970s, the Fed countered with a policy of "tight money," i.e., high interest rates and limits on the money supply. As a consequence of its central role, its chairman has become a major public figure defending the system's monetary policies. Since membership on the board is for a fixed term and not subject to control by the president or by Congress, the Fed has become a powerful quasi-governmental agency, highly influential in the determination of global economic policies. However, the success of the Fed's policies in bringing down inflation in the United States in the 1980s through the maintenance of high interest rates brought on some foreign-policy problems for the Carter and Reagan administrations. Since high American interest rates tend to attract a considerable portion of the global resources available for investment, American allies argued that their own economic recovery was obstructed. At the economic summit conferences in Williamsburg in 1983 and in London in 1984, leaders of the six leading economic partners of the United States called for lower American interest rates, and President Reagan assured them again that interest rates would soon fall.[40]

Thus while the role of the Federal Reserve Board and its chairman may not always be so dramatic or intense as it has been in the past decade, it will remain a vital element of American foreign policy in a world economy that is increasingly interdependent.

The *Office of Management and Budget (OMB)* is responsible for preparing the president's annual budget. It is an instrument for reflecting a president's political and economic choices. Depending on the relationship between its director and the president, OMB can have considerable influence on the utilization of America's resources in the foreign field.[41]

The *Council of Economic Advisers* and its chairman are assigned the task of analyzing economic trends and recommending appropriate economic policies for the president. Although their influence on foreign policy is indirect, their recommendations may substantially affect the strength of the American economy and therefore the availability of resources with which to sustain American foreign and security policy.[42]

A growing number of independent regulatory agencies of the American government also have foreign-policy implications.

The *Federal Communications Commission* has the power to set policies relevant to telephone, telegraph, and telex communications and to regulate the broadcast industry. It allocates the number of radio and TV stations and the amount of power they may radiate. With the introduction of communications satellites, the domestic policy of the United Staes must be coordinated with those of other countries under international agreements.[43]

The *Securities and Exchange Commission* regulates trading in stocks, bonds, and commodities and sets the rules under which trading can occur. This may touch upon the interests of foreigners investing in the United States or Americans investing abroad.[44]

For many years prior to deregulation, the *Civil Aeronautics Board* regulated the airline industry including the operations, rates, and procedures of American lines operating abroad and foreign airlines operating in the United States.[45]

Other regulatory agencies that may impinge on foreign relations are the Nuclear Regulatory Commission, which sets and enforces standards for nuclear power plants, standards that are sometimes emulated by foreign countries; the Canal Zone government; the Export-Import Bank, which provides loans for foreign investment; the Federal Maritime Commission, which deals with regulation of maritime affairs; the Foreign Claims Settlement Commission; NASA, the National Aeronautics and Space Administration; the Overseas Private Investment Corporation, which provides insurance for overseas investors; the Panama Canal Company; and the United States International Trade Commission.[46]

SUMMARY

In the last four chapters we have examined most of the major individuals and structures in the executive branch engaged in the foreign-policy process. As we shall see in the forthcoming chapters, other units of government may also be involved by playing a role, exercising constitutional authority, or making demands upon the process. In addition, many non-governmental actors are engaged in the process. By and large, however, the actors who have been described are the ones who will, one way or another, contribute to the evolution of the policies of a given administration. Setting aside the additional influences on policy for a moment, we might wonder how order can be achieved in shaping policy amid so many actors, structures, and organizations—many of them with competing views and interests. Having observed the operation of politics and conflict within the departments and agencies, among the leading personalities and among the different organizations involved in the process, we may ask whether the system is mere chaos or whether it works at all. If it works, we need to know how and why it succeeds in serving the national interest. Not only do multiple centers of authority and influence compete in the design of policy, but several forms or tracks of policy must be considered and coordinated, all at the same time.

Can all of this be meshed into a coherent and productive policy, and how can it be done? Thoughtful and experienced analysts have debated at some length on the matter of coordination and have offered a variety of recommendations.

Stanley Hoffmann argues that American foreign policy should be developed in the context of what he calls "world order concerns." In this framework American foreign policy "must devise a process that provides for coherence, a capacity for long-range action, and the integration of domestic considerations into foreign affairs (both in preparation and definition of foreign policy and in its enforcement)."[47] In this system less centralized control over policy is required, and the role of the State Department should be "radically transformed."[48] What is required, states Hoffmann, is "a coordinating body more representative of the full range of issues than the National Security Council set up in 1947."[49] He suggests at the top a presidential assistant with responsibilities covering not merely "national security" but all foreign-policy issues, including economic ones, and a staff dealing with interdependence issues as well as traditional ones. This staff, however, would not be "shapers of content."[50] The substance of policy would be the responsibility of each department, under the control of the president. The role of the assistant on national security affairs would be "one of discretion, administrative efficiency, and analytic talent—not advocacy, and certainly not activism."[51] In short, Hoffmann wants to deemphasize the policy-making role of the national security adviser and to restore it to departments.

Two men who have been national security advisers in the recent past have different views. Henry Kissinger argues that it is difficult for a president to make new policy departures through the departmental system.[52] Nor, according to Kissinger, is the State Department equipped to handle interdepartmental machinery.[53] "I have become convinced that the running of interdepartmental machinery ought to be preeminently the responsibility of the security adviser (except perhaps in a case of crisis). . . . The articulation and conduct of foreign policy should be left in the main to the President and the Secretary of State (and, of course, their designees)."[54]

Kissinger believes that the preparation of policy options should also be the work of the national security adviser. Thus Kissinger would have the presidential assistant retain the responsibility for coordination but would place articulation of policy in the president and the secretary of state.

Jimmy Carter's national security adviser, Zbigniew Brzezinski, continues to support the retention of control of foreign policy in the White House and the strengthening of the position of the adviser. Suggesting that the State Department may confuse diplomacy with overall foreign policy, Brzezinski suggests that the president "needs someone close to him who shares his larger 'Presidential' perspective and can rise above narrower bureaucratic concerns." He adds, "This is why coordination is easier to achieve if attempted from the White House than if it is undertaken from one of the key departments, even if a given Secretary possesses a strong personality." Brzezinski also suggests that centralization of national security policy in the White House "can facilitate a closer integration of foreign and domestic policy."[55]

These views by three knowledgeable observers of the executive-branch system do not exhaust the possibilities of the arrangements that might be developed to produce more coordinated and better policy. All three perceive the growing need to coordinate more effectively the various types of policies necessary in today's world—domestic, political, economic, military, and cultural. All agree with the need for a continuation of a special adviser and staff. All agree that the special adviser should not be the person to articulate foreign policy publicly. However, if broader coordination and integration of policies along a broad spectrum of fields are essential, it suggests that the national security adviser must increasingly be experienced in or highly attuned to domestic issues as well as national security concerns. Policy analyses must increasingly include the elements of all fields, and new scholarship is required to investigate the ways in which all levels of policy interrelate. The National Security Council staff must then be constructed to provide it with experts in the various levels of policy so that mutual effects can be analyzed and understood. Indeed, if better coordination and integration of policy are required, some thought must be given to the adequacy of the National Security Council itself as the most effective body to deliberate and decide foreign-policy questions. Although the three analysts cited above express little enthusiasm for the cabinet as a policy-making body, the cabinet may provide a more broadly based structure in which to consider policy. In any case, none of the three analysts is entirely satisfied with the system as it exists or with a return to the more traditional preeminence of the State Department.

Two additional points merit consideration here. First, despite the multiplicity of actors in the process, it is clear that policy decisions are usually taken by a very few individuals and that a president who knows what he wants can get his way. When he is uncertain, the advice of a few key subordinates may be accepted and endorsed by the president. It becomes his decision. Yet most issues are complex, most presidents do not usually know ahead of time what they want to do, and the positions advocated by the key departments and agencies become important parts of the decision-making process. These positions, in turn, are the result of sometimes fierce internal battles within the departments and agencies. In short, to make the second point, policy results most often from a process that is political at many levels. Argumentation, debate, negotiation, marshaling of support of other concerned actors, wheeling and dealing are all part of the interplay that leads to a decision.

Finally, even when the administration has made a policy decision it must prepare to encounter the Congress, the news media, the public, special interests, and occasionally the courts. The battle is not over, especially when strong views opposing administration policy await in the world beyond Washington. A president and his administration are not without powerful weapons in this battle, however, as we have seen in chapter 3. And in many instances they must use all of them.

NOTES

[1] Henry Kissinger, *White House Years* (Boston: Little, Brown & Company, 1979), p. 954.

[2] Ibid., p. 995.

[3] Ibid.

[4] Thomas G. Paterson, J. Garry Clifford, and Kenneth J. Hagan, *American Foreign Policy: A History* (Lexington, Mass: D. C. Heath & Company, 1977), pp. 43–44.

[5] International Monetary Fund; International Bank for Reconstruction and Development; the regional banks: Asian Development Bank, Inter-American Development Bank, and African Development Bank. Charles W. Kegley and Eugene R. Wittkopf, *American Foreign Policy: Pattern and Process*, 2nd ed. (New York: St. Martin's Press, 1982), pp. 385–86.

[6] Clyde H. Farnsworth, "Wealthy Nations Agree to More Aid for Poorer Lands," *New York Times*, September 5, 1982, p. 1.

[7] Farnsworth, "Wealth Nations Agree"; Leonard Silk, "American Plan for the I.M.F.," *New York Times*, September 3, 1982, p. D2.

[8] Bernard Nossiter, "What's the Bottom Line on World Debt?" *New York Times*, May 15, 1983, p. E3; Barnaby J. Feder, "The World Banking Crisis: Phase Two," *New York Times*, March 27, 1983, F1. The terms Third World and Fourth World are used to describe many of the less developed and developing countries of the world. The term Fourth World has been used to identify the poorest twenty-five to thirty countries in resources, per capita income, and developmental rates.

[9] Kegley and Wittkopf, *American Foreign Policy*, p. 385.

[10] Ibid., p. 386.

[11] Ibid., p. 387.

[12] Ibid., p. 388.

[13] Ibid., p. 389.

[14] Clyde Farnsworth, "Trade Department Plan Issued by Reagan," *New York Times*, June 2, 1983, p. D6.

[15] H. Erich Heinemann, "Trying to Avoid Another Versailles," *New York Times*, May 15, 1983, p. F1; and R. W. Apple, Jr., "7 Leaders Discuss East-West Issues at Economic Talks," *New York Times*, June 8, 1984, p. 1.

[16] Cecil Crabb, Jr., *American Foreign Policy in the Nuclear Age*, 4th ed., (New York: Harper & Row, Publishers, 1983), pp. 209–10.

[17] Ibid., pp. 134–44; Henry Nash, *American Foreign Policy: Changing Perspectives on National Security*, rev. ed., (Homewood, Ill.: Dorsey Press, 1978), pp. 201–34.

[18] Kegley and Wittkopf, *American Foreign Policy*, pp. 373–75.

[19] Crabb, *American Foreign Policy*, p. 136.

[20] Ibid.

[21] Henry L. Stimson and McGeorge Bundy, *On Active Service in Peace and War* (New York: Harper and Brothers, 1947), p. 188.

[22] Crabb, *American Foreign Policy*, p. 143; John H. Esterline and Robert Black, *Inside Foreign Policy* (Palo Alto, Calif.: (Mayfield Publishing Co., 1975), pp. 33–37.

[23] Kegley and Wittkopf, *American Foreign Policy*, p. 379.

[24] Roger Hilsman, *To Govern America* (New York: Harper & Row, Publishers, 1979), p. 195; Crabb, *American Foreign Policy* p. 134.

[25] Esterline and Black, *Inside Foreign Policy*, p. 36.

[26] Harry Howe Ransom, "Strategic Intelligence and Intermestic Politics," in Kegley and Wittkopf, *Perspectives on American Foreign Policy* (New York: St. Martin's Press, 1983), p. 318.

[27] Crabb, *American Foreign Policy*, p. 318.

[28] Nash, *American Foreign Policy*, pp. 209–10.

[29] James Bamford, *The Puzzle Palace* (Boston: Houghton Mifflin Company, 1982); David Burnham, "The Silent Power of the NSA," *New York Times Magazine*, March 27, 1983, pp. 60–69.

[30] Bamford, *Puzzle Palace*, pp. 115–235. Bamford reviews the vast array of technological systems available to and under the control of NSA: listening posts, radar, computers, spy satellites of increasing sophistication, listening and photographic capabilities, special aircraft such as the SR-71.

[31] Nash, *American Foreign Policy*, p. 209.

[32] Kegley and Wittkopf, *American Foreign Policy*, p. 377.

[33] Ibid.

[34] Ibid., p. 378.

[35] Crabb, *American Foreign Policy*, p. 138.

[36] Hilsman, *To Govern America*, p. 195; Nash, *American Foreign Policy*, p. 217.

[37] Zbigniew Brzezinski, *Power and Principle* (New York: Farrar, Straus & Giroux, 1983), p. 68.

[38] Ibid., p. 73.

[39] Hilsman, *To Govern America*, pp. 412, 428–29.

[40] Heinemann, "Trying to Avoid Another Versailles." and R. W. Apple Jr., "7 Leaders Discuss East-West Issues at Economic Talks."

[41] Kegley and Wittkopf, *American Foreign Policy*, pp. 345–46.

[42] Peter T. Kilborn, "The Testing of Martin Feldstein," *New York Times*, September 18, 1983, p. F1.

[43] Thomas R. Dye and L. Harmon Zeigler, *American Politics in the Media Age*, (Monterey, Calif.: Brooks/Cole Publishing Co., 1983), pp. 363–66.

[44] David Edwards, *The American Political Experience*, 2nd ed. (Englewood Cliffs, N.J.: Prentice-Hall, 1982), p. 523.

[45] Crabb, *American Foreign Policy*, p. 140.

[46] Ibid., pp. 103–105; Esterline and Black, *Inside Foreign Policy*, p. 13.

[47] Stanley Hoffmann, *Primacy or World Order* (New York: McGraw-Hill Book Company, 1978), p. 234.

[48] Ibid., p. 236.

[49] Ibid., p. 238.

[50] Ibid.

[51] Ibid., p. 239.

[52] Kissinger, *White House Years*, p. 840.

[53] Kissinger, *Years of Upheaval* (Boston: Little, Brown & Company, 1982), p. 435.

[54] Ibid., p. 437.

[55] Brzezinski, *Power and Principle*, p. 535.

CHAPTER SEVEN
THE CONGRESS

Congress should assert its primary responsibility for the determination of substantive foreign policy.

Senator Sam Ervin

Every time the Congress tries to second guess a president on important national security and foreign policy issues—we are wrong.

Senator John Tower

Our system cannot function when Congress and the President have sharply conflicting goals or when the Congress attempts to prescribe day-to-day tactical decisions.

Henry Kissinger

The first American to orbit the earth, John Glenn, now a United States senator, walked into the crowded hearing room of the Senate Foreign Relations Committee on the afternoon of March 14, 1983, and sat at his place in the semicircle of seats reserved for members of the committee. In the glare of television lights the day's witnesses—Assistant Secretary of State Thomas Enders and Under Secretary of Defense Fred C. Ikle—sat at a table on a slightly lower level facing the senators and defended the Reagan administration's position on providing $60 million more aid for the government of El Salvador.[1] With Glenn leading, the Democratic members of the committee one by one lashed out at the administration's proposal and at its broader Central American policy. Glenn, Paul Sarbanes of Maryland, Paul Tsongas of Massachusetts, and Christopher Dodd of Connecticut took turns in cross-examination. Dodd, the committee's junior member, was most lacerating—probing, attacking, and criticizing with piercing, rapid-fire questioning. The theme of the attack by Democrats was that the Reagan policy was too heavily weighted toward a military approach and too little oriented to dealing with the basic human and economic problems of the people of Central America. The two administration officials were armed with aerial photographs of installations in Grenada they claimed were being developed with Cuban and Soviet aid for use against the United States, and the drama was political in many senses. First, it highlighted genuine intellectual differences over strategy and policy. Second, it developed the line to be used by Democrats in the 1984 elections, underscored by the fact that Senator Glenn later announced his candidacy for the Democratic nomination for president.

On a warm September day in 1982 in Washington, House Speaker Thomas P. "Tip" O'Neill stepped down from his Speaker's chair to take the floor to argue that the House of Representatives should override President Reagan's veto of a $14.2 billion money bill, which the Congress had passed a few weeks earlier. Calling the veto "a dastardly political move by a man with a stone heart," O'Neil added that "the president wants us to make a choice between weapons and handicapped children." Shortly thereafter the House voted 301–117 to override the veto; the next day the Senate also voted to overrid the veto by a 60–30 margin, just the two-thirds vote required for an override.[2]

Now the point of the story is not the excessively colorful rhetoric of Tip O'Neill but the exercise of the independent authority of Congress granted by the Constitution to override the judgment of the president of the United States. Although the disputed portions of this particular bill were primarily domestic programs, the bill also included such foreign-policy items as $350 million of American aid for nations in the Caribbean area. The bill also contained $2 billion less in military spending than the president wanted.

These two incidents demonstrate not only the partisan politics that mark the relations between the two parties but also the intense debate that may occur between the executive and legislative branches of government in the field of foreign policy. In the system created by the Constitution some powers are in the hands of the president, others in the Congress, and some in both branches, making accommodation and compromise necessary. Since the 1960s, Congress has sought a larger role in the shaping and conduct of foreign policy. When Congress expands its involvement in the process, it again raises the questions: who is to make foreign policy in the American system, and what is the appropriate role for Congress if the president's capacity to act is not to be obstructed?

Since the president has no power to command the Congress to do anything, and since the Congress may strongly disagree with the president's policy proposals, the danger of a serious deadlock between the branches is always present. It must be resolved through politics—mutual bargaining involving give and take not only on foreign-policy issues but on domestic issues as well. To be sure, there have been long periods in history when the Congress has either gone along passively with the president or when a spirit of bipartisanship has produced widespread cooperation and agreement. The national debate over the Vietnam War set off the latest period of congressional activism in foreign policy and determination to participate more fully in the policy process.

Congressional opposition to the war in Southeast Asia produced a series of actions beginning in 1970 that symbolized the congressional intention to play a larger role in policy.

In 1970 Congress repealed the Gulf of Tonkin Resolution, and the Cooper-Church amendment banned the use of funds for operations in Cambodia. In 1973 Congress prohibited any further bombing in Cambodia and overrode a presidential veto to pass the War Powers Act. Later Congress prevented the extension of most-favored-nation status to the Soviet Union, pending expanded emigration of Jews from that country. It embargoed arms sales to Turkey in 1974 and banned the expenditure of funds for involvement in Angola. During the period from 1976 to 1980 Congress established committees to provide oversight of intelligence activities and required prior notification by the president of covert operations. During the Carter administration Congress blocked the president's policy to reduce troop commitments to South Korea, added conditions and reservations to the Panama Canal Treaty, and challenged the president's right to abrogate the treaty with Taiwan when he recognized the government of the People's Republic of China. In the 1980s Congress seriously challenged the Reagan policies on Central America, on arms control, and on the building of new weapons systems such as the MX missile and the B-1 bomber.

The pattern of congressional activism in foreign policy in the past decade and a half is clear, and the recent debate over Central American policy suggests that there is no end in sight to the conviction in Congress that it should play a critical and an adversarial role in foreign policy.

Cecil Crabb notes:

> The goal has been to make Congress an equal partner with the president in the formulation and administration of American foreign policy, thereby reversing the long period of executive dominance in the diplomatic field.[3]

In this chapter we will inquire about how well equipped Congress is to play this role.

CAUSES OF CONGRESSIONAL ACTIVISM

The latest surge of congressional assertiveness has followed a period of unusual turbulence in American society and in American politics. Dynamic forces of change within the domestic and global systems have produced a realignment of power within the United States and within the world.

One of the major elements in the process has been the reaction to the use of presidential power. As Crabb and Holt put it:

> Presidents Johnson and Nixon were denounced for using the vast powers of the presidency in behalf of ill-conceived foreign policy ventures, as in the

Vietnam affair. By contrast, Presidents Ford and Carter have been criticized widely for failing to use the power at their command to respond forcefully and successfully to external challenges.[4]

Of course, the crisis of confidence in the executive branch in the past two decades has many causes as we shall see. In recent years, public perceptions that major foreign policies of recent presidents have been disastrous have created an opening for Congress to assume a larger role. Moreover, divisions within the executive branch itself or doubts about who was making foreign policy "have invited strong legislative initiatives in foreign affairs."[5] Crabb and Holt argue: "Congress is irresistibly tempted to fill the ensuing vacuum."[6]

The crisis in presidential leadership, however, has run more deeply than the organizational confusion that has sometimes appeared to characterize the executive branch.

The student must consider the total social fabric of the last two decades. In the 1950s and 1960s a profound social revolution had begun, based largely in the civil-rights movement and in changing social mores. This was reflected in decisions by the Supreme Court, by new legislation passed by Congress, and in new patterns of political activity. Television had become national in scope and communicated the forces of change into the living rooms of most Americans. Urban riots in many American cities gave the impression that the facade of American life was being destroyed. The assassination of John F. Kennedy shook the nation's confidence and optimism. In this environment Lyndon Johnson led the country into the war in Vietnam.

By 1966 the costs of the American military involvement in Vietnam had begun to produce serious doubts within the Johnson administration, in Congress, and among the people about the wisdom of the policy. Dissent coalesced by 1968 into a massive political movement and into a challenge to the reelection of Lyndon Johnson. Even after Johnson withdrew from the race, the war lacerated the American psyche for the next six years and prodded growing numbers of congressional representatives to challenge the policy, while at the same time they provided financial support for forces in the field.

When the South Vietnamese forces collapsed in 1975 and North Vietnam took control over South Vietnam, Laos, and Cambodia, American political objectives in Indochina were in ruins, and American confidence was shattered.

The result was what some have called the Vietnam syndrome. This was a set of reactions, responses, attitudes, and convictions, which included (1) shattered public confidence in both presidential and congressional leadership, and (2) a determination not to engage in foreign military commitments again in such ambiguous circumstances. In terms of political leadership, blame was attached to congressional leadership for passing almost unanimously the Tonkin Gulf Resolution giving Johnson a free hand to use military force. Then the president's inability either to win or to maintain sufficient public support for the commitment weakened confidence in the presidency. From the perspective of the future use of American forces abroad, the Vietnam syndrome diverted the Nixon administration from a commitment in Angola and has been a major barrier to President Reagan's Central American policies in the 1980s.

Even as the American forces were being withdrawn from Vietnam in 1973, a new threat to confidence in presidential leadership was slowly developing: the Watergate scandal. Leading to the resignation of a president who faced impeachment, the Watergate scandal revealed a sordid story of misuse of presidential power, obstruction of justice by the president, and the abuse of the justification of national security. When Nixon was pardoned by his successor, Gerald Ford, barring any future prosecution for criminal offenses, public cynicism deepened. In this atmosphere Jimmy Carter came to the White House.

Although in retrospect Carter's record is far more impressive in foreign policy than was perceived during his tenure in the presidency, divisions within his administration and the vacillation of the president on some key issues left the impression that his leadership was weak. Despite the fact that his policies succeeded in getting all the American hostges out of Iran alive, the hostage crisis was generally viewed as a disaster for American prestige and for Carter's hopes for reelection. With the election of Ronald Reagan, Americans got what they saw as strong leadership. However, soon Reagan's strong ideological views on reassertion of American power in the world produced a strong reaction in the Congress.

The intermixture of domestic social turbulence, the Vietnam syndrome, the Watergate affair, public perceptions of the Carter presidency, and strong reaction to Reagan's proposals in foreign policy form the backdrop for a new era of congressional assertiveness.

FORMAL POWERS

On June 23, 1983, the Supreme Court announced its decision that the legislative veto was unconstitutional, a decision that could alter the balance of power between the executive and legislative branches and affect control of foreign policy.[7]

Under the legislative veto, either or both houses were able to block specific actions taken by a president or a federal agency to whom Congress had delegated authority. In the foreign-policy field, the ruling affects the War Powers Act of 1973, the Congressional Budget and Impoundment Control Act of 1974, the Military Appropriation Authorization Act of 1975, the International Security Assistance and Arms Control Act of 1976, and the Nuclear Nonproliferation Act of 1978.[8] Involved in these acts was congressional authority in such fields as the following: commitment of armed forces abroad, the spending of funds appropriated by Congress, military sales and aid to other countries, and transmission of nuclear materials.

Thus the effects on congressional authority in foreign affairs are potentially profound, for many of these acts reflect the increased assertiveness of Congress in foreign policy since the 1970s. However, while the Court stated that the Constitution provides the veto power only to the president, it is clear that Congress still had adequate powers to exercise its authority through the passage of more specifically written legislation. Indeed, some members of Congress viewed the decision as an opportunity for Congress to take greater care in passing legislation in the first place.

While removal of the legislative veto will undoubtedly reduce some of the tactical flexibility available to Congress in responding to presidential initiatives, it has done nothing to reduce Congress's fundamental power over a number of activities.

Since the passage of the War Powers Act, doubts have persisted about its constitutionality and also its effectiveness,[9] doubts intensified by the new Supreme Court decision. A new challenge to the act arose more rapidly than expected when events in Lebanon in 1983 raised new questions about its applicability to the commitment of American forces there as part of an international peace-keeping mission.

Under pressures from Congress, the administration agreed to a limitation of eighteen months on the commitment, although subsequent events led to an early withdrawal of the multinational force, including the American contingent. The affair left unanswered many of the constitutional and operational questions about the act and its effectiveness.

Originally the act was intended by Congress as a way to provide congressional participation in the most vital decision a government can make—the commitment of military forces abroad. Responding to bitter criticism about the ways in which the United States got into Vietnam, Congress also attempted to deal with some form of modernization of one of its most important powers—the declaration of war. In the age of nuclear missiles and guerilla warfare, of covert operations and gradual military escalation, serious doubts had arisen over the adequacy of the declaration-of-war clause as written. Rather than confront a process of constitutional amendment, a process fraught with complexity, Congress constructed the War Powers Act. In general it provides that a president must report any military combat commitment to Congress within forty-eight hours. Theoretically the president was to consult with Congress before the commitment, and Congress, by concurrent resolution, could order the withdrawal of troops. In longer-term situations, an automatic termination of presidential authority would occur in sixty days unless Congress extended the commitment for another thirty days. Whatever its pros and cons, the act was a political response to what was perceived as erosion of congressional authority in the area of military commitment.

In any case, the power to declare war still resides constitutionally with Congress and is potentially Congress's most awesome power. It has not used the power since 1941.

A less authoritative but still important power available to Congress to express its position on foreign-policy questions is the *resolution*. The right of either house of Congrss to pass a "sense of the house" resolution expressing its collective view on any issue, and the power of both houses to pass concurrent resolutions can be effective means of expressing support of, or opposition to, a president's policies.[10] Indeed, a president may seek a congressional resolution to support a policy, as President Johnson did in 1964 with the Gulf of Tonkin Resolution supporting his freedom of action in Vietnam. In the case of Vietnam, the resolution was not an effective substitute for a declaration of war, nor, many believe, was its passage necessary to give the president the authority he needed to commit American forces abroad. However, the limits of presidential authority to commit forces and the extent of congressional constraints on presidential power remain unresolved.

Only the Senate is given the the responsibility to *advise and consent* concerning treaties negotiated by the president, ambassadors to foreign countries, and ministers and advisers or counsels, such as the secretary of state.[11] Treaties require a two-thirds vote of the Senate and acquire the status of American law. Although the Congress is not required to approve of executive agreements, its support for such policies is often sought in other ways: provision of appropriations to pay for the agreements, resolutions affirming a presidential action, or public approval by key individual members of Congress.[12]

The Congress has more frequent opportunities to express its views on the foreign policy of the president, however, through its *control of the nation's purse strings*. Many continuing policies and the financial support of the foreign-policy establishment require formally authorized expenditures.[13] The appropriations for these functions must successfully pass through a legislative obstacle course which provides dozens of places in which administration policies can be opposed or obstructed. In many ways this is, of course, the most powerful function available to the Congress in its political relations with the White House.

Other important instruments of congressional power are *investigations and oversight*.[14] Implicit in its responsibilities to pass laws and to hear of the state of the Union from the president is the power to conduct investigations into matters relating to existing law and new proposals and to evaluate the operations of existing laws and programs. The authority not only allows Congress to inquire publicly and privately into presidential initiatives as they are proposed but permits the regular monitoring of the operations of executive agencies and personnel.

During the Vietnam War the Senate Foreign Relations Committee held a series of hearings on administration policy that served as a forum for the national debate over the commitment to Southeast Asia. In 1983 the Senate Foreign Relations Committee, the House Foreign Affairs Committee, and the Armed Services committees in both houses conducted intensive inquiries into Reagan policies in Central America.

Thus the investigation and oversight functions are among the most important day-to-day powers available to Congress.

The power to *regulate commerce with foreign nations* provides Congress with additional scope that has increased in importance in the late twentieth century, characterized as it is by vast international trade, such as oil from OPEC and cars from Japan. Congress has often authorized the president to negotiate foreign trade and economic matters, but the ultimate constitutional authority rests within the legislative branch.[15]

The broadest grant of constitutional authority is the so-called *necessary and proper clause*, the last paragraph of article I, section 8. It has provided vast authority for Congress to engage in policy formulation in both foreign and domestic areas. It permits Congress to do what is necessary and proper to carry out the powers specifically cited in the Constitution and "all other powers vested by this Constitution in the Government of the United States or in any Department or Officer thereof."[16]

The congressional authority to *raise, support, and regulate armies and navies and the militia* (National Guard or reserves) and to create and support other departments and agencies in the foreign-policy field gives Congress not only oversight capability but considerable influence on the size and shape of the structures of government.[17] In this area the power transcends appropriations authority alone. Inherent in it is the capability to influence policy, and Congress may have divergent views from a president on the necessary size, mixture, and deployment of forces.

In addition to the commerce power, Congress has a broad range of *other economic powers:* raising and collecting taxes, regulating the value of money, setting tariff and trade policy, and punishing piracies and felonies on the high seas and offenses against international law.[18]

It also has the power to regulate immigration and naturalization policies.

Another powerful congressional weapon is the authority to *override presidential vetoes.*[19] As a practical matter, this power cannot be mustered very often, but it can be a potent one in deterring the political power of a president or in preventing a policy initiative that is not convincing to more than two-thirds of either house.

The *general legislative authority* of Congress is an important congressional weapon not only because of how it may relate to foreign-policy questions but also because of how political trade-offs between domestic and foreign matters may be pursued.[20]

Abraham F. Lowenthal describes the trade-off process:

> A proposed measure that penalizes some well-organized group . . . copper companies, sugar or citrus growers, shoe manufacturers, auto or textile workers, church groups, or whatever . . . can be shelved by blocking coalitions within the highly fragmented structure of United States foreign policy making. Although the proposed change may promise substantially to benefit United States society as a whole, a group likely to be influenced often can prevent the measure's adoption; the history of sugar tariffs and quotas amply illustrates this point. Nor does it necessarily require congressional action to frustrate an administration's initiatives. . . .[21]

Clearly the support of some representatives or senators on foreign-policy questions may depend on administration concessions on domestic issues. The process is made possible by the wide general legislative authority inherent in Congress. Congress also has many informal ways of exercising an influence on policy.

INFORMAL POWERS

The *politics* involved in the trade-offs afford Congress a wide array of informal capabilities to influence policy, just as they do for the president.

The process of compromise may result from mutual efforts to intellectually convince each other of the rightness of views on each side. Without question, the process is as useful within Congress as it is between Congress and the White House. Within the Congress differences must be adjusted between leaders and followers, among committees, between Democrats and Republicans, and between House and Senate. When a thrust toward congressional *consensus* seems clear, views must be compromised with those of the president. In the process, such traditional bargaining techniques as distribution of pork barrel, log-rolling, and other rewards and punishments can be as effective in the hands of congressional forces as in the hands of a skillful president.[22]

The *educational capabilities* available to Congress provide means to exercise pressure on an administration and to inform and persuade the public. Although Congress, in general, cannot match the communication potential of an effective president, members have direct access to their constituents through local media coverage, newsletters, personal contacts, and election campaigns, all of which provide access to a wider public.[23] Support or criticism of administration policy can be an effective device for expression of congressional opinion.

Moreover, media coverage of Congress in Washington has increased substantially over the last few decades.[24] Radio and TV facilities were added to each house, to expand upon the printed media capabilities. Studio facilities have been constructed for immediate radio and TV response to presidential speeches and actions. Most recently the House of Representatives inaugurated live television coverage of floor and committee sessions, although the Senate has decided against live floor coverage. House sessions may be televised in their entirety live over cable television or excerpts may be used by the major television networks.

In addition, many in Congress are adept at using news leaks, that is, the passing of confidential information to reporters and commentators.[25]

Beyond the utilization of media and coverage of Congress by the media, members of Congress may air their opinions and ideas on issues in a number of other places. Speeches to organizations, to university audiences, and to party functions provide many opportunities for expression of views.

Usually certain individuals with special expertise, aside from the congressional leaders, provide views contrary to administration policy.[26] During the Vietnam War Senator J. William Fulbright, chairman of the Foreign Relations Committee, became a major focus for congressional and public dissent. In the more recent debate over Central America, Senator Christopher Dodd became a major congressional critic of Reagan policy. Senator Edward Kennedy attracts extensive attention when he comments on foreign or domestic issues.

Still another frequent source for congressional discussion and leadership on foreign-policy questions is *members of Congress positioning themselves for a race for the presidency*, whether or not they are members of key committees dealing with the subject. In the late 1950s a young senator from Massachusetts, John F. Kennedy, made a key speech on the Senate floor in favor of independence for Algeria from France. It brought him attention as a serious commentator on contemporary foreign-policy issues. Since so many candidates for the presidency come from the Congress, particularly the Senate, it is not surprising to find individuals attempting to stake out positions and to establish their credentials and expertise in foreign policy. In recent years many members of Congress have become candidates, among them John Kennedy, Richard Nixon, Lyndon Johnson, Robert Kennedy, George McGovern, Walter Mondale, Henry Jackson, Morris Udall, Robert Dole, Howard Baker, Ted Kennedy, Gerald Ford, John Glenn and Gary Hart. That both Carter and Reagan were state governors has been a break in precedent, but many observers believe that the next changeover will return to the pattern of the past.

In any event, although Congress as a whole and individual members of Congress cannot match the exposure and attention available to a president, Congress has ample resources with which to communicate with the administration, with itself, and with the public.

Still another means of congressional participation in foreign policy is *travel* to other parts of the world.[27] Despite the public skepticism about congressional junkets, travel abroad to meet foreign leaders and to assess public opinion in foreign countries is essentially a useful device to broaden the knowledge and judgment of members of Congress. With or without a presidential request, the members' travel abroad can provide useful information, the opportunity to deliver personal messages, and the opportunity to enhance the members' prestige at home.

A mechanism that has added to the influence of members of Congress is their *participation,* at the request of the president, in important negotiations.[28] From the standpoint of Congress, this may co-opt congressional opposition to a president's policies, but it provides the opportunity to be in on the takeoffs as well as the landings.

A brief point here about *congressional staffs:* The vast increase in the numbers and expertise of personal and committee staffs in the last twenty years has provided Congress with an excellent source of knowledge and information about policy and the policy process. The staff has greatly enhanced congressional capabilities in debating foreign policy.

ORGANIZATION

The constitutional arrangement of the Congress into two houses provided for a check-and-balance system with the executive branch, but it also provides the two houses with a check and balance on each other. The Senate, symbolizing equal representation of all the states, and the House, representing more local and regional interests, have inevitably reflected different levels of experience, belief, and methods. Senators, elected for six years, are somewhat less susceptible to immediate public opinion than are representatives, who must seek reelection every two years. In addition, the powers of each house under the Constitution are somewhat different in foreign policy. The Senate has power in the approval of treaties and the confirmation of officials, while the House has more immediate power in the appropriations process. In general, the Senate has tended in recent years to be somewhat more liberal than the House, although both houses must reconcile differences in final legislation.

Primarily, power is exercised in both houses through committees and subcommittees, and in recent years subcommittees and their chairs have become a major source of policy guidance. Although in the past the general perception has been that the House is less important and less effective in foreign-policy debate, efforts over the past ten years to invigorate House committees involved in foreign policy have produced somewhat expanded attention on the House.

In the 1981–82 session of the 97th Congress, the House maintained 22 standing committees and 141 subcommittees, while the Senate had 15 standing committees with 83 subcommittees.[29] In addition, 3 House select committees had 7 subcommittees, and the Senate had 5 select committees with 12 subcommittees.

With reference to foreign policy, all but 5 House committees and all but 3 Senate committees have some jurisdiction over some aspect of foreign policy.[30] This has led to the problem of multiple referrals, i.e., the consideration by many committees of different aspects of foreign-policy questions, and it has led to the erosion of control by traditional committees.[31] For example, in reference to the House Foreign Affairs Committee, two scholars have noted:

> It shares the Food and Peace Program with Agriculture; foreign intelligence activities with Armed Services and the Select Committee on Intelligence; international banking with Banking, Finance, and Urban Affairs; the ACTION program (including the Peace Corps) and other education programs as well as the United Nation's International Labor Organization with Education and Labor; immigration, claims, and passports with Judiciary; international fishing rights and environmental legislation and the Panama Canal with Merchant Marine and Fisheries; and trade with Ways and Means.[32]

The authors conclude that "the more actors who become involved in the process, the less expeditiously the nation can act."[33]

The fact that almost every congressional committee, like almost every executive-branch department, may occasionally be involved in matters of foreign policy does not preclude the recognition that there are a few major committees whose primary responsibility has long been one of foreign policy and the means to execute it.

In matters of foreign policy, foreign aid, treaties, advice, and consent on appointments, the *Senate Foreign Relations Committee* has considerable authority and prestige. Regarded as one of the most desirable committees on which to serve, the committee has a number of subcommittees organized to deal with specific geographic areas and functional problems. Its counterpart in the House of Representatives, the *House Foreign Affairs Committee,* has somewhat less legislative responsibility but has also become a body of special expertise in matters of foreign policy.

The *Armed Services Committees* in both the Senate and the House have considerable responsibility for consideration of the size and content of the budget for the Department of Defense, for composition and deployment of the armed forces, for defense strategy, and for coordination of military and foreign policy.

Also directly involved in foreign-policy questions are the *appropriations committees* and their subcommittees in both the House and the Senate. It is those committees that must examine, analyze, and decide on the amounts of money to be allocated to all governmental activity, including defense and foreign policy.

In the areas of spending, relatively new *Budget Committees* in both houses play an indirect role by setting budget limitations on the entire Congress. The reconciliation of the congressional budgets drafted by these committees and those drafted by the executive branch open the way for considerable political bargaining between the two branches.

In the area of international economic activity the *Interstate and Foreign Commerce Committee* in the House and the *Commerce, Science and Transportation Committee* in the Senate are concerned with matters of trade, while the *Banking, Housing, and Urban Affairs Committee* in the Senate oversees the question of money in the American system and in the global economy. In addition, the *Joint Economic Committee,* composed of members of both houses, considers broad questions of economic policy for the domestic and foreign areas.

In the areas of science and technology the House *Committee on Science and Technology;* the Senate *Committee on Commerce, Science and Transportation;* and the Senate *Committees on Energy and Natural Resources* deal with questions that relate to foreign policy.

The House *Committee on Agriculture* and the Senate *Committee on Agriculture, Nutrition, and Forestry* deal with questions involving the production and sale of American food products to foreign countries, and the House *Committee on Merchant Marine and Fisheries* also encompasses matters that may have a foreign-policy content.

Finally, each house has a *Select Committee on Intelligence,* which oversees the operations of the American intelligence community, including the CIA, the DIA, and NSA.

In addition, other committees, such as *Government Operations* in the House or *Governmental Affairs* in the Senate may deal with the organizational structure of key departments and agencies involved in foreign policy.

An organizational factor of increasing importance is the professional staff. By 1980 it was estimated that the staff totaled at least eighteen thousand divided among personal staffs, the staffs of the committees and subcommittees, and staffs employed by Congress as a whole.[34] In this last category are such organizations as the General Accounting Office (GAO), the Congressional Budget Office, and the Office of Technology Assessment. Staffs of committees are normally selected by the majority and minority members of committees and reflect the political predispositions of the members. Although the level of special expertise is regarded as high, it is not uniform, and the staff can, therefore, reflect different levels of background and experience.

Nonetheless, whatever the level of interest and expertise of members, their staffs can provide up-to-date information about the legislative calendar, details about issues, and estimates of how other members of the committee stand on given issues.[35] The communication and coordination among staff personnel is extensive, and their daily briefings of members is invaluable. In addition, staff experts review the literature in the field, carry out independent research, and survey the news media. Their primary problem is to get enough time with their members to provide adequate background and briefings on contemporary issues.[36] In the case of members with little interest, experience, or background in foreign policy, the considered judgments of the staff are highly influential in shaping the thinking and the positions of members.

Staff experts frequently travel abroad with their chiefs and are sometimes employed by the executive departments or the National Security Council when they leave their staff jobs. Occasionally they go on to write books or join university faculties.

LIMITATIONS ON CONGRESSIONAL ROLE

As the House of Representatives moved closer in late July 1983 to voting to approve a cut-off of funds for support of antigovernment guerillas in Nicaragua, Americans were aware of the capability of Congress to prevent the administration from carrying out a policy it regarded as necessary to achieve American aims in Central America. What was more difficult for Congress was to determine the policy that would replace it. The problems of 535 members of Congress forging foreign policies are immeasurable. Indeed, the very structure of Congress raises serious questions about its capability to devise and to manage foreign policy independently.

Perhaps the most important constraint on Congress in foreign policy lies in one of its major strengths—the tendency toward agreement. Developing a majority opinion requires the time-consuming task of building coalitions, acquiring allies, and holding the line over a period of months. On particularly difficult and complex issues the problems of building a majority, let alone a consensus, are formidable. If consensus means agreement by a very large proportion of the group, and if consensus would provide the necessary credible foundation for policy initiatives, it is clear that Congress is at a disadvantage in playing a leadership role.

On the question of cutting off aid to guerillas in Nicaragua, for example, the House was nearly evenly divided, and the action carried by only thirty-three votes.[37] Hardly a ringing endorsement for congressional policy contrary to the president's policy. Even during the Vietnam War, majorities to limit the president's policy were frequently small. Thus when Congress acts, it is not only the time-consuming nature of the process that constrains it but the normal absence of sufficient consensus to establish the credible authority of policy alternatives.

The difficulties of forming a majority, let alone a consensus, are multiplied by a number of other elements in the American political culture and in the operations of Congress itself. One of the reasons mass consensus may be absent from the Congress most of the time is that it is absent from the country most of the time. America is a pluralist country in whch many forces, opinions, and interests are at work.[38] Special-interest groups, single-issue lobbies, independent voters, and the mass media contribute to a fragmented political system, resulting in a Congress whose interests are fragmented too. Members of Congress are intensely sensitive to special interests and public opinion, since they are concerned with the next election. Moreover, the large divisions within the country contribute to the fragmented nature of Congress. Geographical differences (north and south, east and west); ethnic, racial, religious, and class differences; and educational differences may not obliterate consensus on many basic American principles; but, they do complicate the formation of coalitions on specific issues.

Within the Congress changes made in the past decade have dispersed power among leaders, committees, subcommittees, and individuals.[39] Delivering the votes can be a most difficult job for leaders. Within the field of foreign policy, as we have seen, responsibilities have been so divided that most committees in both houses deal with some aspect of foreign policy.

Whatever the virtues of the present system, it is clear that it is more difficult than in the past for a president or for congressional leaders to organize a majority on anything.

In terms of foreign policy, one might remember that except when a major crisis threatens, the great majority of the public is dramatically uninterested in foreign policy.[40] While this fact may widen the discretion of both the president and Congress in foreign policy, it also affects the amount of interest and time many members of Congress are prepared to devote to foreign policy questions. Since being a foreign-policy expert is not the major path to reelection most of the time, indifference to foreign policy among most legislators is sizeable.

This factor leads to the parochialism that can be found in the country and in the Congress. Local and individual interests tend to dominate the attention of many members of Congress, especially those in the House, who must campaign every two years.[41] When legislators express an interest in foreign policy or security affairs, it is more likely to stem from budget items for military contracts or bases in the legislator's district or state.[42]

For those in Congress who are interested in foreign policy, the limits on available time impose additional constraints on the capacity to act intelligently. The member's time is necessarily divided among domestic and foreign issues, several committees and subcommittees, servicing constituents, maintaining contacts with his or her district or state, meeting with reporters, and a wide variety of other functions that are part of the agenda of even the newest member of Congress.[43] The time required for reading, background, and discussion with advisers is tightly limited. In short, members of the executive departments in foreign policy spend full time in the field, while the members of Congress can, at best, give efforts in the field only a small percentage of their time.

When discussing the contributions of the professional staffs, we raised the subject of expertise. Even with vastly expanded staffs, congressional capabilities are regarded as meager at best when compared with the resources of the executive branch.[44] Relatively few members come to Congress with background or experience in foreign policy, and once in Congress, there is limited time to acquire the specialized knowledge required to speak with authority.

Even assuming the presence of expert staff and knowledgeable members, access to information may be severely limited on important issues. Control of information and its flow remain in the White House and in the executive departments, and even without considering the volume of "secret" information held within the executive branch and not shared with all members of Congress, access to information may be limited.[45]

Finally, during the 1960s and 1970s, public confidence in the presidency eroded at the same time that the public looked to Congress to correct many of the problems of the period. In the 1980s public confidence in the Congress continued to erode because of a number of scandals, such as ABSCAM, "Koreagate," sex and drug charges, and several individual cases of censure or reprimand.[46]

However, the presidency survived Vietnam and Watergate. The Congress will survive ABSCAM.

Whatever the doubts about presidential leadership in recent years, it is clear that the capability of Congress to play a leadership role in foreign policy is severely limited.

AN INDIVIDUAL PERSPECTIVE

Congressional assertiveness does not appear to motivate some younger members of Congress. For example, Representative Bruce Morrison, a liberal Democrat from the New Haven, Connecticut area, and chairman of the Democratic freshmen caucus in Congress in the 1983–84 term, has expressed reservations about Congress's ability to play more than a veto role over executive actions: "By nature, Congress can't make foreign policy in a meaningful sense; it can check and restrain what the executive does more than it can define what the executive does. It is hard for Congress to play a positive, creative role."[47]

Morrison concluded, after his first six months in Congress, that the role of the members in foreign policy is limited and that the news media and other outside sources provide more information to the representative on foreign-policy questions than does Congress itself. On the virtues of bipartisanship Morrison argues that "consistency over time is an advantage, but bipartisanship just for the label doesn't have any value; it too often is used as a way of saying you're not supposed to criticize the administration." His view is that "there always ought to be a lively debate as consensus is being defined." Morrison regards foreign-policy questions as relatively important among his constituents. Commenting on contemporary issues relating to Central America, Morrison supports the Boland amendment, which prohibits use of covert activities to overthrow foreign governments. "I don't think we should be in the business of overthrowing other people's governments or destabilizing other people's governments," he noted.

These views of a freshman representative in 1983, while not representative of the views of all his 434 colleagues in the House, nonetheless provide some insights into the views of younger members about the appropriate role for Congress in the relationshp with the executive branch.

CONCLUSIONS

One scholar of congressional behavior in foreign policy has written that "by the end of the 1970s even former legislators themselves were expressing serious reservations about Congress' ability to produce unified and effective national policies—especially in the foreign policy realm."[48]

The unified and coherent decision making required in foreign policy calls for an organizational discipline that many believe Congress has yet to demonstrate.[49]

Apart from policy making, the Congress' success in day-to-day management is also regarded as incomplete. One study noted: "This is not a realm into which the legislative branch should intrude regularly, nor is it really equipped to do so."[50]

But if Congress is not equipped to formulate policy or to provide daily management oversight of foreign-policy agencies, what is it to do? What is its most productive role? Can it not lead, too?

In a political framework there is little doubt that the relationship between the executive branch and the Congress is the central one in the American system most of the time. Occasionally the Supreme Court, the mass media, or public opinion may force both the president and the Congress to respond to particular problems. However, Congress is the primary conduit through which most of the forces of America flow into the policy process: the public, special interests, the media. And the consent of Congress is still required for a wide array of presidential actions. Roger Hilsman notes:

> On some specific detail of foreign policy, the President may frequently ignore the Congress with complete impunity, but on the overall, fundamental issues that persist over time, he must have their cooperation and acquiescence, even if he is not required to have their formal and legal consent.[51]

In the past, when we spoke of "Congress" and its role in foreign policy, we might have meant a relatively small group of experts who served on a few relevant committees, even though, to be sure, all members had to vote on foreign-policy questions. Today, with the dispersal of responsibility, the number of experts and the number of issues have expanded to almost every major committee in both houses. Indeed, every member, whatever his or her interest in foreign policy, had to learn enough about it to be able to respond intelligently to questions back home. One member, who didn't know that a neutron bomb was a nuclear weapon and so informed his constituency, was not reelected in 1982.

In general, the responsibility of Congress is to absorb, process, and articulate the concerns, beliefs, and demands of the public it serves and to try to translate that into a response to presidential initiatives. Beyond that, it occasionally has the opportunity to lead public opinion and to take policy initiatives. In the period of 1945–50, had Senators Arthur Vandenberg and Tom Connolly been unwilling to support the policies of the Truman administration, if they had only reflected public opinion, American foreign policy might have been much less creative and effective. Today congressional authority is not so centralized, and 535 voting members constitute 535 centers of power.

Although the era of bipartisanship may be dead, its demise has brought benefits as well as problems. Issues are increasingly complex in a dangerous and interdependent world, and the present system permits a more comprehensive analysis and debate of problems and of proposed solutions. Nonetheless, the loss of bipartisanship means the end of massive broad-based consensus on many issues and erodes the ability of government to make clear, unambiguous, and authoritative statements on policy.

Congressional assertiveness on foreign policy faces another risk: that it will be seen as mere partisan politics. The efforts of many Democrats in Congress in the past few years to oppose Reagan policies in Central America occurred as the 1984 election campaign had already begun. Four Democratic United States Senators were seeking the Democratic party nomination for president: John Glenn, Gary Hart, Alan Cranston, and Ernest Hollings. To what extent were Democrats in Congress playing politics, and to what extent were they expressing sincere and valid criticism of administration policy?

In the debate over Central American policy, for example, Democrats with majority control in the House understood that the Senate, which is controlled by a Republican majority, would support a Republican president on most issues. Therefore, the House was free to take a firm stand against presidential policies, knowing that its actions had no chance of becoming policy. It was "safe" to take an opposing position, which would have little effect on administration policy. House Democrats had the best of all worlds. They could appear fiercely combative, attack the administration, and know they would do no real damage to policy.

In the debate over cutting off funds for support of covert action in Nicaragua in late July 1983, the House majority was in a position to take an independent position, knowing that the measure had no chance of also passing the Senate. Indeed, the compromise measure that the House finally adopted on July 28 encompassed a sleight of hand. It approved the taking away of funds for covert action by anti-Nicaraguan guerillas, but at the same time it approved an additional $80 million in overt aid to friendly Central American governments for halting arms shipments to guerilla forces in the region. Thus the action was hardly a clear-cut expression of House opposition to administration policy.

An attack in Congress on a specific policy or proposal may have broader purposes—electoral politics, dramatization of political differences in order to educate or arouse the public, or a sincere desire to thwart a presidential policy or a presidential ideology regarded as harmful to the national interest. Undoubtedly many congressional Democrats, perhaps most, hold beliefs that strongly differ from the hard-line approach in foreign policy pursued by the Reagan administration, just as in the Carter years many Republicans objected deeply to the president's perceived softer-line approach. Staking out opposing positions may be based in true ideological differences, but it may also contribute to formation of effective issues in the next election. That is politics, too. The effects may not be bad, however, no matter what the basic motivation. Whether for political advantage or for ideological conviction, the system produces policy alternatives, which can be considered by the people. A process that provides, for whatever reason, opposing analysis and alternate policy proposals serves the purposes of democracy and surprisingly often serves the national interest very well.

It is the function of loyal opposition to oppose—whether to gain an advantage for the next election or to suggest abstract policy options. In an increasingly complex world facing difficult and sometimes dangerous choices, there are many different approaches that might be followed by any administration. Congress, through vigorous criticism and debate, helps to articulate the most basic questions required for survival and to suggest alternative paths to serve the national interest. This alone justifies an assertive role by Congress.

Congress, certainly, is not the only voice of the people. The executive branch represents the people, too. But each may hear different messages, and the essence of democracy is to thrash out the differences, find compromise solutions, and acquire legitimacy for the policies that result. It is the provision of legitimacy that justifies the use by Congress of its many formal and informal powers to question, criticize, correct, and constrain presidential action.

Congress can provide funds, as it did in the Vietnam War, but appropriation alone may not necessarily provide the legitimacy for policy that enlists public support, long-term commitment, and sacrifice. Presidents have wide independent latitude to act in foreign policy, but without the support of Congress, their policies will eventually erode.

By itself, Congress cannot lead or manage foreign affairs, but it can examine alternatives in the public arena, identify the costs, and legitimize the results. The process by which it does so couldn't be more political, but if the results include a foreign policy most Americans can support, most would conclude the process is worth the cost.

NOTES

[1] Margot Hornblower, "Salvadoran Aid Opposed in Senate," *Washington Post,* March 15, 1983, p. 1.

[2] "House Approves Overriding Reagan's Veto on Spending," *New York Times,* September 10, 1982, p. 1.

[3] Cecil Crabb, Jr. *American Foreign Policy in the Nuclear Age,* 4th ed. (New York: Harper & Row, Publishers, 1983), p. 188.

[4] Cecil V. Crabb, Jr., and Pat M. Holt, *Invitation to Struggle: Congress, the President, and Foreign Policy* (Washington, D.C.: Congressional Quarterly Press, 1980), p. 197.

[5] Ibid., p. 198.

[6] Ibid.

[7] Linda Greenhouse, "Supreme Court, 7–2, Restricts Congress' Right to Overrule Actions by Executive Branch," *New York Times,* June 24, 1983, p. 1.

[8] "Major Laws with Veto Provisions," *New York Times,* June 24, 1983, p. B5.

[9] Crabb, *American Foreign Policy,* p. 69.

[10] Ibid., pp. 210–12.

[11] Crabb and Holt, *Invitation to Struggle,* p. 201.

[12] Crabb, *American Foreign Policy,* pp. 190–92.

[13] Charles W. Kegley and Eugene R. Wittkopf, *American Foreign Policy: Pattern and Process,* 2nd ed. (New York: St. Martin's Press, 1982), p. 422.

[14] Crabb and Holt, *Invitation to Struggle,* p. 49.

[15] Ibid., p. 47.

[16] Sheldon Goldman, *Constitutional Law and Supreme Court Decision-Making* (New York: Harper & Row, Publishers, 1982), p. 45.

[17] Crabb, *American Foreign Policy*, p. 199.

[18] Crabb and Holt, *Invitation to Struggle*, pp. 47–48.

[19] David V. Edwards, *The American Political Experience*, 2nd ed. (Englewood Cliffs, N. J.: Prentice-Hall, 1982), pp. 310–11.

[20] Crabb, *American Foreign Policy*, pp. 207–208.

[21] Abraham F. Lowenthal, "Ronald Reagan and Latin America: Coping With Hegemony in Decline," in Kenneth A. Oye, Robert J. Lieber, and Donald Rothchild, eds., *Eagle Defiant: United States Foreign Policy in the 1980s* (Boston: Little, Brown and Company, 1983), p. 324.

[22] Roger Hilsman, *To Govern America* (New York: Harper & Row, Publishers, 1979), pp. 128–29.

[23] Thomas R. Dye and L. Harmon Zeigler, *American Politics in the Media Age* (Monterey, Calif.: Brooks/Cole Publishing Co., 1983), pp. 261–62, 267.

[24] Dye and Zeigler, *American Politics*, p. 295; Michael J. Robinson and Kevin R. Appel, "Network News Coverage of Congress," *Political Science Quarterly* (fall 1979), pp. 409–10. Although the media spend more time covering the presidency, they devote an estimated 15 percent of their coverage to Congress, with the Senate receiving twice as much as the House. At the beginning of 1983, over 3,800 reporters and photographers were accredited by Congress.

[25] Kegley and Wittkopf, *American Foreign Policy*, p. 408.

[26] Crabb, *American Foreign Policy*, pp. 212–14.

[27] Ibid., pp. 214–15.

[28] Crabb and Holt, *Invitation to Struggle*, pp. 199–200.

[29] David J. Vogler, *The Politics of Congress*, 4th ed. (Boston: Allyn & Bacon, 1983), p. 148.

[30] Crabb, *American Foreign Policy*, p. 220.

[31] John Spanier and Eric M. Uslaner, *Foreign Policy and the Democratic Dilemmas*, 3rd ed. (New York: Holt, Rinehart, and Winston), 1982, pp. 98–99.

[32] Ibid., p. 99.

[33] Ibid.

[34] Ibid., p. 89.

[35] Ibid.

[36] Personal interview with Robert Dockery, assistant to Senator Christopher Dodd of Connecticut, March 14, 1983, Washington, D.C.

[37] Steven Roberts, "Vote on Aid Cutoff: A House Divided and Confused," *New York Times*, July 30, 1983, p. D3.

[38] Joseph L. Nogee, "Congress and the Presidency: The Dilemmas of Policy Making in a Democracy," in John Spanier and Joseph Nogee, *Congress, the Presidency, and American Foreign Policy* (New York: Pergamon Press, 1981), pp. 191–92.

[39] Spanier and Uslander, *Foreign Policy*, pp. 99–100.

[40] Kegley and Wittkopf, *American Foreign Policy*, p. 273; "New Priority," *New York Times Magazine*, July 25, 1983, p. 15.

[41] Crabb and Holt, *Invitation to Struggle*, p. 212–13.

[42] Vogler, *The Politics of Congress*, pp. 299–300.

[43] Crabb and Holt, *Invitation to Struggle*, p. 212.

[44] Kegley and Wittkopf, *American Foreign Policy*, p. 411.

[45] Ibid., p. 412.

[46] Thomas E. Cronin, "A Resurgent Congress and the Imperial Presidency," in Charles W. Kegley and Eugene R. Wittkopf, *Perspectives on American Foreign Policy* (New York: St. Martin's Press, 1983), p. 337.

[47] Interview by author with Representative Bruce Morrison, Third District of Connecticut, Hamden, Conn., June 15, 1983.

[48] Crabb, *American Foreign Policy*, p. 225.

[49] Ibid., p. 226.

[50] Crabb and Holt, *Invitation to Struggle*, p. 205.

[51] Roger Hilsman, *The Politics of Policy Making in Defense and Foreign Affairs* (New York: Harper & Row, Publishers, 1971), p. 83.

CHAPTER EIGHT
THE JUDICIARY, STATE AND LOCAL GOVERNMENTS, AND INTERNATIONAL ORGANIZATIONS

Normally we don't think of the other parts of the American government—the judiciary and the state and local governments—as part of the foreign-policy process. Normally they are not. At least not directly. And when they are involved, it is usually not at the level of high policy. Nonetheless, they have occasionally played a direct role in important, even vital, foreign policies, and they have an indirect role in the policy process that should be considered more fully. These parts of government are formal components of American federalism and of the checks-and-balances system that allocates power and authority within American society.

In addition, a relatively new set of structures, new in the last forty years, have also become quite important in the American foreign-policy process—Intergovernmental Organizations (IGOs). American membership in an expanding network of groups composed of many nation-states has imposed new international obligations, demands, and challenges on American policy.

In the pages that follow we want to examine and consider the implications of these structures.

THE JUDICIARY

Like the president, the judiciary is not assigned very many specific powers in foreign policy by the Constitution. Indeed, the Constitution as a whole has provided only "spotty" guidelines for the allocation of power and for the authority to do many of the things that two hundred years of national existence have required.[1] The sources of power have been not only the Constitution but national sovereignty and the law of nations. Over time some of the important gaps have been filled in by the courts, but for the most part, the courts have played a limited role in the "politics" of foreign-policy making and in the foreign relations of the United States. Nonetheless, that role has been crucial in sustaining the power of the national government in foreign affairs, in affirming the powers of the president as the "sole organ" of foreign policy, and in clarifying the status of treaties and international agreements made by the government. In the process the courts have also clarified the limits of national and state power in foreign policy and the questions that have arisen between Congress and the president over boundaries of power. On the other hand, the courts have often refrained from interfering in foreign-policy questions because of (1) a claimed lack of jurisdiction, (2) the desire to avoid a confrontation with the other branches, or (3) a lack of authority. The courts have usually regarded foreign-policy questions as matters for the "political" branches or have considered particular issues to be "political questions." In addition, the courts have never systematically developed specialized expertise needed to deal with foreign policy.

In an increasingly complex global system, however, the role of the courts may expand in the future, as they must define customary international law, settling disputes of private parties functioning in other countries or of foreign interests functioning within the United States.

Thus while the courts have not played as active a "political" role in foreign affairs as have the other two branches, it is important to recognize that some of their decisions have been vital to the development of the political process and that any decisions made by the courts have inevitable political consequences.

It may or may not be true that the courts follow the election returns, as claimed by Mr. Dooley, but some constitutional scholars have observed that the courts do, in fact, respond to the changing political, moral, and social realities of the United States. In addition, those appointed to the courts are not usually immune to the political realities and pressures of their time.[2] Mostly, the members of the courts have participated in the political-party system and have learned to be sensitive to the public mood. They are political creatures, and donning austere judicial robes may or may not override their political experience, instincts, and knowledge. At the very least, most judges have developed a political and judicial philosophy that comes to be reflected in their opinions on constitutional issues. Internally the courts reflect some of the same kinds of political, philosophical, and personality conflicts that beset the rest of society.[3] Thus the courts are often likely to be more political than either they or we think, but this need not be a disadvantage in foreign affairs or in general. Many consider it preferable to a system in which judges were ivory-tower types, overly detached, and ignorant of the feelings, needs, and problems of the people.

Another reason for the fact that the judiciary is not as prominent in foreign affairs as are the other branches is that it is not always welcome in these matters. Presidents often wish to act without too much consideration of judicial restraints, and Congress is jealous of its own powers to check and balance.

Whatever the role of the judiciary in different periods, it is useful to understand precisely what powers the courts possess in dealing with foreign affairs.

Article III, section 2, of the Constitution gives the judiciary certain powers:

> The judicial power shall extend to all cases in Law and Equity arising under this Constitution, the Laws of the United States, and Treaties made, or which shall be made, under their Authority; . . . to all Cases affecting Ambassadors, other public Ministers and Consuls; . . . to Controversies . . . to which the United States shall be a party; . . .
>
> In all Cases affecting Ambassadors, other public Ministers and Consuls, and those in which a State shall be a party, the Supreme Court shall have original jurisdiction. In all the other Cases before mentioned, the Supreme Court shall have appellate jurisdiction, both as to Law and Fact, with such Exceptions and under such Regulations as the Congress shall make.[4]

These explicit powers give the courts, and especially the Supreme Court, jurisdiction in suits involving foreign ambassadors, foreign consuls, and state action against aliens. However, the courts also have jurisdiction in cases arising under the Constitution or under laws or treaties involving a wide variety of matters. The courts review the activities of federal administrative agencies involved in foreign relations, the foreign activities of the Departments of the Treasury and of Commerce, problems in coastal and border states that relate to foreign neighbors, and problems of New York State and New York City and the United Nations.[5]

Judicial Review

Although judicial review is not specifically mentioned in the Constitution, it has turned out to be as important as original jurisdiction as a basis for the role of the courts in the foreign-policy process. The power of the courts to declare the acts of the other branches of government unconstitutional has provided them with the broad authority to define the Constitution and has provided the country with the flexibility it has needed to adapt to new conditions.

Basically, in a long history of cases dealing with questions of foreign policy, the judiciary has sustained (1) the exclusive power of the national government in foreign affairs, (2) the foreign-policy power of the national government beyond those specific powers granted by the Constitution, (3) the primary role of the president in the foreign-policy process, (4) the status of treaties and executive agreements, (5) the status of customary international law, (6) the limitations of powers of the state governments, and (7) the scope and limits of government power over individuals in matters stemming from perceived foreign threat. A brief review of the major cases in these key areas is in order.

Power of the National Government and the President.   The most far-reaching ruling made by the Supreme Court in defining the scope of authority of the national government and of the president was set down in the case of *United States* v. *Curtiss-Wright* (1936). In chapter 3 it was noted that the decision designated the president as the "sole organ" of the United States in its relations with other countries. "The president alone has the power to speak or listen as a representative of the nation,"[6] Justice Sutherland stated in his famous opinion (joined by six other judges). However, the decision also supported the existence of sweeping foreign-policy powers in the national government over and above those granted by the constitution. Arguing that the Union existed before the Constitution and was the sole possessor of external sovereignty, the Court said that the Union, therefore, had all the powers inherent in sovereignty and "did not depend upon the affirmative grants of the Constitution."[7] The decision also underscored the view that there is a difference between domestic and foreign powers and that the states possessed no foreign-affairs power. As a result, "there is virtually nothing related to foreign affairs that is beyond the constitutional powers of the federal government."[8]

As we saw in chapter 7, the Constitution also grants Congress foreign-policy powers: the declaration of war, regulation of foreign commerce, advice and consent on the ratification of treaties and the appointment of ambassadors and other key officials, and, of course, the determination of expenditures. But it is clear that policy initiatives clearly rest with the president and with those in the executive branch to whom authority is delegated.

Despite their authority, the courts have often been reluctant to intervene in foreign-policy decisions made by the president and/or Congress. During the Vietnam War, for example, the Supreme Court declined to hear cases challenging President Johnson's policies. In *Mitchell* v. *United States* (1967) the Court declined to consider whether the war was a violation of international law,[9] and in *Luftig* v. *McNamara* (1967),[10] *Mora* v. *McNamara* (1967),[11] and other cases, the Court declined to consider whether the president had exceeded his powers since Congress had not declared war. The political-question doctrine was invoked by the Court in these cases to avoid action.

Treaties and Executive Agreements

The United States enters into formal relationships with other countries through treaties and executive agreements, and at any given time it is involved in thousands of such arrangements. A treaty can be negotiated by the president, but it must undergo "advice and consent" of the Senate, consent based on a two-thirds vote in that body. Executive agreements require no such congressional approval, although presidents may need to acquire majority support in both houses of Congress for approval of expenditures necessary to implement the agreements. Treaties and executive agreements may cover matters from the most important high policy, such as the SALT treaties, to routine functions between countries.

That treaties are "the supreme law of the land" was determined as early in the nation's history as 1796 in *Ware* v. *Hylton*. Nearly a century later, the court ruled in *Whiting* v. *Robertson* (1888) that a treaty is on the same constitutional footing as legislation and that the last one enacted will control the other.[12] Two years later, in 1890, the court said that the treaty power, in the dictum of the court, "does not extend so far as to authorize what the Constitution forbids."[13] Thus, there are limitations to the power of treaties to infringe upon such other parts of the Constitution as the Bill of Rights. That treaties are superior to the actions of states was made clear in the case of *Missouri* v. *Holland* in 1920, although probably no treaty can deny to the states a republican form of government or a state militia guaranteed by the Constitution.[14]

The president's authority to execute, interpret, or to cancel treaties has been upheld. He has the principal responsibility for seeing that treaty provisions are carried out, and the provisions of a treaty mean what he says they mean. Relatively few treaties have been challenged in the courts, but in most such cases, decisions have supported the broad discretion given to the president.[15]

In a recent case, the Supreme Court supported the right of the president to cancel a treaty without the participation and consent of Congress. In 1979 the Supreme Court in *Goldwater* v. *Carter* upheld President Carter's authority to abrogate an American treaty with Taiwan when the administration took steps to recognize the Communist government in China.[16]

However, the courts have enunciated protection of Bill of Rights guarantees. In *Burdell* v. *Canadian Pacific Airlines* (1968) the Supreme Court held that some provisions of the Warsaw Convention were unconstitutional if they limited matters of venue and damage limitations in American courts.[17]

Thus although treaties and the authority of presidents to negotiate, interpret, and cancel them have been given broad support from the courts, that authority is not unlimited.

Nor are there many significant limitations upon executive agreements. Although executive agreements had long been practiced by chief executives, the major statement on the subject by the Supreme Court came in 1937 following a challenge to presidential actions relating to the recognition of the government of the Soviet Union. In *United States* v. *Belmont* the Supreme Court supported the broad authority of the president to engage in agreements with other countries not subject to the treaty-ratification process.[18] Certain matters involving foreign commerce are still reserved to Congress, however.[19]

The president's power to make agreements was again upheld in a major case in 1981.[20] In negotiating the release of hostages from Iran in 1979–80, President Jimmy Carter agreed to an arrangement with Iran in which private legal claims against Iran would not be permitted to proceed in American courts but were to be determined by a special claims tribunal established by Iran and the United States. A California firm had already brought suit against Iran and then filed suit against the United States to prevent enforcement of the Carter agreement. The Supreme Court agreed to hear the case and subsequently decided that "the President was authorized to suspend pending claims pursuant to executive order 12293. . . . In light of the fact that Congress may be considered to have consented to the President's action in suspending claims, we cannot say that action exceeded the President's authority."[21] Still, the Court's decision did not foreclose the firm's right to bring action in the Court of Claims at a later period.

Since precedent and judicial review have long sustained executive agreements, it is clear that restraints on presidential authority must rest in the realm of politics rather than in the law, a realization that places an increasing emphasis on the interplay among the president, Congress, and public opinion.

The courts however, have an impact on foreign policy that goes beyond their power to define the limits and content of the authority of other parts of the federal system and the meaning of written treaties and agreements. Using powers granted by the Constitution and by Congress, the courts have long defined law concerning: the maritime field, requirements of international comity, the rules that decide which of the conflicting laws of different countries should govern a transnational transaction, the rights of governments to sue in domestic courts, and the effect of judgments of foreign courts in the United States.[22]

In the interpretation of customary international law, the courts possess authority of increasing importance. Customary law consists of many of the practices of states over the centuries, which have been accepted as forms of international rules.[23] Many of these remain unwritten and uncodified.[24] Article 38 of the Statute of the International Court of Justice defines international custom as "evidence of a general practice accepted as law," and international custom provides a major source of international law.[25] Brierly notes that some of the important sources of evidence for such practices include: diplomatic correspondence, official instructions to diplomatists, consuls, naval and military commanders, acts of state legislation and decisions of state courts, and opinions of law officers, especially when they are published, as is done in the United States.[26] "It is in the nature of customary law, whether national or international, not to be susceptible of exact or final formulation," writes Brierly.[27]

In addition, rapid social, political, and economic change may produce rapid changes in old practices, create new ones, or mix the old and the new. In this context the courts have broad discretion for interpreting the meaning of customary international law in the present context. In the *Sabbatino* case in 1964, the Supreme Court ruled that it could determine and establish a single uniform rule of customary international law for state courts as well as for the federal system.[28] Although the executive and legislative branches are not constitutionally forbidden to violate international law, the courts have sometimes enforced it against lower-level officials not otherwise directed by the president to violate it.[29]

Thus the power of the courts in foreign relations can be considerable. The courts can interpret the substance of the powers of the other parts of the federal system; they can define the limitations on the states; they can give meaning to treaties, agreements, and customary law; they can, in some areas, define their own power.

In addition, the courts have played an active role in defining the rights of individuals affected by domestic legislation and policy induced by the perception of foreign threats. They have also effectively affirmed the limitations of state powers in foreign relations.

Limitations on the Power
of State Governments

In the next section the role of state and local governments in the foreign-policy process will be examined in more detail. Relevant here, however, is the constitutional interpretation by the court that has confirmed the dominance of the national government. First of all, the Constitution itself is quite clear about the prohibitions of state activity in foreign policy.[30] Two major early cases before the Supreme Court further clarified the question of predominance of national government authority to act in certain fields. In 1816 in the case of *Martin* v. *Hunter's Lessee* the Court held that the Treaty of 1794 with England protected British property (including Martin's) from confiscation by a state.[31] In *McCulloch* v. *Maryland* (1819) the Court invoked the doctrine of the supremacy of national law to prevent Maryland from attempting to destroy an agency of the national government.[32] That treaties are the supreme law of the land was emphasized as early as 1796 in *Ware* v. *Hylton.*[33] A half century before the *United States* v. *Curtiss-Wright* case, the Supreme Court, in the case of *Fong Yue Ting* v. *United States* (1893) ruled not only that the national government had the exclusive authority to deport aliens but also that the national government was supreme in matters of foreign affairs. The opinion, delivered by Justice Gray, stated: "The United States are a sovereign and independent nation, and are vested by the Constitution with the entire control of international relations, and with all the powers of government necessary to maintain that control and make it effective."[34] He also cites the express constitutional prohibitions on state-government action in foreign affairs.

Many additional cases could be cited to demonstrate the judicial support for the supremacy of the national government and the limitations of state power in foreign policy. However, these few basic cases should suffice. The fact that states, nonetheless, are involved in the foreign-policy process will be examined shortly.

Other Courts and Agencies

In discussing the judiciary and its role in American foreign policy, I have concentrated on the Supreme Court. The judiciary consists, however, of dozens of other, lower courts and quasi-judicial agencies, some of which are directly related to foreign affairs. In addition to the Supreme Court, there are 11 Circuit Courts of Appeals, 191 district courts in the fifty states, and such subsidiary courts as the Customs Court and the Court of Customs and Patent Appeals, a Court of Claims, and a Court of Military Appeals, tax courts, and 4 territorial courts.[35]

Quasi-judicial functions are performed in many government agencies, and often those functions relate to foreign policy. The Federal Communications Commission, the Federal Maritime Commission, and the Nuclear Regulatory Commission are among the many such agencies.[36]

Summary

Although the political role of the judiciary has not been as direct in foreign policy as those of the executive and legislative branches or as it has been in the domestic field, its impact has been profound on those occasions when it has acted. In the past the courts have often pursued the conviction that it was necessary and desirable to remain as detached as possible from foreign affairs and from the functioning of the president and Congress.

However, the growth of a more complex global system of customary and codified international law and of the opportunity for judicial legislation in uncharted areas of international life may produce expanded judicial roles.

STATE AND LOCAL
GOVERNMENTS

In the summer of 1982 the small community of Glen Cove, Long Island, in New York State decided to wage its own cold war with the Soviet Union.[37] In May the city council voted by a 6–1 margin to bar Soviet diplomats from using the three city beaches, the eighteen tennis courts, and a golf course. The Soviets own a forty-nine-room mansion there used by members of the Soviet mission to the United Nations. The Glen Cove residents were in their own way protesting Soviet actions in Afghanistan and Poland. Naturally, the Soviet government retaliated against Americans in the Soviet Union, barring American diplomats from a beach on the Moscow River. On August 18, 1982, Glen Cove officials were invited to Washington to talk the situation over with officials at the State Department (but they stood firm). Glen Cove upset the State Department, but it received congratulatory messages from many other Americans. In April 1984 Glen Cove officials reconsidered and dropped the restrictions.

This small flap is a reminder that on occasion, a local government may play a role in the foreign policy and foreign relations of the United States.[38] Such occasions are rare, however, and highlight the fact that state and local governments, as governments, usually play at best a relatively small role in the foreign-policy process. One of the primary reasons is that the Constitution has assigned them few functions. Another is that Constitutional history has deprived them of some of the power and authority they once thought they had or claimed they had.

Originally some of the states assumed that they retained at least some authority to deal with foreign countries, but even the Articles of Confederation left the matter in considerable dispute, and the Constitution and subsequent decisions by the courts removed most lingering notions of power by spelling out what the national government could do and what the states could not.

Article I, section 10, outlines many of the prohibitions on state activity. States cannot: "enter into a Treaty, Alliance, or Confederation; grant Letters of Marque and Reprisal; coin Money; emit Bills of Credit; make any Thing but gold and silver Coin a Tender in Payment of Debts;

pass any Bill of Attainder, ex post facto Law, or Law impairing the Obligation of Contracts, or grant any Title of Nobility."

Also prohibited to the states is the payment of imposts or duties, except what may be absolutely necessary for executing its inspection laws; the net produce of all duties and imports laid by any state on imports and exports "shall be for the use of the treasury of the United States, and all such laws shall be subject to the Revision and control of the Congress."

States are also prohibited from the following without consent of Congress: laying any duty of tonnage, keeping troops or ships of war in time of peace, entering into any agreement or compact with another state or with a foreign power or engaging in war, unless actually invaded or in such imminent danger as will not admit of delay.

Treaties, as noted, are forbidden to states, but agreements or compacts are permissible with the consent of Congress. Relatively few such agreements have occurred, and none appear to have intruded upon national policy. One such agreement is the New York-Canada agreement for a port authority to operate the bridge over the Niagara River.[39] Minnesota has a highway agreement with the Canadian province of Manitoba, and some northeastern states have formed a Northeastern Interstate Forest Fire Protection Compact with adjacent Canadian provinces. Congress would surely prevent any undesirable agreements or compacts created by a state, but few controversies have arisen.

In some areas prohibitions on state activity are less clearly defined, and states may become involved in foreign relations. In regulation of commerce, for example, although much power is given to the national government, states may sometimes possess concurrent power. In general the courts will not uphold state regulations that discriminate against foreign persons or against foreign goods by tariffs, taxation or trade. But in areas where Congress has been silent, states may have somewhat more latitude to legislate and regulate independently.[40] An example of the state role in commerce is the so-called unitary tax imposed by twelve states. It is a state tax on a local company's profits, calculated as a percentage of its total worldwide profits if it is a multinational corporation. In 1984 a team of Japanese business executives began an intense lobbying campaign in several state capitals to abolish the tax. In addition to pressure from Japanese businessmen, the Reagan administration, seeking additional foreign investment in the United States, also urged state governments to remove the tax.[41]

Until 1968 there was no larger principle of state exclusion from foreign affairs, but in *Zschernig* v. *Miller,* a case involving a question about the right of inheritance, the Supreme Court found "an intrusion by the State into the field of foreign affairs which the Constitution entrusts to the President and the Congress." The decision meant that the Constitution excludes state intrusions even when the federal branches have not acted.

Despite this principle, states continue to touch upon foreign relations in a number of ways. They regulate and tax commerce of foreign nations, regulate the rights of aliens, examine state law and policy in determining whether American or foreign law will apply to a transnational transaction, decide whether to give effect to a foreign act of state that imposed a tax or penalty, and whether to enforce a judgment of a foreign court.[42] In addition, the national government often gives the states considerable responsibility for implementing national policy.

Of course, states have the discretion to violate international obligations by denying or obstructing rights of aliens or by failing to fulfill commitments to foreign governments; and under the eleventh amendment to the Constitution states cannot be sued by foreign nationals or foreign governments without their consent.

The principal influence of the states, however, lies more in the political realm than in any other. Foreign affairs touch some states very profoundly. The free-trade policy of the United States opens the way for foreign imports, which may seriously affect American business and labor. For example, the increasing share of the automobile markets captured by the Japanese has had profound effects on Michigan and on cities such as Detroit. Reduced car sales, plus increased imports of foreign steel have deeply touched such states as Ohio and cities such as Youngstown. Unemployment rates have been excessively high in the steel and auto industries for a number of reasons, but international trade agreements and policy have worsened the situation. Pressures arise from state governors and local mayors for relief from the national government for such effects of American foreign relations—slumping sales and increasing unemployment.

On the other hand, the policies that require a strong military establishment may contribute to the economic well-being of those states and communities where military production, military bases, and military research are present.

Some states are deeply affected by the massive flow of immigrants, both legal and illegal, who have entered the United States in the past two decades. The mass exodus of Cubans from the regime of Fidel Castro has produced both positive and negative results for Florida. The tens of thousands of immigrants have created new population pressures on the state. On the one hand, many Cuban immigrants have established prosperous businesses and communities. On the other hand, the immigrant population has imposed new pressures on social-welfare policies and institutions.

For many years a large number of illegal immigrants have crossed the Mexican border into Texas, Oklahoma, and other states of the Southwest. Many are used as inexpensive labor in border areas. Some are exploited by unscrupulous interests. Although many illegal immigrants return to their families in Latin America, many others stay and become the responsibility of domestic social programs.

Pressures by the state governments upon the national government to negotiate agreements with Mexico limiting the flow of immigrants have led to proposals for legislation that would provide many former illegal aliens with legal status in the United States and would establish procedures for utilizing migrant labor.

Another recent wave of immigrants includes those from Southeast Asia who fled the area after the victory of North Vietnam in 1975. Known as the boat people because so many fled in small boats, these immigrants have been admitted to the United States and are reasonably well distributed throughout the country.

Problems caused by mass migrations clearly involve some state and local governments in some of the effects of foreign relations.

Additionally, some states and local communities and their political and business leaders participate actively in pressuring the national government and in negotiating with foreign interests for investment and trade. The efforts of the government of Pennsylvania and local governments in that state in the 1970s to attract a Volkswagen assembly plant symbolize this type of participation.

To a large degree, of course, the political process, especially the electoral process, reflects state and local interests and involvements. Under the system of the electoral college, presidential candidates must base their campaigns on winning enough individual states to be elected. The Senate is based upon, and to some degree reflects, the equality of states. The House of Representatives more often reflects local interests, but frequently both Senate and House races are determined by state or local issues, personalities, and needs. State and local officials exercise considerable pressure upon the Washington establishment and on their own senators and congressional representatives and this will often reflect strong foreign-policy concerns. For example, the agricultural states and their leaders exerted considerable pressure on both the Carter and Reagan administrations to remove the grain embargoes placed on the Soviet Union in retaliation for Soviet intervention in Afghanistan and Poland. Many states retain lobbyists in Washington to articulate state and local interests.

There is a further input of state and local interests into policy. Although state and local governments rarely take formal positions on foreign-policy questions (it happens occasionally), state and local leaders are national citizens, too, and they are likely to have strong views about foreign policies that affect them as Americans and affect their states and localities. In the past few years some local councils have passed resolutions calling for a nuclear freeze, for example.

To summarize: The states and localities have little constitutional authority in foreign policy and foreign relations, but they often perform valuable functions with foreign-affairs implications. They have considerably more influence through the political process, although it may not be dominant very often. The national government still needs the support of state and local leaders—for policies, for elections, and for other domestic legislation. Foreign policy may seem distinct, but in the political arena its formulation and implementation may depend upon support from the states and localities obtained through bargaining over domestic policy. Each side has something to bargain with, and that is the essence of politics.

INTERNATIONAL ORGANIZATIONS

There are literally hundreds of international organizations to which the United States belongs, and each seeks to affect American foreign policy and foreign relations.[43] The great growth of the number, complexity, and variety of these organizations reflects the development of a more complex global system, which was discussed in chapter 2. That this phenomenon has raised new political, constitutional, and philosophical questions for Americans is clear enough. American participation in these organizations has been the result of conscious American policy and of numerous treaties and agreements covering a wide range of political, economic, military, and cultural activities. In most of these organizations, the United States confronts decisions that are not mandatory, in which it is not bound beyond discretion and in which there is no method of outside enforcement.

Few of these organizations, treaties, and agreements have stirred much recent controversy in the United States, although in 1952 the proposed Bricker amendment would have limited the degree to which the United States might be bound by international commitments. It was defeated.

A few of the organizations, however, possess some regulatory power over the signatories, even though it is generally conceded that the president and the Congress have the power to ignore them.

The most comprehensive organization to which the United States belongs is the United Nations. As a treaty signatory to the United Nations Charter, the United States has accepted obligations and responsibilities of some scope. The Security Council, of which the United States is a permanent member, with veto power, can direct military and economic sanctions by members. However, with the veto and because the organization does not possess the means to enforce its decisions, there is little danger that the United States can be compelled to act against its will.

Of major significance in American policy are the North Atlantic Treaty and the NATO military organization. The treaty commits the United States to come to the defense of its European treaty partners if they are attacked. However, it provides for American action only after American constitutional processes are carried out.

A number of international organizations have been assigned some regulatory power by their signatories, and while any government remains free to disregard their rulings, it is usually regarded as in the national interest to cooperate. The International Monetary Fund, the International Bank for Reconstruction and Development (the World Bank), the General Agreement on Tariffs and Trade (the GATT), the International Civil Aeronautics Organization, and world commodity agreements in such areas as wheat, sugar, coffee, and cotton are among the many international agencies with some regulatory power.[44]

In a real sense, however, these organizations have become forums for negotiating agreements to which the members will voluntarily accede. Even when agreements are reached, the United States government must still implement them. In addition, in many of these organizations the United States either has a veto power or a weighted vote so that decisions are rarely contrary to American policy decisions.

Some of these organizations operate in the field of law and adjudication. The United States is a party to the Statute of the International Court of Justice and the Nuremberg Charter, but it has not delegated judicial powers of the United States.[45] In addition, the United States remains free to accept or reject findings of the ICJ or to simply ignore them if they are unfavorable to American interests. Furthermore, decisions apply only to governments, not to individuals, although there is a movement internationally to give the individual a status before the court equal to that of national states.[46]

Constitutionally there is nothing to prohibit the United States from permitting an international tribunal to apply international law to acts of individuals in the United States, nor do these international organizations raise any constitutional difficulties when they impose international obligations for the United States to carry out in accordance with normal constitutional procedures.[47]

In summary, international organizations of whatever nature have no power and in some cases no right to force the United States to do whatever it does not wish to do. Yet the decisions, recommendations, and policies adopted by many of them cannot be easily ignored. They are, in fact, places in which politics on a global basis can be conducted and in which the United States is free to bargain, negotiate, debate, and accept or reject the decisions made. For the most part, acceptance of decisions is regarded by the government as being in the national interest of the United States. That hard bargaining occurs within such organizations and that the United States does not always get everything it wants is clear. Further, even though the United States has the power to reject or ignore decisions of such bodies, it cannot always ignore the political cost of doing so, since decisions often reflect a substantial expression of the policies of allies, of the world community, or even of adversaries. These organizations, therefore, constitute an important influence on American foreign policy and foreign relations, one that has grown in importance in the last four decades as the world has become more interdependently linked. Their views affect the domestic political debate over policy, and they affect the formation of global policy affecting all nations.

SUMMARY

In reviewing the role of the judiciary, of state and local governments, and of international organizations in the foreign-policy process, we have observed actors that may occasionally play a decisive role in American foreign policy and foreign relations.

Their powers and their relationships with the national government have been shown to be relevant to the process. Particularly as the interpretation of customary international law and the formulation of international policy by major organizations increase in importance in the coming decades, it is not incorrect to suggest that the judiciary and the international organizations may soon become far more involved in the politics of policy making than they have been in the past. Further, there seems to be a growing awareness in state and local government that as separate authorities and as citizens, they have a right to participate in and to take a stand on foreign-policy decisions.

In short, the actors examined in this chapter are likely to increase in importance in the future determination of foreign policy and foreign relations.

NOTES

[1] Louis Henkin, *Foreign Affairs and the Constitution* (Mineola, N.Y.: Foundation Press, 1972), p. 19.

[2] Roger Hilsman, *To Govern America* (New York: Harper & Row, Publishers, 1979), pp. 149–51.

[3] Bob Woodward and Scott Armstrong, *The Brethren* (New York: Avon Books, 1979), pp. 525–28.

[4] Gerald Gunther, *Cases and Materials in Constitutional Law*, 10th ed. (Mineola, N.Y.: Foundation Press, 1980), app. B, pp. B7–8.

[5] Henkin, *Foreign Affairs*, p. 208.

[6] Ibid., pp. 45–47.

[7] Gunther, *Cases and Materials*, p. 255.

[8] Henkin, *Foreign Affairs*, p. 27.

[9] Ibid., p. 452, fn. 32.

[10] Ibid., p. 452, fn. 31.

[11] Gunther, *Cases and Materials*, pp. 411–12.

[12] Henkin, *Foreign Affairs*, pp. 163, 410, fn. 111.

[13] Ibid., p. 141.

[14] Gunther, *Cases and Materials*, pp. 250–51.

[15] Henkin, *Foreign Affairs*, pp. 164–67.

[16] Sheldon Goldman, *Constitutional Law and Supreme Court Decision-Making*, (New York: Harper & Row, Publishers, 1982), pp. 746–48.

[17] Henkin, *Foreign Affairs*, p. 383, fn. 34.

[18] Ibid., pp. 177–80.

[19] Ibid., p. 70.

[20] Goldman, *Constitutional Law*, p. 784.

[21] Ibid.

[22] Henkin, *Foreign Affairs*, pp. 187–88, 216–17.

[23] K. J. Holsti, *International Politics: A Framework for Analysis*, 3rd ed. (Englewood Cliffs, N.J.: Prentice-Hall, 1977), pp. 418–49.

[24] Henkin, *Foreign Affairs*, p. 43, fn. 45.

[25] J. L. Brierly, *The Law of Nations*, 5th ed. (London: Oxford University Press, 1955), p. 57.

[26] Ibid., p. 61.

[27] Ibid.

[28] Henkin, *Foreign Affairs*, p. 223.

[29] Ibid., p. 222.

[30] Ibid., pp. 228–29.

[31] Gunther, *Cases and Materials*, pp. 36–44.

[32] Ibid., pp. 78–92.

[33] Robert E. Cushman and Robert F. Cushman, *Cases in Constitutional Law*, 3rd ed. (New York: Appleton-Century-Crofts, 1968), p. 468.

[34] Ibid., p. 144.

[35] David Edwards, *The American Political Experience*, 2nd ed. (Englewood Cliffs, N.J.: Prentice-Hall, 1982), pp. 366–67.

[36] Ibid., pp. 303–5.

[37] "Glen Cove Affair," *New York Times*, May 22, 1983, p. 41.

[38] Samuel G. Freedman, "Local Disputes with Foreign Missions Call for Diplomacy," *New York Times*, January 23, 1983, E7.

[39] Henkin, *Foreign Affairs*, p. 230.

[40] Ibid., pp. 230–48.

[41] David E. Sanger, "Japanese Fight Unitary Tax in U.S.," *New York Times*, June 7, 1984, p. D1.

[42] Henkin, *Foreign Affairs*, pp. 247–48.

[43] Theodore A. Couloumbis and James H. Wolfe, *Introduction to International Relations*, 2nd ed., (Englewood Cliffs, N.J.: Prentice-Hall, 1982), pp. 264–65. According to *Yearbook of International Organizations*, 855 are projected by the year 2000.

[44] Charles W. Kegley and Eugene R. Wittkopf, *American Foreign Policy: Pattern and Process*, 2nd ed. (New York: St. Martin's Press, 1982), pp. 182, 194.

[45] Henkin *Foreign Affairs,* pp. 196–98.
[46] Evan Luard, *The International Protection of Human Rights* (New York: Praeger, Publishers, 1967), pp. 20–21.
[47] Henkin, *Foreign Affairs,* pp. 197–98.

CHAPTER NINE
THE VOICES
OF THE PEOPLE:
THE GENERAL PUBLIC
AND THE MEDIA

Many Americans share an attitude toward government that "you can't fight city hall," so why bother? This attitude seems to apply even more broadly toward foreign policy. Polls indicate that except in wartime, foreign policy is at the bottom of the list of the public's priorities and knowledge. On the basis of recent events, it might be difficult to persuade Presidents Carter and Reagan of the validity of these findings. Public reaction to Carter's leadership during the Iranian hostage crisis was a major factor in his defeat in the 1980 election. Then his successor, Ronald Reagan, discovered that public opinion on the development of nuclear weapons was strong enough to force a modification of his arms-control proposals.

Another view shared by some Americans is that public opinion is controlled by large special interests, so again, why bother to become involved? As one critic of the mass media has suggested: "Far from being vigilant critics, most newspersons share the counterrevolutionary, anticommunist assumptions and vocabulary of the ruling class, which employs them."[1]

As in most cases, the reality is more complex than such judgments suggest. In this chapter, however, we will examine the relationships among public opinion, the mass media, the leaders, and the policy-making process. First of all, there are *many* public voices, and they rarely speak in unison. Second, not all members of the public speak, even in national elections, since in 1976 and 1980 barely more than 50 percent of all eligible voters bothered to go to the polls. When other forms of political activism are studied, the percentages were even lower for joining groups, communicating with officials of the government, or otherwise speaking out.[2] Third, on the matter of having information about policy or interest in it, scholars have found sharp distinctions among Americans and have suggested such categories of citizens as the attentive public, the spectators, and the apathetics to describe the levels of interest and participation.[3] Further, among those Americans who are actively involved, their many loyalties usually create cross-pressures, that is, countervailing and opposing viewpoints. In addition, many public voices become active and outspoken on only a few matters—on issues of private interest rather than of the national interest. Thus patterns of pressure are uneven, inconsistent, and unpredictable.

Still, many questions remain unanswered about the effects that any or all of these voices have on foreign policy. Although scholars have developed sophisticated techniques for understanding the behavior of these groups and their effects on policy, considerable ignorance remains. In the absence of precise knowledge, assumptions that the impact of public voices is substantial continue to be believed and accepted.

One of the problems in measuring the precise effects of nongovernmental groups on policy is the confusion over what is being measured or what ought to be measured. One scholar, after considering the differences between power and influence, concludes that neither is useful in measuring the effects of public voices. Bernard Cohen notes the distinction between mere *efforts* to influence policy and efforts that are *successful*, recognizing the differences between direct and indirect pressures.[4] In his own studies he uses the concept of influence as having an "apparent impact on the direction of policy."[5] Somewhat vague, this definition suggests that influence is to be measured by some evidence that pressure from public groups has had *some* impact on the decision to make a decision or on the content of the decision that is finally made. Interestingly, Cohen connects the concept of influence by private groups with the way in which particular issues are handled by the news media. The longer an issue is "news," the greater is the opportunity for groups to apply pressure successfully.[6]

Clearly, no analysis of the foreign-policy process and the part played in it by any of the important actors can fail to consider the role played by the media and, more particularly, television. Surely, television has changed many of the *forms* of contemporary American politics, but whether it has changed anything fundamental remains an open question requiring much more intensive investigation. Assumptions abound that television has changed a great deal in the policy process, but much less is known than we suppose about the precise ways in which this may occur.

Nonetheless, television is a phenomenon that must be understood more fully. As Richard Reeves comments on the existence of television: "The president, by the end of the 20th century, was seeing the same battlefield on the television news—or the premier's statement, or riots in Poland—at the same time his constituents were."[7] Members of Congress and the people were all briefed simultaneously. "We were all little presidents," concluded Reeves.[8] Whatever the validity of this viewpoint, it is certain that the presence of television in virtually every American home—and before television, radio—has tended to make more Americans than ever aware of developments throughout the world.

Awareness, as important as it is in a democratic society, does not always lead to political activism, and even when it does, activism does not always have an impact on the direction of policy. At best, awareness may lead only to what Almond found to be a broad public mood setting the limits of permissible action by the government.[9] When translated into action, awareness may inspire only limited segments of the general public even in crisis situations such as the Vietnam War. Apart from matters of such general concern, few people are equally informed or aware of complex scientific and technological issues, for example, and many debates involve only groups of "experts." Nonetheless, a growing number of citizens still become active on a wide range of issues.

This concern is reflected in public-opinion polls, in elections, and in the mass media.

THE MASS MEDIA

In March 1968 President Lyndon Johnson sat before the television cameras reporting to the American people on the status of events in the Vietnam War. With a shocking suddenness, he inserted a paragraph into his remarks that stunned the American people. He would not seek and would not accept renomination for the presidency. One month before the speech, an unheralded candidate for the nomination, Senator Eugene McCarthy, a leader of the antiwar protest movement, had almost beaten Johnson in the New Hampshire primary. Johnson's withdrawal signaled his understanding that by 1968 the protest movement had grown so large that he would have to fight very hard to win renomination and that, indeed, there was a good chance that he could be defeated. Behind these events pressed the mass movement of those elements in society that constitute the bulk of the public voice: the mass media, polls, elections, and public opinion.

In one dramatic episode the potential power of the public voice was demonstrated. Linking the public opinion of 1968 to the presidency and expressing its furor were the mass media.

By definition, communications media that reach a mass audience—an audience in the millions—are mass media. Television, radio, newspapers, news magazines, wire services, and motion pictures are the instruments of communication available to audiences of millions. Their basic functions include (1) newsmaking and reporting, (2) interpretation, (3) socialization, (4) persuasion, and (5) agenda setting.[10]

In defining what is "news," the mass media decide which matters are brought to the attention of the public. To provide this material they utilize spot news stories of events, continuing coverage of the governmental and political processes, and feature stories about issues and personalities. Interpretation is provided through the use of editorials, columnists, commentators, documentaries, and discussion programs. Socialization of citizens into the values of the culture occurs through entertainment programs and feature material as well as through news material. In addition, the mass media are instruments for persuasion and propaganda; that is, they provide the outlets for political leaders and others to communicate with the public and motivate them for particular purposes. They are the means by which political opposition can make its counterarguments. Finally, the media, by what they decide to emphasize, play a large role in setting the political agenda. One experienced and knowledgeable Senate aide contends that "90 percent of what they [Congress] react to comes from the front pages of the *New York Times* and the *Washington Post.*"[11]

In most cases the media, then, are the people's most direct link with the world, and the media's definition of reality is a predominant force in the public's perceptions of the world.[12]

However, "the media" contain many different voices. Despite some concentration of ownership and control in the communication industry, considerable diversity among media provides a variety of insights to Americans interested in discovering all sides of contemporary issues.

The Print Media

Notwithstanding the growth and expansion of television, the print media retain a vital role in the communication process.

1. The oldest and most traditional of the mass media are the *newspapers,* and despite a decrease in the number of daily newspapers in the United States, there are still over 1,800 in operation throughout the country.[13] Moreover, there has been a sharp increase in the number of weekly newspapers in many of the nation's small towns and suburbs. Like special-interest groups, their influence is not equal or uniform, but where it is present, it may be impressive. Not all daily newspapers either carry substantial material relating to foreign policy or exercise much influence on policy makers in Washington. However, the members of the House and the Senate are more likely to be aware of a particular newspaper's influence when they return to their home states and districts.

Although with rare exceptions there have been no "national" newspapers, some publications have had circulation in population centers across the country. The *New York Times* publishes a national edition and the *Wall Street Journal* prints and distributes editions from regional centers around the country. However, a relatively new paper, *USA Today,* is the largest attempt to establish a daily paper with national circulation, but it is still too early to know whether it will survive. Nonetheless with new technology, some publishers are confident that successful national newspapers are possible in the near future. In any event major regional newspapers throughout the country remain important sources of information.

Some newspapers are widely recognized as possessing extraordinary influence on policy makers, on elites in many fields, and ultimately on public opinion at large. As a newspaper of record the *New York Times,* despite a smaller circulation than many other American newspapers, is clearly one of the three or four most prestigious and influential sources of news, opinion, and background information, and its editorial views and the views of its leading columnists often provide the attitudinal cues for many segments of American society.[14] Striving to match the position of the *Times* is the *Washington Post,* whose influence was observed during the Watergate crisis, when its coverage maintained public interest in the indiscretions and illegalities of the Nixon administration. Also of considerable influence is the *Wall Street Journal,* whose coverage of foreign-policy affairs is extensive, incisive, and influential.

To be sure, there are many respected and influential local newspapers whose impact is felt not only in their local communities but in government circles as well. However, none is quite as much in the center of journalistic influence as are those mentioned.

2.   In addition to the newspapers, the *news magazines* have developed a wide and interested audience, and many of their stories, features, interviews, and columnists are read by leaders in many fields.[15] The two most prominent news magazines with national circulation are *Time* and *Newsweek*, although *U.S. News and World Report* is also a highly regarded publication. Somewhat more specialized magazines dealing in political and foreign policy questions are the *New Republic*, expressive of liberal views, and the *National Review*, an organ with primarily conservative views. Among other magazines with a serious approach to public affairs and with an influential readership are the *Atlantic, Commentary,* and *Harper's.*

3.   Of somewhat less relevance to the general public are the *specialized magazines* in the field of foreign policy: *Foreign Affairs, Foreign Policy, International Organization,* and scores of other journals directed primarily to professionals in the field.

4.   Of course, *books* are also an important source of information, history, analysis, and debate on foreign-policy issues.[16] Memoirs of leading public officials, special studies by experts in varied subjects, and even textbooks such as this one are important means for informing the wider public of important matters and of calling attention to research and insights into the problems facing the United States in world affairs.

5.   Another element of the print media I have saved for last, partly because its impact is so seldom recognized by the public. The *wire services,* such as Associated Press and United Press International, provide a huge base of information on a twenty-four-hour-a-day, seven-day-a-week basis to virtually all other media.[17] Obtaining information from their own staff and from contributions from all their members, the wire services provide basic information to almost all of the radio, television, and newspaper outlets in the country. They also provide a variety of other features and background material, but their selection of stories and their story sequence may influence thousands of other media throughout the country and the world. In addition, their own staff reporters often provide separate and useful insights into stories covered by many other reporters.

Overall, then, the print media are vital, indispensable and intelligent observers, commentators, and analysts, and their influence on leaders and the people alike remains high.

The Electronic Media

Radio and television are fairly recent additions to the American political process. Nonetheless, many observers regard television as the most important of the mass media today.[18] First of all, key elements of radio and television are national; that is, they consist of networks that broadcast the same programs to all Americans. Second, because of their technology they are capable of delivering the news fast and first, and their great mobility can take the audience to the scene and sounds of news as it is happening.

1.   *Radio* became an effective mass medium in the 1920s, and the development of national networks soon followed.[19] Of all the national networks, CBS, the Columbia Broadcasting System, developed an international news gathering capability first and established the standards for responsibile broadcast journalism. Before the onset of television, radio served as the primary home-entertainment medium as well as a primary source of news. Network news began to play a major role in the American consciousness during the pre-World War II period, and that role grew during the war.

2.   With the first *television* stations on the air by the late 1940s, the new visual medium became national by the mid-1950s. Again CBS established the earliest standards of broadcast journalism, but soon the two other major national networks,

NBC and ABC, expanded their own informational capabilities. Later, in the 1970s, Public Television came to offer a somewhat less ambitious but significant service. In addition, some nine thousand local radio stations and over seven hundred local television stations also developed their own local news capability and frequently covered issues and events related to foreign policy.[20] In the late 1970s cable television networks emerged as new technology had brought wired television signals into millions of homes for a fee. The Cable News Network became the first twenty-four-hour all-news network operation.

During political campaigns the broadcast media have become the center of the candidates' activities, and entire schedules are arranged to obtain maximum coverage by evening television news programs. Although radio has receded in recent decades as a major national influence, nonetheless it provides through news, interview programs, and "talk shows" information about a wide range of subjects, including world affairs and foreign policy.

Probably the impact of television has never been more immediate than during the trip by President Richard M. Nixon to China in 1971. Scores of reporters, technicians, cameramen, and assistants accompanied the president on the historic trip, and few events have been more widely available for viewing by Americans.

Commenting on the television coverage of the Nixon trip to China, Henry Kissinger writes:

> The fact that the excursions were geared to television only reinforced that here, if ever, the medium was the message. In the mind of the American public, television established the reality of the People's Republic and the grandeur of China as no series of diplomatic notes possibly could have. The advance men had, after all, made their own contribution to history in a way that I had not even comprehended or appreciated beforehand.[21]

At the Great Wall of China Nixon was shown as an almost typical tourist. "This is a great wall," he said in a remarkable understatement.[22] But symbolic television diplomacy flowed from the stately and formal banquets held in the Great Hall of the People. The live televising of these events on morning shows in the United States, said Kissinger, "performed a deadly serious purpose. They communicated rapidly and dramatically to the peoples of both countries that a new relationship was being forged."[23] However, Kissinger added, "The symbolism was meaningful only if it could be matched by substance."[24] By the early 1970s the public may have been prepared for a new relationship with the People's Republic of China, but the massive television coverage affected American attitudes by removing all but a fragment of previous American attitudes of hostility toward the PRC.

Television coverage of election campaigns, presidential news conferences and speeches, summit conferences with world leaders, and even the social life of the president and other leaders have become regular features of the process. However, the daily, regular news coverage of issues, events, and personalities at home and abroad constitutes the bulk of television's attention to foreign policy. The daily evening newscasts of the three major networks provide the primary sources of news for the majority of Americans,[25] although the major drawbacks of network news as a primary source of foreign-policy information include a limited amount of

time for coverage amid the demands of domestic events, superficial reporting of events with little emphasis on background and analysis, and limited
expertise by many of those reporting. One critic, commenting on this
point, observes that the responsibilities of reporters

> tend to be defined institutionally rather than substantively; that is to say, they
> cover specific governmental agencies, such as the Department of Defense or
> the Department of State or the White House, but not as a general rule, a
> subject matter (such as security policy) that might require them to go to all of
> these places, plus the Congress and a number of embassies in pursuit of any
> given question on any given day.[26]

Other problems arise from the ways in which journalists define "news," a
process that identifies issues and events that journalists believe are of interest to the public and which the public wants to hear about and see.[27]

At the very least, little in-depth reporting is offered by the major
networks—relatively little commentary, analysis, or documentary programming is presented.[28] On public television the MacNeil-Lehrer News Hour
is one exception, offering detailed analyses of major issues each evening,
often focusing on foreign policy.

Another excellent source of analysis is the public television program
"Washington Week in Review" in which foreign-policy questions of the past
week are regularly included in a general review of government. A more
recent addition to in-depth reporting is ABC's "Nightline."

Despite the shortcomings of television, it makes available more information to more people than any other medium of communication in history. While we cannot be certain how this information affects or motivates
people, it is clear that the vast majority should not be unaware of major
developments in the world and of some of the ways they will affect the
United States.

Certainly for world leaders radio and television offer direct access to
the people, and each president has sought to utilize them to build support
for himself and for his policies. Franklin Roosevelt used "fireside chats" on
radio with superb effect, and in the television age John F. Kennedy,
Richard Nixon, and Ronald Reagan have used television with great skill.
Reagan is regarded by many as the most skilled communicator to occupy
the White House since the coming of television, and the fact that he
retained personal popularity even though the country was involved in a
near depression was partly attributable to the television image he was able
to sustain. At the same time, Lyndon Johnson and Jimmy Carter seemed
unable to adapt their personalities to television with the greatest advantage.

Films

Normally motion pictures are not considered part of the foreign-
policy process, and as a matter of fact, the great majority of films certainly
have nothing to do with issues of war and peace, world politics, or American foreign policy. Even the rare films that address such serious subjects
are not usually intended to affect immediate decisions. All of that having
been said, recognition that drama on the screen has the capability to
inform, arouse, and motivate people suggests that its effects on public

attitudes cannot be wholly disregarded as an element in the formation of the political environment.[29]

Film is one of the major propaganda instruments used by the government to impress and persuade people of other countries of the virtues of the United States. American films and films about the United States are distributed throughout the world, both by the government itself and by private companies. Many are produced by the government for use overseas. Thus government takes film seriously as a tool of foreign policy.

However, motion pictures that deal seriously with aspects of foreign policy may have a profound affect on American attitudes and the American mood. Excellent film biographies of national leaders have often explored their foreign-policy dilemmas. *Wilson, Patton,* and *MacArthur,* are a few modern films made for theaters. Many films have been made for television, including productions about Franklin and Eleanor Roosevelt, Harry Truman, John Kennedy in the Cuban missile crisis (*The Missiles of October*), Richard Nixon, and Dwight Eisenhower. Many of the films made by Ronald Reagan when he was an actor are believed to have played some role in creating his political image or, at the very least, providing him with the skills of communication he later used in politics with considerable success.

During World War II Hollywood turned out dozens of motion pictures about the war, many requested by the government to help motivate Americans in the war effort. Films such as *Bataan, Guadalcanal Diary, Sands of Iwo Jima,* and *They Were Expendable* made Americans aware of the sacrifices made by the armed forces. Forty years later films based on World War II continue to fascinate producers and public alike, and a long list would include *The Battle of the Bulge, Tora, Tora, Tora,* and *The Winds of War* (the last produced for television).

Many of the most noteworthy films relating to foreign policy, however, have dealt with the dangers of accidental nuclear war, the effects of nuclear war, or a breakdown of the military. Few films on any subject have been more stunning than *On the Beach,* based on the novel by Neville Shute. It dealt with the last earthly survivors (Australians) after a nuclear war and their slow death from the deadly nuclear fallout. Both the original version and a remake of *All Quiet on the Western Front* have conveyed powerful messages about the insanity of war. Among those films dramatizing the possibilities of nuclear war by accident or madness are *Fail-Safe, Dr. Strangelove,* and *The Bedford Incident,* and the potential dangers of a military takeover of the government were imagined in *Seven Days in May.* Interestingly, few antiwar films were made during the Vietnam War, but *M–A–S–H,* a Korean War movie, proved to be devastating. It was, of course, turned into an extremely popular TV series.

In short, films can be a powerful element in shaping attitudes and in commenting on important questions facing the United States and the rest of the world.

Summary

The mass-media exercise a role in foreign policy (indeed, in all policy) on a number of levels. As neutral instruments, they report, inform, provide basic information and background. As participants, they offer comment and opinions; they may also behave as a special interest-group seeking to shape government policy in their own behalf. Finally, often without specific intent or without specific knowledge of the implications of what they are doing they shape general attitudes of millions of people through the over-all content of what they present.

The media are not a monolith. Many different and distinct voices come from them. Yet leaders are concerned by, indeed sometimes fearful of, the voices of the media, and they respond to many of the pressures brought by the media.

We may no longer live in an age when a press lord can tell a reporter: "You supply the stories. I'll supply the war,"[30] but neither can we disregard the effects of critical positions taken by the media on important policies. During the Vietnam War, when CBS television anchorman Walter Cronkite shifted his position to oppose the American involvement, Lyndon Johnson came to believe that the had lost the support of "middle America," which he believed Cronkite symbolized.[31]

When any part of the media can still have that effect on the person in the White House, the impact of the media on the direction of policy cannot be overlooked.

PUBLIC OPINION AND POLLS

The causes of public opinion are a complex combination of the different characteristics of source, medium, messages, and audience. The opinions themselves are often fickle, even contradictory; they defy simple summary.[32]

They also defy simple analysis. There are many public voices, and their sources are complex; yet whatever their content, their messages to policy makers cannot be disregarded. At the same time policy makers are in a unique position to shape public opinion in the directions that they desire.

In one analysis the authors contend that "political opinions flow downward. They originate among elites, are picked up and propagated among attentives, then reach and shape the thinking of the mass citizenry."[33] Further, "the mass media are conduits of the elites' visions of America's overseas interests in all but the most exceptional circumstances."[34]

Among leaders, the authors believe, "presidents are especially adept at manipulating public opinion by creating foreign media events" and by exploiting crises, state visits, and dramatic diplomatic initiatives.[35] Media coverage, they contend, "provide[s] pseudo-participation, an illusion of public discussion, a symbol of democratic input and power in this most elitist of policy areas."[36] In the main, they conclude that "foreign news reporting helps the powerful mobilize public opinion (or quiescence) behind the basic goals of policies on which most Americans have little information and less control."[37]

There has always been some question about the extent to which public opinion is a factor in the day-to-day shaping of foreign policy. In his notable study, *The American People and American Foreign Policy*, Gabriel Almond argues that most Americans are neither informed nor concerned about most foreign-policy decisions but that they do have broad and sometimes deeply held attitudes about foreign policy, which set the goals and the parameters of foreign-policy making that leaders must follow.[38] Other observers have concluded that within this general framework, policy makers are, indeed, quite conscious of the acceptability of their policies and actions to the electorate and are always aware of the possible effects of their actions on the next elections.

In 1982 a sizeable nuclear-freeze movement evolved in the United States, and although it appeared to have no perceptible effect on the mid-term congressional elections, some political observers believed that it would be an issue of some consequence in the 1984 presidential election. It was.

Rarely does the public at large react to an issue as intensely as so many people did during the Vietnam War. Still, a broad consensus forms the basis on which policy makers may act. During the 1980 presidential campaign, for example, it became clear that large segments of the public perceived President Jimmy Carter to be insufficiently "tough" with the Soviet Union and with the new revolutionary government in Iran. Voters responded favorably to the proposals by candidate Ronald Reagan to increase defense spending and to take a stronger stance toward the Soviets.

In general, then, the public mood might be interpreted as one that favors a strong defense, a strong stance against Soviet actions, antagonism toward the Soviet Union and communism, and a willingness to negotiate. Since the end of World War II Americans have been willing to bear heavy costs in both money and lives to maintain a balance of power against the Soviet Union and to maintain a commitment to help defend Western Europe in case of attack. This mood was a clear reversal of the isolationist attitudes of the 1930s, which insisted that the United States refrain from making commitments to Europe. In each case policy had to be made within those limits.

However, on matters of detail or on matters not apparently central to the large issue of immediate security, most Americans appear willing to leave the policy making to those responsible for its execution, always reserving the right to hold them to account for their decisions.

Given this view of the role of public opinion in the foreign-policy process, it is important to discuss the systematic ways in which opinion is identified, assessed, and absorbed by policy makers.

Public-Opinion Polls

Most Americans are quite familiar with the preelection polls purporting to show the strength of candidates during a political campaign.[39] Professional pollsters are constantly at work assessing and evaluating public opinion on everything from toothpaste to the arms-control talks. Employed by political leaders and parties, corporations, and news media, professional polling organizations have expanded enormously in numbers and size. The established pollsters, such as Louis Harris, Gallup, and Yankelovich have been joined by polling organizations among the news media: the New York Times/CBS poll, the NBC/Associated Press poll, and the ABC and Washington Post poll.

Pollsters ask foreign-policy questions on a regular basis, and public attitudes on contemporary issues are watched closely by many in the political community.

In February 1983 the New York Times/CBS poll, for example, revealed that a growing number of Americans no longer feared that the United States lagged behind the Soviet Union in military capability and felt that the Reagan administration was spending too much money on sophisticated new weapons systems.[40] The poll also showed that fewer people approved of Mr. Reagan's handling of the Soviet Union than at any time during his administration—45 percent of those polled compared with 62 percent in September 1981.[41]

Of course, it is one thing to acknowledge that the poll results are readily available to policy makers, but it is quite another to know the precise effects that this information may have on particular decisions. In the case of a Vietnam War, it would be hard to believe that the information conveyed by the polls went unheeded in the process that led finally to a change of policy. In most cases, however, it is much more difficult to find a direct relationship.

The type of poll, it can be argued, that has a much more direct effect on the policy process is called an election, and the political parties and public movements that raise the issues in elections are more formal mechanisms for raising the public voice.

Elections

Although elections produce a clear-cut record of winners and losers, and the members of the government may be installed or removed because of the results, they do not always lead to a change of policy. After the 1982 elections, in which the Democratic party gained twenty-six seats in the House of Representatives while the Republican party maintained a four-vote majority in the Senate, there were numerous and varied interpretations of the meaning of the results, but the effects on policy were mixed, working sometimes in support of the president's program and sometimes against it. The point is that elections are not always clear-cut statements from the public voice and that even when they are, there is no assurance that policy will change.

To take the case of the Vietnam War again, the 1966 elections were, at most, a mild rebuke among some Americans who had begun to voice serious opposition to the administration's policy toward the war. In no way could the results have been regarded as a massive repudiation of the policies of President Johnson. By 1968, however, the electoral process had become the center of organized protest against the war. Antiwar candidates arose in 1968 to challenge the president for the Democratic nomination. Senator Eugene McCarthy mounted a candidacy, and in the New Hampshire primary in February of that year, McCarthy received enough votes to suggest that Johnson would have to fight for the nomination against the growing antiwar movement in the Democratic party and in the country. In March President Johnson announced his decision not to run, and this touched off an expanded fight for the nomination among Democrats, including Senator Robert Kennedy and Hubert Humphrey, the vice-president under Johnson. As the campaign wore on, Robert Kennedy gained the upper hand, but on the night he won the primary in California, he was assassinated in Los Angeles by Sirhan Sirhan. McCarthy stayed in the race, but in a bitter party convention in Chicago Humphrey won the nomination. In the November election Republican Richard Nixon, claiming to have a secret plan to end the war, won a narrow victory.

In any event, by 1968 the electoral process and the election had become the center of a debate over one of the most divisive foreign-policy issues in American history. Yet the results were ambiguous, and although President Nixon felt compelled to continue a policy of American withdrawal from the war, the fighting went on intensively for another six years before the American withdrawal was complete.

Did the election debate coalesce American attitudes, produce a clear public voice, and result in a change of policy? In the end, it was by no means a clear-cut voice, and even by 1974, large segments of the public continued to support the war and the idea that the United States should increase the commitment to win it. To the extent that the elections of 1968 focused on the demand to end the American commitment to the war, it took a long time for that demand to be related to policy.

Thus while elections provide a formal and direct outlet for the expression of public opinion and an opportunity to change the composition of the government, they do not always provide a clear-cut direction to government. Mirroring the complex and pluralist nature of the people, elections are likely to send mixed signals to policy makers, neutralizing the potential influence of the public voice and leaving policy makers free to choose whatever course they prefer. Even on an issue as bitter and important as Vietnam, the public voice was heard giving different commands, and few issues produce as much clarity as did the Vietnam War.

No presidential campaign is ever very simple, and the 1980 campaign, which saw Ronald Reagan defeat incumbent President Jimmy Carter, focused on a number of domestic issues as well as on foreign policy. To the extent that foreign policy was an issue, however, it revolved around two basic points: the perception of weak presidential leadership in foreign policy and the argument that the United States should increase defense spending to catch up with the Soviet Union. A public perception that Carter was not a strong foreign-policy leader arose from many complex sources, not least of which was the unsettled crisis resulting from the seizure of American hostages in Iran.

Although Carter's policy of patience, which finally led to the release of all of the hostages alive on the day Carter left office, was one of intense strength, it was perceived by many Americans to be a policy of weakness. Even Carter himself was persuaded at one point of the need to use force and sanctioned a rescue mission, which badly failed, with the loss of eight lives of members of the mission. In addition, although Carter had increased the defense budget slightly in real dollars (over and above inflation), Reagan made a strong case that the Soviets had moved far ahead of the United States and that a massive buildup was essential. Although a number of social, domestic, and personality issues were also involved in the 1980 election, the foreign-policy issues are believed to have played a significant part in Reagan's victory over an incumbent president. In this case the election results did lead to an immediate and direct effort by Reagan to change policy, to vastly increase the defense budget, to "talk tough" to the

Soviets, and to reject the SALT II agreement negotiated by the Ford and Carter administrations. The election results changed policy to a degree because they changed presidents, removing Carter and installing Reagan.

What does all of this tell us about the influence of elections on policy? First, there is not always a cause-and-effect relationship between the public voice and policy, but it can occur in some circumstances. Second, elections do not always produce a clear-cut public voice. Third, policy makers may sometimes ignore or divert the demands made by the public if they wish to do so.

Even if elections do not produce consensus, however, they create the satisfaction among the people that they have had a voice, and this contributes to the ability of the government to act forcefully in its relations with other countries. Willingly accepting the results of elections, even if they are disagreeable, Americans tend to support the winner and his policies in foreign-policy matters, thus reaffirming the legitimacy of the government.

Administrations risk losing this essential support if they verge too far from the beliefs, myths, hopes, and perceptions of the public. Elections reaffirm and reinforce the people's confidence in their own system.

There is a final important function that elections perform, albeit incompletely. They serve as an educational process for millions of Americans who might otherwise remain uninformed and unconcerned about the foreign policies of their country. During campaigns, issues tend to become overemotionalized, oversimplified, and distorted by candidates, but the massive publicity calls the public's attention to some of the important problems facing the country. On the premise that a larger number of better-informed citizens is essential to a democracy, a premise that is not entirely unchallenged, elections tend to create an expanded awareness of the real problems facing the country. On the other hand, the necessity perceived by candidates to oversimplify issues during campaigns risks depriving the people of essential knowledge and information.

What emerges from elections and is reflected by them is a broad public mood that insists upon a few general principles of foreign policy, as Almond suggests. Approval of these principles then permits administrations to act with broad discretion within these boundaries.

Political Parties

In the United States the two major political parties are conglomerations of a wide range of beliefs, philosophies, and approaches to government and policy. On a national basis, the parties of the fifty states and tens of thousands of localities come together every four years to nominate presidential and vice-presidential candidates, to adopt platforms stating their beliefs, and to organize the forthcoming campaign. The purpose of the party is to win elections, and because of the nature of the electorate and the nature of the parties, the proposed programs attempt to appeal to as wide a range of voters as possible. This does not make for very clear distinctions on foreign policy, or for that matter, on anything else. Nonetheless, despite these shortcomings, the parties are instruments for defining broad positions on policy and for coalescing those who share those positions. In the effort to provide a contrast to each other, the parties develop a sufficient number of differences over policy, style, and perception so that occasionally real foreign-policy options will be presented. The 1980 campaign provided at least one such example of contrasts, even as the 1968 campaign did not. However, it is not uncommon that after the election, the successful candidates ignore the platform, overlook campaign pledges, and go about formulating policy on an entirely different basis. After the election, the party, as a national unit, dissolves back into its state and local forms and exercises little, if any, direct influence on the policy process, although party leaders are always available to remind elected officials of the possible political consequences in the next elections of various courses of action.

A more clear-cut influence of the political parties should be apparent in Congress. In recent years, however, party organizations have had less cohesion, and party loyalty by individuals has been eroded. One explanation for this reduction of party control centers on the liberalization of organizational procedures within the Congress in the last decade. Reforms are seen to have reduced the power of the leaders on both sides of the aisles and to have caused a fragmentation of power. A second explanation relates the problem to the increased reliance of individual members on television and on their own fund-raising efforts in the process of getting nominated and elected. After vetoing a public-works bill, President Jimmy Carter received little support from his party in Congress. Later he wrote:

I learned the hard way that there was no party loyalty or discipline when a complicated or controversial issue was at stake . . . none.[42]

He added:

As the Democratic Party has become less able to reward or punish its members, the rewards and punishments offered by special interests have increased in importance.[43]

A more recent instance in which party loyalty suffered occurred in 1981 when some twenty-five Democrats in the House broke with party leaders and fully supported President Reagan's budget proposals. The boll weevils, as they came to be called, received no effective punishment for their actions, although in 1983, one of them, Phil Gramm of Texas, was stripped of a committee assignment. He thereupon resigned from the party, became a Republican, ran for reelection as a Republican, and won.

The point is that the political party as an expression of the public voice may be a myth in specific cases.

In the end, there are many basic agreements between the parties over foreign policy. In the past a considerable portion of American foreign policy has been bipartisan. Still, in certain elections foreign-policy differences can be an important issue, as in 1980, and the parties may play a key role in defining those differences.

Of course, in recent years there have been minor parties of some significance, and they too may bring new perspectives to all national policy. In general, however, none, except in 1968, has been very successful in recent years in influencing foreign policy.

Political Action Committees

As a result of the passage of the Federal Election Campaign Act of 1974 a new type of political organization emerged—political action committees (PACs). Their purpose is to raise and distribute financial support for political candidates of their choice. By 1984 there were nearly 3,000 of them representing a broad spectrum of corporations, unions, single-issue groups, and other interests. Some of the major firms in the defense industry, for example, are major contributors to PACs. Continued attention will be focused on the influence of the PACs and on their particular message in the public voice.

Public Movements

Large political movements can arise over almost any issue that is important to large numbers of people, and in the last few decades many movements have arisen, some to fall again in a relatively short time. Such movements as those in labor, civil rights, and women's rights have become permanent parts of the American scene and are regarded as "special interests." Such other examples as the antiwar, the antidraft, and the antinuclear movements come and go, sometimes with different leadership activating them at different times. In short, these movements may be permanent or transitory, but they can play a notable role at given moments in the political process.

In 1982, for example, a growing nuclear-freeze movement evolved in the United States, activating many who had also participated in previous antinuclear and antiwar movements. By 1965 the anti-Vietnam War movement had evolved among many local groups opposed to the war, and such national figures as the Reverend William Sloane Coffin came to be accepted as national leaders and symbols of the movement.

It is difficult to generalize about the role and the influence of such movements in the policy process. They are often capable of activating and organizing large numbers of partisans in support of or in opposition to the government and its policies. At the very least, they, too, provide an educational function, an alternative point of view, and an important outlet for the public voice.

Summary

How much do the public voices discussed in this chapter have an influence on the direction of policy, and how do they relate to each other? No simple answers are possible. Although a president is in an extremely favorable position to shape public opinion and to win the support of the bulk of the mass media, we have seen dramatic examples of the failure of presidents to do so. Although large special interests may control elements of the media, and other special interests are in a position to influence them, they do not always prevail in the policy process. Some public attitudes change, while others remain impervious to appeals from political leaders, media, or special interests. Although general public opinion seems indifferent to foreign-policy questions except in a time of crisis, it can become aroused over particular issues. Besides, just as there are many different "publics," there are many different opinions among and within groups. Farmers, workers, intellectuals do not all think alike on many issues. On many issues measured in polls and in elections, sharp differences of opinion are found. Still there are indeed broad positions on which most Americans are likely to share perceptions: communism, the Soviet Union, nuclear war, to name just a few. Thus, the simple view that a small elite controls American opinion is open to question. Vigorous dissent abounds in America despite what appears to be a concentration of power over the socialization process.

It seems clear that public opinion, whether created by the media or merely expressed by the media, provides a censor in the American political system, setting some limits on what policy makers may do. The public voice may only reflect latent, unused power, and it may often be manipulated for the purposes of leaders, but it is often a silent (and sometimes not so silent) participant in policy councils—a major part of the political process of arriving at decisions. For public opinion is the ultimate political arbiter of the soundness of decisions or at least of the degree to which they are perceived as satisfactory.

NOTES

[1] Michael Parenti, *Democracy for the Few*, 4th ed. (New York: St. Martin's Press, 1983), p. 185.

[2] Gabriel Almond and Sidney Verba, *The Civic Culture* (Princeton, N.J.: Princeton University Press, 1963), pp. 202–13; William Schambra, "More Buck for the Bang: New Public Attitudes Toward Foreign Policy," *Public Opinion*, January/February 1979, pp. 47–48.

[3] Lester Milbrath, *Political Participation* (Skokie, Ill.: Rand McNally & Co., 1965), pp. 16–18.

[4] Bernard C. Cohen, "The Influence of Special Interest Groups and Mass Media on Security Policy in the United States," in Charles W. Kegley, Jr., and Eugene R. Wittkopf, *Perspectives on American Foreign Policy* (New York: St. Martin's Press, 1983), pp. 222–23.

[5] Ibid., p. 223.

[6] Ibid., p. 239.

[7] Richard Reeves, *American Journey* (New York: Simon & Schuster, 1982), p. 350.

[8] Ibid., p. 351.

[9] Gabriel Almond, *American People and Foreign Policy* (New York: Praeger Publishers, 1960), p. 88.

[10] Thomas R. Dye and L. Harmon Zeigler, *American Politics in the Media Age* (Monterey, Calif.: Brooks/Cole Publishing Co., 1983), p. 11.

[11] Interview with Robert Dockery, foreign affairs assistant to Senator Christopher Dodd of Connecticut, March 16, 1983, Washington, D.C.

[12] Dye and Zeigler, *American Politics*, pp. 11–26; Edward Jay Epstein, "The Selection of Reality," in Elie Abel, ed., *What's News: The Media in American Society*, (San Francisco: Institute for Contemporary Studies, 1981), pp. 119–82.

[13] Dye and Zeigler, *American Politics*, p. 122.

[14] David L. Paletz and Robert M. Entman, *Media Power Politics* (New York: Free Press, 1981), p. 7.

[15] Dye and Zeigler, *American Politics*, p. 122.

[16] Ibid.

[17] Paletz and Entman, *Media Power Politics*, p. 80.

[18] Dye and Zeigler, *American Politics*, pp. 11, 26, 124–34.

[19] Ibid., pp. 122–23.

[20] Ibid.

[21] Henry Kissinger, *White House Years* (Boston: Little, Brown & Company, 1979), p. 1067.

[22] Ibid.

[23] Ibid., p. 1069.

[24] Ibid., p. 1070.

[25] Dye and Zeigler, *American Politics*, p. 8.

[26] Cohen, "The Influence of Special Interest Groups," p. 227.

[27] Paletz and Entman, *Media Power Politics*, pp. 10, 16–17.

[28] Dye and Zeigler, *American Politics*, pp. 132–33.

[29] Ibid., pp. 122–24.

[30] W. A. Swanberg, *Citizen Hearst: A Biography of William Randolph Hearst* (New York: Charles Scribner's Sons, 1961), p. 108.

[31] David Halberstam, *The Powers That Be* (New York: Alfred A. Knopf, 1979), pp. 508, 514.

[32] Paletz and Entman, *Media Power Politics*, p. 185.

[33] Ibid., p. 186.

[34] Ibid., p. 215.

[35] Ibid., p. 231.

[36] Ibid., p. 233.

[37] Ibid.

[38] Almond, *American People*, pp. 88–89.

[39] Dye and Zeigler, *American Politics*, pp. 155–57.

[40] William E. Schmidt, "Poll Shows Lessening of Fear That U.S. Military is Lagging," *New York Times*, February 6, 1983, p. 1.

[41] Ibid.

[42] Jimmy Carter, *Keeping Faith* (New York: Bantam Books, 1982), p. 80.

[43] Ibid.

CHAPTER TEN
PUBLIC VOICES:
THE ATTENTIVE PUBLIC

> Power In America is organized into large institutions—private as well as
> public—corporations, banks, utilities, governmental bureaucracies, broad-
> casting networks, law firms, universities, foundations, cultural and civic
> organizations. The nation's resources are concentrated in a relatively few
> large institutions and control over these institutional resources is the major
> source of power in society. The people at the top of these institutions—those
> who are in a position to direct, manage, and guide institutional programs,
> policies, and activities—compose the nation's elite.[1]

In the summer of 1982 several European allies of the United States defied
an American embargo on the sale of materials to the Soviet Union required
to complete a gas pipeline into Western Europe. A number of American
companies and their affiliates operating in Europe were caught between
American policy and the laws of the countries in which they operated.
When the Reagan administration was not able to prevent the transfer of
technology by the American affiliates in Europe, it eventually dropped its
opposition to the sale. American foreign policy, whether it was the correct
one or not, had been thwarted by the obligations of American-based companies to other countries.

During the last days of 1981 the Polish government imposed martial
law on the country and suppressed the Solidarity labor movement and
arrested its leader Lech Walesa. Solidarity had been receiving considerable
financial support from American labor unions, and viewed as a serious
threat to continued Communist party control of Poland, it was behaving in

a more independent fashion than the Soviet leaders were prepared to permit in Eastern Europe.

In 1970 the International Telephone and Telegraph Company sought to prevent Marxist Salvador Allende from succeeding to the presidency of Chile, and it attempted to enlist the aid of the CIA to achieve its goals.

Since the 1940s the American Jewish community has been active in numerous ways in the support of Israel and in attempts to influence the policy of the United States government to assure the survival of Israel.

These examples of activities of special interests in the United States designed to affect American foreign policy suggest some of the pressures from the American public that can confront policy makers.

In the context of the global system special-interest groups operate not only within the United States but many of them also operate within foreign countries. Organizations representing a special interest, however, hardly comprise the total of the many types of groups and individuals who actively seek to influence policy. Research organizations, special commissions and councils, and even certain key individuals within American society are active at various levels developing and advocating broad policy and program proposals.

The view that leaders of the groups discussed in this chapter form a "power elite" and, in fact, control American policy—a view expressed at the top of this chapter—is not universally accepted. That many of them have an opportunity to present their views to the high councils of government more regularly and more effectively than the general public is beyond dispute. That they always prevail in getting the government to do what they want it to do is much less certain.

Nonetheless, the possibility of unequal influence by parochial interests raises important questions about the process by which the national interest is defined and governmental policies are designed. Whether special interests and their advice coincide with the national interest is not always certain.

In any case, the exercise of pressure is an inherent part of the political process, and the constitution provides any individual or group the right to advocate policies to which they are committed. As a consequence, the guarantee of free expression in the American system has led to the development of a number of techniques for exercising influence. Essentially these techniques involve efforts to elect officials sympathetic to one's beliefs and positions. Through campaign contributions, interests hope to establish opportunities to elect and consult with leaders on a consistent basis. Through the techniques of lobbying—provision of information and testimony, advertising and promotion, social contacts, promotion of specific legislation, among others—special interests target their efforts at officials and at the general public. Further, these techniques can be used not only with the American government but also within other societies.

President Dwight D. Eisenhower in his farewell address warned against the dangers of what he called the military-industrial complex. By that he meant the combination of government agencies and private defense-related industries whose efforts could potentially distort the identification of national priorities and the spending choices of the government. Of course, there are many other parts of American society that have a financial interest in the size of the defense budget, and in the years since Eisenhower left office, many of them have been intense advocates of policies that require increased military spending. For the moment we will refrain from discussion of the soundness of these policies. Suffice to say that the views of the defense advocates are not universally accepted.

What this introduction suggests, then, is the importance of recognizing the role of the nongovernmental actors identified in this chapter and their relevance to the foreign-policy process.

BUSINESS

The most numerous nongovernmental actors are the thousands of private American businesses and corporations operating both within the United States and abroad. A sizeable number of them either do substantial business abroad or operate multinational affiliates in foreign countries. Others are affected by foreign trade, imports, and domestic government economic policy. During a nearly two-hundred-year history, few subjects have aroused more scholarly interest and political controversy than the relationship between business and government in the United States. In a capitalist society dedicated to the principle of private enterprise, in which private interests are given major economic opportunities and responsibilities for the public well-being, business has, in general, sought government support in promotion of its interests and government abstention from limitation of its private powers. Corporate executives may reject the notion of welfare for the poor but at the same time seek tax incentives, exemptions, and government-guaranteed loans. From national policy, business requires that government maintain stable conditions at home and abroad, that it pursue "sound" monetary and fiscal policies, and that it encourage economic growth. As a consequence, business has been active throughout our national experience promoting its own interests, contending that that path is in the national interest as well. This thought was expressed by Charles E. Wilson, secretary of defense in the Eisenhower administration and a former president of General Motors, when he said, "What's good for General Motors is good for the country."[2] Skeptics have noted, however, that what's good for business is not always, nor necessarily, good for the country. Therein lies the source of much of the controversy about the role of business in the policy process.

That business should promote those policies it regards as most useful to its prosperity is not surprising. In the 1980s many businesspeople argued that the United States should emulate the close cooperative government-business relationship that functions in Japan. However, Americans have been historically ambivalent about the relationship between government and business, fluctuating between support for free enterprise and for government regulation or trying to find the best combination of the two policies. In fact, the modern American economy is a mixture of private and governmental policies, each deeply dependent upon the other.

As we have seen, some analysts have concluded that business "runs" America and that foreign and domestic policy is largely determined by business elites and their associates in other key positions. Historically, the link between economic and political power has been a central question of political analysis. It is one of the basic assumptions of Marxism-Leninism that government in a capitalist state is merely the servant of business interests. The empirical evidence, however, provides only a limited basis for such sweeping generalizations. That business interests possess more resources to influence policy and have a profound interest in doing so is hardly arguable. That business does not always win in a pluralistic society, that other interests are often competitive and successful, has also been observed.[3] Furthermore, economic interests are not the only ones pursued by any country, and other interests—such as security, power, prestige— may have as much or more influence in determining policy at any given time.

One recent study by Bruce Russett and Elizabeth Hanson found that among businessmen and businesswomen ideology was a far more powerful factor than business interests in shaping the attitudes of executives toward foreign policy.[4] However, both this study and one at Columbia University found that businesspeople are likely to be more hawkish than some other civilian elite groups. Further, while businesspeople may abhor large wars, they do not so overwhelmingly object to smaller wars for limited goals, according to the study.

It is suggested that these findings are somewhat supportive of the concept of a military-industrial complex.

But business is not a monolith. It does not always speak with one voice on foreign-policy issues, or on domestic issues, for that matter. Manufacturing, trading, investing, and retailing interests may reflect conflicting goals, needs, and methods. For example, American auto manufacturing wishing to buy low-cost steel from abroad promote different policies than does the American steel industry, which seeks protection from steel imports.

With all of this in mind, we may note that most large businesses and an increasing number of smaller ones maintain a capability to influence local, state, national, and international policy. Usually through the operations of a public-relations or legislative-affairs staff but often through the top corporate officers themselves companies seek to influence policy. In the process they also use professional lobbying firms and all of the techniques of persuasion and influence available to them. In short, American business people are well funded and well equipped to effectively articulate and argue for their positions on all issues. Whether they are always successful in getting what they want is another matter.

When American businesses operate abroad as multinational corporations, an added set of factors enters into the consideration of the relationships between business and government. First of all, multinational corporations have been viewed in the past thirty years as (1) creative ways to provide economic assistance to other countries or (2) as exploitative neoimperialistic tools of American domination of foreign societies. On some occasions they have been both. On others, their activities have placed the American government in the middle of unwanted controversies or have created problems for American policy that the government could have done without.[5] Although host governments have placed limits on the political activities of multinational firms and their managers, the companies have often found subtle ways to attempt to influence the policies of their host governments. Beyond political influence are the more indirect changes that an American multinational firm may cause or enhance in host countries. Host-government citizens working for multinational firms, especially at the executive levels, are exposed to new values and new attitudes that may erode their identification with their own country. As they take on the values of the foreign corporations, they may become more efficient economically but less nationalist in their outlook.[6] Certain firms adopt a specific policy to develop a more internationalized value system among host nationals. To be sure, it is difficult to assess the long-term political effects of this process with certainty. However, that American organizations have the capability to alter such basic attitudes among some citizens of other countries has relevance to the foreign-policy process in the years ahead.

American foreign policy since World War II has been designed, in part, to promote American business interests abroad. It was one of the early thrusts of Alexander Hamilton and the Washington administration. Institutions such as the Export-Import Bank, the Overseas Private Investment Corporation, the Office of the President's Special Trade Representative, and the Commerce Department are designed to support American business abroad. Special tax arrangements have been created to encourage overseas investments.

In recent years American business hurt by expanding imports from abroad has sought increased protection from government in such areas as steel, automobiles, and motorcycles. Although the government has provided selective assistance through import quotas and tariff surcharges, no basic change in free-trade principles has been adopted at the insistence of business.

It should be noted that in addition to the individual political efforts of businesses, large business associations have long existed to promote business interests. The American Chamber of Commerce, the National Association of Manufacturers, and numerous specific trade and industry associations are well organized and funded to conduct efforts to protect their constituents. Other groups, such as the Business Round Table, the Conference Board, and the Council on Economic Development, also articulate business interests.

Certainly, business has the means and the motivation to influence domestic and foreign policy. It engages in domestic politics to acquire access to policy makers and to set national priorities. Overseas it has both economic and cultural impact on host countries.

Clearly, then, business is a major actor in the political process, and decision makers cannot easily disregard its voice.

Banks

In the summer of 1982, as the economy of Mexico appeared to border on collapse, Americans took note of the fact that many of the countries of the so-called Third World had accumulated nearly $700 billion of debt, much of it to Western banks.[7] The Mexican debt, $80 billion, was among the largest. More seriously, many analysts believed that the bulk of the debt was bad debt, that is, uncollectible. Of the $700 billion, it was estimated that up to $400 billion was owed to American banks. To explain this situation, one must recognize the policies of successive American administrations in seeking to (1) help Third World countries, (2) help American business to operate abroad, and (3) promote free-enterprise economies tied to the United States.

In pursuit of these objectives, the government has encouraged American banks and foreign governments to cooperate to establish the banks in foreign countries as multinational corporations. This has provided many governments with additional sources of capital and many banks with additional markets.

It has also facilitated the ability of Americans to do business and to travel abroad. However, the presence of American banks and their role in foreign countries occasionally has led to sharp criticism by national political opposition groups and to charges that the banks are instruments of American foreign policy designed to perpetuate neoimperialist attempts to control the governments. Without doubt, these charges and criticisms have often complicated relations between the United States and some of these host countries. While the presence of the banks may, in fact, be an expression of American policy, the charge that the policy is intended to maintain neoimperialist control by the United States is, at the very least, open to question. Indeed, a strong case exists that American policy encouraging the establishment of American multinational corporations, and especially banks, is an immediate and tangible method by which the United States can contribute to the development of many countries.

On the broader question of the extent to which banks and bankers have an impact on the direction of American foreign policy, some scholars have argued that through access to policy makers, through interlocking corporate directorships with other key elites, and through other devices, major American banks have a substantial influence on the direction and content of overall American policy.[8] Those propounding this view often suggest that, indeed, the influence of major banking firms exceeds that of any other interest group in the United States.

It is impossible to argue with the evidence that considerable concentration of economic power has evolved in the United States, in banking as well as in other areas of economic life. Just how this economic power translates into political power and into the capability of making foreign policy is much less clear.

Agriculture

The American farmer, according to myth, has always been one of the most influential interests seeking to shape government policy. In the last half of the twentieth century, the American farmer has often become part of large corporations in the field of agribusiness, and American food has become one of the most important American exports to world markets.[9] Farming interests have, in general, protected themselves quite well in terms of domestic policy, and as their role in foreign affairs has increased in importance, they have managed to be an effective voice in foreign policy as well.

In October 1982 President Ronald Reagan announced that the United States would be willing to sell up to 23 million metric tons of grain to the Soviet Union in addition to the 8 million tons already contracted for. The immensely productive American agriculture sector not only produces surpluses far in excess of American needs but produces resources that are now often used in the high-policy bargaining of major states.

In response to the Soviet intervention in Afghanistan, President Jimmy Carter imposed an embargo on grain sales to the Soviets. American farmers, aggrieved because they felt singled out to carry the burden of the embargo, pressured the new administration of Ronald Reagan to withdraw it, and Reagan eventually did so.

Of course, when the Nixon administration decided during the 1970s to sell large amounts of grain to the Soviet Union, the four largest grain sales companies precipitously sold supplies for a very low price, rapidly depleting supplies in the United States and driving up prices for bread, feed grains, and meat.[10] Thus the impact of agricultural interests was felt by almost every American.

In addition, a number of agricultural organizations articulate the interests of the agricultural sector. The American Farm Bureau and the National Grange are the two leading associations in the field.

To summarize, American food surpluses and techniques are inevitable elements in American foreign policy, and those who control them and the knowledge that produces them have considerable impact on the thinking of policy makers.

LABOR

The organized American labor movement has long been a major force in American domestic politics and in the nomination and election of candidates. Although the labor movement has had its largest influence within and upon the Democratic party, Republican leaders have also had to be responsive to concerns of labor and opportunistic in seeking labor support.

American labor has long participated in international labor organizations, and many of the largest American labor unions are organized on an international basis. For example, on November 6, 1982 Canadian members of the United Auto Workers Union chose to strike against Chrysler Corporation operations in Canada, much to the chagrin of American members of the union who had chosen not to strike Chrysler in the United States, at least not until after the Christmas holidays. On occasion, of course, the influence is reversed.

On another issue, there is considerable evidence that American unions provided over a number of years financial, moral, and planning support for Solidarity and its goals in Poland. When the Soviet Union induced the Polish government to impose martial law, the United States responded with a limited embargo on materials necessary for construction of the European pipeline.

Like business, labor has occasionally been criticized for advocating national policies affecting America's role in the world and its relations with the Soviet Union. Members of some unions refused to unload Soviet goods after the intervention in Afghanistan.

But like other special interests, labor is not monolithic, and its concerns have centered on the legitimate needs of American workers. Pressures by the AFL-CIO, the United Auto Workers Union and the United Steelworkers' Union, among others, have frequently centered on such foreign-policy questions as the transfer overseas by multinational corporations of thousands of jobs that would be unavailable to American workers, the massive exports of American jobs, and the discrimination against American-made products in overseas markets.

On broader foreign-policy questions, the influence of labor is no less sporadic than that of other special interests.

RACIAL, ETHNIC, AND RELIGIOUS GROUPS

Americans, except for Native Americans, can trace their roots to various foreign countries. Some of their forebears came to America voluntarily, and some did not. In addition, many present-day Americans are direct immigrants. In recent years, for example, there have been sharp increases in immigrants from Cuba, Mexico, Haiti, Southeast Asia, and other Third World areas. Immigrants and the American-born alike often retain an identification with their racial, religious, and ethnic origins, and when matters of foreign policy arise relating to these areas, many of these citizens become politically active on behalf of those interests.

In recent years many American blacks, for example, have been politically active not only in their own behalf within the United States but also on behalf of black independence movements in Africa and in opposition to the apartheid policies of South Africa. These pressures have contributed to the adoption of policies by the United States government in support of the black populations of these countries. In a move designed to improve the relationship between the United States and the nonwhite countries of the world, President Jimmy Carter named Andrew Young, a noted black civil-rights leader and politician, as ambassador to the United Nations.

Before the state of Israel was created in 1948, the American Jewish community worked toward the goal of a Jewish nation, and since then it has provided political and financial support for Israel and has worked diligently to influence an American foreign policy supportive of that country. In both ethnic and religious terms, the American government has been responsive to this influence.

During the war between Greece and Turkey over Cyprus in the 1970s both the Greek-American and Turkish-American communities were actively involved in trying to influence American policy toward the interests of their "old country."

Many Americans of Irish-Catholic origin have supported the efforts of nationalists in Northern Ireland to establish control by Catholics of the area, and many American Catholics were supportive of the large Catholic community in South Vietnam in the effort to prevent control by the Communist regime in the North.

OTHER GROUPS

Many other types of groups develop positions relating to foreign policy and exert every effort to advocate their adoption.

Human-rights groups, such as the Amnesty International, the National Council of Churches, the Red Cross; associations of scientists, scholars, and artists; specific movements of individual citizens, such as those formed during the Vietnam War, may all become active at given times to influence the direction of foreign policy or the effectiveness of its implementation. Professional associations that identify a foreign-policy concern as a matter of their interest will not hesitate to inform the government of their views. For example, the viewpoints of the medical and bar associations on the standards of training in foreign schools and on the admission of professionals from other countries into the United States to practice have foreign-policy implications.

Professional standards involved in the organization of efforts to provide medical care to foreign countries through church-related or World Health Organization-related enterprises are also a matter of legitimate concern of the medical associations.

Scientists, scholars, and artists concerned with promoting freedom of their professions in other countries and in sharing knowledge with those in other countries may also play an influential role, especially in matters of cultural-exchange policy.

In short, in an increasingly interdependent and transnational global system, virtually any group may develop a specific interest in matters of foreign policy and may not hesitate to exert pressure on their government. When functioning in foreign countries, these interests may serve as effective communicators of American ideals and of knowledge about foreign countries to Americans.

UNIVERSITIES, FOUNDATIONS, AND THINK-TANKS

1.   When undergraduates take their first class in foreign policy and are assigned to read a textbook or an assortment of other readings, *American colleges and universities* are playing one of their less glamorous, but important, roles.[11] The teaching function of institutions of higher education is a long-term influence on the foreign-policy process. In the first place, it acquaints a broad base of young Americans with the basic elements of the foreign-policy process, the structure of government, and the elements of contemporary issues. One of the by-products of this process is a more broadly and better informed public in areas of foreign policy. Second, the colleges and universities provide much of the basis for the education of those who will ultimately teach in higher education, work in government, or become researchers.

The training of informed laypersons and of future professionals is not an unimportant function of higher education. Beyond the teaching function, the research that is supported and encouraged in many universities and colleges is sometimes reflected in special institutes, in organized acquisition of research grants, and not infrequently in the interests of individual scholars. Much of the important research and literature in the fields of foreign policy, international relations, and comparative government, among other subjects, originates in these institutions. They provide important data, theory, and analysis to scholars and governments alike as well as important insights from perspectives outside the government.

It is not by accident that many of the leading policy makers in recent years have come into government from a university setting. Recent national security advisers Henry Kissinger, Zbigniew Brzezinski, and Richard Allen are among those who have had university experience.

As institutions, universities and colleges rarely take corporate positions on foreign-policy issues, but they have been centers of political activism by students, faculty, and administrators. During the Vietnam period many campuses were scenes of protest and other organized activities, and indeed the universities themselves were frequently the objects of demonstrations, scorn, and seizures of offices. The single most tragic occurrence of the domestic protest movement took place on a university campus. On May 4, 1970, four students at Kent State University were killed by National Guardsmen during an antiwar protest.

In the 1980s university campuses have become centers of the nuclear freeze movements, although the administrations still avoid participation in issues. In early November, 1982, Yale University refused to sanction a recording by the Yale Glee Club of the anthem of Solidarity, the Polish labor movement under repression by the martial law government. The recording was to be used on Voice of America for transmission to Poland and Eastern Europe. There was some disappointment among Polish-American groups, but the university administration defended its position of nonpolitical involvement.

In any case, the academic environment remains an important source of talent, research, activism, and teaching.

2.   Almost seven thousand *private foundations* organized by individuals and corporations operate in the United States, and many of them play an active role in the foreign-policy process.[12] The names of the major foundations include the founders of some of the largest enterprises in the United States: Ford, Lilly, Rockefeller, Duke, Kresge, Kellogg, Mott, Pew, Hartford, Sloan, Carnegie, Mellon. Those foundations channel resources into universities, into research projects, and into various other philanthropies. Some play a more direct role than others in foreign-policy matters.

According to Thomas Dye, the Rockefeller family interest in foreign affairs is especially strong. Rockefeller interests in foreign oil and in foreign banking provide substantial motivation for their interest in foreign affairs, and Rockefeller organizations have been the base of support for many individuals who have become top foreign-affairs advisers.[13] Indeed, Dye regards David Rockefeller as "the single most powerful private citizen in America today,"[14] although Rockefeller resigned as chairman of the Chase Manhattan Bank in 1981. In general, foundations, according to Dye, determine "policy objectives—strategic arms limitations, relations with the Soviet Union and China, defense strategies," among other social goals.[15] They accomplish this by providing seed money for research and for determination of new policy directions.

3.   Of growing importance in the policy process are other organizations engaged in policy research called *think-tanks*, institutions in which groups of scholars are engaged in study and writing on public-policy issues of consequence. The Brookings Institution, established in 1916, has been characterized as the "dominant pol-

icy-planning group for American domestic policy."[16] But Brookings scholars also explore elements of foreign policy, and their publications are regarded as among the most serious in the field.

More recently the American Enterprise Institute has evolved into a major research institution sponsoring studies across domestic- and foreign-policy questions.[17] Other research and policy-planning organizations include the RAND Corporation, the Hudson Institute, and Stanford Research Institute, although they are somewhat less involved in policy planning than such organizations as the Council on Foreign Relations and Brookings.[18]

COMMISSIONS, ASSOCIATIONS, AND COUNCILS

In late July 1983, in the midst of the national debate over American policy in Central America, President Ronald Reagan called upon Henry Kissinger to head a twelve-person commission to study the question of long-term policy in the region.[19] Formally called the National Bipartisan Commission on Central America, the group became the latest and most newsworthy use of the civilian study commission to find acceptable solutions for complex and difficult national problems. Suggestions that "government by commission" by-passes the Congress tend to overlook the fact that such commissions may be able to reach compromise recommendations that can be more easily accepted by Congress and by the president. Major presidential commissions on Social Security and on the MX missile produced compromise solutions to complex issues.

In such cases the president and the Congress are free to reject the commission's findings or to accept them in whole or in part. They can be stacked to support solutions that a president wanted anyway, but in the case of Social Security and MX, their recommendations made agreement possible between the president and Congress. In late 1982, responding to Congress' rejection of the dense-pack basing system for the proposed MX missile, President Reagan appointed a commission headed by former National Security Adviser General Brent Scowcroft and including former officials Harold Brown and Alexander Haig.[20] The commission report was a major factor in the approval of the MX system by Congress in 1983.

Another type of commission that may affect foreign policy is the private commission composed of leading citizens. *The Trilateral Commission*, organized by Rockefeller interests, seeks the expansion of economic coordination among the United States, Western Europe, and Japan.[21] By one count, nineteen members of the Carter administration had been among the commission's sixty-five members, including Carter himself, National Security Adviser Zbigniew Brzezinski, Secretary of State Cyrus Vance, Secretary of Defense Harold Brown, Secretary of the Treasury Michael Blumenthal, and Vice-President Walter Mondale.[22]

Among the most important organizations actively engaged in the study of foreign policy is the *Council on Foreign Relations*. Its commissions study policy questions and help to set the major directions of policy.[23] The council publishes *Foreign Affairs*, a periodical regarded by many as one of the most influential publications in the field of foreign policy. The council also provides consulting services and information, holds seminars, and offers memberships for corporate clients. Its members have included former or future cabinet members of both Democratic and Republican administrations.

Business maintains a number of organizations capable of articulating its interests. The chief executives of some two hundred of the nation's largest corporations operate the *Business Roundtable*, an organization that involves top executives of large firms in the effort to influence policy. The *Council on Economic Development*, founded during World War II, continues to function today as a representative of its business members.[24] The *Conference Board* is an independent business-research organization founded more than sixty years ago to provide for continuing research to more than four thousand members and forty thousand others around the world.[25]

A wide range of professional and civic associations participate in the study and discussion of foreign policy. The *Foreign Policy Association* organizes public discussion of issues in foreign policy and publishes books and pamphlets in the field.[26] The *United Nations Association* conducts various activities to acquaint the public with the work of the U.N. *The American Assembly* also studies and presents materials dealing with foreign policy.

In the field of professional scholarship, a number of national and regional associations invite and disseminate research relating to foreign policy. The *American Political Science Association* invites research papers for presentation at annual meetings and publishes the *American Political Science Review* as a forum for new research in many specializations, including foreign policy. The *American Academy of Political and Social Science* publishes the *Annals*, and the *Academy of Political Science* publishes *Political Science Quarterly*.

In addition, regional political science associations also publish scholarly research.

This partial list of some of the major commissions, associations, and councils engaged in research, discussion, or advocacy of foreign-policy views suggests the range of activity by private citizens in the field to influence policy, policy makers, and the general public.[27]

While they may often be dissimilar in motivations, intentions, and resources, they constitute a body of knowledge and opinion that cannot be easily disregarded or ignored by government officials.

KEY INDIVIDUALS

Occasionally certain individuals, not connected formally with the government, play a role at critical points in the foreign-policy process. Precisely when their role is itself a critical one is much more difficult to determine, and it can be argued that they have no ultimate influence at all. However, it is worth examining some of these people.

In the 1930s, during the administration of Franklin D. Roosevelt, a Roman Catholic priest named Father Charles E. Coughlin became a severe critic of the New Deal in both domestic and foreign policy.[28] Utilizing radio, then the major national broadcast medium, Coughlin supported the views of isolationists on a number of questions and attacked Roosevelt on a wide range of issues.

From the 1920s onward, Walter Lippmann was regarded as much more than a journalist. Through his newspaper columns, books, and intimate contacts with leaders for over five decades, Lippmann became a major public voice on American foreign policy, and his criticisms of the policy of the Johnson administration during the Vietnam War were a major influence on the antiwar movement and on thinking within the Johnson administration.[29] His importance in the foreign-policy discussion was unique; no journalist in either print or broadcast media, no scholar, and no independent expert from any quarter has yet achieved the place that Lippmann had in American political life, and none has matched his prestige.

Although Armand Hammer does not speak out publicly very often on foreign-policy issues, he has played a unique and independent role in relations with the Soviet Union.[30] As founder of Occidental Petroleum, Hammer has maintained contacts with Soviet leaders since the Revolution in 1917 and has provided valuable insights into their personalities and character. In addition, he has promoted the idea of good relations and trade between the two powers.

Another individual with national recognition who maintained close contact with many presidents was financier Bernard Baruch. Although he rarely engaged in public debate over issues, several twentieth-century presidents received his advice and counsel.

Apart from these independent national voices, presidents may also seek counsel with old friends or "cronies," people in whom the president has confidence and with whom he can share his problems with no fear that his confidant will breach secrecy. Richard M. Nixon spent considerable time with Charles "Bebe" Rebozo, and Jimmy Carter confided in Charles Curbow, an associate from Atlanta. Publisher Walter Annenberg has been reported to be a close personal and social acquaintance of both Richard Nixon and Ronald Reagan. What is clear is that these old and close friends may have a kind of contact and a level of trust that few governmental associates of a president share. In any case, whatever their influence on specific policies, there is little doubt that this type of relationship has the potential for coloring a president's evaluations of problems, personalities, and policies.

Beyond friends and cronies, there are many other outside advisers available to counsel a president. Views may be solicited from retired foreign-policy experts, academic experts with unique knowledge, professional consultants, and key political leaders throughout the country.

A special kind of adviser is the "grey eminence," the highly distinguished American who may have special expertise and experience in policy making. Former presidents are often consulted, their support sought for particular policies or their participation requested for specific missions. Usually former living presidents are kept informed and advised of important policy matters and are provided with the latest confidential information.

In addition to former presidents, other public officials may be recruited for specific missions, for advice, or to provide useful and timely public support. Former Secretary of State Dean Acheson was asked to join the discussions during the Cuban missile crisis, and such former officials as Clark Clifford and Averell Harriman have been recalled to serve or to provide advice.

THE INDIVIDUAL CITIZEN

> To influence the conduct of the government in a significant way, citizens nearly always need an organization of some sort. Organizations are important for anyone who wishes to influence government, but they are particularly crucial for those who lack great individual resources.[31]

As Robert Dahl notes, many citizens do not participate in organizations of any kind. Many never take any overt action at all to express their views, if they have any, to government officials.[32]

But is there anything individuals can do by themselves to affect policy? Actually citizens are free to write, telephone, or send telegrams to representatives, senators, or the White House. The individual's hope for influence is likely to be most effective with the local congressional representative, who is usually reasonably accessible to constituents. All representatives vote on foreign-policy issues, and many are active in committees with special involvement in foreign policy. U.S. senators may be equally accessible, and all senators are also involved with some aspects of foreign policy. Thus the individual has the freedom and the opportunity to communicate his or her views to the Congress; and the vote is still an important expression of views.

Communications that are informed, reasoned, and factual may in fact have an impression on those in Congress, and citizen communications are also read and tabulated in the White House.

The individual can also decide to run for public office, to work for a cause, and to speak forthrightly with friends, associates, and coworkers. Most of all, the individual can become well informed and remain knowledgeable about the challenges that face the United States in the world and the policies that are in place to deal with them.

The individual is not powerless, by any means, but it would be an exaggeration to conclude that individuals, acting alone, can cause policies to be created or changed. But individuals can always find like-minded persons to form groups, and as we have seen, citizens' groups can indeed have an impact on the direction of policy under some circumstances.

SUMMARY

As we have seen in this and the preceding chapter, many public voices seek to influence the foreign-policy process. Their purposes range from efforts to strengthen the national interest and capabilities to the narrowest kind of self-interest. Utilizing political means, many of these public voices constitute an important element in the political process by which policy options are recognized, considered, and decided, and some of them are not regarded kindly by policy makers. For example, Jimmy Carter argues that "the lobbies are a growing menace to our democratic system of government."[33] He adds: ". . . when the interests of powerful lobbyists were at stake, a majority of the members [of Congress] often yielded to a combination of political threats and blandishments of heavy campaign contributions."[34] He concludes: "Ultimately something will have to be done to control the influence of special interests."[35]

Certainly, not all observers share Carter's dim view of the operations of special interests. Bernard Cohen notes that "the weight of current judgment is that interest groups of all kinds, including those that are economic in nature, have little influence on issues of security policy."[36] He points to three reasons cited by Lester Milbrath to explain this belief. Security decisions are more intellective and less subject to social processes and open to group influence. In addition, the more intense the public scrutiny and the greater the importance of the issues, the less likelihood that group interest will be effective. Although Cohen suggests that these limitations on group influence may not necessarily apply to other aspects of foreign policy, he suggests that in a time when consensus is lacking among Americans, "interest groups may be an increasingly important means of creating and mobilizing significant public opinion with respect to specific and unforeseen issues of external policy that arise between elections and have threatening consequences for the whole society."[37]

This suggests that special interests may serve a more constructive purpose than their critics imagine.

Between Carter's view of alarm and Cohen's more sanguine hypotheses lie the requirements for a better understanding of special interests and their role in the policy process. In terms of foreign and security policy, their impact is generally regarded as less effective than in the domestic sphere. However, in a time when there are increasing crossovers between foreign and domestic policy, this might suggest that special interests will gain influence in the future.

In terms of the other public voices considered in this chapter, their influence is likely to be more indirect. Through the generation of ideas, knowledge, methods, and advice, they can affect the perceptions of options, limits, and capabilities available to policy makers. In providing support for spokespersons of one view or another, they become part of the political process in which policy choices are made.

Underlying consideration of all of the governmental and public voices contributing to the process lie the questions of what is the national interest, who should define it, and how should it be defined. In a free society everyone has the right to offer his or her version.

NOTES

[1] Thomas R. Dye, *Who's Running America?* 3rd ed., (Englewood Cliffs, N.J.: Prentice-Hall, 1983), p. 265.

[2] E. Bruce Geelhold, *Charles E. Wilson and Controversy at the Pentagon, 1953 to 1957* (Detroit: Wayne State University Press, 1979), pp. 46–47.

[3] Robert A. Dahl, *Democracy in the United States: Promise and Performance*, 3rd ed. (Chicago: Rand McNally & Co., 1976), pp. 41–59.

[4] Bruce M. Russett and Elizabeth C. Hanson, *Interest and Ideology* (San Francisco: W.H. Freeman and Co., 1975), pp. 244–50; Bruce M. Russett and Harvey Starr, *World Politics: The Menu for Choice* (San Francisco: W.H. Freeman and Co., 1981), pp. 224–28.

[5] David Leyton-Brown, "Governments of Developed Countries as Hosts to Multinational Corporations: The Canadian, British, and French Policy Experiences," Ph.D. dissertation (unpublished), department of government, Harvard University, 1975.

[6] James Dull, "Effects of Multinational Corporations on the Attitudes of Mexican Executives," Ph.D. dissertation (unpublished), department of political science, Graduate School of Arts and Science, Columbia University, 1981.

[7] Barnaby J. Feder, "The World Banking Crisis: Phase Two," *New York Times*, March 27, 1983, p. F12; Leonard Silk, "Avalanche of Debt Threatens Global Economy," *New York Times*, September 12, 1982, p. E3.

[8] Dye, *Who's Running America?* pp. 269–71, 175–90.

[9] Michael Parenti, *Democracy for the Few*, 4th ed. (New York: St. Martin's Press, 1983), p. 13.

[10] Charles W. Kegley and Eugene R. Wittkopf, *American Foreign Policy: Pattern and Process*, 2nd ed. (New York: St. Martin's Press, 1982), pp. 213, 228.

[11] Dye, *Who's Running America?*, pp. 157–60.

[12] Ibid., pp. 142–47.

[13] Ibid., pp. 145–46, 181–82.

[14] Ibid., p. 183; The role of David Rockefeller in seeking admittance of the Shah of Iran into the United States for medical treatment in 1979 is described by former President Jimmy Carter in *Keeping Faith*, (New York: Bantam Books, 1982) pp. 452–68.

[15] Dye, *Who's Running America?*, p. 241.

[16] Ibid., p. 251.

[17] Ibid., p. 254.

[18] Ibid., p. 241.

[19] Steven Strassner and others, "The Return of Kissinger," *Newsweek*, August 1, 1983, pp. 18–22.

[20] Theodore H. White, "Weinberger on the Ramparts," *New York Times Magazine*, February 6, 1983, pp. 64–65.

[21] Dye, *Who's Running America?* p. 247; Kegley and Wittkopf, *American Foreign Policy*, pp. 251–53.

[22] Kegley and Wittkopf, *American Foreign Policy*, p. 252.

[23] Dye, *Who's Running America?*, pp. 151–54, 244–47.

[24] Ibid., pp. 247–51.

[25] Joseph LaPalombara and Stephan Blank, *Multinational Corporations in Comparative Perspective* (New York: Conference Board, 1977), inside front cover.

[26] David V. Edwards, *The American Political Experience*, 2nd ed. (Englewood Cliffs, N.J.: pp. 627–28.

[27] Ibid.

[28] William Manchester, *The Glory and the Dream* (New York: Bantam Books, 1975, pp. 108–11; Arthur Schlesinger, Jr., *The Politics of Upheaval* (Boston: Houghton & Mifflin Company: 1960), pp. 5, 16–28.

[29] Ronald Steel, *Walter Lippmann and the American Century* (Boston: Little, Brown & Company, 1980), pp. xiii–xvii.

[30] Bob Considine, *The Remarkable Life of Armand Hammer* (New York: Harper & Row, Publishers, 1975), pp. 176–88.

[31] Robert Dahl, *Democracy in the United States*, p. 460.

[32] Ibid.

[33] Jimmy Carter, *Keeping Faith*, p. 80.

[34] Ibid., p. 88.

[35] Ibid.

[36] Bernard C. Cohen, "The Influence of Special Interest Groups and Mass Media on Security Policy in the United States," in Charles W. Kegley and Eugene B. Wittkopf, *Perspectives on American Foreign Policy* (New York: St. Martin's Press, 1983), p. 224.

[37] Ibid., p. 238.

CHAPTER ELEVEN
THE GRAND
FRAMEWORKS

By the time men and women arrive at positions of power, they bring with them more or less well defined views of reality. These ideas constitute the core of their beliefs about how the world works and how the United States should behave in it. The successful political leader, like all rational individuals, has customarily developed an organizing intellectual order based on experience, knowledge, and observation. Therein lies the power of ideas. From ancient philosophies to the models of contemporary social science, ideas provide a foundation upon which the leader defines and explains the meaning of contemporary events, personalities, and conflicts. Ideas themselves become intrinsic actors in the process and the stuff of political debate.

History is rich in these intellectual guideposts to action, and contemporary research seeks to expand the knowledge on which policy can be based. Having examined the numerous individuals and groups exercising power or influence in the policy process, we will now review many of the ideas available to policy makers—philosophies, ideologies, theories, hypotheses, models—and explore their functions in the making of policy and in the conduct of foreign relations.

Some leaders arrive at positions of power with strong and clear-cut beliefs, while some rely on other sources to provide guidance and background. Jimmy Carter was one of the latter; Zbigniew Brzezinski feels that he lacked a sense of history.[1] President Ronald Reagan entered the White

House with some broad but deeply held attitudes about the Soviet Union and about the proper relationship between it and the United States.

When a president has fewer and less well defined ideas about foreign policy, he tends to rely more heavily on the knowledge of key advisers or on the experiences he has had in domestic politics. When this occurs, analytic emphasis must be placed upon the ideas of key advisers.

Analysis of the sources of all of the ideas held by leaders is beyond the scope of this book, but at a minimum it must be remembered that beliefs have many roots beyond political philosophies and theories. Religion, culture, experience, new knowledge, and personality all contribute to the socialization of leaders and their followers. How they all blend together within individuals to form a belief system, which ones are dominant at any given time, and how beliefs relate to specific policies are impossible to determine with analytic tools presently available. Still the comments and actions of leaders provide clues to the importance of some of the ideas that have emerged from theory and experience.

Regrettably, no single theory or model exists that is capable of explaining all human or political behavior because every theory and model (1) contains flaws in conception, comprehensiveness, and completeness; (2) can be supported by the evidence only partially, or not at all; (3) has exceptions too numerous to permit unquestioned acceptance. Nevertheless, many of the intellectual attempts to find and impose conceptual order on political behavior constitute meaningful but fragmentary guideposts to the achievement of a better understanding of the processes and content of policy. Each discovers one or more segments of reality and serves as a building block on which more complete analysis may be constructed to create a safer and more humane world.

In this chapter we will examine some of the most comprehensive ideas confronting policy makers in the contemporary world—broad concepts that purport to explain political behavior among states and to advocate the norms by which states should act, leaders should govern, and policies should evolve.

Realism and the balance of power, idealism, interdependence, geopolitics, Marxism-Leninism, capitalism, imperialism, nationalism, transnationalism, world community, American liberalism and conservatism, democracy, authoritarianism, liberty, equality, self-determination, nonalignment, messianism—all constitute sets of ideas that have motivated leaders in the twentieth century or have been used to explain this behavior.

Providing considerable insight into political behavior, the ideas embodied in the foregoing list can be traced in many of the American foreign policies pursued in the past two centuries. In some cases they have been the basis for American actions. In others they have afforded challenges to American policies and interests.

REALISM AND THE BALANCE OF POWER

Based on the view that the nature of man is sinful, aggressive, and conflictual, realism holds that political theory must flow from observation of the history and experience of people and of states and that these show a pattern of violent, aggressive behavior.[2] In this environment the highest moral duty of the state is its own preservation. To accomplish this, states must utilize power, power being defined as anything that establishes and maintains control of man over man. The interest of the state, defined in terms of power, is the primary moral guide by which policies are developed, but prudence in pursuing that interest is the primary ethical guide for policy makers and is what is called the supreme virtue in politics. In a world of power politics, states must arrange their power to provide for survival, according to realist theory, and this provides the justification for balance of power arrangements, which realists contend are the most effective techniques for managing power. Thus the goals of state have come to include the search for ways to acquire and keep power, increase power, and demonstrate power. In short, in a world of conflicting states seeking power, a world confirmed by historical experience and by the nature of man, states must engage in power politics in order to survive, and they should do anything prudent to achieve that goal.

If power politics leads to the formation of balances to deter potential aggressors and to preserve the existence of states, a useful definition of a *balance of power* is required.[3] Regrettably, the term has many meanings and interpretations, any of which might be accurate in one setting but misleading in another. Although balance of power, like realism, is an old concept and practice, it has many modern applications. In an important analysis of the concept, Inis Claude has suggested at least six ways in which the term has traditionally been used.[4] It has described both the concept of equilibrium and disequilibrium of power among states, that is, (1) situations in which power is perceived to be relatively equally balanced among states or groups of states and (2) those in which one state or group of states has sufficient superior power over another so that aggression may be deterred.

The achievement and maintenance of a balance of power have also been regarded as a necessary policy of states in pursuit of survival. In addition, the term has been applied to the concept of a system, that is, a set of relationships and arrangements among states that imposes rules, restraints, and rewards for acceptable behavior. Balance of power has also been used to describe the actual distribution of power among states at a given moment, and it has been advocated as a symbol of wise and prudent interpretation of history, a philosophy likely to produce the most order and peace among states.

Aside from the difficulties resulting from the various uses to which the term *balance of power* has been put, the student of foreign policy is confronted with other problems in understanding the concept and applying it to contemporary behavior.

Few concepts have provoked as much disagreement as "power." Power is seen as the capability of *A* to get *B* to do what *B* would otherwise not do.[5] It may be exercised in numerous ways: the use or threat of the use of force, influence, threats, promises, mutual interest, among others. But if the exercise of power involves a relationship among two or more parties, the content of power is what produces the capability to act. Here again, considerable disagreement about the nature of the content of power persists. Many people believe that power is synonymous with military capability, but the content of national power is composed of far more than military forces alone. At least five broad dimensions of factors contribute to a nation-state's power: geography, population, economic base, military capability, and national character.[6] The size, topography, natural resources, arability, and geological balance of a state; the natural frontiers and barriers it possesses; and the climate all contribute to power since they relate to independent satisfaction of basic needs (food, raw materials, living space, water).

In terms of population, such factors as its size, age distribution, growth rates, mobility, health, and skills set limits on the capabilities of states in world affairs. The productive use of geographic and population factors to create wealth makes the economic base a most important element in national power. A country's capability to develop a wide range of skills among its labor force, to provide for research and development of new techniques of management and production, and to support purposes in the national interest (such as education, health, transportation) relate directly to its means to act in foreign affairs and to maintain effective military capability.

The size, balance, and modernity of the military capability are, to be sure, important to American power. The development of new weapons systems, the access to military personnel, the availability of adequate leadership and the availability of strong allies constitute significant parts of the military capability, along with the economic resources to support it. Finally, for want of a better term to describe the motivational characteristics of a people, we use the term *national character*. That does not refer to national stereotypes. Rather, national character can be conceived of as meaning the combination of dominant values, beliefs, and attitudes that impel a people to develop and support national power and its use under specific circumstances. When America went to war in 1941, the bulk of the American people supported the crusade against the Axis powers. After the United States government made a military commitment to defend South Vietnam in 1964–65, popular support rapidly eroded as the war continued. The national willingness to support governmental exercise of national power abroad is thus a central element in the nation's overall power. The public resistance to Reagan administration policies in Lebanon and in Central America in 1983 reflects the importance of this factor.

Assuming agreement on these elements of power, we might, nonetheless, find it difficult to measure power with precision or to compare it with that of other countries. Each year at budget time in Congress, a lot of discussion is heard contending that the United States has "fallen behind" the Soviet Union in power. Much emphasis is placed on this or that weapons system in which Soviet numbers exceed those of the United States. But measuring power with precision is no small task. Is a Soviet SS-20 intermediate-range missile more or less powerful than a division of troops? Even if there are some Soviet systems superior in quality and quantity, how important is the strength of the American economy versus the Soviet economy?

Thus when we speak of *balance of power*, it is necessary to be clear about what we mean by *balance* and *power*. Even when we are clear about it, what is a balance? How can it be measured? When does it exist? Are all factors of power equally important, or are some more important than others under some varying circumstances?

In this uncertain and imprecise process, it may be enough to know that a balance of power is what leaders think it is and that it exists when they perceive that it does. If the existing American power capability deters adversaries from doing what we want to prevent them from doing, then it can be assumed that the balance of power, however imprecisely measured, is working.

TYPES OF BALANCE-
OF-POWER SYSTEMS

The acceptance of the basic concept of balance of power by scholars and by leaders has led to their efforts to elaborate on it, to identify different patterns of the balance, and to suggest ways in which these different patterns operate to promote world order.

One of the most interesting elaborations of the classical balance of power model is that offered by Morton Kaplan.[7] Suggesting that the period between 1815 and 1914 was the representative period in which this system functioned, Kaplan believes that the system required the presence of at least five major powers of relative equality engaged in the formation of rapidly shifting alliances. This system was also characterized by a "balancer" nation, which entered on the side of the weaker alliance to deter the stronger ones. Another element in this system was the absence of regional or international organizations.

The concept of bipolarity has produced some imaginative theorizing and some vigorous scholarly debate.[8] One view contends that the balance of power is presently organized around two poles, the United States and the Soviet Union. However, there has been disagreement over whether the term *poles* should refer to the balance between single states or between two blocs of states. In most contemporary analysis there is a tendency to regard bipolarity as the balance of blocs rather than one of individual states. Kaplan goes further and postulates two different kinds of bipolar systems—a tight system and a loose system.[9] In the tight system all nonaligned nations would become part of one bloc or the other, and the central power would exercise rigid, or tight, control over the members. The loose bipolar system involves alliances and associations of many nations around each of the superpowers, although many other nations remained nonaligned. Within the system there is considerable diversity and autonomy of bloc members. The loose bipolar-system concept comes the closest to describing the world power system since the mid-1940s. One of the leading advocates and proponents of bipolarity, Kenneth Waltz, argues tht such a system provides more security and stability than any other, since neither bloc will seek domination over the other.[10]

However, another school of thought holds that bipolarity is the most dangerous system of all. Karl Deutsch and J. David Singer suggested in their study on the functioning of multipolar systems, that is, systems in which there are several poles of power, that wars are likely to be less frequent and less massive in multipolar systems than in other systems.[11] The concept of multipolarity has assumed increased importance in the late twentieth century, as observers have noted an increase in the number of power centers, i.e., polycentrism. In 1973 Secretary of State Henry Kissinger claimed that while there are just two superpowers, there are at least five major groupings of states in the world.[12] Countries can exert political influence even when they have neither military nor economic strength, he said.[13] Among the states and groups believed to possess independent power in the 1980s, in addition to the two superpowers, are Japan, West Germany, the Common Market, China, and OPEC, with at least the first four believed capable of achieving superpower status in the future.

An attempt to reconcile the competing claims of bipolarity and multipolarity has been made by Richard Rosencrance.[14] Although he suggests that his view of what he calls bi-multipolarity should not be confused with the present world order, he argues that a system which includes bipolarity at the nuclear level and multipolarity at the levels of politics, economics, and conventional military force would be the most likely to minimize violence.

Not only have many other hypothetical models of past or future systems been suggested, but there are other ways in which the concept of *system* has been used, aside from those associated with the operation of a balance of power. For some the entire earth is seen as a single system in which nations, blocs, and regions are regarded as subsystems.[15] In this hypothesized unit the activities of individual actors affect the whole system in innumerable ways. Wars, trade, and pollution are believed to have an impact on the entire global system.

Yet another way in which the term *system* has been applied to the global structure has been the suggestion of a process by which demands are made on the total system, and they in turn are converted into outputs—policies, programs, agreements, treaties, and so on.[16] The capacity of the system to respond to the demands of its parts and to the global environment is a test of its stability and adaptability. Power is a factor in the process of the system since it may determine the force of demands made upon it and increase the ability of those with disproportionate power to obtain outputs most favorable to themselves and least favorable to adversaries.

In any event, the concepts of balance, power, system, balance of power, and balance-of-power system have not only provided scholars with the subjects of endless study and debate, but they continue to provide guideposts to policy makers. Realist notions of human nature and of the behavior of states abound in the writings and policies of many leaders everywhere. Balance of power, both as a descriptive device in picturing the distribution of power in the world and as a wise and prudent basis for policy, remains a vital concept in world affairs and in foreign policy.

Despite the imprecision of the doctrine, the fact that it has been accepted and utilized in many of its forms by American policy makers since 1945 is abundantly clear. Beginning with the analysis of the Soviet Union offered in 1946 by former ambassador to the Soviet Union George Kennan, the United States government developed what has been called the containment policy.[17] Simply put, containment has come to mean a balance-of-power policy designed to confine perceived expansion of the Soviet Union. Although originally designed to apply to Western Europe, the concept has been utilized to justify a balance with the Soviets on a global scale. Acceptance of the idea of containment subsequently led to the development of specific American programs designed to limit Soviet power and expansion. The Truman Doctrine in 1946 not only offered $400 million to Greece and Turkey to assist in defeating Communist-supported uprisings, but it also proclaimed the intention of the American government to oppose Soviet expansion elsewhere. In 1947 it was followed by the Marshall Plan, a vast economic-aid program designed to support the recovery of Western Europe and to strengthen it against Soviet expansion. Later a military component was added to containment policy with the creation of the North Atlantic Treaty Organization, combining the military forces of the United States and Western Europe and committing the United States to the protection and defense of its allies against Soviet attack. Long after this period, Kissinger commented:

> Like it or not, we were assuming the historical responsibility for preserving the balance of power, and we were poorly prepared for the task.[18]

He defined clearly the requirements of maintaining a balance of power policy:

> . . . the management of a balance of power is a permanent undertaking, not an exertion that has a forseeable end. To a great extent it is a psychological phenomenon; if an equality of power is perceived, it will not be tested. Calculations must include potential as well as actual power, not only the possession of power but the will to bring it to bear. Management of the balance requires perseverance, subtlety, not a little courage, and above all understanding of its requirements.[19]

Arguing that the balance of power has been a "precondition of peace," Henry Kissinger contends that "throughout history the political influence of nations has been roughly correlative to their military power."[20] The emphasis on military power has been repeatedly expressed by President Ronald Reagan. On March 31, 1982, in a news conference, Reagan discounted the proposal for a freeze on the development of nuclear weapons until the United States has again achieved "superiority."[21]

The point is that from 1946 to the present moment, the concept of balance of power, in all of its forms, has been a major element in the thinking and in the policies of American presidents and most of their major advisers. It also remains a central idea in the perceptions of the public, as reflected in the 1980 elections and in public-opinion polls. It has been by no means the only major concept at work in policy making, as we shall see, but most objective analyses of the statements, writings, and policies offered by the majority of leaders in the postwar world suggests that it is probably the most persistent and persuasive framework in the minds of those who determine policy and set the conditions for foreign relations of all types.

IDEALISM

Another major theme in American foreign policy and in American foreign relations, especially in the twentieth century, is idealism.[22] As a philosophy and as a basis for policy, idealism differs sharply from realism in many of its impulses, premises, values, and perceptions. Like realism, its philosophical roots are ancient and deep in human experience. Many of its antecedents can be found in the teachings of Christ and in the search of the Greco-Roman culture for order based on law. In the America of the twentieth century, no more effective advocate of its principles lived than President Woodrow Wilson, whose proposed foreign policies were based on moral, legal, and humanitarian principles. Others advocating idealist principles include pacifists, world federalists, and religionists.

Taking a more benign view of the nature of man and of the human experience than the realists, idealists believe that people are essentially good, cooperative, and perfectible; that humanity has the capacity to learn, to change, and control its behavior; that individuals seek peace, justice, mutual respect, and a just order. On the basis of this interpretation, idealists believe that it is possible to govern according to moral principles for the purpose of creating a good life through the creation of just laws, the abandonment of force as a means of settling disputes, acceptance of peaceful change, and creation of equal rights for all citizens and states.

Structurally, idealists believe that these principles can be achieved through the establishment of and adherence to international law and through reliance on international organizations, especially those capable of providing for the adjudication, mediation, and arbitration of disputes. Others go even further in advocating the creation of a world government with the authority to settle disputes among states.

As a means of preserving order, idealists support the concept of collective security, a process in which all members of the community join to deter or to punish those who resort to violence and aggression. Although some idealists are totally pacifist and nonviolent, many others concede that there is a need to provide an international structure with authority and legitimate force to maintain peace.

Repulsed by the horrors and the costs inflicted by modern war, idealists hold the view that the balance-of-power system and the realist views underlying it have not only failed to prevent the wars of the nineteenth and twentieth centuries but have contributed to the causes and the destructiveness of those wars. In the search for a more successful and a more humane system, idealists supported the creation of the League of Nations and the United Nations as well as an expanded system of international law and collective security.

Two American presidents in the twentieth century were particularly intent upon inclusion of idealist tenets in American foreign policy. For Woodrow Wilson a League of Nations following World War I was an essential instrument to help safeguard peace after 1918. He was perfectly aware that it was a mechanism that might require the use of force. But when force was required, it would be applied with the legitimacy that comes from world law and world organization. Although Wilson failed to get the American Congress to accept American participation in the organization, and although the organization failed ultimately to prevent World War II, it provided inspiration for another American president a generation later, Franklin D. Roosevelt.

Persuaded of the soundness of Wilson's ideas despite the earlier failures, Roosevelt made the creation of the United Nations one of his major postwar goals during the Second World War. This time, although Roosevelt died before the end of the war, the United States, under the leadership of Harry Truman, became a founding member of the new world organization and participated in all of its associated international agencies. Later in 1950 Truman relied on the collective-security authority of the United Nations Charter to organize armed resistance to an invasion of South Korea by North Korea and by the People's Republic of China. In addition, the United States supported the creation of the International Court of Justice and has occasionally utilized its processes.

The United States also played a leadership role in the creation of the Universal Declaration of Human Rights. Eleanor Roosevelt, as a delegate to the United Nations, was in the forefront of the passage of the document expressing many of the same human rights that had long been part of the American Constitution and American law. Conventions establishing international economic and social rights were also supported by the United States, although many of these have not been effective.

Following the experience of the Korean War, the American government has relied less on the collective-security arrangements of the U.N. Charter for two reasons: the anticipated veto by the Soviet Union in the Security Council and doubts about the practical workability of the system in the present U.N.; more than one hundred new nations have joined since 1945 reflecting varied and complex viewpoints about security issues.

As for the question of world government, relatively few Americans and no American presidents have actively supported the idea. However, as part of the doctrine of idealism, world federalism and world government retain some support in the United States.

Idealist principles have been pursued in other aspects of American policy in the twentieth century. As part of his peace plan in 1918, the so-called fourteen points, President Woodrow Wilson advocated the idea of self-determination for all the peoples of the world. This ideal provided some of the impetus for the anticolonialist movements of the post-World War II period. American presidents, including Ronald Reagan, have proclaimed the American interest in extending human rights, self-determination, and economic progress to all of mankind. Indeed, one of the key elements of the foreign policies of a recent president, Jimmy Carter (1977–81), was an emphasis on human-rights issues, and despite some inconsistencies in the definition and application of the doctrine to specific countries, many observers regard the approach by Carter as productive.

The belief in the soundness and effectiveness of idealist principles and structures is still strong among many Americans, and although few believe that the United Nations is capable of guaranteeing peace, they have accepted the more limited peace-keeping capability of the world organization as a welcome addition to world politics.

The belief in law, in the peaceful settlement of disputes, in the danger of arms races and the awesome cost of nuclear war, and in the cooperative side of human nature continues to lend support and substance to much in American foreign policy, and at the same time, to influence the ways in which policy is made.

INTERDEPENDENCE

A third set of ideas has emerged in recent years as a framework in which foreign policy and foreign relations can develop. Interdependence is the term used to designate the intricate set of political, economic, cultural, and psychological relationships that have evolved in the modern world among states, peoples, private organizations, international agencies, and political systems. Broadly defined, interdependence in world politics "refers to situations characterized by reciprocal effects among countries or among actors in different countries."[23] Robert Keohane and Joseph Nye contend that "where there are reciprocal (although not necessarily symmetrical) costly effects of transactions, there is interdependence."[24] Other analysts of interdependence have described it in these terms:

> National political authorities in one nation are no longer able to insulate their sovereign jurisdictions from the effects of economic policies engineered by political authorities or private-sector actors located abroad. But other transnational linkages have also become part of what it means to live in an interdependent world. Military alliances have become entangling and permanent. Heads of state visit each other with such frequency that the practice of summitry and shuttle diplomacy are now commonplace. Private citizens increasingly participate in intercultural experiences, whether by mail and telecommunications or through business travel and tourism. National economies have become internationalized, as trade and capital flows among them have expanded geometrically. . . . Global interdependence is likely to continue to describe the world political system, at least in the short run.[25]

There are those who question whether perceptions of the increasing numbers of linkages among actors in the world system add up to satisfactory theory or indeed to any theory at all. One major criticism of some of the models of interdependence is that the multiple linkages that are observed constitute not interdependence but rather either independence of some states or dominance/subservience, i.e., dependent relationships. At the very least, it is argued, interdependence is as likely to produce conflict as cooperation among states.[26]

Underlying the belief that interdependence is a valid concept are two powerful facts. First, since the end of World War II, the number, variety, and importance of linkages among actors in the global system have expanded dramatically, and second, no nation-state, not even a superpower, is entirely independent of others for security, materials, products, or other basic needs. Some countries, like the United States, may be somewhat more independent than others, but not only have linkages expanded and multiplied, but the perception of a single global system has slowly emerged.

To be sure, as a theory, interdependence has not yet been completely or satisfactorily formulated despite some substantial efforts to do so. However, an examination of the premises, roots, models, and claims of interdependence provides the material with which a theory can be constructed. It suggests that in viewing human nature, one can conclude that whether humanity is essentially good and cooperative or sinful and conflictual, it is also practical, pragmatic, and rational; that people will act in their own self-interest in the most cost-effective way, and if that involves reciprocity in order to achieve goals, they will accept it through peaceful means.

The roots of the concept are relatively modern. The free-trade liberalism of the mid-nineteenth century carried over into the post-1945 world, in which the United States promoted a series of arrangements designed to create a system of free and open trade among states. As a concept, interdependence arose first as an economic perception of the mutual dependence among states in the postwar period. More recently it came to be applied to a broader range of relationships—political, strategic, military, cultural, and social.

Underlying the belief in interdependence as a basis for maintaining peace and for providing the foundations for economic development in the world is the view that mutual self-interest produces mutual satisfaction and mutual rewards and is a more effective instrument than power and war, international law and organization, balance of power, or collective security. It affirms the belief that there are practical, pragmatic things that countries can do to avert war, short of building mass armies and weapons of destruction.

Some critics of interdependence as a theory regard it as even more utopian and unworkable than idealism because most linkages that have evolved in the system are not truly reciprocal but are unequal and even exploitative, perpetuating dominance/subservience relationships and neo-imperialism.[27]

Giving added impetus to the rise of the concept of interdependence in American awareness, however, was the 1973 oil boycott by member states of OPEC. This brought home to Americans that not even the United States is immune to dependency on other states for vital resources. Energy is just one such resource. Copper, bauxite, and other metals are others. Even at that, the United States is much less dependent upon other countries than the great majority of states of the world.

As scholarly refinement of the concept proceeds, it is clear that as an explanation of the linkages in the present global system and as a policy direction for the United States interdependence has had considerable acceptance. In the spring of 1981 President Ronald Reagan proposed a new set of relationships between the United States and Latin American states of the Caribbean Basin.[28] In return for economic aid, the United States is seeking political stability and the exclusion of Soviet and Cuban influence among the states of Central America. Is this interdependence? Many students of foreign policy and foreign relations will think so.

IMPERIALISM,
NEOIMPERIALISM,
AND SPHERES OF INFLUENCE

By definition, writes Richard Sterling, imperialism "established a government by strangers. Alien rule is the hallmark of empire. The key decisions for the colony are made by persons, processes, and institutions foreign to the colony."[29]

Implicit in the idea of imperialism is exploitation. "All the rationalizations and justifications for empire cannot disguise the fact that the basic imperial impulse is to conquer and to enjoy the benefits that accrue to conquerors," writes Sterling.[30]

Not infrequently the conquerors were proud of their enterprise and viewed it as a duty to bring the benefits of civilization to backward and savage lands.

Contrary to the Marxist-Leninist view that imperialism emerged from the predatory drives of exploitative capitalists, other analysts, such as Joseph Schumpeter, see the cause of imperialism stemming from the irrational nature of man and in the precapitalist factors that still persist in modern states.

As Sterling views imperialism:

> Desires for security, wealth and glory, the hankering after adventure and crusades, and the readiness to gratify these ambitions at the expense of freedom and dignity for others are human characteristics transcending all distinctions among races or socioeconomic systems.[31]

In short, there are many causes of imperialism in history and at present. Kenneth N. Waltz notes:

> "Republics (Athens and Rome), divine-right monarchies (Bourbon France and Meijian Japan), modern democracies (Britain and America) have all at times been imperialist. Similarly, economies of great variety—pastoral, feudal, mercantilist, capitalist, socialist—have sustained imperialist enterprises. To explain imperialism by capitalism is parochial at best.[32]

The phrase that expresses the root cause that operates across directly organized economies is "the imperialism of great power," writes Waltz. "Where one finds empires," he contends, "one notices that they are built by those who have organized themselves and exploited their resources more effectively." Where gross imbalances of power exist and where the means of transportation permit the export of goods and of the instruments of rule, the more capable peoples ordinarily exert a considerable influence over those less able to produce surpluses."[33]

Thus imperialism is a potential result of the gross disparities in power and capabilities among political entities of any era and may arise from within whatever economic system exists at the time.

When the identification of imperialism with capitalism failed to hold up under intense scrutiny, some theorists in the last half of the twentieth century developed the theory of neoimperialism. In this new era private business replaces government as the instrument of imperialism, and multi-national corporations are viewed as maintaining a dominance/dependence relationship over weak countries, resulting in the perpetuation of economic backwardness in these countries. Waltz argues: "The effort to save Lenin's thesis has led to such a broadening of the definition of imperialism that almost any relation among unequals can be termed 'imperialism'".[34]

An additional theoretical difficulty with imperialism and neoimperialism lies in the fact that most states may be expansionist.

But can expansionism always be equated with imperialism? Small states as well as large ones often seek to establish alliances, trade relationships, religious or cultural influence, or even military bases with other countries. Is this imperialism, especially when the other states participate in these arrangements voluntarily? Hardly.

Still, the conceptions and misconceptions about imperialism constitute powerful ideas about how states behave. Although the attractions of empire have eroded considerably as the result of the costly and violent revolutions that have confronted imperialist countries in the last half of the twentieth century, the appeal of empire may not be entirely dead. In the United States, however, the appeal seems weak to those who realize the limitations on the resources of the nation or to those for whom the idea is repugnant. Expanded American influence in many parts of the world and the view that the United States should play a leadership role in providing guidelines for world economic and political development are characteristics of powerful states, but they do not necessarily constitute either imperialism or neoimperialism. To the extent that American policy in some countries may attempt through either overt or covert activity to determine major policies of other countries, the purpose is as often to thwart the expansionist activities of the Soviet Union as to maintain control for its own sake. A central problem is trying to determine whether the activity of one government toward another amounts to imperialism; one has to examine not only the level of activity which one state may maintain within the borders of others but also how much control it has achieved over the policies of the others. What do we mean by *control*? How does it differ from *influence*?

If, as Sterling suggests, control involves the making of "key" decisions for the colony by persons, processes, and institutions foreign to the colony,[35] the definition seems clear enough. However, in a world where, with the exception of the Soviet empire in Eastern and Central Europe, key decisions in many countries are not made by outside forces through the presence of military rulers or the external threat to impose military authority, classical imperialism would seem to have almost disappeared. Reality is a bit more subtle and complex. Relatively little consensus exists over the ways control is measured. What decisions are key decisions, and which key decisions must be made by external powers if an imperialist or neoimperialist situation is concluded to exist? Must all, or only some key decisions be made by external forces, and if only some key decisions are made externally, which ones? If key decisions appear to be made exclusively by the government of the alleged colony, what role does the external power have to play to create control, and at what point is the relationship one only of influence, not of control?

As events of the last three decades suggest, the United States hardly controls the policies of even its closest allies. Sharp diagreements of policy are represented by the unsuccessful efforts of successive American administrations to get the Europeans to open their markets to American farm products, to induce the Japanese to open their markets to a wider range of American products, or to persuade the government in Israel to accept American views on settlement of the Palestinian problem. Even in other states where American control is alleged to be more effective—in Latin America, the Philippines, or South Korea, for example—there is ample evidence to suggest that national independence on vital issues is not always subject to American control.

That the United States has influence on policies in many countries is quite clear. But that does not constitute either imperialism or neoimperialism.

If influence is defined as the capability to have an impact on the direction of the policies of other governments, then American influence on many countries abounds. But, then, many other countries have a profound influence on American policies, too. That is interdependence, not neoimperialism, for in an imperialist or neoimperialist relationship, the influence is overwhelmingly one way.

There are patterns of spheres of influence among great powers, however, and the concept of spheres of influence describes relationships that may or may not include classical empire or neoimperialism.[36] The Yalta and Potsdam agreements at the end of World War II generally recognized postwar spheres of influence among victorious powers in which each was to be dominant in specified geographical areas of the world through whatever means they chose to use. The agreements hardly prevented them from promoting their own influence in the spheres of others. In any case, a sphere of influence is not usually a rigid, neatly defined, and organized structure, but it is an area in which a great power is acknowledged by others to be free to exercise as much influence on the policies of other countries in the sphere as it can, whatever these other countries may think about it.

Clearly, many regard imperialism, neoimperialism, or spheres of influence as immoral, unjust, and illegal in any form. As concepts of international behavior and of foreign policy, however, they remain deeply embedded in the experience and thought of leaders.

GEOPOLITICS

The belief that the connection between politics and geography is an important one is at least as old as Aristotle and as new as the work of Harold and Margaret Sprout, who have emphasized the relevance of humanity's relationship with the entire physical environment.[37]

Admiral Alfred Thayer Mahan, contemplating a nineteenth-century world based so heavily on sea power, suggested that control of the seas was fundamental to great-power status for countries aspiring to it.[38] Halford Mackinder developed the "heartland theory" around the view that the great Eurasian land mass was the "pivot area" of the world's politics and that the power who controlled this land mass commands the world.[39] In the 1920s, Karl Haushofer, a retired German army officer, developed the doctrine that great nations had a need to expand their frontiers to provide for raw materials, industry, markets, and population growth. *Lebensraum*, a doctrine that came to play a major part in Nazi policies in Germany under Adolph Hitler,[40] was an outgrowth of that theory. Counterposed to the heartland theory was the rimland theory offered by Nicholas Spykman, who suggested that the rimlands around the Eurasian land mass were essential to the control of Eurasia and thus the world.[41]

An extension of geopolitical thinking brought about by new technology was reflected in theories of air power, developed by such individuals as Guilio Douhet and General Billy Mitchell and first adopted in the twentieth century by the Germans prior to World War II.[42] The view that the country that controlled the air controlled the land has advanced into the space age in which the belief that the country that controls space or at least is capable of exploiting it successfully can control the world. In their work on the relationship between people and their entire environment the Sprouts state their belief that political accomplishment is limited by geographic configuration and the distribution and arrangement of phenomena over the earth's surface.[43]

The continuing relevance of geopolitical thinking to contemporary foreign policy can be seen from a few examples. The energy crisis of the 1970s once again highlighted the importance of those geographical areas in which huge deposits of oil are to be found. This has contributed to the complex and disputed politics of the Middle East since the 1940s and was a factor in the Carter Doctrine proposed by the former president, which drew a line of American national interest in the Persian Gulf region. Much of American foreign policy toward Latin America in the last three decades has centered on the removal of Soviet influence from countries close to the United States, and the single most threatening episode of the cold war, the Cuban missile crisis, resulted, in part, from Soviet attempts to use Cuba as a missile base against the United States. Efforts to maintain such key facilities as the Panama and Suez Canals emphasize the importance of geographical factors. Lest contemporary Americans think that the sea-power doctrines of Mahan are obsolete, they should examine the defense budget for expenditures on nuclear-powered Trident missile submarines and the vital role of the SLBMs in American strategic military thinking.

The cold war and the American doctrine of containment may be viewed as a modern clash of the heartland and rimland theories. The Soviet Union controls a substantial part of the Eurasian land mass, but in turn is contained around its rim by NATO in the West, the United States in the Middle East and Southwest Asia, China in the South, and American contacts with Japan, the Philippines, and South Korea in the East.

The geopolitical perspective remains, therefore, one of considerable importance and utility in creating the framework of beliefs that guide and motivate policy makers.

Beyond these five broad frameworks additional powerful ideas motivate national behavior. Some of these will be examined in the next chapters.

NOTES

[1] Zbigniew Brzezinski, *Power and Principle* (New York: Farrar, Straus & Giroux, 1983), pp. 522–24.

[2] Hans Morgenthau, *Politics Among Nations*, 5th ed., rev. (New York: Alfred A. Knopf, 1978), pp. 4–15, 29–38.

[3] Ibid., pp. 173–228.

[4] Inis L. Claude, Jr., *Power and International Relations* (New York: Random House, 1962), pp. 13–39.

[5] Robert Dahl, "The Concept of Power," *Behavioral Science* 2 (1957), 201–15.

[6] Karl Deutsch, *The Analysis of International Relations* (Englewood Cliffs, N.J.: Prentice-Hall, 1968), pp. 21–39; Morgenthau, *Politics Among Nations*, pp. 117–54.

[7] Morton Kaplan, *Systems and Process in International Politics* (New York: John Wiley, 1962), pp. 22–23.

[8] Kaplan, *Systems and Process*, pp. 45–58; Kenneth Waltz, *Theory of International Relations* (Reading, Mass.: Addison-Wesley Publishing Co., 1979), pp. 204–9; Karl W. Deutsch and J. David Singer, "Multipolar Power Systems and International Stability," *World Politics* 16 (1964), 390–406.

[9] Kaplan, *Systems and Process*, pp. 45–58.

[10] Waltz, *Theory of International Relations*, pp. 204–9.

[11] Deutsch and Singer, "Multipolar Power Systems."

[12] Henry Kissinger, *White House Years* (Boston: Little, Brown & Company, 1979), pp. 67–68; Kissinger, *American Foreign Policy*, 3rd ed. (New York: W. W. Norton & Company, 1977), pp. 59–90; Charles W. Kegley and Eugene R. Wittkopf, *World Politics: Trend and Transformation* (New York: St. Martin's Press, 1981), p. 396.

[13] Kissinger, *American Foreign Policy*, pp. 53–54.

[14] Richard Rosencrance, "Bipolarity, Multipolarity, and the Future," *Journal of Conflict Resolution* 10 (1966), 314–27.

[15] Harold and Margaret Sprout, *The Ecological Perspective on Human Affairs with Special Reference to International Politics* (Princeton, N.J.: Princeton University Press, 1965), p. 27; Sprout and Sprout, *The Context of Environmental Politics: Unfinished Business for America's Third Century* (Lexington: University Press of Kentucky, 1978), pp. 107–24; Richard W. Sterling, *Macropolitics* (New York: Alfred A. Knopf, 1974), pp. 3–7.

[16] David Easton, *A Framework for Political Analysis* (Englewood Cliffs, N.J.: Prentice-Hall, 1965), pp. 25–50.

[17] James A. Nathan and James K. Oliver, *United States Foreign Policy and World Order*, 2nd ed. (Boston: Little, Brown & Company, 1981), pp. 57–58.

[18] Kissinger, *White House Years*, p. 115.

[19] Ibid.

[20] Ibid., p. 195.

[21] Alexander Dallin and Gail W. Lapidus, "Reagan and the Russians: United States Policy Toward the Soviet Union and Eastern Europe," in Kenneth A. Oye, Robert J. Lieber, and Donald Rothchild, *Eagle Defiant: United States Foreign Policy in the 1980s* (Boston: Little, Brown & Company, 1983), pp. 204–5.

[22] Theodore A. Couloumbis and James H. Wolfe, *Introduction to International Relations: Power and Justice*, 2nd ed. (Englewood Cliffs, N.J.: Prentice-Hall, 1982), pp. 9–11, 243; Morgenthau, *Politics Among Nations*, pp. 3, 39–41.

[23] Robert O. Keohane and Joseph S. Nye, Jr., *Power and Interdependence* (Boston: Little, Brown & Company, 1977), p. 8.

[24] Ibid., p. 9.

[25] Kegley and Wittkopf, *World Politics*, p. 487.

[26] Ibid., p. 488.

[27] Waltz, *Theory of International Relations*, pp. 156–60.

[28] Allan Riding, "The Central American Quagmire," *Foreign Affairs* 61: 640–41.

[29] Sterling, *Macropolitics*, p. 204.

[30] Ibid., p. 206.

[31] Ibid., p. 230.

[32] Waltz, *Theory of International Relations*, p. 26.

[33] Ibid., pp. 26–27.

[34] Ibid., p. 33.

35 Sterling, *Macropolitics*, p. 204.

36 Morgenthau, *Politics Among Nations*, pp. 56–57, 173.

37 James E. Dougherty and Robert L. Pfaltzgraff, *Contending Theories of International Relations* (J. B. Lippincott Co., 1971), pp. 57–63.

38 Ibid., pp. 50–52; Alfred Thayer Mahan, *The Influence of Seapower Upon History* (Boston: Little, Brown & Company, 1897).

39 Dougherty and Pfaltzgraff, *Contending Theories*, pp. 52–54; Harold Mackinder, "The Geographical Pivot of History," *Geographic Journal* 23 (April 1904).

40 Dougherty and Pfaltzgraff, *Contending Theories*, pp. 56–57.

41 Ibid., pp. 72–74; Nicholas J. Spykman, *American Strategy in World Politics: The United States and the Balance of Power* (New York: Harcourt, Brace and Co., 1942).

42 Robert E. Osgood, "The Expansion of Force," in Robert J. Art and Kenneth W. Waltz, *The Use of Force* (Boston: Little, Brown & Company, 1971), pp. 51–52; Roger Hilsman, *To Govern America* (New York: Harper & Row, Publishers, 1977), p. 479.

43 Dougherty and Pfaltzgraff, *Contending Theories*, p. 59.

CHAPTER TWELVE
DRIVING FORCES

Other broad ideas and ideologies have shaped the behavior of people and states and their foreign policies. In the twentieth century they have influenced American foreign policy because they have motivated the American people or because they have activated other peoples around the world to adopt either cooperative or conflicting postures toward the United States.

Marxism-Leninism and capitalism offer conflicting conceptions of how human beings should organize their lives, their economies, and their governments, each providing the impetus to industrialism and modernization. The ideals of nationalism have driven peoples to extraordinary efforts to create states and to promote their national interests. Ideas of transnationalism, world community, and world government have evolved from the expansions of linkages among countries. Human aspirations for democracy, liberty, equality, justice have moved peoples and their leaders to intense activity, but at the same time the appeals of authoritarianism and messianism have been strong in many places.

Within the United States sets of ideas of how to operate a democratic system—liberalism and conservatism—have provided differing views of how to govern America and how to relate to the rest of the world.

A brief review of these powerful ideas is in order.

MARXISM-LENINISM

Marxism-Leninism is both a theory of power and an ideology for those who believe it. The difference is that a theory is a hypothesis or model purporting to explain behavior. Ideology carries with it the conviction that the hypothesis and the specific beliefs it implies are correct.

In his major works, *Capital* and *The Communist Manifesto,* Karl Marx argued that private property led to class divisions between those who owned and controlled it and those who did not.[1] He further argued that ownership of property inevitably led to the exploitation by the ownership class of the nonownership class, thereby establishing class conflict and class warfare in which the working class would eventually triumph. Marxism implied that in countries where private capital existed the governments were merely the tools of the capitalist class and would serve to protect the interests of those who owned property.

To the basic views of Marx, Lenin added an international element explaining how and why capitalist countries behaved in the world and developed their particular foreign policies. Based strongly on the views of imperialism developed by Joseph Hobson, Lenin's argument was that it was in the nature of capitalist societies to produce more than they could consume, necessitating the acquisition of foreign markets and access to raw materials unavailable at home.[2] This necessity was the basis for imperialism, for the establishment of colonial empires, and for the conflict among capitalist countries over colonies.

Thus the basic view of Marxism-Leninism is that the foreign policy of capitalist states is based on economic necessity and that economic determinism is the most powerful factor in explaining foreign policy, especially policies of capitalist states.

It must be noted that as an explanation of imperialism, Marxism-Leninism fails to deal with the fact that imperialism existed long before the development of capitalism and that it continues to exist long after the classical empires have all disappeared, with the exception, ironically, of the Soviet empire in Eastern and Central Europe. As a theory of foreign policy, it has been adapted several times in the twentieth century into theories of neoimperialism, i.e., the maintenance of economic influence and domination of former colonies by means of economic dominance/dependence relationships. Even here, unless definitions are stretched to fit the circumstances, the Marxist-Leninist views of the bases of foreign-policy behavior of capitalist states leave sizeable gaps in explanation, for in 1982 former colonies and other newer, developing nations had accumulated some $700 billion in debt to capitalist states that had lent them the money. In addition, international agencies, consisting of many former colonial powers, had provided billions in additional financing to many countries. The situation at least raised questions about who was exploiting whom.

Despite the problems with Marxism-Leninism as a theory of imperialism, however, many analysts feel that it offers a hypothetical model of foreign policy that has some validity through its insistence on economic determinism as a motive force in foreign policy. Marxism-Leninism, i.e., communism, thus tends to explain the causes of war as the consequences of capitalist imperialist tendencies. From the standpoint of American foreign policy in the last fifty years, however, several elements of Communist doctrine also posed aggressive challenges to American interests. First, the doctrine predicts and supports Communist revolutions throughout the world against capitalist interests and capitalist countries, viewing the triumph of communism as the inevitable wave of history. In the post-World War II period this doctrine has led to the encouragement and support of "wars of liberation" by the Soviet Union in many parts of the world. The appeal of the doctrine itself to masses of people throughout the world has posed a number of policy problems and crises for American foreign policy. The poor, who constitute more than half of the world's population, have found powerful incentives to believe in a system that promises to provide equal resources, an end to exploitation by a few oligarchs, and a voice in their own lives. Although some contemporary analysts believe that Communist-Socialist ideology has lost its appeal and that the Soviet model is no longer a powerful attraction, challenges posed by dedicated Marxist-Leninists continue to face the United States in Central America, Asia, and Africa. For example, since 1981 the Reagan administration has confronted a challenge from the Communist-led Sandinista government in Nicaragua, which according to the administration, has fomented revolution in El Salvador with the aid of Fidel Castro of Cuba and the Soviet Union. Cuban and Soviet aid and advisers, it is claimed, are supporting and encouraging the Sandinista government in the attempt to establish Communist strongholds in Central America.

In the poverty, injustice, and inequality of many Third and Fourth World countries, Soviet-supported revolutionary forces have exploited conditions, often challenging regimes supported by the United States. The Soviet success rate in some of these countries is not perfect, but one of the primary challenges facing American foreign policy since 1945 has been how best to deal with the turbulent expectations of less developed countries, promote political order, and contain Soviet influence, all at the same time. As with the Soviets, the American record is a mixture of success and failure.

Thus Marxism-Leninism remains a major political, spiritual, and ideological challenge to the United States, quite apart from Soviet behavior in the world in behalf of the national interest of the Soviet Union and of its status as a superpower.

CAPITALISM

The idea that property, materials, and labor can be combined by private individuals to produce goods that may be sold at a profit is the basis of capitalism.[3] Beyond this basic idea, the view that capital itself is a product and that profit should be used to produce additional profit either through rent or through further investment produced the basic theory on which many nation-states of the Western world developed in the modern era.

Although capitalist theory is vague on foreign policy, a few generalizations appear possible. Those who own the means of production and distribution in capitalist societies are likely to believe in a government that seeks (1) to protect property interests domestically, (2) to protect American business from attacks by pirates or by other states, (3) to support capitalist interests in developing new markets and acquiring needed raw materials from foreign sources, (4) to facilitate establishment of American business interests abroad, and (5) to protect those business interests once established. In short, private interests seek security and support for their business goals. They have also supported the doctrine of free trade throughout the world—the concept that all states should remove barriers to each others' products.

Another place where the analyst may look for elements of capitalist theory is in the theory of the firm. The concept that in an environment in which it is permitted, the growth, expansion, and merger of firms into ever larger institutions is inevitable and desirable has not only resulted in the formation of gigantic conglomerates but has also led to the evolution of new forms of corporate organization, such as the multinational or transnational corporation.[4]

The development of these new forms has a decided foreign-policy content. It requires that the government negotiate agreements with other states permitting multinational corporations to operate in a foreign environment and that it protect American interests in those countries.

Another theoretical impulse in capitalism has to do with the internationalization of capital and the development of a global monetary system in which American capitalist interests may lend money and affect the values of money from country to country. With large capital resources, capitalist interests are prepared and eager to lend money to foreign states, individuals, and corporations and to attract foreign investments to American banks at the same time. In addition, those controlling capital are highly interested in the maintenance of a stable international monetary and exchange-rate system that can establish the precise value of currencies at any given moment. Finally, capitalist interests have been willing to cooperate in multilateral international organizations with the capability of providing temporary and long-term financial support for other states. Such agencies as the International Monetary Fund and the World Bank are engaged in this type of activity.

To be sure, these efforts have sometimes been regarded as neoimperialistic by critics of capitalism, but they have provided financial resources for many countries seeking to develop their own economies.

In any case, capitalist theory has many foreign-policy implications. An underlying principle is that states should establish and pursue politico-economic systems that embody the free-enterprise principle—the idea that private businesses and entrepreneurs, operating with the private profit motive, constitute the most efficient and productive means to develop economic resources, create wealth, and produce an improved standard of living for the people. It rejects the Marxist-Leninist view that the state should own, control, and develop the economic system of a country.

NATIONALISM

Like so many of the concepts we have examined, nationalism has been used to describe a number of attitudes, activities, and policies of states. As a theory that seeks to explain foreign policy, however, it has some identifiable features. First of all, a nation is a group of people who think of themselves as a nation seeking to have or to maintain a state, and nationalism can be defined as the process of doing so.[5] The individual's commitment to the nation-state, sometimes called patriotism, is another element of nationalism.[6] Specific goals of the group are said to be based on national interest, and these goals include foreign policy.

Some scholars have contended that the nation-state is the largest political unit to which people give their loyalty and that service to the national interest is the highest possible ethic.[7]

In the last two centuries the drive of groups to establish and maintain an independent, sovereign nation-state has been among the most common and the most powerful impulses operative in world politics. To do so has often involved foreign policy—wars of independence, negotiated decolonization, separation from other states. Not infrequently nationalism has led to a sense of national destiny that implies expansion or trade or empire.

Nationalism, in all of its ramifications, thereby provides a theoretical explanation of some of the behavior and foreign policies of states. The many goals of a national state, as they are defined and implemented by policy makers, are based on the imperatives of nationalism—the safeguarding, prosperity, and development of the state.

TRANSNATIONALISM AND INTEGRATION

A world in which nation-states are no longer the primary objects of loyalty of people, in which commitment evolves toward some form of political organization beyond the nation-state, is a model of limited but growing force.[8] Based on the idea of expanding integration among peoples into larger political units, transnationalism suggests that the process of social organization will lead to one of the following: (1) the merger of two or more separate states, (2) the formation of regional groups of states sharing political and economic functions, (3) the development of a capability to act in common for common purposes, and (4) the ultimate unification of the separate peoples.

At another level transnationalism is also used to describe the expanding interlinkages among states, peoples, and other institutions without the prospect of merger, amalgamation, or unification of institutions and peoples.

WORLD COMMUNITY/WORLD GOVERNMENT

The evolution of peoples, states, and regions into one world community is envisioned by those who regard the growing number of international organizations as a prelude to world government.[9] The assumption that a world community supporting a world government is the most stable assurance of world order and the assumption that such a result will evolve offer another theoretical model to explain foreign policies. In reality, no contemporary government actively pursues foreign policies with world government in mind, but this does not preclude the possibility that it may one day become a goal of national leaders. Nor does it preclude the possibility that the present and future policies of governments to support international institutions will *not* inexorably lead toward the gradual creation of a sense of world community and citizenship among peoples, or the foundations of institutions that can be expanded to contain features of world government.

Organizations such as IMF, IBRD, and GATT already constitute significant elements of a world order capable of exercising governmental-type functions.

In the final analysis, this theory would appear not to explain much about foreign policy or to occupy the serious attention of most policy makers. However, it provides another set of ideas that could influence leaders of the future.

LIBERALISM AND CONSERVATISM

Somewhat more limited in scope are two sets of ideas that relate to American political attitudes—liberalism and conservatism. Although the meaning of the two terms is imprecise and changes from time to time, they are used to identify contemporary political attitudes or philosophies of government.

In general, liberalism includes such attitudes as the following: a belief in the use of the national government to identify and solve major national problems, a willingness to permit the use of deficit financing to support social programs, a belief in rapid change of existing conditions, a belief in the regulation of private interests in the public interest, a commitment to a broad interpretation of individual civil rights and liberties, and a sense of egalitarianism.[10]

Broadly speaking, conservatism in the United States in the twentieth century has implied the following: a mistrust of extensive, centralized activity by the national government; a belief in the efficacy of decentralized government and in the role of state and local governments; a commitment to the principle of balanced budgets; a belief in free enterprise with a minimum of government regulation; a sense of elitism and meritocracy.[11]

In terms of foreign policy, there have been some ironic transfers in beliefs between liberals and conservatives in the past fifty years. During the period from the 1930s to 1968 liberals tended to (1) support a role of strong American leadership in the international community, (2) emphasize the need for a buildup of American military power, and (3) urge the importance of a global balance of power against the Axis powers and then the Soviet Union. In this sense liberals tended to support increased military budgets, a commitment to defend Europe, and a broad commitment to Asia.

For some of this period conservatives tended to be isolationist, i.e., wishing to keep the United States aloof from participation in European or global affairs. Many tended to oppose increased military spending, increased cold war commitments to Europe, President Truman's commitment to Korea, and American support of the emerging Third World.

Ironically, Democratic liberal presidents Franklin Roosevelt, Harry Truman, John Kennedy, and Lyndon Johnson built American military power and the systems of alliances that were designed to contain foreign powers, first the German-Italian-Japanese Axis powers, and then the Soviet Union and Communist China.

During the period of the cold war, conservatives became more anti-Communist, hard-line, and militarily supportive, while many liberals became less confrontational, less committed to large defense budgets, and more interested in seeking accommodation with the Soviet Union. The watershed of liberal change came during the Vietnam War, when many younger Americans, supporting the so-called New Left, provided the strength for the challenge to liberal assumptions by Senator Eugene McCarthy in his 1968 campaign for the presidential nomination. The process propelled Senator George McGovern into the Democratic nomination in 1972 in what came to be a major redefinition of liberal principles of foreign policy.

In the meantime, many conservatives were becoming more hard-line toward the Soviet Union, although, again ironically, it was a conservative president, Richard Nixon, who created a policy of détente (relaxation of tensions) with the Soviet Union and made the first major contacts with the government of Red China since 1949.

Thus the use of contemporary liberal or conservative thinking as a reliable model of foreign policy is troublesome. Not only is it difficult to define the terms with precision, but even where that is possible, liberals and conservatives have sometimes exchanged positions in given periods. A further complication: Many liberals and conservatives have *shared* other beliefs and attitudes about foreign policy. Both have supported economic-aid and trade programs, the doctrine of free trade, and participation in global economic organizations. Both have supported cultural-exchange programs. Both have occasionally supported the use of economic sanctions against the Soviet Union.

How then can we summarize the important foreign-policy concepts implicit in the two sets of ideas? In the 1980s liberals tend to take a more conciliatory posture toward the Soviet Union with less emphasis on military power, especially nuclear-weapon power. Conservatives tend to be more confrontational in their perceptions of the Soviet threat and more committed to a large military establishment. These generalizations risk overlooking exceptions and subtleties. To some extent, however, they were present in the presidential campaign of 1980 and contributed to the victory by conservative Ronald Reagan over a more liberal Jimmy Carter.

As theoretical guides to or descriptions of decision making, they may be less useful for the student than some others we have discussed. Yet liberalism and conservatism, as defined at any specific time, are elements of some significance in understanding foreign policy and the decision-making process. They are one of the bases of American politics, and the differences between them provide the outlines of the political debates over the definition of foreign policy.

DEMOCRACY

The belief that the sovereign power of a state should lie with the people and that they, through representative institutions, should govern themselves is the essence of democracy.[12] It implies the existence of free speech and free press, free elections, separation and balance of governmental powers, politics by consensus, and the sense that the people predominate over the state.

Ever since Woodrow Wilson argued that World War I was waged to "make the world safe for democracy" the impulse of leaders of democratic countries to promote democracy in other countries has been a source of American foreign policy and an element in the value systems of leaders. Part of the American political creed has been the belief that democracy in conjunction with capitalism is the preferable model for political development throughout the world.

In practice American foreign policy has accommodated to states that reject democracy or practice it imperfectly. Yet the encouragement of democratic institutions and free enterprise remains the model the United States urges upon others. As recently as the conference of twenty-two Third World countries at Cancun, Mexico, in 1981 President Ronald Reagan urged the adoption of this model upon other countries, and American policy toward Poland in the 1980s encouraged the increased democratization of that country through freedom for the Solidarity labor movement.

Clearly, the importance of democratic ideals as part of the belief system of leaders cannot be ignored.

AUTHORITARIANISM

In contrast to the principles of democracy is the model of authoritarianism.[13] From Plato to Chernenko, it has been argued that populations require strong, directive, expert leadership from the top. Various forms of authoritarian rule in history provide examples of the variety of possibilities within the model. Monarchy, civilian or military dictatorship, totalitarianism, or long-term one-party control may still be found in the 1980s in different parts of the world. As a model, authoritarianism may seem less related to foreign policy than to internal politics. In the modern world, however, American foreign policy may accommodate or even encourage authoritarian regimes in countries that are part of the American global-alliance system, and popular reaction against authoritarian regimes may affect American interests. For example, the United States supported for several decades the authoritarian regime of the Shah of Iran, and also supported a series of authoritarian elements in South Vietnam. The revolution in Iran was directed almost as much against the United States as it was against the shah, and in Vietnam massive American support failed to sustain a regime in Saigon that was regarded as unacceptable by sizeable portions of the population.

Thus, even acceptance of and acquiescence to authoritarian regimes may not always work to sustain American interests. In some cases it can be argued that American policy has promoted creation of regimes that are authoritarian as long as they cooperate with American policy. There are some indications that the Nixon administration did not discourage the establishment of martial law and authoritarian rule in the Philippines by Ferdinand Marcos in 1972.[14]

Although the authoritarian model of power has not usually affected American policy makers' views in terms of the United States, it may have been a source of policy making in regard to American interests elsewhere in the world.

LIBERTY, EQUALITY, AND SELF-DETERMINATION

Certain single ideas may be relevant in devising foreign policies, either because they have particular intrinsic appeal to human beings elsewhere and thus have policy utility, or because they form part of the American belief system and require that American policies be justified in their terms. In themselves they do not constitute models or theories of policy making, nor are they full-blown ideologies. However, they are independent, objective ideas that can justify policies and even create an increased receptivity abroad to particular foreign policies. Some writers include them as intrinsic elements of democracy. Even in places where democratic institutions may not exist or have much contemporary appeal, the ideals embodied in liberty, equality, and self-determination are powerful elements in many cultures.

Liberty, at the very least, suggests the idea of political freedom of individuals to think, speak and act politically in their own societies. More broadly, it also means the freedom of individuals to fulfill their personal ambitions and to express themselves freely as nonpolitical individuals.

A sense of equality in a world of cultures in which inequality has been the rule has also had a powerful appeal in the twentieth century. Beyond the ideal of personal equality, the growing desire for national equality has been a powerful impetus to the behavior of many states in the post-World War II world.

A third idea with powerful force in this century has been that of self-determination. As part of Woodrow Wilson's fourteen points, self-determination was a battle cry to peoples who wanted their countries to be free and independent of foreign control.

It was a rallying cry behind the anticolonial movement of the last forty years and a powerful argument in American foreign policy.

These three ideals, singly or together, have not been absent from the minds of policy makers who shared the ideals and wanted others to enjoy them. At the very least leaders sought to use them to legitimize American foreign policy. This is not to suggest that all policy makers are do-gooders or base all American policies on such ideals. In many cases, however, American policy has been shaped with these ideals in the forefront. The League of Nations, the United Nations, the Universal Declaration of Human Rights are just a few of the specific foreign policies advocated by Americans in this century formed, in part, on idealist sentiment and conviction.

MESSIANISM

The desire to expand, proselytize, and disseminate one's own religion, philosophy, form of government, form of economy, and prestige is as old as human organizations. It has often led to imperialism of a cultural as well as a military-economic nature, and although it is hardly a developed theory or model, it is a demonstrable element in the motivation of some states. Indeed, it has been part of the American policy in the past. From "manifest destiny" to the demand in the late nineteenth century for American control over the entire Western Hemisphere, messianism has been a force of some consequence. Even Wilson's view that the First World War was to "make the world safe for democracy" had its element of national, cultural, and political evangelism.

The impulse to make the world just like us implies the belief that our way is not only superior to the ways of others but that it is indispensable to the perfection of human society.

The Vietnam experience was far more complicated than an exercise in messianism, but surely, the desire to build a society in the South based on the American model contained elements of it.

Even where messianism may be absent from American motives in foreign policy, its presence in other states may affect American foreign policy. The declared intent of Marxism-Leninism and the rulers of the Soviet Union to create a Communist world or the policy of Adolph Hitler to impose membership in the Third Reich upon the peoples of Europe whether they wished it or not are major examples of messianism that posed confrontations with American policy.

Thus, as an impulse that may color the making of foreign policy, messianism should be recognized.

SUMMARY

The broad theories, ideologies, concepts, and ideas examined in this chapter constitute significant parts of the belief systems of leaders. It is impossible to know, of course, the exact weight of any one of them or their exact mixture in the minds of individuals. However, many of them can be found in policies adopted by the United States in this century and in the justifications of those policies offered by decision makers.

From the standpont of present and future American foreign policy, it is essential to try to understand more fully how leaders integrate these ideas into their perceptions of reality and into their judgments about how the United States should respond. To be sure, as we shall see in the next chapter, the policy-making process often involves a clash of views among leaders about the existence of problems, the costs of solving them, and the virtues of alternative options. More important, it is essential that policy makers themselves recognize the need to coordinate and to orchestrate the many different perspectives that confront them and forge those perspectives into workable, pragmatic, and principled tools for the management of American affairs abroad.

States are not yet willing to abandon the power concepts of realism, even as they fitfully evolve a system based on idealism and interdependence. Indeed, American foreign policy in the last four decades has been a mixture of all three perspectives, buttressed by the force of such powerful ideas as democracy, nationalism, self-determination, liberty, equality, and capitalism. Some American policy has also been based on convictions grounded in geopolitics, spheres of influence, transnationalism, and world community. American liberalism and conservatism, despite the fluctuations in their foreign-policy content, have also afforded policy guidelines based, in part, on the imperatives of electoral politics. American leaders have had to respond to the appeals and successes of Marxism-Leninism, imperialism, and authoritarianism, and they have sometimes been carried away with the bravado of messianism.

The choice of beliefs by individual leaders comprises an important part of the politics of making foreign policy and conducting foreign relations. Although it is sometimes alleged that most policy makers share the same essential beliefs, the evidence to which we will refer in the next chapter dealing with the politics of the decision-making process indicates that policy makers bring to the process sharply different interpretations of problems, solutions, and options based on important differences of beliefs.

In the final analysis, the beliefs of policy makers play an important part in the making of policy.

NOTES

[1] James E. Dougherty and Robert L. Pfaltzgraff, Jr., *Contending Theories of International Relations* (Philadelphia: J. B. Lippincott Co., 1971), pp. 172–76.

[2] Ibid., pp. 176–81.

[3] David Edwards, *The American Political Experience*, 2nd ed., (Englewood Cliffs, N.J.: Prentice-Hall, 1982), pp. 509–14; Adam Smith, *The Wealth of Nations*, ed. Edwin Cannan (New York: Modern Library, 1937).

[4] Joan Edelman Spero, *The Politics of International Economic Relations* (New York: St. Martin's Press, 1977), pp. 88–115.

[5] Rupert Emerson, *From Empire to Nation* (Boston: Beacon Press, 1960), p. 102.

[6] Leonard Doob, *Patriotism and Nationalism: Their Psychological Foundations* (New Haven: Yale University Press, 1964), pp. 114–46; Roger Hilsman, *The Crouching Future* (Garden City, N.Y.: Doubleday and Co., 1975), pp. 228–83; Louis Snyder, *The Meaning of Nationalism* (New York: Greenwood Press, 1968), p. 160.

[7] Emerson, *From Empire to Nation*, pp. 95–96.

[8] Robert Keohane and Joseph S. Nye, Jr., "Transnational Relations: An Introduction," in Robert Keohane and Joseph S. Nye, Jr., eds, *Transnational Relations and World Politics* (Cambridge, Mass.: Harvard University Press, 1972), pp. xii–xvi; Karl W. Deutsch et al., *Political Community and the North Atlantic Area*, (Princeton, N.J.: Princeton University Press, 1957); Ernst Haas, *Beyond the Nation-State* (Stanford, Calif.: Stanford University Press, 1958).

⁹ Inis L. Claude, Jr., *Power and International Relations* (New York: Random House, 1962), pp. 205–42; Hans Morgenthau, *Politics Among Nations*, 5th ed., rev. (New York: Alfred A. Knopf, 1973), pp. 499–525.

¹⁰ Edwards, *American Political Experience*, pp. 131–34.

¹¹ Ibid.

¹² Edwards, *American Political Experience*, pp. 10, 630–34; Hilsman, *To Govern America* (New York: Harper & Row, Publishers, 1977), pp. 19–30.

¹³ Theodore A. Couloumbis and James H. Wolfe, *Introduction to International Relations: Power and Justice*, 2nd ed. (Englewood Cliffs, N.J.: Prentice-Hall, 1982), pp. 83–84; Morgenthau, *Politics Among Nations*, pp. 268–69.

¹⁴ Primitivo Mijores, *The Conjugal Dictatorship of Ferdinand and Imelda Marcos I*, cited in Carl H. Lande, "Authoritarian Rule in the Philippines: Some Critical Views," a review article, *Pacific Affairs*, 55: 80–93. Mijores, portraying himself as a former confidant of Imelda Marcos, reports that she told him of a telephone conversation between Ferdinand Marcos and President Richard Nixon in which Nixon was alleged to have given his personal blessing to the imposition of martial law, supposedly because Nixon might find a need for a model he could adopt later in the United States.

CHAPTER THIRTEEN
MODELS OF POLICY
SOURCES

The broad theoretical and philosophical frameworks, ideas, and ideologies considered in the previous chapters point to large and powerful forces that shape the thinking of policy makers. In recent years research has provided new insights into the policy process that focus on a smaller base—the individual and the decision-making group. Still other research has probed somewhat more comprehensive sources of policy: the distribution of power within the state and the effects of the characteristics of states, particularly large ones. The extent to which the findings of this research have become intellectual guideposts to policy making is not easily determined. However, new knowledge flowing from it cannot be easily dismissed by policy makers seeking more effective and rational ways to develop effective foreign policy or by scholars trying to understand the process. Informed observers have identified all four levels of activity—the individual, the decision-making group, competing national power centers, and the nature of the state—as important sources of national behavior in foreign policy.

One recent study of the determinants of foreign policy surveyed a number of experts in the field of foreign policy to attempt to identify the major sources of American foreign policy and foreign relations. Lloyd Jensen surveyed 43 newspaper and radio correspondents based in Washington, New York, and Boston; 48 officials from the State Department; and 41 from the Defense Department.[1] Seventy percent of the 171 respondents regarded the national power capabilities of the United States as a very important factor in American policy. In the mid-to-upper 40 percent range were such other factors as the internal economic and political situation; the behavior of other states; and the personality of leaders. Ranked as somewhat less important factors were ideology, the decision-making structure, and the country's historical tradition.

Whatever the validity of the attitudes of Jensen's respondents, all four levels of analysis are reflected in the beliefs of informed observers: personality, the decision-making structure, the internal power distribution, and the nature of states. The personalities of presidents, the determination of premises and policies by leaders within the administration, the interests of powerful groups, and the implications of America's size and power since the 1940s all contributed to American policies. While other observers might disagree with the emphasis of Jensen's respondents on the relative importance of the factors they identified, the fact that they perceived the importance of several causes of policy suggests how essential is modern research into the sources of policy.

Let us begin by focusing on the individual.

IDIOSYNCRATIC AND PSYCHOPOLITICAL MODELS

In early August 1974 Richard Nixon considered placing the 82nd Airborne Division around the White House to protect the president. Under intense stress from the Watergate investigations and the move in Congress for impeachment, Nixon had been boasting about his authority to order a nuclear strike within twenty minutes. Discreetly, Defense Secretary James Schlesinger ordered the military not to act on nuclear-strike orders even if they came from the president.[2]

Few events in American history have so sharply underscored the importance of personality factors in the decision-making process or have come so close to confirming the fears of Americans and others throughout the world since the beginning of the nuclear age that one day, under immense personal stress, an emotionally unstable leader might plunge the world into nuclear catastrophe.

The image of a madman in control in the White House or in the Kremlin pushing a button or ordering nuclear attack has haunted people for almost forty years. Fortunately, the image has not yet become reality, and the possibility remains remote, although one study suggests that in the last four hundred years at least seventy-five heads of state have been emotionally disturbed while they exercised power.[3] To be sure, it can be argued that this is a small percentage of the thousands of individuals who have governed countries in the last four centuries and that the proportion of mentally disturbed leaders is no greater than that in the general population and is probably less. Further, except in hereditary monarchies, where the crown is automatically conferred upon kings, the political path to power in most countries usually screens out all but the emotionally stable and strong individuals, those capable of acquiring and handling awesome responsibility.

The study of the role of personality in the policy process is complicated by the fact that psychology itself is still a developing science and much remains unknown about human personality and its sources. Second, the study of the personality of leaders suffers from the fact that it is generally impossible to conduct personal studies, necessitating the use of secondary sources. Third, even where personality types among leaders have been identified, there is a lack of theory and evidence to demonstrate the connection between the psychology of the decision makers and the ultimate policies they select. With these reservations in mind, a brief review of some of the efforts in the field will be helpful.

Individual Studies

Starting with the ground-breaking work of Harold Lasswell in the 1930s, the study of psychological and personality factors among decision makers has attracted increasing attention. According to Lasswell, the political personality pursues power as a means of compensation against deprivation. "Power is expected to overcome low estimates of the self, by changing either the traits of the self or the environment in which it functions," writes Lasswell.[4] Thus policies advocated by such a leader may be designed to achieve these goals.

Following Lasswell's work, several other studies concentrated on particular leaders from a psychological perspective—John Foster Dulles, Woodrow Wilson, America's first Secretary of Defense James Forrestal, John Kennedy, Lyndon Johnson, Henry Kissinger, and Richard Nixon. The psychological theme running through these works was the premise that personality characteristics, shaped by childhood experiences and by socialization, produced adult personalities who responded to foreign-policy crises in particular and possibly dangerous ways. Dulles and Wilson were said to have become inflexible in their images and attitudes and incapable of reasonable compromise.[5] Forrestal, it is contended, became paranoid, seeing enemies all around him.[6] Kennedy and Johnson were each allegedly compensating for an incomplete sense of personal worth and self-esteem.[7] Kissinger, said to be personally insecure, yet egocentric, developed a pessimistic view of the world and a conviction about the conflict between states.[8] Nixon, regarded as a disturbed personality, had suffered an unhappy childhood and was insecure.[9] As Kissinger writes of Nixon: "No modern president could have been less equipped by nature for political life. Painfully shy, Nixon dreaded meeting with new people. . . ."[10] Fear of rejection, fierce pride, and deep insecurity were attributes Kissinger perceived in Nixon.[11]

Whatever the validity of these psychological insights, they represent serious attempts to identify characteristics of the behavior of particular leaders observed occasionally, but not always, at first hand. Further, the hypothesized connections between these characteristics, even if valid, and the policies promoted by the leaders who possessed them are hardly convincing evidence of a cause-and-effect relationship, considering all of the other elements involved in the policy process.

Types

Another intriguing approach to the analysis of the relationships between psychological factors and policy is the development of particular types of leaders. Lasswell suggested that there were three types: the agitator, the administrator, and the theorist.[12] John Stoessinger suggests that there were two types of leaders: crusaders and pragmatists.[13] Kegley and Wittkopf, summarizing a number of other types developed by scholars, found ten: the nationalist, the militarist, the conservative, the pragmatist, the paranoid, the Machiavellian, the true believer, the authoritarian, the antiauthoritarian, and the dogmatist.[14]

One of the most provocative attempts to create categories or types of leaders has been made by James David Barber.[15] Using the criteria of how active a president is and how much he seems to enjoy his work, Barber has suggested four types: active-positive, active-negative, passive-positive, and passive-negative.

Active-positives are vigorous, creative leaders, who immensely enjoy the job. Active-negative leaders may be vigorous but do not generally gain much personal satisfaction or enjoyment from it. The passive-positive may not be a vigorous, dynamic leader but may gain satisfaction from the job, while the passive-negative neither does much nor enjoys the experience. Barber suggests that active-positives include Franklin Roosevelt, Truman, Kennedy, Ford, and Carter. Active-negatives include Wilson, Hoover, Johnson, Nixon. Passive-positives would be Harding and Taft, while passive-negatives include Coolidge and Eisenhower.

Barber regards Reagan as a passive-positive. Certainly, other interpretations of each of these presidents is possible, but the typology provides a useful device for thinking about the possible relationship between personality and policy.

An attempt to match personality characteristics with different types of foreign policies has been made by Margaret Hermann. Looking at such characteristics as a need for power, conceptual complexity, trust-distrust of others, need for affiliation, belief of control over events, and nationalism, she found that (1) the greater the need of the decision maker for power, the more aggressive government policy will be; (2) the greater the ability of leaders to deal with complexity, the more cooperative the government policy will tend to be.[16]

Interestingly, studies of lower-level officials in the bureaucracy found that both those who were ambitious and had high self-esteem and those who were mistrustful and had low self-esteem were likely to advocate the use of force to settle disputes.[17]

These exploratory probes into the possible relationships between the personalities of leaders and the policies they produce are intriguing insights into a relatively unknown area of the sources of policy. With all of their acknowledged limitations, they could well provide a productive way to find satisfactory explanations of the decisions of leaders. However, another approach to the idiosyncratic explanation of policy provides a more substantial explanation of the policy process—the investigation of the perceptions and misperceptions of reality developed by elites and masses alike.

Perception, Misperception, and Images

Americans sometimes think of the Soviets as ten feet tall and the United States as weak and helpless in the face of Soviet pressure. This is a function of perception and misperception that can often produce a distorted picture of reality. Karl Deutsch has written that 50 to 60 percent of major foreign-policy decisions are the consequence of fundamental misperceptions and misjudgments of the intentions and capabilities of states.[18] Perception is a process by which an individual selects, organizes, and evaluates incoming information concerning the surrounding world, while misreading or misinterpretation of that information leads to misperception.[19] Concluding a study of several major wars in the twentieth century, John Stoessinger writes: " . . . perhaps the most important single precipitating factor in the outbreak of war is misperception. Such distortion may manifest itself in four different ways: in a leader's image of himself; a leader's view of his adversary's character; a leader's view of his adversary's intentions toward himself; and, finally, a leader's views of his capabilities and power.[20]

According to Ole Holsti, perceptions are affected by the individual's images of reality. Holsti suggests that there are important differences among types of images. An open image can permit absorption of new information and lead to a change of image of reality. A closed image is one that resists new information, screens it, and seeks to retain the existing image.[21] Further, Robert Jervis has argued that screening information selectively is a characteristic of general populations and not just of leaders.[22]

In the development of images and perceptions individuals may resort to defense mechanisms to protect themselves from uncomfortable feelings. Projection occurs when the individual attributes his or her own emotions to others.[23] This can result in seeking a scapegoat or an enemy. The need to see others as adversaries or enemies (us-them) arises from the difficulty with ambiguity and from the wish to see reality in either-or terms.[24] An intriguing aspect of the process is what has been called the mirror image. Uri Bronfenbrenner suggests that adversaries see the same things, but in reverse.[25] Using a study of people of the United States and the Soviet Union, Bronfenbrenner found that each saw themselves as moral and the other side as aggressive. DeRivera and Janis have argued that policy makers should try to put themselves in the places of opponents to achieve better understanding of conflict.[26]

Operational Codes

Another concept that has been of interest in understanding the foreign-policy decisions of leaders is that of operational codes. Defined as the attitudes, values, beliefs, ideologies, and analogies held by individuals, the operational code creates a core of responses to reality. Developed originally by Nathan Leites and elaborated by Alexander George, the approach is useful for tracing the development of the political goals and the procedural rules adopted by leaders.[27] In any case, the personality characteristics and beliefs of leaders are found to be more operative in crisis situations, in complex and ambiguous situations, and in cases where there is wide latitude for policy.

Stress and Health

Americans frequently note that their presidents seem to "age" rapidly in office. The image of a robust Franklin Roosevelt deteriorating to a gaunt shadow of his former self could be seen by all, despite wartime efforts to minimize the decline evident in photographs and films. Similar aging could be seen in most recent presidents, including Ronald Reagan.

One study of the medical histories of leaders found a very high rate of medical disabilities, which, combined with the drugs taken to treat them, can have devastating effects on the individual and can affect his or her policies.[28] Roosevelt's condition, it is often contended, may have affected his performance at the critical Yalta Conference near the end of World War II.

In some cases immense stress is associated with crisis situations, those events in which there are these factors: high threat, limited time for decision, and massive information.[29] Such circumstances can lead the policy maker to overreact or underreact and can have a heavy physiological cost.

Aside from crisis situations, the heavy burden of the daily workload of national leaders, the limited rest and relaxation available to them, the mass of domestic issues confronting them, the travel, the election process, and family obligations leave little time for reflection or physical recuperation from fatigue. In this context psychological pressures are inevitably increased as tension tests the limits of physical and mental endurance. Inevitably this can lead to a reliance on basic impulses and established responses, or it can distort the judgment of those who must make critical decisions. Note former Secretary of State Cyrus Vance's account of a single day during his service—the day after the Camp David accords were signed:

> That morning, after two weeks of round-the-clock negotiations at Camp David, the president and I met with the Chinese Ambassador to discuss a critical issue about the normalization of relations with China. At that point we were still enmeshed in the problems of the Middle East, as we had not yet received Prime Minister Menachem Begin's letter confirming our agreement for a freeze on construction of new settlements in the West Bank. Moreover, that afternoon I had to return again to urgent matters pertaining to the SALT negotiations, which were entering a crucial phase, and to grapple with negotiations relating to southern Africa that demanded immediate attention. A day like that was not unusual.[30]

In many cases a president's schedule is even more demanding, since he must confront an even wider range of problems than does the secretary of state.

With limited sleep, it is apparent that psychological pressures can intensify on any office holder and affect his or her thinking.

Ethology and Biopolitics

The recent study of the effects of biological and biochemical processes on the behavior of individuals and especially on those involved in the political process has been called sociobiology or biopolitics.[31]

Studies of the functioning of the brain and the glands, of genetics, and of the effects of drugs and nutrition have sought explanations of political behavior in the processes of the human organism. The attempt has been made to relate new knowledge about these physiological and chemical processes to such behavioral effects as aggressiveness, violence, and other psychological patterns.

The attempt to study the instinctual behavior of animals and to draw analogies with human behavior is called ethology.[32] The work of scholars such as Robert Ardrey, Konrad Lorenz, and Desmond Morris suggests that other living creatures commit violence only for food and survival but that human beings commit violence for reasons unrelated to survival.

The implication is that gratuitous violence is an instinct of human beings. Considerable controversy surrounds this issue, and critics would argue that (1) human beings cannot be compared to birds, fish, dogs or other animals and that (2) sufficient evidence exists to the contrary to refute the implication. Although history is filled with records of war, it also contains countless examples where leaders avoided aggressive responses to varied challenges.

Effects of Individuals
on Policy

Kegley and Wittkopf have summarized the conditions found in the contemporary literature under which the personality of leaders can have extraordinary effects. It occurs when (1) the leader is high in the decision-making structure, (2) the situation is ambiguous and complex, (3) the individual has great self-confidence and ego, (4) the individual is intensely involved in the situation, (5) minimal information is available, and (6) the individual is relatively new in power.[33]

However, leaders often tend to conform to prevailing beliefs, to the views of superiors, and to past policies.

Whatever the degree of validity of the psychological analysis of leaders that may exist in the studies, it has been impossible to determine with any accuracy precisely how personality characteristics explain policy since, as we have seen, there are so many elements involved in the policy process. Yet the evidence that does exist, as speculative as it may be, is suggestive that further inquiry into these processes may be fruitful. Psychological analysis of leaders may provide not only for a better understanding of ourselves but for insights into the leaders of other states. This clearly would facilitate the capability of negotiation and peaceful resolution of outstanding issues.

Of course, these personality and character differences may make little, if any, difference to American foreign policy. Policy has remained essentially stable through nine presidents since World War II despite the presence in the Oval Office of men of widely different personalities and backgrounds. According to this view, policy has changed from president to president only in style, emphasis, and tactics rather than in broad content. Despite a broad stable pattern in global policy, however, one is still left to wonder whether other presidents would have accepted world leadership in 1945, committed American Forces to Korea or Vietnam, dropped the nuclear bomb, opened relations with China, or taken any one of a number of other key decisions that profoundly affected the people. Speculation of this type may be unproductive, but it serves to raise the question of the effects of particular personalities on events.

DECISION-MAKING GROUPS

Key leaders, including presidents, operate within decision-making groups. They bring with them their philosophies, pathologies, operational codes, images, perceptions, their physical state, their ability to cope with stress, and their tendency to conform.

Participation in a group, however, creates a new set of psychological dynamics, and this too can affect the policy decisions that emerge from the process.

Considerable research has developed since the 1940s into the processes and politics of intragroup and intergroup behavior, and in the following pages some of these insights will be reviewed.

THE DECISION-MAKING MODEL

What James Rosenau called "the first systematic treatment of decision-making phenomena in the study of foreign policy and international politics"[34] emerged in the early 1950s in the work of Richard C. Snyder, who with junior colleagues H. W. Bruck and Burton Sapin, proposed a broad framework of analysis that included the internal factors acting on policy makers, the external environment that provides opportunities and limitations upon action, and the decision-making process by which policy makers reach decisions.[35] The thesis that policy making involved "a complex and interdependent set of social, political, and psychological processes"[36] was new in the study of foreign policy.

In short, the model proposed that motivations of leaders and the elements of the world as they saw it was the comprehensive framework required to produce a better understanding of policy.

Although the new model led to only limited testing, it produced continuing attempts to refine it, the most important of which was developed by Rosenau himself.

The Rosenau Framework

Recognizing that innumerable factors may be relevant to the policy-making process, James Rosenau developed an analytical framework of five major sources of influence on foreign policy ranging from the individual decision makers to the entire global system.[37] As inputs to foreign policy Rosenau posited (1) external sources, including events from throughout the global system; (2) idiosyncratic or individual sources, including the values, personality, and perceptions of leaders; (3) role sources, involving the outlines of the roles to be played by leaders in specific positions of power; (4) societal sources, encompassing national values, interest groups, and the like; and (5) governmental sources, including the structure of American government and politics and the ways in which they interrelate in the policy process.

Within the external environment are the other nation-states of the world, their policies, their needs, their behavior; nonstate or nongovernmental actors, such as multinational corporations, churches, and private nongovernmental institutions; the common problems facing humanity: nuclear threat, overpopulation, pollution, energy. In short, external factors may include anything that exists outside the United States.

Among the characteristics of individuals that may become factors in decision making are their psychology, their moral values, their knowledge and experience, and the level of rationality of their judgment.

Among the societal sources of influence, Rosenau includes elements such as national values and beliefs, the nation's cohesiveness, the people's confidence in their system and in their government, and their support of general foreign-policy goals identified by the government.

The governmental system establishes the broad powers and limitations of power that governmental leaders must accept. The Constitution, the checks-and-balances system, federalism, and specific statutes relating to foreign policy all impose responsibilities and constraints on what leaders may and may not do.

In addition, within the system there are certain roles that have evolved for leaders, who are expected to act in certain established ways (within the Constitution for example). Roles condition their occupants to absorb certain patterns from the past.

That the decision makers consciously or unconsciously face all of these factors when they define and confront a foreign-policy problem is not arguable, and key leaders are well aware of the complexity of what they attempt.

The serious problem with these all-encompassing decision-making frameworks is the danger that while they include so much, they may explain so little. Which of Rosenau's five major elements is predominant most of the time? Is there any consistent pattern to the effects that idiosyncratic or societal or role factors have on policy, or do they, in fact, have any measurable effects at all?

Their great value, of course, lies in the fact that they identify the countless factors that may at one time or another be critical in shaping particular policies of intense national interest.

The Rational-Actor Model

In contrast to the Rosenau model is the rational-actor model.[38] Where Rosenau suggests the multiple factors involved in foreign policy, the rational-actor model emphasizes one factor: the policy that is finally enunciated and pursued by one state vis-à-vis others. The rational-actor model assumes that policy is (1) the result of a rational consideration by decision makers of the objectives, costs, and possible attainments of a given policy, (2) the product of careful consideration of options and of all the information essential to choice, and (3) the ideal way to produce maximum benefits at minimal cost in response to the actions of others.

In the past, diplomatic historians and political scientists have often used this model with some success in explaining foreign policy. However, the model tells us little about *how* the policy was decided upon and the politics of deciding upon it. It suggests implicitly that how a policy was arrived at is less important than the policy itself and than whether the policy achieves the purposes for which it was designed.

The "Muddling-Through" Model

Among the major problems with the rational-actor model pointed out by Lindblom and Braybrooke is that policy is rarely made in the ideal circumstances of carefully considered decisions based upon complete information, adequate time for calm analysis and reflection, and full discussion of the advantages and disadvantages of policy options.[39] At best, they argue, there is never very much time to consider any problem and its solutions, and in many cases of crisis there is almost no time at all. Information is always imperfect, and discussion is limited and sometimes uninformed. Therefore, Lindblom and Braybrooke argue, most decisions are made on the basis of limited time, information, and reflection, and all policy makers can do is to muddle through and hope for the best. In this imperfect system, decisions are more likely to be incremental, i.e., small changes in existing policy rather than sweeping, radical, or new actions.

In any case, many students of the subject suspect that the "muddling-through" version of policy-making is closer to reality than is the ideal rational-actor model. Nonetheless, each approach represents one way to understand policy and to assess its results, and flaws in each do not necessarily remove their utility as explanations or guidelines for policy.

Groupthink

According to Irving Janis, groupthink is a psychological set of factors characteristic of some decision-making groups that leads to erroneous or ineffective policies. Among its characteristics are the following:[40]

1. An illusion of invulnerability, shared by most or all of the members, which creates excessive optimism and encourages taking extreme risks.

2. Collective efforts to rationalize in order to discount warnings that might lead members to reconsider their assumptions before they recommit themselves to their past policy decisions.

3. An unquestioned belief in the group's inherent morality, inclining the members to ignore the ethical or moral consequences of their decisions.

4. Stereotyped views of enemy leaders as too evil to warrant genuine attempts to negotiate or as too weak and stupid to counter whatever attempts are made to defeat their purposes.

5. Direct pressure on any member who expressed strong arguments against any of the group's stereotypes, illusions, or commitments, making clear that this type of dissent is contrary to what is expected of all loyal members.

6. Self-censorship of deviations from the apparent group consensus.

7. A shared illusion of unanimity concerning judgments conforming to the majority view.

8. The emergence of self-appointed mind-guards—members who protect the group from adverse information that might shatter their shared complacency about the effectiveness and morality of their decisions.

Janis concludes: "The greater the threats to the self-esteem of the members of a cohesive decision-making body, the greater will be their inclination to resort to concurrence-seeking at the expense of critical thinking."[41]

To deter the operation of groupthink, Janis suggests use of a number of steps in the policy process that would more objectively evaluate the problem, the options, the adversary, and the internal consensus.

The Cybernetic Model

The more or less comprehensive consideration of issues, policy options, costs, and benefits implicit in the rational-actor and muddling-through models may be somewhat irrelevant, according to the cybernetic model of decision making. The model suggests that decisions are relatively automatic responses triggered by perceived threats to survival and that they focus on a very narrow range of information relevant to survival.[42] Decision-making mechanisms, whether individuals or groups, possess existing or preprogrammed responses to external challenge, and these screen out information perceived as not essential to the decision. According to Steinbruner, "The essential criterion is simply survival as directly reflected in the internal state of the decision-making mechanism and whatever actions are performed are motivated by that basic value."[43]

If the model is correct, it could result in the failure of leaders to recognize several important elements of key events. For example, in arms-control negotiations, the model suggests that participants will fall back on those positions that it is believed will best guarantee survival rather than to explore novel arrangements that may have more peaceful long-term effects. Still, it may partially explain the phenomenon found in other studies of decision-making groups in which new information is either distorted or ignored.

The Bureaucratic-Politics Model

Another view of the internal interaction of the decision-making process is the bureaucratic-politics model suggested by Graham Allison and others.[44] It tends to suggest that, in fact, considerable and lively debate occurs within policy-making groups but that the options proposed reflect the views, positions, and attitudes of particular bureaucrats and bureaucracies. In any event, the debate that occurs is a conflict among established bureaucratic positions rather than an open examination of other alternatives.

According to this model, different bureaucracies present alternative positions, argue them out among themselves, and seek presidential choice of their particular option. In some cases the stakes are the personal or institutional prestige of the advocate. In other cases it is the genuine belief that their proposal is truly the one most likely to produce a desired outcome of policy.

This process may produce a clear-cut choice by the president, but it may also involve a compromise among competing positions that may weaken the ultimate policy. On the other hand, by accepting parts of the proposals from different sources, a president may strengthen execution of policy by making it more comprehensive and broadly based.

The Operational-Process Model

The organizational-process model contains the view that in the implementation of broad policy, those departments and agencies designated to carry out the policy make part of the policy through their standard operating procedures. Once in action, they may reject interference by superiors.[45] This model takes the policy process from the competition among departments into the internal workings of the active departments, placing an emphasis on their views of how the policy should actually work in practice.

Again, the Cuban missile crisis affords an example. When the policy of "quarantine" of ships entering Cuba had been decided upon, the main task of implementing it fell to the Navy, which turned to its standard operating procedures for performing the task. The fact that the president wished to retain precise control of when ships should be stopped and searched interfered with the Navy's operation of the quarantine "by the book," and at least one conflict was noted between the secretary of defense and the chief of naval operations over the question of whether the operation should remain in the hands of the navy or the president.

Since implementation of policy can indeed provide the content of policy itself, this model provides insights into another important element of the policy process.

A Prescriptive Model

As a result of the Cuban missile crisis and of the successful decision-making process that John Kennedy had organized to develop a policy, many scholars looked toward the lessons of the experience to define a decision-making model that could effectively serve a president in the modern era.[46] Among the elements of the model are the following: the establishment of open, improvised channels of communication expanding the time required to develop solutions; the pacing of the events of the crisis to provide additional time for settlement; the application of flexibility to the adversary and the avoidance of forcing the adversary to choose; placing options within the context of international law and historical national morality; consultation with allies; close supervision of the crisis operations; the use of a collegial style of management; selection of the decision group on an ad hoc basis from both inside and outside the government; consideration of a diversity of views, options, and consequences of varied policies and encouragement of participants to shift positions; intense efforts by the president to seek support for implementation among the agencies involved.

Presumably President Ronald Reagan's organization of a "crisis-management" team under Vice-President George Bush was an effort to put into place organizational machinery capable of dealing rapidly with foreign crisis.

In any case, consideration by a president of a planned system capable of dealing with crises appears to be a necessity. Presidents clearly have used different combinations of advisers in crisis situations, but the prescriptive model offers some clear guidelines for one possible and effective way the problem can be handled.

The Issue Paradigm

A relatively new approach to the explanation of decision making suggests that the nature of the issue under consideration is a powerful factor in shaping the decision-making process. As Mansbach and Vasquez explain it:

> An issue paradigm looks first at how issues are defined, what values they are supposed to embody, the proposals that being made for their resolution, and the issue position each actor takes on the various proposals. It then looks at the interaction process. How and why do actors contend over the competing proposals, what types of techniques are employed to achieve resolution, and how does the process itself influence the relationship among actors and the way they define the issues?[47]

The politics involved is not so much concerned with struggling for power as for making "a collective decision for the purpose of allocating values in an authoritative manner."[48]

It would appear that consideration of the nature of the issue can be a most important element in the analysis of the decision-making process.

It should be clear that there are psychological dynamics operating within decision-making groups that can affect the ultimate decision, but it is not clear under what circumstances the group will tend to conform with past practice or will vigorously debate options on the basis of bureaucratic position, personal ambition, or conviction. Different issues are likely to affect the ways in which decisions are debated and reached. Nonetheless, because of the confusing signals that the scholarship in the decision-making process conveys, continued study would be fruitful.

THEORIES OF POWER

Who has the power to make decisions, and in whose behalf are decisions made? These questions have spawned considerable research, analysis, and disagreement among scholars.

In discussing special-interest groups, we raised some of the issues about the sources and distribution of political power and influence in the United States. In this chapter, thus far, we have looked at analyses of how decisions are made. At this point, it is necessary to examine the question, For whom are decisions made?

We have noted the Marxist viewpoint that those who control capital control the state in capitalist societies. A recent expression of this view is to be found in the work of Ralph Miliband:

> The most important political fact about advanced capitalist societies . . . is the continued existence in them of private and ever more concentrated economic power. As a result of that power, the men . . . owners and controllers—in whose hands it lies enjoy a massive preponderance in society, in the political system, and in the determination of the state's policies and actions.[49]

The implication is that American foreign policy usually reflects the needs and the interests of this elite class of Americans. However, views that power and influence are more widely distributed than the Marxist perspective indicates also abound.

The Power-Elite Theory

The power-elite theory, whose major advocate was the late C. Wright Mills, holds that a relatively small group of citizens with special power positions constitute a power elite who determine more or less consciously among themselves what the philosophies and the policies of the country should be.[50] An offshoot of Marxist-Leninist doctrine, the power-elite theory suggests that a relatively few bankers, industrialists, political leaders, and opinion leaders share certain basic values and goals, and through their prestige, their connections, and the resources they control, they establish the national value system, the governmental agenda, and the national mood. Either through deliberate consultation, shared interests, or coincidentally held beliefs, they determine the policies to be pursued, and they effectively communicate their preferences through other levels of the society. Their foreign-policy preferences would be drafted with the view of expanding and protecting their own interests.

Pluralism/Polyarchy

In contrast to the power-elite theory are the views of those who argue that there are many competing centers of power in the United States. Robert Dahl, among others, has effectively argued that several major centers of power not only exist but operate in differing issue areas.[51] Where interests conflict, the power centers wage battles, form coalitions, and seek preference. No one power center wins all policy conflicts all the time, and most enjoy victories some of the time and suffer losses at others. The net result, according to the theory, is to disprove the existence of a single, small power elite and its domination of the policy process. Another implication of pluralist theory, however, is that not all individual citizens or smaller groups necessarily participate in the competition and that usually their influence is negligible. The people, it is said, exercise influence by their power to vote and to elect leaders or by their membership in one of the larger, powerful, participant blocs of power, such as the labor unions.

Oligarchy

A third view, which combines elements of a power elite and a pluralist model, has been offered by Thomas Dye. Called the oligarchical model, it posits that there is, in fact, an elite whose members have more power and influence than others but that it is a much larger group than that suggested by Mills. Indeed, Dye claims that the exact number of the elite is 7,314—leaders of business corporations, government, journalism, academia.[52] However, he also perceives the influence of numerous other groups and interests in pluralist form and suggests that the sway of the elites is not complete or uniform.

The study of the locus and the distribution of political power in the United States has identified a complex structure in which a power elite of debatable size functions concurrently with many other large forces that exercise power and influence. While small numbers of elite leaders seem to possess disproportionate influence on policy, other groups compete vigorously in the political process, and no interest is predominant all of the time.

The general mass public is not usually regarded as a leading part of the power structure. Decisions are almost always made by leaders, although public opinion establishes limits on leader's actions.[53] In general, changes in public opinion follow government action. Yet a growing number of Americans are becoming part of the attentive public, and many are increasingly active in the foreign-policy debate. The nuclear-freeze movement that has developed in the 1980s is an example of public influence and power.

While the models of power reviewed here suggest that power and influence in the United States are not equally shared among Americans, neither are they possessed only by one group.

POWER AND THE NATURE OF THE STATE

Is there something inherent in the nature of states, especially large ones, that shapes their foreign policies? Does the United States fit the patterns of the behavior exhibited by large states in terms of participation in foreign activity, war, or aggressive behavior?

   A considerable body of recent evidence suggests that (1) large states are more active in foreign policy,[54] (2) large states are more frequently involved in war,[55] (3) democracies are as likely to wage war as are authoritarian regimes,[56] and (4) there is no clear relationship between internal turmoil and foreign war.[57]

   Thus the study of comparative foreign policies has provided some confirmation of some broad characteristics of the behavior of large states. Although exceptions can be found to each of these findings, all of them, more or less, characterize American foreign policy in the twentieth century. The United States, although one of the world's largest and most potentially powerful countries in the world by the early part of the century, only gradually expanded its foreign-policy activity around the globe. A democracy, it has, in fact, been involved in four major wars since 1917 and has become militarily involved in many other crisis situations throughout the world since 1945. However, American behavior abroad has led to internal turmoil more frequently than internal troubles have led to American military involvement abroad.

   If the size of a state, in this case the United States, is a most important factor in determining the amount and the kinds of its foreign activity, then the United States is clearly destined to remain an active, involved, and ambitious country for the foreseeable future. However, a new phenomenon of the twentieth century is the increased foreign-policy activity of smaller states. Rapid technological change and the shifting patterns of internal life among almost 160 countries have led to activist foreign policies among the smaller states of OPEC and among states such as Libya, Cuba, and Israel. Thus the small size of a state is not necessarily an impediment to an active foreign policy or even to waging war.

   That large states are more likely to engage in more foreign-policy activity and in war is, nevertheless, not surprising. With political relations with most countries, with economic links with virtually all other states, the United States has developed interests in every part of the globe and possesses the resources to pursue its interests wherever it must. American foreign policy is in large measure a response to these realities.

   Just as sovereignty confers certain rights, characteristics, and qualities upon states, the existence of the state imposes certain imperatives on the formulation of policy. The United States is what history has made it, and Americans must live with the reality of superpower status with all that that implies. Conscious policy may ease some of the more dangerous burdens of that status, but it cannot easily or quickly change it. Nor can the nature of allies and adversaries be changed either. In this way what we have become affects what we can and must do. We are not left without choice, but the nature of states and the state system certainly influences the shape of foreign policy.

CONCLUSION

Whether we consider the impact of the individual personality or the nature of the national state, the import of group processes or the distribution of power within the state, we are enriched by much of the recent research into the foreign-policy behavior of states.

The provocative new theories and models of political behavior have confirmed some older impressions and have opened up new avenues for understanding the sources and effects of policies.

The idiosyncratic or psychopolitics models and theories have identified the potential connection between the psychology of individual leaders and the policies pursued by a government.

Research into the decision-making processes in groups has identified some important obstacles to creating successful foreign policy but also suggests some productive guideposts to rational decision making.

Studies seeking the sources and distribution of power have helped to identify important influences on the policy process.

And systematic study of the nature of states and their foreign behavior has shown that there are more similarities than differences among large states.

Whether these new theories, models, and designs are known to leaders and whether they offer new clarity to their choices and methods cannot be easily determined. It is a reasonable assumption that many of the ideas embodied in these approaches will come to the attention of policy makers seeking to develop sound and successful policies.

Taken as a whole, the research reviewed in this chapter suggests some powerful reasons why policy appears to change so slowly, why innovation and creativity seem so often missing from the policy process. From the personality characteristics of individual leaders, to the decision process within groups, to the distribution of power among those benefiting from the status quo, to the nature of states, we have seen powerful forces working to maintain the existing order. The individual tends to fall back on what he or she knows or what gives him or her psychic satisfaction, groups tend to conform to previous patterns, power centers seek to maintain their favored status, and large states tend to preserve the existing structure of things. When new demands arise in the international system, the capability to respond is limited. Foreign policies are not created or adjusted easily to accommodate to new challenges.

For those individuals, groups, power centers, and states that wish to create new policies and to adapt to new realities, the political struggle must include intense efforts to change perceptions, attitudes, and images and to persuade others to depart from mere incremental change from patterns of the past.

How have these factors related to American foreign policy since the end of World War II? Certainly the Truman administration became convinced of the aggressive intentions and the expansionist policy of the Soviet Union. It persuaded the American people that communism and the Soviets posed a serious challenge, branding them as the new enemies, and it mobilized public opinion into an anti-Communist, anti-Soviet crusade. Was this an accurate picture of the Soviet Union, and was the cold war the best response to postwar Soviet behavior? The preponderance of opinion in the leadership and among the people ever since has answered that it was.

Whether it was or not, did the response by President Truman, George Kennan, George Marshall, Dean Acheson and other key leaders reflect predominant personality characteristics or a reasoned and objective analysis of reality? Can it be explained by looking for childhood deprivation of self-esteem, misperception, mirror images or any of the other provocative psychological insights we have examined? Was there some ulterior motive of an economic power elite wishing to retain power and to stimulate the postwar economy with large defense expenditures? Was there something in the nature of the two major survivors of World War II that inherently tended toward competition and conflict? Were alternative strategies and policies possible under the circumstances? Did we have a realistic choice in 1945–46 or since?

In subsequent years to what degree did the personality traits of John Kennedy or Lyndon Johnson or Richard Nixon determine the policies and the challenges they presented to the Soviet Union?

Belief systems and perceptions have many sources, but the ideas surveyed in the last two chapters are among the most important of them.

NOTES

[1] Lloyd Jensen, *Explaining Foreign Policy* (Englewood Cliffs, N.J.: Prentice-Hall, 1982), pp. 264–66.

[2] Jensen, *Explaining Foreign Policy*, p. 31; Henry Kissinger, *Years of Upheaval* (Boston: Little, Brown & Company, 1982), p. 1199.

[3] Jerome Frank, *Sanity or Survival: Psychological Aspects of War and Peace* (New York: Random House, 1967), p. 59.

[4] Harold Lasswell, *Power and Personality* (New York: W. W. Norton & Company, 1948), p. 39.

[5] Ole Holsti, "The Belief System and National Images: A Case Study," *Journal of Conflict Resolution* 6 (1962), 244–52; Alexander and Juliet George, *Woodrow Wilson and Colonel House: A Personality Study* (New York: Dover, 1964).

[6] Arnold A. Rogow, *James Forrestal: A Study in Personality, Politics, and Policy* (New York: Macmillan Company, 1963), pp. 328–41.

[7] Thomas M. Mongar, "Personality and Decision-Making: John F. Kennedy in Four Crisis Decisions," in Gordon DiRenzo, ed., *Personality and Politics* (Garden City, N.Y.: Doubleday-Anchor, 1974), pp. 334–72; James David Barber, *The Presidential Character* (Englewood Cliffs, N.J.: Prentice-Hall, 1977), pp. 295–304.

[8] Harvey Starr, "The Kissinger Years: Studying Individuals and Foreign Policy," *International Studies Quarterly* 24 (December 1980), 465–95.

[9] David Abrahamsen, *Nixon v. Nixon: An Emotional Tragedy* (New York: Farrar, Straus, & Giroux, 1977), pp. 225–27; Barber, *Presidential Character*, pp. 396-417.

[10] Kissinger, *Years of Upheaval*, p. 1181.

[11] Ibid., pp. 1181–82.

[12] Lasswell, *Power and Personality*, pp. 59–92.

[13] John Stoessinger, *Crusaders and Pragmatists: Movers of Modern American Foreign Policy* (New York: W. W. Norton & Company, 1973), pp. 288.

[14] Charles W. Kegley and Eugene R. Wittkopf, *American Foreign Policy: Pattern and Process*, 2nd Ed. (New York: St. Martin's Press, 1982), pp. 504–6.

[15] Barber, *Presidential Character*, pp. 11–14, 58, 146, 174, 211.

[16] Margaret G. Hermann, "Leader Personality and Foreign Policy Behavior," in James Rosenau, ed., *Comparing Foreign Policies* (New York: Halsted, 1974), pp. 201–33; and *A Psychological Examination of Political Leaders* (New York: Free Press, 1976).

[17] Lloyd Etheridge, "Personality and Foreign Policy: Bullies in the State Department," *Psychology Today*, March 1975, p. 38.

[18] Cited in Bruce M. Russett and Harvey Starr, *World Politics: The Menu for Choice* (San Francisco: W. H. Freeman and Co. Publishers, 1981), p. 301.

[19] Russett and Starr, *World Politics*, pp. 300–302.

[20] John Stoessinger, *Why Nations Go to War* (New York: St. Martin's Press, 1974), p. 223.

[21] Russett and Starr, *World Politics*, p. 300.

[22] Robert Jervis, *Perception and Misperception* (Princeton, N.J.: Princeton University Press, 1976), pp. 288–315.

[23] Arthur Gladstone, "The Concept of the Enemy," *Journal of Conflict Resolution* 3 (1959), 132–37.

[24] Ralph K. White, *Nobody Wanted War: Misperception in Vietnam and Other Wars* (New York: Doubleday & Company, 1970).

[25] Uri Bronfenbrenner, "The Mirror Image in Soviet-American Relations," *Journal of Social Issues* 17 (1961), 45–46.

[26] Irvin L. Janis, *Groupthink* (Boston: Houghton Mifflin Company, 1982), pp. 215–18; Joseph DeRivera, *The Psychological Dimensions of Foreign Policy* (Columbus, Ohio: Charles E. Merrill Publishing Co., 1968), pp. 61–64.

[27] K. J. Holsti, *International Politics: A Framework for Analysis*, 3rd ed. (Englewood Cliffs, N.J.: Prentice-Hall, 1977), pp. 377–78.

[28] Hugh L'Etang, *The Pathology of Leadership* (New York: Hawthorne Books, 1970), pp. 9–12. At the time L'Etang published his study he estimated that since 1908, eleven of thirteen British prime ministers and six of ten American presidents had some major physical problems. Since 1970, President Nixon, late in his term, was afflicted with phlebitis, and President Reagan was temporarily incapacitated in an assassination attempt in 1981.

[29] Russett and Starr, *World Politics*, pp. 320–21.

[30] Cyrus Vance, *Hard Choices* (New York: Simon & Schuster, 1983), preface, pp. 13–14.

[31] Robert Travers, "Sociobiology and Politics," in Elliot White, ed., *Sociobiology and Human Politics* (Lexington, Mass.: Lexington Books, 1981), pp. 1–43; Edward Wilson, *Sociobiology: The New Synthesis* (Cambridge, Mass.: Belknap Press of Harvard University Press, 1975), pp. 7–31; Ralph Pettman, *Human Behavior and World Politics* (New York: St. Martin's Press, 1975), pp. 153–75.

[32] Pettman, *Human Behavior*, pp. 176–99.

[33] Kegley and Wittkopf, *American Foreign Policy*, pp. 513–14.

[34] James Rosenau, "The Premise and Promises of Decision-Making Analysis," in James C. Charlesworth, ed., *Contemporary Political Analysis* (New York: Free Press, 1967), p. 193.

[35] Ibid., pp. 195–96.

[36] Ibid., p. 196.

[37] James Rosenau, "Pre-Theories and Theories of Foreign Policy," in R. Barry Farrell, ed., *Approaches to Comparative and International Politics* (Evanston, Ill.: Northwestern University Press, 1966), pp. 27–92; and Rosenau, "The Study of Foreign Policy," in Rosenau, Kenneth W. Thompson, and Gavin Boyd, *World Politics: An Introduction* (New York: Free Press, 1976), pp. 15–35.

[38] Graham Allison, *Essence of Decision* (Boston: Little, Brown & Company, 1971), pp. 11–38.

[39] Charles E. Lindblom, "The Science of Muddling Through," *Public Administration Review* 19 (spring 1959), 79–88; David Braybrooke and Charles Lindblom, *A Strategy of Decision: Policy Evaluation As a Social Process* (New York: Free Press of Glencoe, 1963), pp. 81–110.

[40] Janis, *Groupthink*, pp. 197–98.

[41] Ibid., p. 206.

[42] Karl W. Deutsch, *The Nerves of Government* (New York: Free Press, 1966); John D. Steinbruner, *The Cybernetic Theory of Decision* (Princeton, N.J.: Princeton University Press, 1974), pp. 47–87.

[43] Steinbruner, *Cybernetic Theory of Decision*, p. 65.

[44] Allison, *Essence of Decision*, pp. 144–86.

[45] Ibid., pp. 67–100.

[46] Joshua Sandman, "A Prescriptive Model for Handling Nuclear Age Crises in the Executive Office," *Presidential Studies Quarterly* 13 (winter 1983), 121–28.

[47] Richard W. Mansbach and John A. Vasquez, *In Search of Theory: A New Paradigm for Global Politics* (New York: Columbia University Press, 1981), pp. 38–83.

[48] Ibid., p. 72.

[49] Ralph Miliband, *The State in Capitalist Society* (New York: Basic Books, 1969), p. 265.

[50] C. Wright Mills, *The Power Elite* (New York: Oxford University Press, 1956), pp. 3–29, 274–97.

[51] Robert A. Dahl, "A Critique of the Ruling Elite Model," *American Political Science Review* (June 1958), 463–69; also *Who Governs: Democracy and Power in an American City* (New Haven: Yale University Press, 1961), pp. 228, 296–301; also *Polyarchy* (New Haven: Yale University Press, 1971), pp. 8–16, 202–7.

[52] Thomas R. Dye, *Who's Running America* 3rd ed. (Englewood Cliffs, N.J.: Prentice-Hall, 1983), pp. 14, 274.

[53] K. J. Holsti, *International Politics*, pp. 396–97.

[54] Rudolph Rummel, *Dimensions of Nations* (Beverly Hills, Calif.: Sage Publications, 1972); Maurice East and Charles Hermann, "Do Nation-Types Account for Foreign Policy Behavior," in Rosenau, *Comparing Foreign Policies*, p. 299; Melvin Small and J. David Singer, "The Diplomatic Importance of States, 1816–1970: An Extension and Refinement of the Indicator," *World Politics* 25 (1973), 577–99.

[55] Lewis Richardson, *Statistics of Deadly Quarrels* (Chicago: Quadrangle Books, 1960), pp. 173–75; Quincy Wright, *The Study of War*, 2nd ed. (Chicago: University of Chicago Press, 1965), pp. 647–50.

[56] J. David Singer and Melvin Small, *The Wages of War 1816-1965: A Statistical Handbook* (New York: John Wiley and Sons, Inc., 1972), pp. 257–86, 374–78; Jonathan Wilkenfeld, "Domestic and Foreign Conflict Behavior of Nations," *Journal of Peace Research* 5 (1968), pp. 56–59.

[57] Rummel, "The Relationship Between National Attitudes and Foreign Conflict Behavior," in J. David Singer, ed., *Quantitative International Politics: Insights and Evidence* (New York: Free Press, 1968), pp. 187–214; Raymond Tanter, "Dimensions of Conflict Behavior Within and Between Nations, 1958–1960," *Journal of Conflict Resolution* 10 (1966), 61–62; Jonathan Wilkenfeld, "Domestic and Foreign Conflict Behavior of Nations," *Journal of Peace Research* 1 (1961), 56–59; Dina A. Zinnes and Jonathan Wilkenfeld, "An Analysis of Foreign Conflict Behavior of Nations," in Wolfram Hanreider, ed., *Comparative Foreign Policy: Theoretical Essays* (New York: David McKay Co., 1971), pp. 167–213.

CHAPTER FOURTEEN
THE POLITICAL TRACK

In 1983 the American invasion of Grenada and the introduction of U.S. military forces into Lebanon brought Americans face to face with the difficult choices facing the country in defining American political objectives and in choosing the most effective means of achieving them. Throughout the 1980s debate continued over the nature of American political interests in Central America and the Middle East, much as, some twenty years earlier, Presidents John F. Kennedy and Lyndon Johnson grappled with the identification of American interests in Southeast Asia and the best means for pursuing them.

In the two periods, twenty years apart, American presidents proclaimed that vital American national interests were at stake in countries far beyond American borders and came down on the side of military tools as the most effective means to deal with events.

American interests in the world encompass a much broader spectrum than these examples suggest, however. American policy reflects interests in four major tracks: political, economic, military, and cultural. Each track contains its own specific tools or instruments of action. Although a good deal of the history of the past four decades seems to indicate a tendency on the part of presidents to emphasize the military track, the totality of American relations with other countries reveals extensive reliance on the other tracks as well. In the broadest sense, all four tracks are political and have political objectives and political consequences.

In modern America the term *politics* is used to describe a wide range of human activity. From individual maneuvering in "office politics" to the glad-handing of ward politicians seeking votes at election time to the highest levels of summit diplomacy, politics is at work. On the broadest level, of course, politics is a form of human behavior in which individuals and groups develop and articulate interests and goals and attempt to resolve conflicts nonviolently. But politics is also a method by which human beings organize their societies, establishing government and other structures, forging rules and procedures, and determining how power and authority shall be allocated. In doing this, societies create the process by which groups or individuals may seek the power and authority to make policy choices and to impose their preferences on the whole citizenry.

Hilsman notes: "Politics concerns the activities and relationships of groups of people that are organized as societies. Thus, we may consider a political process as a device for making group decisions."[1] He refers to matters of government and of the national state.

A political system, then, provides the mechanisms for making choices and for the resolution of conflicts over (1) power and authority; (2) interests, wants, needs, goals; (3) ideas, perceptions, theories, images, philosophies; and (4) personal, group, or institutional ambitions. The American political system, as we have seen, is structured to permit virtually unrestricted expression of conflicting positions through the mechanisms discussed in part II. The process, based in the national Constitution, is regarded as legally, politically, and morally legitimate, and it has the support and loyalty of all citizens, who accept the resulting decisions and policies and give material and personal support to them. Hilsman notes, the political system "provides a way of accomplishing social and political change with at least a minimum of violence—and, if it is working—without any of the large-scale, organized violence of war or civil war."[2]

However, only a part of the foreign-policy process functions within the domestic American political system. The rest of it operates within a global political system that differs quite markedly from the national system. Within the global community there is no central government, constitution, executive, legislature, or judiciary. No legitimate central authority exists, and each of the 160 or so sovereign states regards itself as the final arbiter of its own actions. Thus politics within the global system requires different forms, methods, and goals. Politics at the international level—diplomacy—necessitates the use of other devices to reconcile differences and to settle disputes. This is one function of the political track.

Three major concepts shape the political track of American foreign policy: the national interest, the status of world leadership, and the cold war. Each provokes considerable political controversy within the United States and between the United States and other countries. Each contains elements that have spanned the last forty years and other elements that are subject to change by succeeding presidents and administrations. Considered together, they explain a great deal about the political interests of the United States in the 1980s.

THE NATIONAL INTEREST

For almost a decade the nations of the world worked on creating a new Law of the Sea Treaty, which would detail the rights and obligations of countries on the oceans, seas, and waterways of the globe. In December 1982, 117 states signed the treaty.[3] The United States refused to do so. The major obstacle was the definition of the rights of the seabed. Most countries agreed to the access by all states to the seabeds and to their minerals. Present technology permits only a few countries, including the United States, to mine these resources. Thus the American choice lay between retaining almost complete access to these resources for the foreseeable future or agreeing to share them with other states. Which option is in the American national interest? The administrations from Lyndon Johnson through Jimmy Carter agreed with the latter position. The Reagan administration decided, however, that the American national interest lies in keeping nearly exclusive access to the seabed resources as long as possible. Which decision is correct? Unless Americans perceive that the resources provided to less developed countries will benefit the United States in the long run, they are likely to agree with Reagan's decision. However, the issue is not just one of kindliness to less developed countries. With money available from distribution of profits from the seabed, many of these countries can increase their economic security, purchase goods and services made in the United States, and cooperate with the United States on other issues. The question of whether this situation serves the long-term American national interest more fully than monopolization of immediate profits suggests the dilemma faced by those who define the national interest and by the Americans who are affected by the decisions.

Just what the national interest is at any given time, who decides what it is, and what factors affect it are matters of some disagreement.

Hans Morgenthau, contending that statesmen "think and act in terms of interest defined as power,"[4] believes that international politics is a process in which national interests are adjusted. In a world of states, Morgenthau argues, "national interest is indeed the last word in world politics."[5] Interest is the essence of politics. Survival is the primary national interest, but states also pursue lesser interests.

Frederick Hartmann says national interests are those things that states could or do seek to protect or achieve vis-à-vis other states. According to Hartmann, states have *vital* interests, ones for which the state is normally willing to fight immediately or ultimately and which are "always bound up first and foremost with the preservation of the nation's status quo." They include at a minimum the protection of their existing territory and the preservation of their prestige. All other interests are *secondary*, i.e., not worth a war. States may be mistaken in defining their vital interests, but states may have common interests or opposed interests with other states. Hartmann suggests that a state's concept of its national interests arises out of a complex and not entirely rational interaction between the lessons its people absorb from the external environment and the nature of its own society.[6]

How valid is the concept of national interest? How does it affect American foreign policy? Is there such a thing?

First of all, the global system is organized around the nation-state, and some 160 of them are joined by new ones every year. Nationalism and the creation of the nation-state encompass basic goals and objectives of peoples everywhere: survival, security, prosperity, prestige, and friendship, among others.[7] The process by which each state must accommodate its national interests with those of other countries is the stuff of international politics. The interests of various countries may conflict with each other, but their definitions of their interests may change over time. New leaders may impose new perceptions on the definition of national interests or may emphasize the use of different sets of tools to achieve their goals. Other new forces may impose the need to redefine interests. For example, the invention of nuclear bombs and the intercontinental capability to deliver them altered the definition of the national interests in the United States and in many other countries. Occasionally major elements of the public may reject definitions proposed by leaders, and elections in democratic states provide the opportunity to select new leaders.

Emerging from the isolation of the 1930s, the United States defined its political interest after 1945 to encompass global, regional, hemispheric, and continental responsibilities and needs. The formation of the United Nations and various alliances, the expansion of trade, the search for security, and the cultural contact with many other states required political relationships that far exceeded in number and complexity the pre-World War II system.

Thus what countries want and need in the world becomes part of their national interest. Difficult to define and articulate, to measure with accuracy, or to agree upon, the concept of the national interest is admittedly volatile, but valid, nonetheless.

Despite some changes in the definition of the American national interest, a remarkable continuity has characterized it for the past four decades. Opposition to communism and to its expansion, and promotion of free trade throughout the world have been goals of both liberal and conservative and both Democratic and Republican administrations.

With the American and Soviet blocs more or less solidified in Europe since the 1950s, the most intense area of disagreement about the American national interest has centered on the question of importance of the Third and Fourth Worlds to American interests. Consequently, many of the newly independent states of Asia, Africa, and Latin America have become arenas of superpower competition. Recent crises in Central America and in Lebanon in which American military forces were committed to action represented the judgment of the Reagan administration about adverse effects of Soviet, Cuban, or Syrian behavior in these regions on the American national interest.

Whether it is in the American national interest to be involved in virtually every part of the world and what the substance of that "involvement" should be remain central questions in the debate over the definition of the national interest. Intensified considerably by the unsuccessful American intervention in Vietnam, the debate has produced a division of American opinion into "hawks" and "doves." Although this rather crude measure of opinion obscures the many shadings of belief and opinion among Americans about the country's role in the world, it helps to illustrate the options that confront Americans in the 1980s. Among many doves American involvement beyond normal diplomatic relations with other countries, involvement that may impose excessive pressures to conform with American political objectives, is unacceptable. This attitude is especially applicable to the use of American military tools. On the other hand, most hawks accept the view that since the United States has global responsibilities, it has the need and the right to intervene in ways that serve American interests anywhere in the world and with military force, if necessary.

In addition to the differences posed by these two sets of attitudes lies an even more complex problem. What is a *vital* interest? If attacked directly, most Americans support the right of self-defense. However, to what extent do distant lands constitute a part of American self-defense? During the bitter American debate over Vietnam and, more recently, in the debates over Grenada and Lebanon, these questions prompted an extensive examination of American interests, purposes, and policies. Were Vietnam, Grenada, and Lebanon American vital interests? At the time, presidents said they were. Consequently, a vital interest is one for which a country will go to war; the definition of what constitutes a *vital* interest is among the most important a country and its government can make.

As the story about the Law of the Sea Treaty suggests, knowledgeable individuals can disagree about the definition of vital interests or, indeed, about secondary, peripheral, or private interests as well. Given the American position in the world in the 1980s, it is clear that the United States does have vital interests in many parts of the world. Just what they are and why they are vital are subject to debate. Avoidance of war, especially nuclear war, with the Soviet Union is a vital interest. Pending development of alternate sources of energy, access to Middle East oil is a vital interest of the United States and its major allies. A better standard of living for all people of the world can also be defined as a vital interest. Pursuit of all of these vital interests necessitates more than just a casual involvement with other countries.

In the United States national interests, including the vital interests, are defined through the political process, with final decisions in the hands of the president. They are articulated through presidential speeches and policy statements, reports of major departments and agencies, comments by top officials, and reports and legislation provided by Congress. With some major notable exceptions, these interests have sustained considerable bipartisan support and a sufficient consensus among the public to enable presidents to act vigorously in the area of foreign policy. Broad-based agreement on the definition of national interests abroad, however, runs the risk of failure to question and challenge existing premises, policies, and political goals. An open political process reduces these risks, but as the long debate over Vietnam suggests, changing fundamental definitions of the national interest can be exceedingly difficult.

In any case, definition of the national interest and of vital interest will continue to be shaped for some time to come by two other major factors: America's role as world leader and the cold war.

WORLD LEADERSHIP

In the early 1940s the United States did not set out to become the leader of the Western world, a postwar superpower, or the strongest nation on earth. Eager to return to prewar isolationism in 1945, Americans demanded rapid demobilization of wartime forces. However, with the prewar political system in shambles, the major actors desperately weakened or destroyed, and the threat of disorder, revolution, and chaos in the wind, the events of history had placed the United States in a position in which it could either take the lead in rebuilding world order or return to isolation. Physically untouched by war, enriched by a vibrant economy, militarily more power-ful than any other survivor of the war, the United States chose to assume a leadership role.

The decision took place in the framework of the global political sys-tem. Historically the system, in the absence of central world government and with each state sovereign to determine its own behavior, required makeshift arrangements to provide rudimentary order, deterrence of aggressive ambitions of states, and a few operational rules under which all states could function. These arrangements—balance of power, alliances, international law—provide mechanisms to create stability and order from legal and political anarchy. They were created and led by the strongest states, and in 1945 the United States and the Soviet Union emerged from the war with greater strength than others. When the relationship between the two countries came to preclude a partnership in the effort to produce global order, each state became the leader of its own bloc.

The American decision to provide the leadership for the non-Com-munist bloc and to seek peace through containment of Soviet ambitions led to a series of American policies designed to exercise that leadership. What was involved in this decision was a permanent American political commit-ment abroad, a drastic departure from the role the United States had previously played. The burden of world leadership was to involve a com-mitment of political, economic, military, and cultural resources for the foreseeable future. On the other hand, world leadership brought with it the opportunity to promote the ideals of democracy and capitalism, to strengthen the American economy by providing new foreign markets, and to solidify access to essential raw materials.

It was a new position for the United States, and it shaped the ways in which the national interest came to be defined. Had the older European powers resumed their previous roles in the world order, the United States might have resumed its isolation and defined its national interests in quite different terms.

Clearly history, and not just particular leaders, had shaped the reality confronting the United States in the mid-1940s. Personalities, of course, played their role in interpreting the world of the period and in designing an American response to it. Roosevelt was deeply committed to the creation of the United Nations and to the establishment of a postwar economic system. Some others may well have seen the opportunity for the expansion of American influence throughout the world. Others were moved to act by the bitter economic hardship created by the war on millions of people in Europe. The motives behind the definitions of the national interest that flowed from the period varied, but among the most powerful was the bitter reaction to the behavior of the Soviet Union in Europe. Soviet actions and the response of American leaders to them in the critical period of 1944–47 produced another profound influence on the definition of American national interests: the cold war.

THE COLD WAR

Since 1945 American relations with the Soviet Union have been at the very center of American foreign policy.

In view of the many interpretations of the onset of the cold war, some of which contend that the United States provoked the Soviet Union into belligerent behavior,[8] what is clear is that the Truman administration began to react strongly against Soviet actions in the territories it occupied during World War II. The imposition of Communist governments in many of the states of Eastern and Central Europe and the intensity of Communist party agitation in countries of Western Europe convinced the new president and most of his key advisers that meaningful cooperation between the two countries was impossible. Indeed, the Soviets had their own internal debate in these critical years, the Varga debate,[9], over policy toward the West and toward its own occupied countries. The Truman administration discerned an expansionist pattern by the Soviet Union and developed the "containment" policy designed to resist Soviet expansion, based on the analysis by Ambassador George Kennan of Soviet intentions. Relations between the two powers deteriorated, rhetoric grew more hostile, and the Soviet government chose to isolate itself from the Western economic and political system. President Truman pressured the Soviets to leave Iran, assumed support for anti-Communist forces in Greece and Turkey in the Truman Doctrine, and initiated the Marshall Plan, the Berlin airlift, the North Atlantic Treaty Organization, and American intervention in the Korean War as steps to counter what he regarded as Communist aggression. The cold war was in high gear, and its effect on the definition of American national interests was profound.

Three broad factors that persist to the present day form the basis of the cold war: ideological challenge, the conflict of national interests, and the competition for preeminence in the world system.

Many Americans originally saw the cold war in terms of the ideological challenge to the American system posed by communism. Long a target among Americans, communism was viewed as a challenge to religion, property, and democracy, offering in their stead an entirely different way of life and of government. The appeal of the ideas of communism was a cutting edge in Soviet postwar efforts to expand its influence. Indeed, some analysts have regarded Communist ideology primarily as a weapon in the pursuit of Soviet national interests which long predated the Communist government of the Soviet Union.

Enduring repeated invasions from the West, the Soviets were eager to establish a protective zone in Eastern Europe to deter invasion. This involved control of the countries occupied during the war and the continued division of Germany, a country that had invaded the Soviet Union twice in the twentieth century. In addition, the Soviets were eager for warm-water ports that would provide year-round access to the oceans and seas. Inevitably these territorial ambitions came in conflict with what Americans believed were the rights of the peoples of Eastern and Central Europe to freedom from foreign domination. Further, the Truman administration came to the conclusion, one that has been held ever since, that the Soviets were also eager to expand as far into Western Europe as possible or at least to extend their influence through the success of national Communist parties in France, Italy, Greece, and elsewhere.

However, a third major foundation of the cold war is the competition between the two countries for preeminence in the global system. Once victorious in World War II, the Soviets saw opportunities for the expansion of their influence not only in Europe but throughout the world. Thus the competition became global. Furthermore, Soviet leaders frequently announced their intentions of overtaking the United States in power, influence, wealth, and prestige.

Other elements have also contributed to the Soviet-American relationship: personal ambitions, technological change, domestic affairs.

Nearly forty years later, it is useful to ask whether the definitions of Soviet intentions and of the American national interest by virtually all top government officials were correct and whether an alternative policy toward the Soviet Union was possible. A number of American scholars, the so-called revisionist school, have recently questioned the premises and assumptions that led to the Cold War. Henry Nash points out:

> During the earliest post-war years, sustained and forceful policy dissent came only from Secretary [of Commerce Henry] Wallace. There was disagreement from time to time, but, other than the views of Henry Wallace, there was no outspoken criticism of the means and objectives of the new design of America's foreign policy.[10]

As suggested in the last two chapters, how leaders see and define reality and how they believe they should respond to it depends on a number of factors: psychological predispositions, personality, experience, the history of how states have behaved in the past, and domestic pressures. Was the definition of reality by the Truman administration in 1945-47 correct, or was a cooperative relationship with the Soviet Union possible?

Was Henry Wallace right after all? First, it must be noted that virtually all high-level policy makers have agreed that the Soviet intentions were aggressive and expansionist. Consensus does not necessarily imply correctness. Decision-making groups can be confident and certain of their analysis, and they can be wrong. The Yalta agreement had seemed to the Soviets to legitimize their sphere of influence in the territories occupied during the war. Subsequent American protests that the Soviets were not providing democratically elected governments as stipulated in the agreement overlooked the fact that Soviet definitions of democratic elections differed substantially from Western ones. With many American constituencies composed of natives of many of the occupied countries, the Truman administration protested that the agreements were being violated. From the Soviet viewpoint, the American actions might well have been interpreted as an attempt to renege on the agreement. Americans, having just finished one war against aggressive dictators, saw Soviet behavior as expansionist and unacceptable. In any case, American leaders saw ample justification for their interpretations of contemporary reality. Were they right? If it is correct that the three basic elements of the Cold War were conflicts over ideology, national interests, and global preeminence, it seems clear that unless the United States had agreed to satisfy fully all of the interests of the Soviet Union, normal, cooperative relations were not likely, and friction would have occurred in any case. Perhaps it might have been more muted or more mixed with cooperation in the events that followed, but the essentially competitive relationship seems to have been inevitable.

The result is that these three major elements—a national interest linked to every part of the globe, the role of world leadership, and the Cold War—provide the framework of the political track of American foreign policy. The United States maintained extensive linkages with many parts of the world prior to World War II—trade, trusteeship over scattered territories, military bases—but these expanded dramatically after the war when the role of world leadership and the cold war required additional contacts throughout the world.

One of the major results of the three dimensions of the political track is the impulse to oppose Soviet expansion everywhere. Through the use of the tools of policy in the four tracks, American policy makers have sought to close the doors of opportunity to Soviet initiatives throughout the world. The range of political tools available to serve political objectives provides considerable flexibility in the formulation and implementation of American foreign policy.

POLITICAL TOOLS

The multiplicity of tools available in the political track includes the following: diplomacy, international law, recognition, establishment and maintenance of diplomatic relations, treaties, trade agreements, participation in international or regional organizations, blocs or alliances, political warfare, covert operations. The basic tool of international politics is diplomacy.

Diplomacy

Diplomacy is politics among nation-states within the global system. Political scientist Richard Sterling regards it as "the oldest method that men have devised for coping with the problems of war and peace," and defines it as "the politics of international relations; it is international politics in the most precise sense of the term." Pointing to the differences between national systems and the global system, Sterling comments: "The purposes of politics and diplomacy are identical. Both seek to unite a plurality of interests or at least make them compatible—or both seek to make some interests prevail over others." Both diplomacy and politics encompass three basic modes of behavior: cooperation, accommodation, and opposition.[11]

In the absence of an established political order among states similar to the constitutional order of nation-states, diplomacy, nonetheless, has not only forged instruments by which states interact and mutually regulate their own behavior, but it more or less effectively follows the less integrated political procedures operating within the global system.

It is not unusual to hear people equate the term *diplomacy* with the foreign policy of the United States. Certainly when policy makers choose to rely on diplomacy instead of war, diplomacy is not only the means of policy but is policy itself. When diplomacy is chosen, it encompasses a wide range of subsidiary policies that may also be regarded as instruments of policy: recognition, friendship, cooperation, coordination of policies, treaties, alliance or bloc formation, mutual communications on a regular basis. Of course, diplomacy can also lead to other forms of friendly interaction among states: trade, travel, mutual security agreements, cultural ties.

In essence, foreign policy results from a process that takes into account the politics among states and the ways in which domestic politics evolves responses to them. Hans Morgenthau saw the task of diplomacy (in both its internal and foreign processes) as four-fold: (1) It must determine objectives in the light of the power actually and potentially available for the pursuit of these objectives; (2) it must assess the objectives of other nations and the power actually and potentially available for the pursuit of these objectives; (3) it must determine to what extent these different objectives are compatible with each other; and (4) it must employ the means suited to the pursuit of its objectives. "Failure in any of these tasks," Morgenthau writes, "may jeopardize the success of foreign policy and with it the peace of the world."[12]

Inherent in these comments about diplomacy are two distinct levels at which diplomacy must be understood. First, it involves the overall policy of a country and the process by which it was formed. Second, it encompasses the means utilized to carry out those policies.

Basically, most of the actions states may take toward each other range among cooperation, competition, conflict, or some combination of all of these. They include pledges, threats, promises, rewards and punishment.

In the World Events Interaction Survey (WEIS), twenty-two major foreign-policy responses and many subcategories were identified and tested. Among them are the following: yield, comment, consult, approve, promise, grant, reward, agree, request, propose, reject, accuse, protest, deny, demand, warn, threaten, demonstrate, reduce the relationship, expel, seize, and force.[13]

States may also choose to appease the demands of others, to seek the isolation of unfriendly states from normal contact with other states, to apply sanctions (such as American grain embargoes on the Soviet Union), or to inflict other forms of punishment.

These varied diplomatic options provide policy makers with considerable flexibility in fulfilling the major functions of diplomacy.

The Functions of Diplomacy   In the examination of the elaborate machinery of diplomacy in chapters 4 and 5 I emphasized the importance of diplomatic missions stationed in foreign countries and in international organizations, of the many agencies active in the missions, and in the policy-making machinery in Washington.

As Sterling suggests, this machinery performs the three classic functions of diplomacy: representation, intelligence, and negotiation.[14]

As part of the *representational function*, diplomats are expected to communicate regularly with officials of other governments and to articulate the policies of the United States.[15] They are also expected to explain American policies within their host countries as widely as possible. In another sense, they must also represent the views of the host government, or at the very least, report them accurately to Washington. Officials of a mission are also expected to represent the interests of Americans living in, traveling through, or doing business in their assigned country. With thousands of American corporate subsidiaries and affiliates functioning in foreign countries, with American tourists traveling abroad in record numbers, and with sizeable foreign-exchange programs, diplomats are broadly engaged in representing both governmental and private interests.

The intelligence function encompasses a wide range of activities abroad.[16] Information can be gathered from a number of formal and informal, public and confidential, governmental and nongovernmental sources. Basic information about other countries, their problems, their leaders and potential leaders is essential to the formulation of foreign policy, and the American capability to obtain information is extensive. Standard diplomacy, professional intelligence agencies, and complex electronic surveillance techniques are among the instruments available to gather necessary information throughout the world, and the United States has the resources to support a large and complex system, which can be focused as necessary for particular problems.

Intelligence is also *shared* with allies, although this can frequently lead to leaks of important information. A series of spy scandals in Great Britain, for example, has demonstrated that there are dangers as well as benefits in sharing certain types of intelligence with others.

Negotiation can range from attempts to solve a visa problem for an American tourist to the attempt to reestablish the independence of Lebanon. Matters large and small come under the negotiation function of diplomats, and the forms of diplomacy that have evolved in the twentieth century are varied.[17]

Traditional diplomacy involves negotiations between the American ambassador or a delegated official with officials of the host government. In the past, when transportation and communication were less developed than at present, the ambassador possessed a good deal of discretion and authority to negotiate major questions with other governments. In the jet age and in the era of instant communications, high government officials can retain control of negotiations, either through continuous communication or through direct travel to negotiate personally. One extreme form of this new diplomacy is "shuttle diplomacy," the intense travel by high officials between contending forces in an international crisis in order to produce a settlement of a dispute. In mid-1983, Secretary of State George Shultz made several trips to countries in the Middle East in order to find a diplomatic solution to the crisis in Lebanon.

Another form of diplomacy is "summitry," the meetings of heads of state, usually to sign some agreement that has been reached by lower-level diplomats.

In addition, the use of *personal envoys* representing the president, envoys who may or may not be permanent members of the governmental structure, has increased in the twentieth century.

Mass diplomacy takes place in the growing number of international organizations formed since the end of World War II. Such institutions as the United Nations, the International Monetary Fund, and the General Agreement on Tariffs and Trade provide the forums for negotiating important agreements among scores of states.

In the last analysis, while the overall power of ambassadors and envoys may have diminished, it is clear that the negotiating function of diplomacy has increased in both volume and importance in recent decades. Conferences, negotiations, and other communications are taking place somewhere in the world with American participation on a daily basis.

Recognition

On December 15, 1978, President Jimmy Carter announced that the United States and the People's Republic of China had agreed to establish normal diplomatic relations.[18] It was the end of almost thirty years of strained relations between the two countries, thirty years in which neither country formally recognized the other. During that period the American government had recognized the Nationalist government based on Taiwan as the formal government of China, and the dramatic turnabout was a recognition of the reality of the control of China by the Marxist government. Gradually, beginning in 1971, relations with the Beijing government had improved, leading to President Richard Nixon's historic trip there in 1971. However, a number of events slowed down the process leading to formal recognition and to the establishment of diplomatic relations, not least of which was the changeover in the government leadership in China following the death of Mao Zedung and Chou En-lai. In any case, the entire affair demonstrates the importance of the tools of recognition and formal diplomatic relations in the hands of the president, for these moves carry with them not only formal legal meaning but a sense of political legitimacy. In the case of China, the government had been recognized by many other countries in the world, but formal acceptance by the United States was an important additional legitimizing action opening the way for other relationships.

To grant recognition or to withhold it can be an important tool in a nation-state's relations with others.[19] Agreeing to recognize the existence of a new state or the legitimacy of a particular government of an existing state opens the way to regular, formal diplomatic relations, the establishment of embassies or missions in each other's country, and the beginning of trade, cultural exchange, and cooperation on a wide range of issues.

International Law and Treaties

Formal recognition of the sovereignty of other states and of the legitimacy of their governments, the establishment and maintenance of formal diplomatic relations involving the exchange of ambassadors, and the creation of treaties are among the most fundamental political-legal aspects of the relations between the United States and other countries.[20] They are part of the fabric of international law, which constitutes both part of the American national interest and an instrument of American foreign policy.

The United States invokes references to international law to dissuade other states from acting in ways that are objectionable to American interests, and it uses the proposals of new legal arrangements as inducements to cooperation with American interests.

The most basic legal-diplomatic arrangements proposed are treaties or executive agreements.[21] Although the Senate must consent to ratification of treaties but takes no part in agreements, the two instruments have practically equal status in American law. Treaties of friendship, commerce, and navigation or treaties of mutual security constitute the major legal arrangements made by the United States with other states.

Trade agreements will be explored in more detail in the next chapter.

International Organizations

In addition to bilateral relations, the United States participates in literally hundreds of international organizations and agrees to abide by their rules.[22] Clearly, the most comprehensive of these is the United Nations, where the United States has direct contact with member states. It may also have indirect contact with political movements it does not yet formally recognize, such as the Palestine Liberation Organization, which has been given observer status at the U.N. One former American ambassador to the United Nations, Andrew Young, was severely criticized at one point for holding discussions with a representative of the PLO in New York.[23] Since the PLO does not have the formal status of a nation-state, and since the United States does not formally recognize it, any contacts must properly take place through third parties.

In a more recent case, following the seizure of American hostages and of the American embassy in Teheran, Iran, in November 1979, during the Iranian Revolution, the United States broke diplomatic relations with the new Iranian government, and negotiations for the release of the hostages were conducted through a number of third parties, particularly Algeria.[24]

Alliances and Blocs

Since World War II, the United States has helped to organize a wide range of alliances and blocs. The alliance is a formal and legal set of arrangements by which states undertake mutual obligations of various sorts.[25] Blocs may be less formal arrangements in which states organize themselves for varied reasons: voting in the United Nations, regional development, or economic cooperation to name just a few.

The North Atlantic alliance, formed in a treaty among the United States and several states of Western Europe in 1949, is the major American military-political alliance. It provides for creation of a joint military organization, the North Atlantic Treaty Organization (NATO) supported by financial and military contributions from the member states.

A regional organization, the Organization of American States (OAS), was formed to provide common consultation among the countries of North and South America.

NATO and OAS are among the most important alliances to which the United States is a member.

Alliances and blocs entail both costs and rewards. The obligations undertaken by the United States when it participates require a willingness to accommodate American views to those of allies. However, the political strength produced by the joint action of like-minded states exceeds that of the United States alone. Still, the problems of politics within the alliances and blocs constitute distinct foreign-policy questions. NATO, for example, has been said for over thirty years to be in "disarray" with one or another partner engaged in independent action that may or may not be consistent with American goals. Although differences with the French government have been most pronounced within NATO, the United States has occasionally had serious differences with almost every other member of the alliance.

Aside from the necessity to keep American alliances in good working order, leaders may also try to limit the size and effectiveness of the alliances of an adversary.[26] Efforts to persuade countries from joining the Soviet bloc and to detach existing allies from it has been part of American cold war policy, as the notable successes of the last decade with Egypt and China have demonstrated.

In the final analysis, maintenance of allies requires great skill in sustaining common purpose and common action, but alliances remain one of the most important tools of American foreign policy.

Political Warfare and Covert Operations

Somewhere between peaceful, normal relations and war, the United States has developed a variety of tools of policy that can be termed political warfare, that is, a way to pursue political objectives short of war. These techniques include a wide range of both overt and covert techniques for promoting the interests of the United States and for obstructing the pursuit of the interests of an adversary. Some of the tools of political warfare may also be directed at allies in order to retain their support of American goals and their opposition to Soviet pressures, but the bulk of the techniques are directed primarily either at the Soviet Union or at states in which the superpowers are in competition.

Political warfare may include various forms of covert operations, psychological strategies, propaganda, infiltration, subversion, espionage, assassination, bribery, and sanctions.[27] Even more extreme measures— military or paramilitary—may also be used to achieve political objectives.[28] Sabotage, terrorism, guerilla war, support of coups d'état, or the attempt to prevent them are some of the techniques employing force.

Political warfare is defined as a controlled form of physical and psychological action that is directed against specific foreign personalities or publics. It may be applied on a scale of increasing intensity—from public and benign activity such as psychological strategies, economic aid, propaganda, and information-gathering all the way to covert, secret support of civil war in another country.

Covert operations customarily encompass spying, espionage, infiltration, subversion, bribery, terrorism, and sabotage.[29]

Some intelligence activities still require the use of spies, either foreign or national, whose cooperation is achieved through bribery, blackmail, personal conviction or ambition. The infiltration of agents of one country into the key sectors of another or into military operations and the infiltration of soldiers behind enemy lines are methods of attacking the enemy's position from within. The use of subversion to either influence the behavior of a foreign government or to cause a decline in public confidence in the government and subvert its policies constitutes an effective covert method of political warfare. Financial support of various types, such as outright bribery, paid advertising, or campaign contributions, is designed to assist a regime to stay in power, keep it from cooperating with the Soviet Union, or help remove it from power. On occasion assassination of foreign leaders has been considered.

Psychological warfare consists of efforts to create, sustain, or change attitudes of foreign leaders or publics in ways that will promote the foreign-policy interests of the United States.[30]

Although governments have many means with which to communicate privately as well as publicly with each other, propaganda—the public announcement and discussion of their objectives and policies—is an essential part of the process.[31] The public news media of the world are a massive forum for the communication of psychological strategies, but in addition, the United States is one of many governments with the capability to communicate directly with other peoples and their leaders.

Since the end of the Second World War, the United States has maintained elaborate propaganda machinery under the U.S. Information Agency (USIA). Among its functions are the maintenance of libraries, publications, and other printed informational services; the operation of the Voice of America, a worldwide radio-broadcast service; the distribution of film, videotape, and television programs; communication through provision of speakers to local groups; and exchange programs. In its operations it provides some level of entertainment as well as information. Two other broadcast services—Radio Free Europe and Radio Liberty—directed at the nations of Eastern Europe and the Soviet Union were largely funded in the past with CIA support, but subsequently have been placed under the government's Board of International Broadcasting.

Another worldwide American informational system, one less specifically dedicated to propaganda, is the Armed Forces Press, Radio, and TV Service. Designed originally to provide "back home" entertainment and information for American military personnel abroad, AFPRTS soon attracted substantial audiences among the civilian populations of the many countries in which it operates. In general, it has been of propaganda value because of its basically nonpropaganda nature.

The use of the tools of political warfare and covert operations has long been a controversial aspect of American foreign policy. On the one hand, it is argued that, given the responsibilities that the United States has acquired as a superpower, instruments short of war are essential if the government is to defend American interests abroad. On the other hand, many Americans have been deeply disturbed over the use of secret and violent techniques by a democracy. Investigations by the Senate in the 1970s of CIA activities produced intense public criticism of the covert operations of the intelligence system, and many argued that not only were these operations not representative of American thinking but they could also be a domestic danger if turned against Americans. The revelations of the Senate hearings about American activities in Chile in 1970–73 and of the Watergate hearings concerning the domestic activities of the Nixon administration deepened the skepticism of many Americans about the use of such tools of policy. Intelligence activities have been brought under somewhat closer scrutiny by the creation of special committees within the House of Representatives and the Senate. However, the Reagan administration has moved to strengthen the intelligence system and to make it a crime to reveal the names of agents abroad. Congress has legislated that the United States government may do nothing to overthrow or help to overthrow a legitimate government, but a major controversy arose in 1983 about American covert support of antigovernment forces in Nicaragua. American support for the government of El Salvador includes both overt and covert operations against a growing rebel force.

Clearly, the government has no intention of relinquishing the tools of political warfare or covert operations.

CONCLUSION

As we have seen, the political track of American foreign policy is largely shaped by the definition of the national interest. Therefore, the specific content of that definition is one of the most important political decisions that American policy makers can make. Affected by the cold war relationship with the Soviet Union and by the reality of a world leadership role, the national interest is subject to various interpretations as leaders and world conditions change.

In the real world of nation-states, all countries are free to define their own national interests, and the essence of international politics and of the foreign policies of all states is the adjustment of their national interests to those of other countries. How this is done depends upon whether states perceive that they share mutual interests or whether they have fundamentally opposing interests. The challenge for American foreign policy, as it is designed to serve the American national interest, is to maximize the development of mutual interests and correctly identify and respond to opposing interests.

In confronting opposing interests, three options are possible: (1) ignore them; (2) combat them; or (3) seek to change them into mutual interests through peaceful means (reconciliation).

Given the status of the United States as a superpower, Americans must carefully consider, as they define the national interest, what is the right, moral, and effective role the United States must play in the political track of the global system. What rights, responsibilities, authority, and power should the United States have to intervene in the development of the global system as it considers the three options cited above?

The way we answer such questions will be a powerful determinant of how we define the national interest and how we devise foreign policies appropriate to the definition. If we conclude that the United States has no special leadership role in the global system, we might define the national interest in a way that minimizes American political, military, economic, and cultural activity throughout the world. On the other hand, a conclusion that the United States, because of its size, wealth, and power must play a leadership role in maintaining world order, in promoting peaceful economic and social change, and in promoting the expansion of human rights everywhere, would support a role that entails broad-based involvement in world affairs. Between these two views—detachment and full commitment—lie many other possible choices.

The crises in Central America and Lebanon in 1983 and the response of the Reagan administration to them, resulting in the deaths of nearly three hundred Americans, painfully raised questions again about the American role in the world and the relevance of such areas to the American national interest. Why does a tiny island such as Grenada and a small country in the distant Middle East such as Lebanon require an American military commitment and the loss of American lives? What is the political objective? Were political tools not sufficient to deal with the problems? In the thinking of the Reagan administration, Grenada was in the process of becoming a base for Cuban and Soviet expansion in the Caribbean area and in the Western Hemisphere. The stability of Lebanon was concluded to be vital to the security of Israel, to the American position in the Middle East so critical to maintaining access to oil, and to the exclusion of Soviet influence from the region. Is there validity in these conclusions and in the assumptions that led to them? Even granting the validity of the assumptions, was military force the most effective tool available to deal with the problem and to accomplish political objectives? Can the United States ignore political developments in distant regions that seem to affect American national interests, and how do we decide which developments do, in fact, adversely affect American national interests? Is there a limit to the effectiveness of nonmilitary tools, and when are military tools to be utilized? Should the United States remain detached from political developments in other countries and refrain from interference in any way? Would the ultimate costs of involvement be larger than the costs of detachment?

Americans have many differing views about the answers to such questions, and these are reflected in the American political process, in the debates in the country and in the Congress, and in the struggle between Congress and the president. American reaction to the tragedy in Vietnam has deeply influenced the debate about how best to exercise American influence and over whether American influence should be exercised at all in distant places. But at the bottom of every debate lies the question of the ambitions and intentions of the Soviet Union and the relevance of its actions to world peace.

As the twentieth century draws to an end, however, there are other challenges to the status quo (and some would argue to American interests) from other quarters. Cuba, although strongly allied to the Soviet Union, represents the challenge by many peoples in Central America to the past domination by the United States. Libya, under Muammar Quaddafi, represents a powerful thrust to Islamic and Pan-Arab sentiment for independence and power in a world dominated by Western Christian powers and by Eastern non-Islamic powers. Iran, under the control of Ayatollah Khomeini, symbolizes the drive of Moslem fundamentalism to reassert independence from Western political and cultural influence. In these cases the Soviet Union did not create the ambitions and movements of others, but has often skillfully exploited them against the United States and the West in its own interests. Thus it is not merely Soviet imperialism that challenges a world order desired by the United States.

But is every local or regional movement a challenge to American interests? Can't such movements be accepted as inevitable parts of the world order, which can be accommodated by the United States? Further, is there no way in which the legitimate interests of the superpowers can be reconciled, in which each can recognize and accept the vital interests of each other? Short of the destruction of the Soviet Union or a massive transformation of its society and government, it will remain an active, ambitious, and growing country. Its interests will inevitably conflict with those of the United States in many parts of the world. Resistance to its ambitions is often seen as a zero-sum game. But need it be? The political track involves the need to seek ways to peacefully reconcile conflicting interests and ambitions and to convert opposing interests into mutual ones. The effort will require a change in the mixture of cooperation, conflict, and competition between the super-powers, with the acquiescence of both. This was one goal of the period of détente in the 1970s. In the 1980s such issues as arms control, trade, and cultural exchange are areas in which mutuality of interests exists but agreement is difficult, and both powers are required to make concessions.

Cooperation on providing nonmilitary aid to the less developed countries of the world would be in the national interests of both sides.

On a wide range of grounds—humanitarian, moral, political, economic—it is essential that American policy be continued toward organizing and distributing development support: investment, loans, training, technical assistance.

The revolutions of peoples of less developed countries have long constituted a political challenge to American leadership. How to lead them rather than repress them has been a puzzle for most administrations since 1945. Opposition to revolutions because they are Marxist in nature has not only been counterproductive much of the time but has often failed to distinguish between those that are truly nonaligned and those that are likely to become strategic bases for the Soviet Union. For American policy makers, acceptance of Marxist regimes in the Soviet Union and China has been easier than acceptance of Marxist governments in Third World areas. This approach is not only inconsistent but potentially dangerous.

In a world system in which there is no central government or central authority, the great powers have always played a major political role in maintaining whatever order and peace that has been achieved. It is hardly the most rational model for political life that humanity can devise, but it is one with which the world must live for the foreseeable future. In such a system great powers have assumed great prerogatives and great responsibilities, based on their interests and capabilities. Thus each superpower assumes the right to establish and maintain its influence throughout the world, both for its own interest and to balance or resist the influence of the other. In the process each seeks to exert pressure, to manipulate, and to mold the system according to its own definitions of its national interest. To find the best balance between the interests of superpowers and those of other states is a primary challenge of the political track since the interests of each superpower may not coincide with the interests of all other states nor with each other.

Thus, developing new mutual interests and reconciling opposing interests not only with the Soviet Union but with all other states is a primary function of the political track.

NOTES

[1] Roger Hilsman, *To Govern America* (New York: Harper & Row, Publishers, 1979), p. 11.

[2] Ibid., pp. 18–19.

[3] Bernard D. Nossiter, "Sea Law Signed by 117 Nations: U.S. Opposes It," *New York Times*, December 11, 1982, p. 1.

[4] Hans Morgenthau, *Politics Among Nations: The Struggle for Power and Peace*, 5th ed., rev. (New York: Alfred A. Knopf, 1978), p. 5.

[5] Morgenthau, "Another Great Debate: The National Interest of the United States," *American Political Science Review* LXVI (December 1952), 961–98.

[6] Frederick H. Hartmann, *The Relations of Nations*, 6th ed. (New York: Macmillan Company, 1983), pp. xxiv–xxv, 7–12.

[7] See chapter 2, pp. 20–32.

[8] Representative of these views are the following: Gabriel Kolko, *The Roots of American Foreign Policy* (Boston: Beacon Press, 1969), and William Appleman Williams, *The Tragedy of American Diplomacy*, 2nd ed. (New York: Delta, 1972).

[9] Alvin Z. Rubenstein, *Soviet Foreign Policy Since World War II: Imperial and Global* (Cambridge, Mass.: Winthrop Publishers, 1981), p. 52; Adam B. Ulam, *Expansion and Coexistence: Soviet Foreign Policy 1917–73*, 2nd ed. (New York: Praeger Publishers, 1974), p. 410.

Varga, director of the Institute of the World Economics and World Politics, argued after the war that capitalism would not collapse and that the Soviet Union should maintain more open relationships with the West and with its satellite countries. He eventually lost the argument to Kremlin hardliners, including Stalin, who decided on a more combative posture toward the West.

[10] Henry T. Nash, *American Foreign Policy: Changing Perspectives on National Security*, rev. ed. (Homewood, Ill.: Dorsey Press, 1978), p. 33.

[11] Richard W. Sterling, *Macropolitics: International Relations in a Global Society* (New York: Alfred A. Knopf, 1974), p. 233.

[12] Morgenthau, *Politics Among Nations*, pp. 529–31.

[13] World Events Interaction Survey, cited in Bruce M. Russett and Harvey Starr, *World Politics: The Menu for Choice* (San Francisco: W. H. Freeman and Co., Publishers, 1981), pp. 189–91.

[14] Sterling, *Macropolitics*, p. 233.

[15] Ibid., p. 234.

[16] Theodore A. Couloumbis and James H. Wolfe, *Introduction to International Relations: Power and Justice*, 2nd ed. (Englewood Cliffs, N.J.: Prentice-Hall, 1982), pp. 154–60.

[17] Sterling, *Macropolitics*, pp. 235–36, 249.

[18] Jimmy Carter, *Keeping Faith* (New York: Bantam Books, 1982), pp. 199–200.

[19] Couloumbis and Wolfe, *Introduction to International Relations*, pp. 248–50.

[20] Ibid., pp. 244–56.

[21] Ibid., pp. 254–56.

[22] Charles W. Kegley and Eugene R. Wittkopf, *American Foreign Policy: Pattern and Process*, 2nd ed. (New York: St. Martin's Press, 1982), pp. 168–75.

[23] Carter, *Keeping Faith*, p. 491.

[24] Ibid., pp. 524–81.

[25] Couloumbis and Wolfe, *Introduction to International Relations*, pp. 225-26.

[26] Hartmann, *The Relations of Nations*, pp. 324–25.

[27] Couloumbis and Wolfe, *Introduction to International Relations*, pp. 152–54.

[28] K. J. Holsti, *International Politics: A Framework for Analysis*, 3rd ed. (Englewood Cliffs, N.J.: Prentice-Hall, 1977), pp. 274–76.

[29] Kegley and Wittkopf, *American Foreign Policy*, pp. 110–16.

[30] Cecil V. Crabb, Jr., *American Foreign Policy in the Nuclear Age*, 4th ed. (New York: Harper & Row, Publishers, 1983), pp. 149–53.

[31] Ibid., pp. 151–59.

CHAPTER FIFTEEN
THE ECONOMIC TRACK

> Just as economic factors shape political outcomes, so political factors shape economic outcomes.
>
> Joan Edelman Spero

Since the 1770s the government of the United States has engaged in first, the creation, and then, the development of the American economy, and over the years its responsibility for the economic well-being of the country has expanded dramatically. The process has included foreign policy. The acquisition of foreign loans to sustain the struggling new republic, the negotiation and maintenance of colonial trade with Europe, and fragmentary efforts to support development of the domestic economy constituted a major part of the agenda of the Continental Congress. The American government then had to determine the shape and structure of the economic system, principally the relationship between government and the private sector. The choice was to leave the basic responsibility for economic development in the hands of private citizens in a free-enterprise system. However, the coming of the welfare state and the increasing number of responsibilities assumed by the national government, the onset of world leadership functions in the twentieth century, and new demands by the public have all contributed to a larger governmental role in economic affairs. By now, in the 1980s, the government's economic activity has come to include regulation along a broad spectrum of economic activity and a budget that constitutes about one-third of the gross national product.

Indeed, government spending is now the largest single part of the national economy.

Few would argue that by the early twentieth century, the country's economic well-being had become one of the primary responsibilities of the United States government. Yet much of the drive for economic activity also comes from the private sector—from private entrepreneurs and corporations primarily interested in making a profit, much of it in business abroad. Their interests necessarily involve the government, reflect upon national interests, and have ripple effects in other countries.

The operation of private economic interests raises the old and controversial issue of whether business follows the flag or whether the flag follows business. Convinced of their doctrine of economic determinism, Marxist-Leninists argue that economic motives lie behind all domestic and foreign political activity, including imperialism. The realist school, on the other hand, contends that power is the driving force behind national behavior.

This "chicken-or-egg" argument is a fascinating one, but in many ways an irrelevant one in the contemporary world. Both Marxist and non-Marxist systems engage in a web of global economic activity in which it is nearly impossible to separate economic motives from political ones or, indeed, to know how to do so. States act both for economic and political purposes using economic tools. Whatever the validity of claims that economic interests motivate political behavior, Spero contends that there are equally powerful ways in which political factors shape economic policy.[1] First, she argues, the political system shapes the economic system. As nations rise and fall, as new international structures of power emerge, new economic systems arise. Second, political concerns often shape economic policy, utilizing economic tools to promote larger strategic or security interests. Third, international economic relations, in and of themselves, are political relations. The negotiation of economic matters and the purposes for which they are negotiated involve political processes.

If the connection between international politics and the economic track is clear, the relationship between the domestic economy and foreign policy should be even more apparent. Economic strength is one of the major foundations of political power. It is fundamental to the capability of the United States to play a leadership role in the world. The resources required to sustain military capability, technological research and development, a mass public-education system, and general personal comfort are massive, and only a vibrant economy can produce them.

Finally, the economic base of the United States provides adequate resources to support and to utilize a wide range of economic tools to serve American national interests abroad. Their availability to use as rewards or punishments provides considerable flexibility to policy makers in dealing with other countries.

In pursuit of the economic well-being of the American people and of the United States, the goals of the United States in the economic track include the following: (1) maintaining the competition between capitalism and communism; (2) supporting the doctrine of free trade and the free market; (3) integrating the three economic systems operative in the world;

(4) strengthening the interdependence of the global system; (5) utilizing and expanding the international machinery designed for economic management; (6) facilitating the transfer of technology, food, and other resources throughout the system, and (7) maintaining the strength and growth of the domestic economy, including the development of an industrial policy.

To achieve these objectives the United States may apply a number of tools: monetary management and policy; trade and access to American markets; investment; multinational corporations; loans, grants, and credits; commodity agreements; technical assistance; financing of facilities and bases in other countries; embargoes and sanctions; immigration; and tourism.

In analyzing the economic track of policy and the tools relating to it, the student must keep in mind that although government policy is required to permit it, private economic interests provide a major part of the economic activity performed by Americans abroad. Occasionally the interests of private enterprise in seeking profit and those of the government may conflict or, at the very least, may not be coordinated. This inconsistency of interests poses serious problems in the utilization of economic tools for maximum results in foreign policy.

An examination of the issues inherent in the economic track follows.

CAPITALISM AND COMMUNISM

The ideological aspect of conflict between the United States and the Soviet Union, as suggested in the previous chapter, is an important part of the cold war. It encompasses competing models of political, economic, and social organization, and it has been used to serve the broader political purposes of both sides. Although some analysts believe that the power of the Communist ideology has diminished, even in the Soviet Union, it continues to produce observable effects in many countries of the world that quickly adopted Marxist politico-economic models; but in the 1980s, faced by economic stagnation, some have appeared to experiment with a greater reliance on the market and on a free-enterprise approach to development. The most notable example in recent years has been the People's Republic of China, which has sought to utilize some market mechanisms and to move rapidly away from dogmatic Maoist communism in economics, and even the Soviet Union has moved toward the market.[2]

Anticommunism has been one of the major foundations of American foreign policy since 1945, not only because of American rejection of the ideology but also as opposition to the expansion of Soviet influence in every area of the globe grew. Rejection of the economic premises of communism and enthusiastic advocacy of the capitalist system remain a major part of American foreign policy.

Communism offers a critique of capitalism that depicts it as a system supporting the property of a few who exploit the many. In a search for profits capitalists promote a foreign policy of imperialism, and war occurs in the search for conquest or in the competition among capitalists for colonies.[3] The Communist model of a domestic economy includes the premise that the people as a whole own all property; that public property is to be administered by the Communist party in the name of the people; and that central direction of the economy will determine production priorities, prices, wages, and use of profit.

Capitalism is based in the belief in the existence of private property, the development of the economy by private individuals seeking profit, and the operation of the privately owned sector with a minimum of interference by the state.[4] This decentralized, pluralist system of economic activity is regulated not by central government direction but by the free market. The market mechanism is a system that determines production, prices, wages, and profit through the interplay of supply and demand.

In theory and in practice, many countries have experimented with mixtures of the two systems, and the variety of permutations is too extensive to review in detail in this context.[5] One country that has long maintained a system blending both private and public ownership of the means of production is Great Britain. Communist states have often integrated elements of the market mechanism in them, and the United States has, in fact, developed many characteristics of governmental direction and influence on the economy.

FREE TRADE
AND THE FREE MARKET

Two of the essential principles in the economic track of American foreign policy are the concepts of free trade and the free market.

The principle of free trade was an outgrowth of British philosophical and economic thinking during the period of Great Britain's colonial expansion.[6] In the twentieth century it was adopted by Americans, including Secretary of State Cordell Hull, who saw in the unrestricted trade among countries a way to avoid the costly and deadly wars that had plagued Europeans for four centuries. On the assumption that conflict over trade was both a cause of war and an expression of hostility among states, supporters of the concept of free trade saw the possibility that in the post-1945 world, a system could be established in which all states opened their markets to products of other countries. This would require a removal or lowering of tariffs, the end of quotas, and the reduction of all barriers to an open global market. The doctrine became an integral part of American postwar policy, and American leadership used it in organizing the General Agreement on Tariffs and Trade. Extensive and lengthy rounds of negotiations were held among member-states in the 1960s in the so-called Kennedy Round and in the 1970s in the Tokyo Round. In a world of increasing economic competition and new and complex products and services, the GATT mechanism has helped to mediate some serious problems, although the use of nontariff barriers and of government subsidy of specific industries by some countries has tended to undercut the intentions of free-trade doctrine. American protests against the efforts of Japan and of the European Common Market to exclude a wide range of American products, for example, suggest the continuing difficulties posed by contemporary international trade.

The free-market doctrine is an essential element of capitalist thinking. Based on the assumption that sales, prices, and production will respond to the forces of supply and demand, the free market is seen as an objective regulator of economic activity.[7] When a demand is perceived for some good or service, producers will respond by producing them. Prices will be set that customers are willing to pay and that will be regulated by the supply of the product available in comparison to the demand for it. The process will produce a profit adequate to make production worthwhile for the seller, who may then use the profit to reinvest. One basic criticism of the market is that because it responds to public demand, it may neglect urgent needs or unprofitable functions needed for the public welfare. Another criticism suggests that the market can be created and manipulated by producers for items with less than vital social utility. Thus the market results in a wasteful allocation of raw materials, wealth, and resources.

Theoretically, there should be no conflict between the free market and free trade. Under the concept of comparative advantage, each country should be able to sell its unique products to those who need them in an open market and thereby acquire the resources to buy the products of all countries. In reality, not all countries possess equal resources either to sell or to buy, and some are at a distinct disadvantage in an open-market system. In some cases major consumer states can keep prices low for products from poorer countries and keep prices high for manufactured goods. On the other hand, producer cartels, such as OPEC, may control the production of a product in order to drive the price higher. Thus the temptation to manipulate the system for special advantage.

Despite the shortcomings of the concepts of free trade and free market and of the efforts to practice them, many defenders of both concepts continue to make the case for them.

THREE SYSTEMS

Spero argues that the global economic system consists of three separate systems: (1) the Western system, consisting of the industrial powers of North America, Western Europe, and Japan; (2) the North-South system, involving relations among the Western system and the less developed states of Asia, Africa, and Latin America; and (3) the East-West system, in which more limited relations exist between the West and the Communist bloc.[8]

The Western system embodies the bulk of global economic relations. Trade is massive, and interdependence is deeply rooted.

The North-South system reflects wide differences among countries in terms of power, resources, and development. The South itself consists of more than one hundred countries of great diversity. Some of these developing countries have reached a high level of development and approach the category of developed states. Close to three dozen are intensely poor and bereft of resources. The majority, however, seem to have the capacities for impressive economic growth.

In the mid-1940s, the Soviet Union decided to remain outside the Western system and to create one of its own with the satellites acquired in World War II. To match the coordinating mechanisms of the West, the Soviet Union formed the Council for Mutual Economic Assistance (COMECON) to facilitate coordination of mutual monetary and trade policies. In the 1970s the policy of détente between the superpowers led to an effort to negotiate a major trade agreement between the superpowers, but events in both countries led to its ultimate rejection.

Nevertheless, the United States has continued to trade actively with the Soviet bloc, as we shall see later in this chapter, and Soviet interest in Western grain and technology has kept trade contacts active.

The concept of three systems is a useful one, although long-term trends suggest increasing interrelationships among them.

INTERDEPENDENCE

The world system since 1945 has been one of dynamic and unprecedented change. Although massive world trade existed prior to 1945, the post war period encompassed the creation and expansion of economic linkages among states, and new developments in transportation and communications made global economic relations easier and quicker. Since 1945 more than one hundred new nation-states have emerged from the wreckage of former colonial empires, each with its own national economic interests. With the exception of the Communist bloc of states, most countries became linked in international systems of money, trade, aid, and investment—a system that is sometimes called interdependence.[9]

In political terms, the system is regarded by critics as a new form of neocolonialism and neoimperialism since, it is said, what has emerged are not equal relationships between and among states but the perpetuation of dominance/dependence relationships. The arguments have been presented elsewhere in this book.[10]

Factually, interdependence includes not only the relationships between the developed and less developed countries but also the changing relationships among the developed countries themselves. Partly as a result of American economic policies in the immediate postwar periods, many of the major countries engaged in World War II were able to recover quickly and to become highly competitive in world trade with the United States.

In the four decades since the establishment of the Bretton Woods system, the nations of the world have muddled through the process of creating a system that is capable of successfully managing this complex world economy, and the United States has been in the forefront of these efforts. For about fifteen years, from 1945 to 1960, the United States could very largely set the rules of the game and intervene to solve problems. With the rise of other states with major economic forces, a form of global pluralism emerged in which the United States remained the most important element but no longer the commanding one. Since the 1960s the non-

Communist world has sought, through trial and error, through negotiation, and through politics to agree upon arrangements to manage the economic system. It is a process laced with national interest, prestige, preference, and power, but it has produced some stability.

From the standpoint of American foreign policy, the forging of a global system has afforded both opportunities and constraints on American global interests. Decisions affecting American domestic affairs have repercussions throughout the entire system, and many activities of foreign countries, such as the OPEC price increases, have profound effects on the United States.

In the 1980s, despite the turbulence and change within the global economic system, the American dollar remains the central currency of international economic life; the American market is the most tempting target for trade; American investment remains a desired goal; and American leadership is still required, although it must now work with other countries on a more political basis.

It is in this global search for a management system for a system of interdependence that the United States continues to play a leading role.

The emerging system has induced the increased economic demands of the less developed countries of the world (LDCs) and has provided them with access to the system and to some degree of power and influence within it. The problems of the LDCs form a large part of the agenda of the system.

INTERNATIONAL MACHINERY

As states have sought to construct an effective system to manage international economic affairs since 1945, they have created a number of new institutions and have posed new responsibilities on older ones.

The Bretton Woods Agreement led to the formation of the International Monetary Fund and the International Bank for Reconstruction and Development (the World Bank).[11] The IMF was created to provide short-term loans to countries to meet balance-of-payments deficits, and the World Bank was designed to provide loans for reconstruction and development of the industrial capacity of states. Later, in response to the needs of many of the newer, less developed countries, the International Finance Corporation and the International Development Association were established.

In recent years the older Bank of International Settlements, in Basel, Switzerland, has played an increasing role in regulating the international monetary system,[12] and in 1983 the United States Congress moved to approve formal American membership.

Within the IMF, a group of ten major industrial states formed the Group of Ten in 1961, largely to provide a means for other states to participate in monetary decision making.[13] Under IMF jurisdiction, less developed countries succeeded in gaining participation in the decision-making group, which was expanded and called the Group of Twenty.

The LDCs, partly in response to what they saw as control of the GATT by the major powers, pressured for the establishment of the United

National Conference on Trade and Development (UNCTAD) in 1964, which would provide a mechanism for the less developed countries.[14] They also established the Group of 77 within the United Nations (which now totals more than 110).[15] In 1974 the group developed and proposed a program for a "New International Economic Order" and has pressed its economic demands on the industrial states.

The industrial states organized their own coordinating institution— The Organization for Economic Cooperation and Development (OECD),[16] and more recently, heads of state of the Group of Five major economic powers, plus Canada and Italy, instituted a series of annual summit conferences to discuss common economic problems.

In addition to intergovernmental machinery, private banks and bank consortia have played an increasingly large role in international economic operations.[17]

These are just a few of the more important structures involved in the world economy in the 1980s; there are many other institutions that can prove useful or, indeed, indispensable to the developing system.

In most of these structures, the United States no longer possesses commanding power and must negotiate with other states to develop major economic policies. Nonetheless, the financial contribution of the United States is often the largest one, and American influence is still substantial.

In the last fifteen years the IMF has come to play an increasingly important role in providing loans to developed and less developed countries involved in either balance-of-payments problems or in serious economic difficulties internally. However, the imposition of conditions on its loans is not always welcome.[18]

It seems clear that this international machinery will play additional roles in the future and that it is already a significant feature which must be integrated into American foreign policy.

TECHNOLOGY, FOOD,
AND OTHER RESOURCES

The desire of other countries to share in the technological revolution and to obtain adequate basic needs such as food and energy constitutes important elements of the international environment that relate to American foreign policy.

Modern technology, developed largely by the United States, has changed many things in our lives, not the least of which are methods of creation and production of wealth. These methods promise to transform the industrial basis of American life. Considerable attention is now focused on the projected transformation of advanced capitalist countries from the industrial to the postindustrial process.[19] Although the change will not occur quickly, some scholars view it as irreversible, similar to the transformation of agricultural economies to industrial ones a century ago. Since the countries of the world are at such disparate stages of development, the transformations that lie ahead pose international realities of considerable magnitude. This means new and immense challenges and opportunities for Americans in both the international and domestic economies. The demand from less developed countries for an increased transfer of technology is just one result of this process, and how the United States responds depends in large measure on how the new conditions affect the definition of the national interest.[20]

The long-term limitations upon food and energy created, in part, by an expanding global population make resource scarcity a problem of increasing intensity to which the United States cannot be indifferent.[21] With a surplus of food but a diminishing supply of fossil energy, the United States faces the need to develop foreign policies that respond to both conditions.

THE DOMESTIC ECONOMY

Whatever the role of international realities in shaping the economic track of policy, the basis of American strength and capability to serve the national interest lies in the domestic economy.[22]

Gifted with a rich and favored geography laced with minerals and raw materials, populated by an ambitious and hard-working people, managed by creative economic entrepreneurs, the United States quickly became a land of wealth. Although wealth was not always fairly distributed among the population, a fact that led to the formation of gigantic labor unions, the economic foundation of highly productive industrial society was in place by the early twentieth century.

How to keep an economy of increasing size and complexity productive remains a major problem not only for domestic policy but for foreign policy as well.

In a capitalist society the state gives the private sector the primary responsibility for creating the economic well-being of the nation. At the same time, in the twentieth century governments have retained the responsibility for creating the conditions in which the economy develops. However responsibility for economic well-being is divided between the private and the government sectors, it is clear that knowledgeable, skilled, and imaginative *leadership* is essential in both sectors to retain the economic strength of the United States.

Finally, it is said that the United States government does not have an industrial policy, that reliance on the decentralized private sector to work out a national economic strategy on its own fails to take into account the broad national interests of the United States.[23] Further, such reliance fails to provide the strategic planning necessary to determine how to make the industrial transition required in the next several decades from an industrial to a post-industrial economy. Proposals for creation of a new reindustrialization agency capable of supporting new industries and defining national economic strategy have produced considerable controversy.[24] Opposition to national governmental planning of any sort remains strong in a free-enterprise system. However, the need for broad, long-term goals and for some informed understanding of how the economic track should best serve the interests of the United States is a real one.

TOOLS OF POLICY

The nature of the global politico-economic system, as we have just seen, provides ideological, environmental, and institutional factors which shape and are shaped by the American domestic economy.

Within this context specific economic capabilities inherent in the system provide American policy makers with a variety of tools with which to deal with the rest of the world. Among these are monetary policy, trade policy (including sanctions and embargoes), investment policy, the transfer of technology and other resources, immigration, and tourism. On the other hand, global economic activity imposes some constraints on American policy especially when the American balance of payments and the balance of trade reflect sizeable deficits.

In the following pages of this chapter, we will assess several of these economic tools.

Money

The amount of money in the world system (liquidity) and the value of money (exchange rates) are two of the major economic problems of the global system.[25] Since 1945 the American dollar has remained the basic reserve currency of the system and a standard for international trade, even after convertibility into gold was abandoned in 1971.

Through the manipulation of monetary policy the United States exercises a powerful influence on the economies and on the domestic politics of most other countries in the system. However, since 1944 the United States has attempted to create and maintain a number of structures within the system to provide an orderly process of monetary control.

While World War II continued, the United States and other countries created the Bretton Woods system. Basically, it established an international system for determining the value of money through fixed exchange rates. Based on the value of gold and of the dollar in relation to gold, the value of other currencies was agreed upon. Changes in exchange rates were permitted only within a very narrow range of value. In addition, the Bretton Woods Agreement provided for the creation of the IMF and the World Bank as institutions capable of providing short-term loans to countries with balance-of-payments deficits and to those seeking development loans with which to rebuild their economies after World War II. Although the system never did work quite as planned, it provided the major monetary mechanisms that led to recovery. By the 1960s, however, many countries had recovered and were becoming increasingly competitive in world trade. Yet exchange rates remained fixed to valuations made in 1945. This caused inevitable pressures in the system, and especially upon the United States, whose payments deficits were growing massive. From 1945 to 1960 these deficits were welcome because they provided needed liquidity to other countries, that is, they provided sources for loans, investment, and industrial expansion abroad. However, once recovery had occurred in Western Europe and Japan, the increasing American deficits became troublesome.

American money spent abroad through a number of mechanisms—military spending, the Marshall Plan, imports, tourism—had left large pools of dollars abroad. As the 1960s wore on, American expenditures for the Vietnam War, the operations of the American corporations and American banks abroad, and American domestic inflation expanded the deficits. By 1970 these and other factors made American products abroad less competitive, and for the first time the United States suffered a deficit in the balance of trade; that is, Americans bought more foreign products than they sold abroad. This increased the balance-of-payments deficits even further.

Theoretically, in order to achieve international monetary stability, countries are expected to attain a balance of payments; that is, they are expected to take in as much as they spend. A balance-of-payments surplus or deficit is expected to be adjusted toward balance either by adjustments in the domestic economy or by borrowing from international agencies or private banks. When adjustments in deficits are not made, the value of the dollar is reduced through inflation, and those holding dollars abroad feel the impact of American domestic policies. During much of the 1960s the United States did little to halt the process, but by the early 1970s the Nixon administration decided to act.

Spero relates what happened:

> On August 15, 1971, President Nixon, without consulting the other members of the international monetary system, and, indeed, without consulting his own State Department, announced his New Economic Policy; henceforth the dollar would no longer be convertible into gold, and the United States would impose a 10 percent surcharge on dutiable imports. August 5, 1971 marked the end of the Bretton Woods period.[26]

Throughout the next several months the United States conducted intense negotiations with other countries, which resulted in the Smithsonian Agreement in December 1971.[27] The United States agreed to devalue the dollar in relation to gold, and other exchange rates were realigned and were permitted to float on a broader range than the Bretton Woods Agreement permitted (2¼ percent plus or minus). It was a patchwork solution, and it was temporary. By late 1972 many countries had decided to permit their currencies to "float" on open markets to determine their value. What emerged was the "managed float," which permits the valuation of currencies daily on the world money markets. It is a free float up to a point, but governments intervene to adjust the exchange-rate mechanism where circumstances warrant. In many ways it has made the international system more interdependent, and for more than a decade it has proved to be more stable than some critics had predicted, but whether it is the ideal way for the global system to manage its monetary affairs is debatable. From the American standpoint, the system had permitted the Japanese yen to remain undervalued, thereby making it possible for the Japanese to sell their products on the world market at lower prices than would have been possible if the yen were valued to reflect the strength of the Japanese economy. In May 1984 the United States and Japan reached an agreement which would result in an increase of the value of the yen in relation to the

American dollar. The agreement provides that Japan would open its capital markets to foreign investors and that the yen would be used as a principal currency in international trade. One anticipated result of these moves is to make Japanese goods more expensive, thus reducing massive Japanese balance of trade surpluses with the rest of the world.[28]

The United States took the leadership in the 1960s to create a new form of international currency called special drawing rights (SDRs), sometimes called paper gold. Fearing an inadequate amount of liquidity in the 1960s, the countries of the Group of Ten (ten major industrial states, including the United States), created a fund of ten billion dollars worth of SDRs to provide credit to applying nations.[29] As time went on there was less need for the SDRs than had been anticipated. Still it was the first creation of an international asset.

The creation of vast new flows of funds followed the price increases in oil begun by OPEC nations in 1973[30] and produced the need for recycling: spending by the OPEC countries, OPEC grants and loans to other countries, and OPEC investment in the banks and in the economies of the industrial societies.

More recently the system has been jolted by the realization that the less developed countries have borrowed some $700 billion from private bankers in the industrial countries and from international agencies.[31] In the 1980s fears that much of this debt is uncollectible, that many countries may declare bankruptcy, and that Western lenders might be left holding the bag has prompted crisis action on the part of lenders and debtors alike. The United States provided an emergency $1 billion advance on oil purchases from Mexico, and the IMF moved to provide emergency funding in some cases. The American contribution to the IMF was increased by $8.5 billion.[32]

By late 1983 the crisis seemed to have subsided, but many experts became aware of the need for mechanisms to monitor and report on the level of total international debt in the future. Some private bankers defended the loans to less developed countries on the basis that their inherent long-term economic potential is sufficient to warrant confidence in lending and that the prospect of default in most cases is minimal. Nonetheless, bankers have been in the position of having to "roll over" the debts, i.e., to lend the debtor countries even more money in order to prevent economic failures of gigantic proportions.

However, the power of the United States to affect the system was evident in the past few years as the Federal Reserve Board, seeking to control American inflation, sharply tightened the money supply and induced high interest rates. The effect of these actions was extensive. First, by inducing a major American recession and high unemployment, the Fed succeeded in reducing the inflation rate from nearly 13 percent to less than 4 percent by 1983. In the process high interest rates attracted capital from many other countries, limiting their own investment capabilities and inducing severe protests to President Reagan. Further, the American recession reduced the purchase of imports from abroad, further weakening economies of trading partners.

Thus in terms of influence on the monetary system and on foreign policy, the United States remains preeminent.

Trade and Markets

Trade is not only a goal of foreign policy, it is an instrument of policy. All countries need to acquire certain things from others. To buy what one needs and to sell what one produces is one of the essential elements of international life and one of the primary objectives of a nation's foreign policy.[33] Nowhere is this more apparent in contemporary life than in the field of energy. Since oil and gas are essential to the efficient functioning of the entire American economy, acquisition of adequate supplies is a matter whose importance far transcends personal convenience in avoiding gasoline lines in the United States. For other countries, access to American markets is essential to their ability to earn enough money to buy what they need from the United States and from manufacturers and sellers in other countries.

Since World War II the United States has supported the doctrine of free trade, i.e., the view that all countries should be able to sell in other countries with minimum tariff and quota barriers. To operationalize this view the United States took the lead in creating the basis on which the non-Communist economic order was established, first with the Bretton Woods Agreement, which established the monetary system of the postwar world, and later with the General Agreement on Tariffs and Trade (GAAT), which created the means by which lower tariffs could be negotiated on a wide variety of products.

A major part of the system was the provision of access to the growing American market for the products of other countries.

In the negotiation of trade arrangements, one of the important tools available to policy makers is the status of most-favored nation (MFN).[34] With it the United States is able to confer on another state trading arrangements equal to those given to the most-favored nations with whom the United States trades. This removes a range of legal, political, and military limitations upon the kinds of products that may be traded; affords prices as favorable as those offered to the most favored trading partners; and removes limitations to the American market.

Thus it is a useful device, particularly in negotiating new agreements with states with whom either limited trade or no trade had existed in the past.

The capability to deny the American market to certain states and to apply economic sanctions such as embargoes is another important weapon in the hands of policy makers. The United States Export Control Act of 1949, for example, sought to regulate the sale of exports to Communist countries and to impose embargoes on any Western state violating it.[35] It banned certain strategic goods from sale to the Communist bloc. In the Mutual Defense Assistance Act Congress authorized the president to deny foreign aid to countries knowingly shipping strategic goods to Communist countries, although these restrictions were eased in the mid-1950s.[36] Nonetheless, the Trade Agreements Act of 1951 withdrew all trade concessions to the Soviet Union.[37] The Trade Reform Act of 1974 gave the president wide authority to impose trade restrictions against states committing unfair trade practices against the United States.[38]

In 1980, after the Soviet invasion of Afghanistan, the Carter administration applied an embargo on grain sales to the Soviet Union in excess of the 8 million tons required under existing agreements, and controls were placed on the sale of advanced technology.[39]

Cooperation from allies and from other countries was minimal, and the embargo was not believed to have hurt the Soviet Union substantially. Also, in the 1979–80 period, during the hostage crisis, the Carter administration imposed a wide range of economic sanctions on Iran, and willingness to remove some of them became part of the deal with Iran that ultimately led to the release of the hostages.[40]

When the Reagan administration came into office in 1981, it removed the embargo on grain to the Soviet Union.[41] When events in Poland brought on martial law, however, the administration imposed trade sanctions on both Poland and the Soviet Union,[42] but President Reagan announced his intention to consider removal of the sanctions when martial law was lifted in July 1983.

In addition, the Reagan administration signed a five-year agreement on August 25, 1983, to sell the Soviet Union a minimum of 9 million and a maximum of 12 million tons of grain a year.[43] Also in August of 1983 the Reagan administration ordered an end to export controls on the sale of certain pipeline equipment to the Soviets.[44] Neither action was affected by the shooting down by a Soviet fighter plane of a Korean airliner, with 269 civilians killed, in late August 1983.

The most serious trade problem facing the United States, however, results from the very structure of the present global economy.[45] Practices that Americans regard as unfair but which other states regard as fair implementation of the free-trade and free-market concepts have caused serious frictions between the United States and Japan and between the United States and Western Europe. Successive American administrations have claimed that Japanese restrictions on American entry into certain Japanese product areas and investment and Common Market resistance to the entry of American farm products have worked to the disadvantage of the United States. The increasing share of the American market by foreign manufacturers in autos, steel, television sets, and footwear, among other things, is seen as a sign of unfair competition. It is charged that some foreign governments unfairly support their export sectors with subsidies, maintain lower wage rates, and impose a number of nontariff barriers on American products. The United States has taken its case occasionally to GATT, to no avail. To be sure, some of the decline in sales of American products on world markets is attributable to the lower prices of foreign goods made possible by lower wage rates. Another factor in higher American prices has been the alleged imbalance in exchange rates, the charge being that the yen and the mark are undervalued, making the prices of their products less than those of the United States.

This has given rise in the United States to pressure for protectionism, that is, efforts by the government to restrict imports in key areas.[46] In the 1980s the Japanese were induced to restrict their automobile exports to the United States voluntarily to permit the American auto industry to recover from the severe recession of 1981–83. Whether this will solve the underlying problems of competitiveness of American cars remains to be seen. In mid-1983 the Reagan administration also permitted restrictions on the import of motorcycles and on specialized steel products. In the search for increased productivity many American industries have turned to the expanded use of robotization, but the long-term impact on employment in the United States is under intense scrutiny in many quarters.

These then are some of the major issues in the trade area. They suggest some of the tools available to American policy makers, some of the constraints on use of those tools, and some of the opportunities they afford. Trade agreements are among the most important political/economic instruments negotiated by governments, and the processes by which they are created are intensely political. Access to the American market, to certain American products, and to the opportunity to earn dollars can be used as rewards and as punishments. On the other hand, American sales abroad constitute a growing part of the American GNP and of American national strength. Foreign trade—exports and imports—accounts for some 20 percent of the GNP. While trade with the major industrial states constitutes the great bulk of American activity, trade with the less developed world is also increasing in economic as well as political importance.

Commodity Agreements

When both producers and consumers of a given product wish to establish long-term stability in both supply and price of a product, they may form a commodity arrangement.[47] Producers agree to produce only a certain amount of the product, and consumers agree to purchase guaranteed amounts over a specific time period. Each side agrees on a range of prices to protect the producers from a sudden fall of prices and consumers from a sudden rise in prices. In the 1970s the United States signed commodity agreements in tin and coffee but declined to do so in cocoa. The European Common Market in a meeting at Lomé created extensive agreements with forty-six associated states in Africa, the Caribbean, and the Pacific. Agreements of this type are a mechanism that can be used productively in the future.[48]

Investment

In the United States investment is usually done by private individuals and corporations, not by the government. However, foreign policy sets the tone for the favorability of investments in other countries, and some foreign companies offer their stock for sale in the United States. In addition, government is often requested to provide advice, information, and recommendations for investment abroad. Thus a policy that encourages investment in particular countries is another instrument the government possesses in its dealings with other countries.

There are two basic forms of investment: purchase of stocks, securities, currencies, and shares of foreign enterprises and direct foreign investment, such as the establishment of American-owned and operated firms in other countries—multinational corporations, a subject that will be discussed separately.

In any case, investment constitutes a valuable resource of development capital for enterprises in other countries. The other side of the coin is that the United States benefits from foreign investment here, and foreign policy also includes the effort to induce foreign interests with capital to invest in American enterprises.

For example, when the OPEC countries came to acquire vast new capital reserves as a result of the quadrupling of oil prices in 1973–74, the Nixon administration took energetic steps to encourage "recycling" of the capital in the United States and in other consuming countries of the West.[49] The productive American economy and favorable interest rates did, in fact, lead to a massive reinvestment of OPEC capital, much of it in stable long-term investment. Some of these resources were used to buy stocks in American corporations, to buy real estate, and to absorb government securities. In this sense the attraction of the American economy for foreign investors can be an element in the relations with other states, facilitated by friendly and cooperative relations between the United States and other countries.

Although private investment is not quite so directly in the control of policy makers as are other elements of economic policy, it is clear that they can have some influence on the flow of capital abroad, either through restrictive legislation or by persuading major investors not to invest in certain places.

Multinational Corporations

Probably no economic activity abroad has been more controversial in the past few decades than multinational corporations.[50] The organization of corporations on a multinational basis, the operation of branches, affiliates, and subsidiaries in other countries, according to theory about the development of the business enterprise, has been part of the inevitable evolution of the corporate form. In its broadest sense a multinational corporation is a company based in one country with the capability of manufacturing, selling or assembling products and services in another country.

Again, like monetary investment, the development of direct foreign investment (DFI) in the form of multinational enterprises is most directly in the hands of private sectors of the American economy. Private corporations have increasingly expanded operations into other countries and have structured their production processes on an international basis. That is to say, they decide to manufacture parts in different countries, to assemble products in yet other countries, and use yet other states as their foreign bases for organizational and tax purposes. Thus a single multinational corporation can operate in many countries simultaneously, and most of the major American corporations are organized in this way.

The economic and political effects of the presence of these firms can be profound, and in many places they are regarded as direct instruments of the American government, although much of the empirical evidence available suggests that this is not so. Indeed, there are some analysts who regard the multinationals as too independent of the American government and too unresponsive to the foreign-policy interests of the United States.

The truth appears to be more complex than either of these views. Some multinational corporations appear to be more responsive to American policy directions than others, and some create more demands upon American foreign policy than others. In terms of their political impact in the host country, again the situation is complex. In the more industrial and older countries the political influence of American multinationals appears to be less impressive than in some of the less developed countries, although the evidence suggests that, in fact, all host countries are increasingly able to control and regulate the multinationals quite effectively when they choose to do so.

As for the purely economic impact on host countries, again it may be said to vary from country to country, depending upon the level of economic development in particular countries. In any case the firms bring to a host country additional jobs, taxes, management expertise, technology, and business for local suppliers. Sometimes this may disrupt local economies, place local manufacturers at a distinct disadvantage, and appear to give control of key parts of a local economy to foreign interests. In many places this has produced a nationalist reaction that has imposed new conditions on the multinationals. For example, most countries have created legislation requiring local affiliates of multinationals to be owned primarily by nationals, and most multinationals have adjusted to this requirement successfully. Many countries demand the employment of nationals as executives of the affiliates, and this too has been accomplished with increasing success in many countries. Thus while arguments persist over the benefits and costs of the presence of American multinationals, few countries have required them to leave or have prohibited their establishment.

From the standpoint of political influence, critics of multinationals contend that they have achieved undue influence. While in most countries the multinationals tend to avoid direct political activity, they have developed more subtle means by which to obtain support of policies favorable to their own interests. They maintain large and expert staffs of legislative and public-relations personnel. Their executives mingle socially with prominent national leaders, and they may offer positions on the boards of affiliate companies to key political leaders.

The charge that the political influence of multinationals in host countries is excessive usually rests on the evidence arising from the behavior of ITT and other American companies in seeking to thwart the election and the presidency of Salvador Allende in Chile. Briefly, massive testimony before a special committee of the United States Senate indicated that some of the firms attempted to elicit the support of the Nixon administration, and particularly of the CIA, to support opponents of Allende and to encourage opposition to his administration. In most countries, however, the attempt of private firms to enlist the United States government to engage in political activities of this sort is less objectionable and blatant. It can be argued that any American company has the right to seek the support of the American government to protect its interests, and indeed there are legitimate steps government can take to support those interests. The point is, though, that these firms may involve the government in political controversy in host countries as often as the government is said to involve the firms in the implementation of American foreign policy.

In general, of course, the U.S. government has the power to permit or prohibit the operation of American-based companies or to restrict the kinds of business and technology they may transfer abroad. Host countries also have the power to decide which businesses they will permit to operate within their borders and the conditions under which they may operate.

It can be argued that multinationals, even if they are, in fact, basically independent, do serve American foreign policy in some important ways. First, they establish or expand direct contacts between the United States and other countries, linkages that may be of considerable importance in the development of cooperative relations between states. Second, they are valuable instruments of economic development for many countries of the world and can contribute to American policy purposes, especially in the less developed countries, by serving as demonstrations of American economic support. Third, they transmit certain American political and economic values into countries that may be inherently suspicious of capitalism, colonialism, and exploitation. In short, no matter how directly or indirectly, how intentionally or unintentionally, the multinationals often do come to symbolize and in many ways to represent the United States in the eyes of foreign nationals.

Some observers have argued that the policy makers of the United States should utilize the benefits of the multinationals more unashamedly and more effectively to serve American policy purposes.[51]

Taking the position that encouraging multinationals to locate in developing countries is one of the most beneficial things that the United States can do to provide immediate economic help to these countries, some argue that American foreign policy should more consciously promote the expansion of multinationals throughout the world. Indeed, this was the position taken by President Ronald Reagan at a conference of developed and underdeveloped countries in Cancun, Mexico, in 1982.

As with other investment, the government of the United States has the capability to persuade private corporations to invest in certain countries and to advise and encourage them to do so. To be sure, there have been cases where American multinationals have provided less favorable relations between the host government and the United States rather than greater cooperation. But the balance sheet appears to reflect far more successes than failures. On the whole, multinational corporations can serve broader American policy interests effectively and, as a tool of policy, may be used in the future with more subtlety and awareness.

Aid

Since the end of World War II, the United States has provided, as part of its foreign policy, more than $200 billion to foreign countries in the form of government loans, grants, credits, or rents.[52] It has done so on both a bilateral and multinational basis—both directly and through international organizations. In addition, governmental policy has permitted, encouraged, and supported massive lending by private American banks and other lending institutions to governments, enterprises, and individuals throughout the world, including countries behind the Iron Curtain. For example, during the period in which the Reagan administration was publicly attacking martial law in Poland, it was also working in conjunction with private banks to prevent Poland from going bankrupt on some $27 billion in debts to the United States and other Western countries.[53] In 1982 a financial crisis in Mexico threatened the $80 billion in debts that Mexico owed to the United States and to international lenders.[54]

Still, these forms of economic assistance are likely to continue because they are believed to serve varied American foreign-policy interests, among them containment of Communist expansion, maintenance of good relations with countries possessing essential raw materials, encouragement of human rights, and belief in the need for real economic development in Third and Fourth Worlds.

In the past two decades, since 1962, economic assistance has been provided under the Foreign Assistance Act, much of it administered by the Agency for International Development (AID).[55] In addition to grants and loans, AID provides technical and administrative expertise and advice to recipient governments. Under this program, for example, the United States has agreed to provide funds to the Philippine government to complete a nuclear power project in Bataan, which will provide power and jobs in the future.[56] In addition, available under the AID administration is the Food for Peace program, which provides food, supplies, and knowledge.[57] The Peace Corps provides training in numerous skills to villagers in host countries. Assistance is also available to countries for refugees, for disaster relief, and for other humanitarian purposes.[58]

The bulk of foreign aid between 1945 and 1960 went to the developed countries recovering from World War II, and new and less developed countries protested that insufficient aid was being directed to them.[59] Furthermore, during the 1950s foreign aid became a controversial political issue in the United States, necessitating the increasing reliance on multilateral lending agencies and the creation of new facilities.[60] Although the amount of this aid is still regarded as inadequate by less developed countries, the mechanism of international distribution reduced some of the nationalist frictions between donor and recipient countries. It also muted the effect of American aid as an instrument of American policy. Still, the United States remains committed to continuing these forms of aid. In 1983 Congress agreed to increase contributions to IMF considerably.[61]

Another important form of economic assistance is that of credits, the agreement to lend another country the resources to buy certain products in the United States. During the 1970s the Nixon administration negotiated a trade treaty with the Soviet Union, one of the key provisions of which was the extension of $300 million in credits to the Soviet Union.[62] The treaty was subsequently rejected by the Soviets. Credit provisions, therefore, are important parts of many bilateral arrangements.

Still another form of American assistance is the rent that the government pays for the use of certain facilities in other countries. For example, in the Philippines the United States provides over $475 million in nonmilitary grants under terms of the new 1983 agreement for use of military bases.[63] In addition to paying the rent, the United States employs thousands of nationals directly, and base operations and Americans stationed there generate millions more in economic activity. Thus in a country such as the Philippines the American military presence generates as much as 5 percent of the gross national product, clearly an important form of economic assistance.[64] To be sure, such economic activity is essential to the global military posture of the United States and to its political position in the Far East. In purely economic terms, however, its withdrawal from the Philippines would be a severe blow to that economy.

During the Carter administration aid was increasingly related to a country's record in human rights and produced some frictions with allies and other countries.[65] With the Reagan administration in power, the linkage between human rights and foreign aid was deemphasized.

Immigration

The flow of immigrants from other countries to the United States has been one of the foundations of the richness, diversity, and productivity of the United States. In recent years immigration policy has come to be more associated with foreign policy designed to relieve unbearable pressures on the economies of neighboring countries than with the needs of American domestic policy, as was the case in the nineteenth century.

In the past decade the flow of immigrants from Latin America, both legal and illegal, has been an important element in foreign policy. Although the American government has attempted to obstruct the flow of illegal immigrants, the Reagan administration has pursued new domestic policies to legalize many thousands already here. To some extent, however, the American government has not been harsh on the matter with such neighbors as Mexico and other Latin American countries. It has at least tacitly permitted some of the immigration to occur to help relieve intense economic pressures on Latin American countries where the United States seeks to maintain influence and cooperation and to provide workers to farms and businesses in the southwest.

In addition, there have been sizeable increases in the immigration of Asians, especially those adversely affected by political events in Southeast Asia—those fleeing from Vietnam or from martial law in the Philippines in the 1970s.

The point is that immigration policy can be an important foreign-policy mechanism to provide aid to those countries to which the government wishes to extend it.

Tourism

A kind of travel that is quite different from immigration is tourism. Still one of America's largest businesses, the travel of Americans abroad constitutes the biggest industry for some countries of the world and a sizeable percentage of the GNP for others.[66] For example, prior to the increase in energy prices in the 1970s tourism was the largest industry in Mexico, and since then it has remained the second largest source of foreign exchange.

In 1984 twenty-four million Americans traveled overseas, while twenty-two million foreign travelers came to the United States. Of those coming to the United States in 1983, forty percent came from Western Europe; twenty-nine percent were from the Far East; and Middle Eastern citizens accounted for nine percent.

Thus the massive interchange among people constitutes a major economic force in the contemporary world.

CONCLUSION

For American foreign policy, the economic track implies nothing less than the continued leadership role in building a global economic system of the next century. In a world of economic as well as political pluralism, that means the necessity to employ political negotiation to agree upon economic matters and to use economic tools to promote political agreement.

In relation to the other major industrial countries, American foreign policy faces increasingly complex tasks of coordination and cooperation. Toward the less developed world American policy confronts the need for flexibility, creativity, and imagination in finding the mechanisms to help accelerate economic development. In terms of the relations with the Soviet Union and the Soviet bloc, American economic inducements have not yet had much observable impact on Soviet political-strategic behavior, and mutual efforts to expand economic contacts have been sporadic and often frictional. Nonetheless, although the Soviets do not yet appear ready to become a partner in the non-Communist system, their own economic dependencies hold the prospect for increased future economic relations. Although sound economic linkages may have to await improved political relations, the barriers may be surmountable, and economic linkages could contribute to political improvements.

How the United States goes about the job of providing continued world leadership may determine the effectiveness of the result. If Americans cannot totally agree on the shape of their own national economy, how can they persuade other states to accept the American vision of a world economy? In one sense, they can't. The evolution of the global economic system will proceed not only on the basis of blueprints offered by either the Soviet Union or the United States but also on a pragmatic search for productive methods, whatever their source.

In the economic track the American national interest consists of acquiring and maintaining access to markets and raw materials, contributing to the development of economies in less developed countries and the improvement in the standard of living of their peoples, and participating in international organizations capable of managing a complex world economy. It also consists of carefully relating American foreign-policy objectives to available national resources. In the aftermath of the Vietnam War Americans became aware of the relationship between costs and benefits from a foreign-policy commitment and the military expenditures required to carry it out. Annual defense expenditures, the costs of support of foreign loans through the IMF and other agencies, the budgets for direct foreign-aid programs, and military commitments (such as those in Lebanon and the Caribbean) constitute a large aggregate burden on American resources and create pressures on the domestic economy. All of this suggests that foreign-policy commitments require a careful analysis of the economic effects on the United States and of the resources available to meet the commitments that are under consideration.

The national interest, in the final analysis, lies in helping to develop economic opportunity for all peoples, and foreign policy related to that objective is essential. American well-being is inextricably linked with the economic development of others, and American foreign policy that continues to recognize the linkage serves the national interest effectively.

NOTES

[1] Joan Edelman Spero, *The Politics of International Economic Relations,* 2nd ed. (New York: St. Martin's Press, 1981), pp. 4–5.

[2] John F. Burns, "Moscow Will Try Again to Widen the Powers of Factory Managers," *New York Times,* July 27, 1983, p. 1.

[3] Richard Sterling, *Macropolitics: International Relations in a Global Society* (New York: Alfred A. Knopf, 1974), pp. 216–22.

[4] Raymond Aron, *Peace and War* (New York: Praeger Publishers, 1966), pp. 268–78; David V. Edwards, *The American Political Experience* (Englewood Cliffs, N.J.: Prentice-Hall, 1982), pp. 509–13.

[5] Charles E. Lindblom, *Power and Markets* (New York: Basic Books, 1977), pp. 107–16, 237–90.

[6] Spero, *International Economic Relations,* pp. 75–76.

[7] John Kenneth Galbraith, *Economics and the Public Purpose* (Boston: Houghton Mifflin Company, 1973), pp. 11–59.

[8] Spero, *International Economic Relations,* pp. 12–18.

[9] Richard Cooper, "Economic Interdependence and Foreign Policy in the Seventies," *World Politics* 24 (January 1972), 159–81; Cooper, *The Economics of Interdependence: Economic Policy in the Atlantic Community* (New York: McGraw-Hill Book Company, 1968), pp. 3–23.

[10] See chapter 11, pp. 163–64.

[11] Spero, *International Economic Relations,* pp. 33–37.

[12] Ibid., pp. 42–43.

[13] Ibid.

[14] Ibid., pp. 188–95.

[15] Ibid., pp. 191–93, 200–208.

[16] Cecil V. Crabb, Jr., *American Foreign Policy in the Nuclear Age,* 4th ed. (New York: Harper & Row, Publishers, 1983) p. 386.

[17] Spero, *International Economic Relations,* p. 46.

[18] Ibid., p. 69.

[19] Daniel Bell, *The Coming of Post-Industrial Society: A Venture in Social Forecasting* (New York: Basic Books, 1973), pp. 12–44.

[20] David H. Blake and Robert S. Walters, *The Politics of Global Economic Relations,* 2nd ed. (Englewood Cliffs, N.J.: Prentice-Hall, 1983), pp. 150–66.

[21] Sterling, *Macropolitics,* pp. 349–53, 376–83.

[22] Edwards, *American Political Experience,* pp. 508–15.

[23] Ibid., pp. 520–21.

[24] Ibid., p. 521.

[25] Blake and Walters, *Global Economic Relations,* pp. 51–82; Spero, *International Economic Relations,* pp. 33–70.

[26] Spero, *International Economic Relations,* p. 52.

[27] Ibid., pp. 52–69.

[28] "U.S. and Japan In Yen Accord," *New York Times,* May 24, 1984, p. D16.

[29] Spero, *International Economic Relations*, p. 45.

[30] Blake and Walters, *Global Economic Relations*, p. 183.

[31] Kenneth N. Gilpin, "Talking Business: Third World's Debt Burden," *New York Times*, July 19, 1983, p. D2; Leonard Silk, "Avalanche of Debt Threatens Global Economy," *New York Times*, September 12, 1983, p. E3.

[32] Clyde H. Farnsworth, "Congress Passes $8.4 Billion in Aid to Monetary Fund," *New York Times*, November 19, 1983, p. 1.

[33] Blake and Walters, *Global Economic Relations*, pp. 11–50; Spero, *International Economic Relations*, pp. 74–101; Charles W. Kegley and Eugene R. Wittkopf, *American Foreign Policy: Pattern and Process* (New York: St. Martin's Press, 1982), pp. 194–202.

[34] Spero, *International Economic Relations*, p. 87.

[35] Ibid., p. 294.

[36] Ibid., p. 295.

[37] Ibid., p. 296.

[38] Ibid., p. 92.

[39] Kegley and Wittkopf, *American Foreign Policy*, pp. 223–24.

[40] Jimmy Carter, *Keeping Faith* (New York: Bantam Books, 1982), pp. 462-65, 505.

[41] Alexander Dallin and Gail W. Lapidus, "Reagan and the Russians: United States Policy Toward the Soviet Union and Eastern Europe," in Kenneth A. Oye, Robert J. Lieber, and Donald Rothchild, eds., *Eagle Defiant: United States Foreign Policy in the 1980s* (Boston: Little, Brown & Company, 1983), pp. 213–14.

[42] Ibid., pp. 217–18.

[43] John F. Burns, "Grain Pact Signed; U.S. Assures Soviet of Steady Supply," *New York Times*, August 26, 1983, p. D1.

[44] Clyde H. Farnsworth, "U.S. Lifts Its Curbs on Sale to Soviet of Pipeline Gear," *New York Times*, August 21, 1983, p. 1.

[45] Benjamin J. Cohen, "An Explosion in the Kitchen? Economic Relations with Other Advanced Industrial States," in Oye et al., *Eagle Defiant*, pp. 120–123.

[46] Spero, *International Economic Relations*, p. 93.

[47] Ibid., pp. 200-208.

[48] Ibid., p. 206.

[49] Blake and Walters, *Global Economic Relations*, pp. 182-83.

[50] The literature on multinational corporations is extensive. An excellent review is to be found in Spero, *International Economic Relations*, pp. 102-129, 222-41; among other major studies that explore the issues from a critical perspective is Richard Barnet and Ronald Muller, *Global Reach* (New York: Simon and Schuster, 1974). More favorable studies of the multinationals include those by Joseph LaPalombara and Stephan Blank, *Multinational Corporations and Developing Countries* (New York: Conference Board, 1979), and *Multinational Corporations in Comparative Perspective* (New York: Conference Board, 1977). Other major studies include Raymond Vernon, *Sovereignty at Bay* (New York: Basic Books, 1971).

[51] Joseph LaPalombara, paper delivered at conference, "American Foreign Policy Issues: A Current Discussion in Commemoration of Dean Acheson," Yale University, April 24, 1982.

[52] Kegley and Wittkopf, *American Foreign Policy*, p. 127; Crabb, *American Foreign Policy*, p. 161.

[53] Dallin and Lapidus, "Reagan and the Russians," pp. 217-18.

[54] Silk, "Avalanche of Debt."

[55] Kegley and Wittkopf, *American Foreign Policy*, pp. 128-30.

[56] "Marcos Gets Boost in Washington," *New York Times*, September 19, 1982, p. E2; Clark D. Neher, "The Philippines in 1980: The Gathering Storm," *Asian Survey* xxi (February 1981), p. 271.

[57] Kegley and Wittkopf, *American Foreign Policy*, p. 126.

[58] Ibid.

[59] Spero, *International Economic Relations*, pp. 149-159.

[60] Ibid., p. 162.

[61] Kenneth N. Gilpin, "Parts of IMF Bill Assailed," *New York Times*, August 6, 1983, p. 43; "Lending Restrictions on IMF Legislation," *New York Times*, August 6, 1983, p. 43.

[62] Kegley and Wittkopf, *American Foreign Policy*, pp. 228-29.

63 "Manila to Get $900 Million in Accord on Bases," *New York Times*, June 1, 1983, p. 6; Philip Taubman, "Shultz in Manila, Affirms Support of U.S. for Marcos," *New York Times*, June 26, 1983, p. 1.

64 James Dull, "Philippine Politics and American Strategy in the 1980s," seminar paper, (Newport, R.I.: Naval War College, 1983).

65 Kegley and Wittkopf, *American Foreign Policy*, pp. 400-401, 550, 557.

66 Michael Demarest and others, "Americans Everywhere: They're Taking Off in Record Numbers, and Europe Is the Big Bonanza," *Time*, July 25, 1983, pp. 40-49.

CHAPTER SIXTEEN
THE MILITARY TRACK

War, it has been said, is too important to be left to the generals, and in a democracy military policy is under the control of civilian authority and subject to public support. But even in a democracy war and the preparation for war are permanent parts of the nation's agenda.

The dictum of von Clausewitz—that war is diplomacy by other means[1]—seems to explain the prevalence of war in history. When wars were relatively limited in size, scope, and the number of combatants involved, war seemed a rational decision by which to apply an extra measure of pressure to an adversary. When war became nationalized in the Napoleonic era, engaging hundreds of thousands of people over an entire continent, the costs of war multiplied, but the lesson remained unheeded. Not until the devastation of World War II—with the shambles of Hiroshima and Nagasaki forewarning of the prospect of global nuclear annihilation—did the calculation of the costs and benefits of global war begin to change. Victory no longer appeared to be more beneficial than defeat, and nuclear war promised that there would be no winners. Still, war continues. Some forty-five states are involved in wars underway at this writing in one place or another,[2] although the world has managed to avoid mass destruction through nuclear war for forty years.

Nevertheless, in a world of nation-states, each devoted to its own survival and security and convinced that force may be used against it, the belief in the need for military policies and for the tools of force remains an entrenched conviction of governments, leaders, and peoples.

Because the military track carries with it its own perceptions of reality and of the most effective ways to deal with that reality, it must be considered as a separate track of foreign policy. Just as we considered whether economic forces drive the foreign policy of the United States, we must assess the degree to which the imperatives of the military track determine the definition of the national interest and the policy goals of the government.

As part of the military track, then, the national security policy of the United States encompasses the interpretation of Soviet behavior in largely military terms, the globalization of the perceived military challenge, the establishment of a global military system, and the use of military capabilities for political purposes with other states. Some elaboration on these points follows.

NATIONAL SECURITY POLICY

National survival and security are the primary goals of the United States and of any nation-state. In order to achieve these goals the United States maintains military power sufficient to deter aggression against itself, to successfully defend itself in case of attack, and to win a war if one should erupt. In the modern world of global commitments and missile capabilities, national security is defined in ways that encompass areas far beyond America's borders. Consequently, the content of national security policy and the tools it provides may affect the definition of the national interest and the broader political objectives of the United States.

But should the military capability of the United States be only a tool of foreign policy, or should it determine foreign policy? The question is relevant to Americans for two basic reasons. First, the Constitution established civilian control over the military, and even in the most serious national crises of the past two hundred years there has been no meaningful challenge to that principle. In the novel *Seven Days in May* the military takeover of the government is imagined, but even here civilian authority and the Constitution prevail. The second reason why the question is important to Americans in the last part of the twentieth century is that if the civilian leaders come to think primarily in military terms and to consider military options the most effective way of solving foreign-policy problems, then the military track may become predominant over other techniques.[3]

Assuming that the military track will remain subservient to the political interests of the United States, however, we will examine some of the ways in which policy makers utilize military capabilities to serve broader political objectives.

Theoretically, then, military capability should be the servant of American foreign policy, not its master. Nevertheless, policy makers frequently believe that foreign policy is largely dependent upon military power. Henry Kissinger writes:

Throughout history the political influence of nations has been roughly correlative to their military power. While states might differ in the moral worth and prestige of their institutions, diplomatic skill could augment but never substitute for military strength.[4]

Is this true? Need it be true? The evidence of history persuades most leaders of most states that Kissinger's view is accurate. It is believed to be true. Whether it need be true may be debatable, but the incessant use of force by nation-states of all sizes up to the present moment is evidence that states believe that the need for military power is real. Most Americans and most of their leaders also believe it to be so, and this provides the foundation on which American military policy functions.[5] This was not always so. Prior to World War I and between 1918 and 1941 the majority of Americans sought to avoid a military role in Europe and to maintain as small a military establishment as possible. Once having made the commitment to the containment policy in 1946, however, American willingness to engage in foreign affairs and to support an expanding military system increased. Behind this sharp reversal of attitudes was the perception that the challenge from the Soviet Union was primarily a military threat. Therefore the military track took on an importance in foreign policy that it previously had possessed only in wartime. But in 1946 this was war—the Cold War—and the military track became a large part of it.

In making the commitment to contain Soviet expansion, American leaders devised a broad range of tools with which to operate in the military track. First there was a need for doctrine, a set of politico-military concepts that would mold military thinking and its place in the world. Then came the reliance on technology to develop a new range of modern weapons in order to stay ahead of the adversary. In short order the desirability of new military alliances became apparent, and new forms of military aid and assistance flowed from Washington. American force levels had to be increased and new strategies developed.

THE MILITARY DEFINITION
OF THE GLOBAL SYSTEM

When political relations with the Soviet Union soured following World War II, many American leaders feared that Soviet forces would roll over the weakened countries of Western Europe. As a result, American policy embodied the creation of massive economic aid to strengthen West European countries and of a permanent American commitment to defend them militarily in case of attack by Soviet forces. The Soviet leaders, fearing an attack from the West, massed most of their armies in Eastern Europe to defend against such an attack. Each side perceived an immediate military threat from the other, or at least their leaders said that they did, and their actions deepened convictions on the other side.

Sharp differences have been expressed among scholars over each side's responsibility for the Cold War,[6] but in retrospect, there were decidedly enough structural and political differences between the two powers to have caused considerable postwar friction.

In the first few years of the Cold War period, American attention was focused on Europe. Americans were outraged at the Soviet domination of Eastern Europe and fearful about Soviet intentions toward Western Europe. By 1949, after the Soviet attempt to blockade West Berlin (located within Soviet-occupied East Germany) a political-military stalemate seemed to have settled on the Continent, marked by the creation of the North Atlantic Treaty Organization and by the intention to return West Germany to independence and to include it in the NATO alliance.

Soon, however, the focus of American-Soviet conflict moved to Asia, when the Soviet-supported government of North Korea invaded American-supported South Korea. To the surprise of many, President Truman decided to respond, and with United Nations authority, committed American forces to hurl back the aggressor.[7] Before the United States was able to assemble sufficient force to accomplish that objective, North Korea occupied most of the South. When American forces under General Douglas MacArthur regrouped and reorganized, they drove the North Koreans back across the 38th parallel into North Korea and close to the Chinese border. At that point the Chinese entered the conflict, and after American and other United Nations forces were pushed back into South Korea, the line stabilized around the 38th parallel that separated North and South Korea and on which the war had begun. Lengthy negotiations led to a truce in the early days of Eisenhower administration, and the situation in Korea has remained fundamentally stable ever since.

Korea was not the only part of the world outside of Europe where the Soviets sought to increase and expand their influence. In the so-called Third World the Soviets engaged in intense anticolonialism. They supported independence movements in Asia, Africa, and Latin America and sought to exploit the unrest and to gain allies and adherents, with some success.

By the mid-1950s, in short, the Cold War had become global. In 1949 the Chinese Communists won the civil war in China and formed an alliance with the Soviet Union. Later, Communist-leaning governments or governments allying themselves with the Soviet Union included Indonesia, Egypt, and Cuba. Soviet pressures have been intense in such other places as the Congo, Angola, Afghanistan, Somalia, Ethiopia, South Yemen, Syria, Iraq, Guatemala, and Nicaragua, to name just a few.

The most prolonged and painful conflict of the last four decades was the war in Vietnam. The American effort to support the existence of an independent non-Communist government in South Vietnam in the face of the intense effort of the Soviet-supported regime of North Vietnam to unify the country under Communist control provided a complex challenge to American policy makers. President John F. Kennedy authorized sending sixteen thousand American military advisers to South Vietnam. Claims that Kennedy had decided by late 1963 to end direct American participation have been disputed.[8] After Kennedy's assassination in November 1963, President Lyndon Johnson decided to massively increase the American role in the war.

In the end, American political dissent over the war forced the Nixon administration to gradually withdraw American forces, and in 1975 the forces of South Vietnam collapsed; North Vietnam occupied the South.

Contrary to the impression conveyed by many writers, the United States was not defeated militarily in South Vietnam. However, the ultimate North Vietnamese victory over the South was a major *political* defeat for the United States. Today, as an ally of the Soviet Union, Vietnam provides substantial forces and facilities (many of them built in the South by the United States) from which Soviet policy in Asia, the Indian Ocean, and the Persian Gulf region can be pursued. South Vietnamese facilities have, at last, provided the Soviet Union with warm-water ports. The extent to which the victory of the North has severely damaged vital American interests is, however, open to question, raising the issue of the wisdom of choosing a military policy to pursue American political objectives in Southeast Asia. The policy choice—military escalation—and the effectiveness with which it was pursued will long remain subjects of analysis and debate in the United States.

By 1945 American interests had become global, and American military capabilities were established in Asia, Africa, and Latin America. The concept that a superpower should maintain global military capabilities with bases, troops, and facilities in each part of the global system grew. Communist ideology and the rapid political flux of new countries emerging from colonialism provided opportunities for the Soviets to match American outreach throughout the global system. In short, the entire world became the chessboard on which each side developed interests and military capabilities. In the case of the Soviets, the determination to expand military capabilities on a global basis accelerated after the Cuban missile crisis and continues at the present moment.

Thus a competition that began in European context has rapidly become universal.

In the four decades of competition the superpowers have also taken their efforts into space. In the field of military missiles as well as in space exploration, each side has attempted to surpass the other in space technology. The Soviets were the first to get men into space, but the United States was the first (and at the moment, the only) state to put men on the moon. In the last few years increased attention has been devoted in both countries to the militarization of space. In March 1983 President Reagan announced a plan to study creation of a ballistic missile defense system (BMD) in space. The plan came to be called "Star Wars," named after the popular movie of futuristic space-age warfare.[9] It was not the first time an American president had proposed a major antiballistic missile system. President Lyndon Johnson proposed a system called The Sentinel, and the Nixon administration came up with the idea for an improved system called The Safeguard. Because of Congressional and public opposition and because of the negotiation of the SALT I Treaty limiting ABM deployment, progress on a space system languished for several years, although both superpowers continued research. The Soviets are believed to have tested a system based on a nuclear blast designed to destroy incoming missiles and a system based on ground-to-air laser beams. Particle beam and laser research also proceeded in the United States.

On Sunday, June 10, 1984, the U.S. Army, firing an experimental antiballistic missile, successfully destroyed an incoming dummy missile in a test in the Pacific. Almost simultaneously, Soviet leader Konstantin Chernenko called for negotiations with the United States to ban antisatellite and other space weapons.[10]

Originally, Reagan proposed sharing knowledge of new defensive systems with the Soviets so that each side would have a comparable defensive capability and development of the system would not destabilize the balance of terror. Reagan proposed a long-term evolution into a defensive strategic balance instead of an offensive one based on offensive missiles in the MAD doctrine. However, given the state of Soviet-American relations throughout 1984, agreement on anti-missile and anti-satellite space weapons seemed remote, and a new arms race in space seemed inevitable.

The universalization of the conflict and competition between the United States and the Soviet Union has put severe strains on the national resources of both countries and their allies, but it has more than ever emphasized the military track in the relations between them.

Ironically, both sides have confronted challenges in which their great military power has been inapplicable or in which there have been constraints on its maximum use. The American role in Korea and Vietnam and the Soviet involvement in Afghanistan are clear cases where overwhelming military power has failed to solve underlying political problems, and indeed, the full military power of the superpowers was not applied. Most recently the Soviet Union was constrained from military intervention in Poland by a number of external factors, and the United States government is facing opposition to the application of military solutions to conditions in Central America.

The superpowers have used their massive power to deter each other, but when they have become engaged in limited conflict abroad, their military power has been less effective than might have been expected.

Still, within the United States, belief in the need for military capability and confidence in its availability remain high.

First, it is believed that massive military power is essential to maintain the security of the United States and its allies if war should occur. Second, the thesis persists that military power-in-being has political and diplomatic consequences even in the absence of war; that it contributes to attitudes in other countries of fear, awe, respect, and willingness to cooperate with American policies. The extent to which the linkage is valid is debatable, but belief in it is very real. Even after the failure of American military policy in Vietnam, there appears to be little decrease in the political and diplomatic influence of the United States in most areas of the world. Third, many people regard the maintenance of military power as an essential element of a strong domestic policy.

For all of these reasons the range of military tools developed by the United States is extensive.

TOOLS OF POLICY

Apart from the political objectives for which military tools may be utilized, the United States has pursued a number of doctrines of military organization and purpose. As organizing principles around which to design strategic and tactical military tools and operational plans, doctrines also provide effective ways to government leaders to explain policy aims to the public and to encourage congressional and public support. A review of some of the major doctrines follows.

Deterrence, Defense, Offense

Three military strategies are available to the United States in its military track: deterrence, defense, and offense.[11]

Deterrence is the concept of creating and maintaining sufficient force and deliberate policy to deter a potential aggressor from initiating war. Although the elements of nuclear deterrence have become central in modern military thinking, the desire to dissuade potential aggressors from attacking is an old one in affairs among states. The overwhelming capability to prevent an attack is an essential ingredient of the doctrine of deterrence.

Defense is a concept based on the view that a state should have adequate military force to successfully defend itself and its allies if deterrence should fail and if war should erupt. The capability to withstand attack, repel invaders, and defeat aggressors once war has occurred is a central principle of defense. In the missile age it includes the necessity to absorb nuclear attack and to survive.

Conceptually, offense is the capability to inflict unacceptable damage on an enemy, defeat its military forces, occupy its country, and impose conditions of settlement upon it. The capability to attack and to prevail against an enemy is the essence of offense.

American policy since World War II has encompassed all three strategies. It is based on the effort to prevent and deter the Soviet Union from starting a war with the United States and its allies, to have force adequate to repel invaders and prevent them from occupying the United States or any of its allies, and to maintain the capability to defeat the adversary on its own territory.

Of course, the separation of these three strategies may appear arbitrary and unjustified since it can be argued that the best offense is a good defense, or vice versa, and that capabilities for offense and defense are required for deterrence. That all three strategies may, indeed, be one is not unrealistic, although different mixes of weapons and capabilities are required for each. In any case, the United States has pursued all three strategies during the Cold War period.

Balance of Power
and Containment

The guiding doctrine of the past four decades has been one of maintaining a balance, indeed a preponderance, of power over the Soviet system, and anticommunism and Soviet containment have provided the foundations for much of American policy.

Whatever its content, it is clear that a doctrine is an invaluable tool in creating sufficient support to maintain a large military force over a long period of time to implement the doctrine or, indeed, to support any policy, foreign or domestic.

The need perceived by leaders of the Truman administration to reverse the existing favorable public attitudes toward the Soviet Union in 1945-46, attitudes formed by the World War II alliance between the two countries, was reflected in the intensity of the attacks on Soviet actions and intentions. The result was the inculcation of attitudes so hostile toward the Soviet Union and toward communism that nearly forty years later the Soviet Union is still perceived by Americans as the greatest threat to American security and to world peace.

Among the fundamental reasons for an emphasis on military tools are the prevailing beliefs and ideas about the causes of war and the methods of preventing it. Without question, one of the most deeply held sets of beliefs among Americans who participate in the foreign-policy process is that of realism with its principles of power and the balance of power.[12] In the immediate post-World War II period American leaders concluded that (1) the Soviet Union was an aggressive, expansionist system and that (2) countervailing power was needed to prevent it from overrunning Western Europe and other areas of the world. The decision was made, therefore, to construct a balance-of-power system, which would confront the Soviet system with a countervailing force of predominant power.

Although George Kennan later repudiated the military element that evolved from the original containment doctrine he proposed, most other leaders defined containment as a balance-of-power doctrine.[13] This implied the creation of military forces sufficient to counter those of the Soviet Union. In the late 1940s it was defined to mean the existence of limited American forces-in-being, reliance on the American monopoly of the nuclear bomb, on the future formation of an alliance with Western European countries, and to a lesser extent, on the possibility of collective security embodied in the charter of the United Nations. Skeptical from the start about the likelihood of all nations of the United Nations massing to impose military and economic sanctions, some leaders regarded the demonstration of collective security in the Korean War (only nineteen nations took part) as a less than reliable mechanism to guarantee American security. With the veto available to the Soviet Union in the Security Council, it was argued that not only was collective security unreliable, the chances of its being used against Soviet interests in the future was nonexistent.

An early result of the containment policy—the Truman Doctrine—addressed the specific problems then existing in Greece and Turkey and also proclaimed the American intention of opposing Soviet and Communist expansion in the world.

The military component of the containment policy was developed in 1948 and 1949 with some assistance from the threat implicit in the Soviet blockade of West Berlin in 1948. Nations of Western Europe enthusiastically joined in signing the North Atlantic Treaty, which established a military organization (NATO) under American command.

Massive Retaliation

By the time the Eisenhower administration came into office in 1953, the Soviet Union had broken the American nuclear monopoly, but with a nuclear advantage and the capability of the Strategic Air Command (SAC) to deliver nuclear destruction, the administration proclaimed the doctrine of "massive retaliation." It implied that if the Soviets caused trouble or threatened Western Europe, the United States would respond with nuclear attack at a time and place of American choice. At the same time Secretary of State John Foster Dulles threatened to "roll back" Soviet control of the nations of Eastern and Central Europe.

Enmeshed in the concept of NATO and of massive retaliation was the "trip-wire" mechanism. Limited but sizeable numbers of American troops would remain assigned to Europe, especially in West Germany. A Soviet attack would necessarily confront these troops and set off the trip-wire of American nuclear response. This "first use" of nuclear weapons has, therefore, been a part of American strategic doctrine since the beginning of the Cold War. Arguments about its wisdom and effectiveness persist, but it is nothing new.

Until the late 1950s the capability of the Soviet Union to strike the United States directly was extremely limited since the Soviets possessed no long-range bombers that were capable of hitting major population or production centers. However, in 1957, with the successful Soviet launching of Sputnik, the first manmade satellite ever to be thrust into space, it was clear that the Soviets possessed not only nuclear weapons but the missile capacity to reach the United States.

More Flexible Response and MAD

The idea of massive retaliation, already under attack for its limitations on American capabilities to respond to less than massive Soviet attacks, gave way in the Kennedy administration to the doctrine of "more flexible response." However, the Kennedy administration was also faced with developing doctrine to cover the new reality of mutual vulnerability to nuclear attack.

Kennedy was determined to expand and diversify the military capability of the United States. He was especially interested in developing new anti-guerilla special forces capable of dealing with uprisings in Third World areas. Beyond these new forces, Kennedy was committed to a strengthening of conventional forces and a repair of the "missile gap" which his campaign alleged the Eisenhower administration had permitted to occur.

Discovering that any "gap" which existed in 1961 was in favor of the United States, Kennedy nonetheless was faced with the need for a new doctrine to encompass the new reality posed by the possession of intercontinental ballistic missiles by both superpowers. The answer was MAD, mutual assured destruction, a doctrine based on the view that American capability to retaliate had to be sufficient to inflict on an enemy damages so unacceptable as to make a Soviet first strike unthinkable.[14]

Implicit in the new state of affairs of the missile age was another name for mutual assured destruction — the balance of terror.[15] Recognition that the two superpowers possessed nuclear weapons and the means to deliver them anywhere in the world suggests the terror that inhibits the use of these weapons. It might be argued that the balance of terror constitutes a new and modern form of balance of power with its roots in the technological developments of the nuclear and missile ages.

In any case, with mutual assured destruction came the subsidiary doctrines of first- and second-strike nuclear capabilities and of such strategies in the use of nuclear weapons as counter-force, counter-city, counter-combatant, and countervailing strikes. That effects of nuclear attack can be confined with surgical precision to military bases and military forces or to cities or to any other specific targets is unlikely. Although advances in technology have improved the accuracy of targeting, the effects of nuclear explosions can hardly be limited.

The Domino Theory, Vietnamization, and Pacification

When President Lyndon Johnson decided to escalate the American commitment to Vietnam, he often cited the domino theory for justification. Originating in the Eisenhower era, the domino theory suggested that if a country were to fall under the control of communists, other countries would also fall like a row of dominoes. In the Johnson administration, the theory was used to suggest that if South Vietnam fell to the Viet Cong and to the North Vietnamese, then all of Southeast Asia would fall to communist forces. When American forces withdrew from Vietnam and the armies of South Vietnam collapsed, communist forces took control of Laos, Kampuchea (formerly Cambodia), and South Vietnam. For more than a decade following the communist victory in Indo-China, however, no additional dominoes have fallen under communist control.

A second major theme that accompanied the American escalation in Vietnam was the intention to train the South Vietnamese military and to transfer the primary responsibility to them—Vietnamization. This became the basis on which both the Johnson and Nixon administrations pursued the gradual withdrawal of American forces.

A third doctrine proclaimed early in the war was that of pacification. Intending to gather scattered villagers and peasants into protected strategic hamlets, pacification was meant to isolate the population from Viet Cong terror in the countryside. The results of the program were mixed.

The Nixon Doctrine and Detente

With the Nixon administration came the Nixon Doctrine, which in essence proclaimed the removal of American forces from future involvements in Asia. More important was the doctrine of detente, the intellectual justification for relaxing tensions with the Soviet Union by negotiation of arms-control agreements, trade, and increased contacts among peoples. Although the trade agreement failed, the Strategic Arms Limitation Talks led to a treaty, SALT I; and the Ford administration, after the resignation of Nixon, laid the groundwork for SALT II. In addition, detente also included the reestablishment of contacts with the People's Republic of China, contacts that led in the Carter administration to formal recognition and formal diplomatic relations.

Human Rights and the Carter
Doctrine

The Carter administration, refining military doctrine and adopting the strategy of countervailing power, changed relatively little of existing accumulated doctrine with two exceptions—an emphasis on human rights and the Carter doctrine.[16] Although not expressly a doctrine relating to military policy the concept of human rights, nonetheless, touched occasionally on military aid to several American allies.

The most important departure in the Carter years from the standpoint of military policy, however, was the Carter Doctrine: the policy that free flow of oil through the Persian Gulf was an American vital interest and would be protected by American power. The move to create a rapid deployment force capable of responding to crisis in the most sensitive areas of the Middle East became an important tactical initiative in the Carter years.

Reagan and a Return
to Superiority

Since the inauguration of Ronald Reagan in 1981, the prevailing doctrine has been the closing of what the president perceived as a "window of vulnerability" in which the United States is seen as militarily inferior to the Soviet Union.[17]

A Reagan proposal with broader long-term implications for the military track is the plan to develop antiballistic missile defenses in space.[18] Conceptually, this could constitute a change of emphasis from the offensive doctrine embodied in mutual assured destruction to a defensive one, originally proposed in the antiballistic missile systems developed in the Johnson administration. The idea is under scrutiny in many quarters.

These, then, are a few of the key politico-military doctrines that have developed since 1945. They have served to mobilize public support, to give direction to policy, and to communicate with the rest of the world. Most are still subject to controversy, but few are likely to be abandoned in the immediate future.

Inevitably, doctrine is subject to intense political debate, but it provides a framework in which other tools of military policy are developed. The size of the defense budget (over $300 billion for fiscal year 1985), the kinds of weapons systems Congress is willing to support (the MX missile and the B-1 bomber for example), and the levels and mixture of other capabilities depend upon the acceptance and support of doctrines by the people and by the Congress.

Force, the Threat of Force,
and the Arms Race

The maintenance of large military forces has been part of American foreign policy for the last four decades. That military force is necessary to deter war or to win one if deterrence fails is one of the basic tenets of the balance-of-power doctrine.[19] The capability to extend American military protection and support to other countries and to threaten potential adversaries provides policy makers with additional options in pursuit of national interests abroad.

The invasion of Grenada by American forces in 1983 to get rid of Cuban and Soviet influence in the Eastern Caribbean marked the sixth time since the end of World War II that military capabilities had been directly employed by American presidents. In Korea in 1950, in Lebanon in 1958 and 1983, in the Dominican Republic in 1965, and in Vietnam, force was employed to achieve political objectives, with mixed results.

American military force was used in more limited ways in the Berlin Airlift of 1948 and in the Cuban Missile Crisis of 1962. When the Soviets blocked all access to West Berlin in 1948, the Truman administration used an airlift to provide supplies to the city until the crisis ended. In 1962 the Kennedy administration used a blockade of Cuba to prevent further installation of missiles and to persuade the Soviets to withdraw those already there. Frequently in the past, so-called gunboat diplomacy has been used to display power through the presence of naval forces in a troubled area, and large-scale military maneuvers are a public means of displaying a military threat. In Central America, large and continuing military maneuvers have provided the Reagan administration with the means to assert American concern with events in the region.

The use of American forces, even in limited ways, however, can create a trap for policy makers and lead to the necessity for deeper and larger commitments of forces or to situations from which they cannot be withdrawn without severe damage to American prestige. The modest program of providing military advisers to Vietnam led to the commitment of over 550,000 men. Participation in a multinational peacekeeping force in Lebanon in 1983-84 and subsequent withdrawal of that force are believed by some observers to have damaged the American position in the Middle East, at least temporarily. Concern about possible escalation of the American military role in Central America in the 1980s has increased because of the modest commitments made in the region by the Reagan administration.

In some cases the mere threat of the use of existing force is sufficient to accomplish policy aims,[20] as the resolution of the Cuban missile crisis in 1962 demonstrated. Another example was the military alert in the Middle East war of 1973 when both Soviet and American leaders threatened intervention.[21]

Indeed, deterrence is based on the threat of nuclear retaliation if the Soviet Union should attempt to overrun Western Europe.

The levels of force required to achieve security and the influence to shape events throughout the global system have led to a major arms race between the superpowers and among smaller countries throughout the world. In an action-reaction process, each superpower has sought to match or to balance forces on the other side. In the 1980s the arms-race issue has focused on the decision by NATO to install modern intermediate-range Pershing II and cruise missiles in Western Europe to match a new generation of SS-20 missiles developed by the Soviet Union. However, the arms race has proceeded on many fronts, both conventional and nuclear. During the period of détente in the 1970s the United States agreed to the principle of strategic parity with the Soviet Union. From 1966 to 1976 American analysts believe that Soviet military spending substantially exceeded that of the United States, as the Soviets attempted to match and to surpass the United States in a wide range of weapons systems. American attempts to limit defense expenditures during the 1970s were sharply criticized by candidate Ronald Reagan in the 1980 presidential campaign, and once elected, President Reagan proposed a vast $1.5 trillion military budget for the next five years. Despite arguments that the deployment of the new intermediate-range missiles in Europe will have little real effect on the balance of power, the unsuccessful negotiations in Geneva over arms control became a symbol of American-Soviet conflict and underscored the deeper political conflicts between the two countries. Meantime, alarm increased among those who believe that arms races in and of themselves constitute dangerous components of political relations and are both a cause of increased arms production and a provocation of more hostile attitudes. In this context the decision to engage in arms-control negotiations not only maintains a moderating link between the two sides but is a policy option containing incentives. Rejection of arms-control negotiations, conversely, is a threat.

Despite the dangers that reside in the maintenance of large forces and the possible escalation of hostility that results from the threats to use them, little inclination is apparent on either side to agree on reductions. The growth of the nuclear-freeze movement in the West in the 1980s has created some political pressures on the United States but has left the Soviet government unmoved.

Beyond the arms races between the superpowers, the increase in arms and the forces to use them has proceeded rapidly throughout the rest of the world. The arming of scores of countries by the United States and the Soviet Union and the development of nuclear capabilities throughout the Third World pose additional dangers to world peace. At the same time the supply of arms to allies, friends, and client states is a formidable tool of policy in the search for support of American or Soviet interests. Whether the provision of arms increases or decreases the security of either superpower is a matter of opinion. In the Middle East, in Central America, in Vietnam, the arming of national forces with the purpose of promoting American and Soviet interests has frequently involved both countries in costly and dangerous events, many of which have the potential for directly involving American and Soviet forces.

Thus force, the use of force, the threat of force, and the arms race provide policy makers with tools of policy, but they constitute the most dangerous instruments of all in their hands.

Covert and Paramilitary Activity

War and the direct involvement of American military forces are the most extreme measures available to policy makers. In most situations their use is unjustified, inappropriate, or inapplicable. For this reason the capability to act covertly in ways short of war provides the means to exercise political influence on events.

While military force has been directly used only six times since 1946 and the threat of force has been used more than two hundred times in the same period by the United States, one estimate indicates that various forms of covert means were used to achieve American goals several thousand times since 1961.[22] In 1983 and 1984, for example, American support of guerilla forces opposed to the Sandinista regime in Nicaragua was sharply debated in Congress, and the Democratic-controlled House of Representatives twice voted to cut American support for covert action.

A wide range of activities fall under the category of covert military operations: assassination, terrorism, sabotage, the use of guerilla forces, and support of coups d'état or civil war. In some cases, as in El Salvador, covert efforts may be used on behalf of the government, while in others, such as Chile or Nicaragua, they may be used against an incumbent government.[23]

The use of covert tools has often been controversial or has produced controversial results. The secret bombing of Cambodia during the Vietnam War, American support for the unsuccessful Bay of Pigs invasion of Cuba by anti-Castro dissidents, the American role in opposing the presidency of Salvador Allende in Chile and in support of the coup d'état that removed him are among the most bitterly debated covert activities undertaken in the last three decades. Equally controversial were revelations that the CIA had considered attempts to assassinate Fidel Castro and other leaders.

The necessity, morality, and wisdom of a democracy conducting such activities will always remain questionable, but the temptation to use the vast American capability for such actions will always be difficult to resist for presidents facing intractable foreign-policy problems.

Congress has prohibited the use of assassination and has attempted to bring covert plans under more direct scrutiny. However, as the Nicaraguan affair of the 1980s suggests, there is little inclination among leaders to discard the tools available in the covert kit.

Modern Technology

The American capability to remain in the forefront of the development of new military technology has been a basic element in the maintenance of the nation's military strength. Access to these modern systems sought by other states affords political leverage to policy makers. The intense political arguments over both of these aspects of new military technology will be examined a bit later. For the moment, a brief survey of the major technological developments in both the strategic and the conventional systems available to policy makers is in order.

Much of the contemporary balance of power with the Soviet Union rests on what is called the strategic triad: intercontinental ballistic missiles (ICBMs), submarine-launched ballistic missiles (SLBMs), and long-range manned bombers (B-52s and the proposed new B-1s). However, a large part of the balance consists of conventional forces: standing armies, surface navies, and tactical air forces.

Inherent in the strategic portion of the military balance is the capability to possess and deliver nuclear weapons. After the creation of the atomic bomb in 1945, the United States moved ahead to develop the far more powerful hydrogen bomb. Technical developments made it possible to create ever larger bombs, but work also continued on the production of smaller bombs for tactical use in more limited areas of battle between armies.[24] More recently scientists produced a neutron bomb, a small-scale weapon capable of destroying people but not equipment or buildings.[25]

Until the late 1950s, although the Soviet Union had also developed nuclear weapons, only the United States had the capability of delivering them with the long-range bomber force of the Strategic Air Command. After the launching of the Sputnik by the Soviets in 1957, it was clear that they had the capability to deliver nuclear bombs to the United States. Efforts in both the Soviet Union and the United States to produce missiles for varying purposes led to succeeding generations of land-based missiles, intermediate-range missiles, antiballistic missiles (ABMs), submarine-launched missiles, ground-to-air antiaircraft missiles, and cruise missiles.[26] In 1983 Congress approved an improved land-based ICBM, the MX, and is considering a new, smaller ICBM, the Midgetman, recommended by the Scowcroft Commission.[27] The cruise missile, a smaller missile capable of launching from aircraft and of flying undetected below enemy radar is being deployed.[28]

Throughout the 1960s the United States developed missiles capable of carrying and firing a number of separate warheads—multiple independently targeted reentry vehicles (MIRVs)[29]—and experimentation proceeded on building maneuverable reentry vehicles (MARVs), warheads that could be maneuvered after launching from missiles.

Research and development has proceeded toward construction of a new long-range manned bomber, the B-1, to replace the B-52 as the major manned component of the strategic triad. President Reagan successfully reinstituted the program after it was shelved by President Carter.[30] Opposition continues in Congress based on some reservations about the continued utility of manned bombers and on the prospect that a new bomber under development, the so-called STEALTH, will be more effective and virtually undetectable.[31] But in late 1983 Congress approved funds for the production of the B-1.

In terms of balance of strategic weapons in the summer of 1983, the *New York Times* estimated that the United States had 1,052 ICBMs to 1398 for the Soviet Union.[32] The Soviet Union had 950 SLBMs, while the United States had 520. The United States had an edge in manned bombers—347 to 156. Under proposals by the Reagan administration, the number of warheads on American missiles will total 14,000 if no arms agreement is reached. The Soviet Union is believed to have fewer warheads.

Although the numbers change somewhat rapidly, and there are many caveats and interpretations necessary to carefully assess the balance, the numbers constitute the basis for negotiations between the superpowers.

On the more conventional level new fighter aircraft such as the F-15 and F16, equipped with sophisticated computers, radar, and "smart" missiles (heat seeking or laser-guided projectiles) have proved to be effective in combat in the Middle East.[33]

Developed for the purpose of surveillance, the AWACs aircraft is equipped with the latest equipment to provide radar, sonar, and photographic capabilities.[34]

For naval forces facing obsolescence in the missile age, the development of nuclear-powered submarines capable of launching missiles created a new mission and a major responsibility in the strategic triad. Three generations of larger subs with longer-range missile capabilities have been developed in the past two decades—the Polaris, the Poseidon, and the Trident—and President Reagan has proposed expanded development and production of the Trident.[35] After the inauguration of President Reagan, the administration gave a new thrust to expansion of the surface fleet and reactivated a few battleships.[36] However, some analysts within the Defense Department remain skeptical of surface vessels in the missile age. Regarding surface ships as highly vulnerable, one analyst has proposed that submersible vessels be developed including missile-carrying ships and aircraft carriers.[37] In the Reagan administration intensive support has continued for a 600-ship fleet with large conventional aircraft carriers.[38]

Although the size of the army has remained fairly stable in recent years, based on a system of volunteer enlistments, Army leaders have sought to define a new doctrine and have proposed new technology to carry it out. The new doctrine, called air-land battle, is based on the premise of tactical flexibility and the attack on enemy forces behind the enemy's lines. The doctrine requires mobility, maneuverability, and surprise.[39] The Bradley armored vehicle and the new Apache AH-64 helicopter are key technological components of the new doctrine. The AH-64 is seen as an antitank weapon and as an effective support of troops.[40] Another new army weapon—the M-1 tank—has been troubled by production problems, although Congress in 1983 approved an increase in output from 720 to 840 tanks per year.[41]

Military technology has also proceeded to develop capabilities in space. Spy satellites provide useful military information and potential verification of arms-control agreements.[42] Research on new weapons for space—laser beams or nuclear-particle beams capable of destroying an enemy's missiles—continues,[43] and President Reagan, as noted, has proposed development of an antimissile system in space early in the twenty-first century. Further, successful flights by the Columbia, Challenger, and Discovery space-shuttle craft suggest possible military uses.[44]

Despite the technological capabilities suggested in the foregoing review of major modern weapons systems, some observers have noted that something as mundane as a lack of spare parts and of maintenance reduces the effectiveness and readiness of all of this sophisticated equipment and, further, that personnel policies inhibit the military's access to enough people as well as the retention of qualified technical specialists. In any case, the technological advancement of weapons systems is awesome and constitutes a significant component of American military strength and political influence.

To be sure, the political debate over these developments focuses on the desirability of an unending technological arms race with the Soviet Union and of the distribution of modern weapons to a variety of countries around the world. It is argued that this produces not stability and a balance of power but rather instability and imbalance.

Alliances

Alliances have historically been among the primary tools of foreign policy.[45] They are designed to enhance the strength and security of their members and to provide guarantees of mutual and common response to external threat. In addition, they are also designed to promote cooperation rather than conflict among their members. Membership in alliances may, in fact, increase the dangers of one's own country, and surely they will increase their members' responsibilities to each other and to the group.[46] Alliances tend to have the greatest cohesion when the external threat is perceived to be the greatest, but remarkably, some of the major alliances in which the United States has participated since 1945 have held up very well, although some others have disappeared. In the late 1940s America's willingness to join in an alliance with Western European countries was considered as an assurance of their security, and it was welcomed with great enthusiasm.

The primary military alliance created by the United States was formed under the terms of the North Atlantic Treaty, which provided for the creation of a unified military alliance, NATO, under the leadership of an American military officer.

During the 1950s and 1960s, alliances were also formed in other parts of the world as elements of the American global-security system: the southeast Asia Treaty Organization, SEATO, formed under the Manila Pact of 1954; the Central Treaty Organization (CENTO), formed in Southwest Asia and the Middle East; the ANZUS Pact, formed among Australia, New Zealand, and the United States; and the Organization of American States, OAS, formed with some of the countries of Latin America. These alliances created global treaty obligations around the world.

SEATO was eroding even before the Vietnam War and then collapsed entirely, CENTO disintegrated many years ago. However, NATO, ANZUS, and OAS remain active and relevant, and more recently a group of Asian nations—the Philippines, Thailand, Malaysia, Indonesia, and Singapore—formed the Association of Southeast Asian Nations (ASEAN), which has had American support and has in turn provided some support to American interests in Asia and the Pacific.[47]

Technically, the United States is also part of the United Nations system of collective security, and as a member, it can be called upon to send forces to serve United Nations objectives when sanctioned by the Security Council. Except for the war in Korea, however, American forces have usually not been required to participate in United Nations military operations.

In any case, the alliance is a continuing and vital mechanism for implementation of foreign policy, and indeed the alliance is one of the actors exerting pressure on the policy process. Still, American willingness to participate in a military alliance is one of the inducements policy makers may utilize in pursuing political objectives.

Military Bases

Some countries are eager to have an American base on their soil, and some are not. For some it may increase their own danger, and for others it may enhance their own security, their income, and their prestige. Military agreements, treaties, and alliance relationships all provide the basis for the presence of American bases, but occasionally new governments will wish to withdraw from these commitments.

From the American perspective, certain bases are essential for the global responsibilities carried on by the United States. For example, with the loss of Vietnam, the American bases in the Philippines—Clark Air Base and Subic Bay Naval Base assumed increased importance to American operations in the Far East. Before Philippine independence in 1946, the United States controlled the bases and once even held sovereignty over them. However, in recent years, the United States has recognized Philippine sovereignty and has negotiated a series of agreements with the Philippines to use the bases.[48]

In Western Europe several American bases remain in operation under the NATO treaty and constitute a major element of NATO defense strategy.

However, bases are sometimes lost. In Vietnam several major naval and air facilities were lost to the victorious Hanoi forces. The United States was asked to leave Libya in the 1960s. In Cuba the United States retains possession of Guantanamo Bay because of an old treaty, although the Castro government would like to end the arrangement. To facilitate naval operations in the Indian Ocean and in the Persian Gulf, the United States has established a base on the small island of Diego Garcia. Recently the trend toward temporary basing arrangements for the rapid deployment force has resulted in agreements with Egypt, Kenya, and Somalia.[49]

There are some three hundred American bases all over the world.[50] Where bases are desired or welcomed, they can facilitate cooperation with other countries. Even where they are not wanted, they may be essential elements in the military structure and in implementing foreign policy.

Military Assistance

Since the end of World War II, the United States has provided several hundred billion dollars worth of military assistance to friends and allies, including arms, equipment, services, and training.[51]

Much of this aid was provided under the Military Assistance Program (MAP) in the form of grants.[52] Military training came under the International Military Education and Training Program in the mid-70s. Foreign military sales (FMS) have become a much larger portion of military aid, and a sizeable portion of sales also include credits to recipient countries to help them purchase what they seek.[53]

Since 1945 the United States has helped to form a number of alliances that provided mutual security arrangements including the transfer of arms and training.

By the mid-1960s the emphasis had shifted from grants to sales, and by 1980, the United States was the world's largest arms supplier.[54] The role of military sales in American policy is well summarized as follows:

> Over time FMS became a multipurpose instrument of policy designed to symbolize American resolve, to protect American credibility, and to strengthen American allies generally, and in the case of Europe, to encourage greater logistical cooperation, upgrade European defense systems, and spread the financial burdens of the collective defense. Among developing nations, FMS was viewed as a vehicle for generating regional power balances, controlling arms races, maintaining American influence, and selectively modifying recipients' policies regarding human rights.[55]

One estimate placed the number of countries with which the United States had some form of military commitment at ninety-two.[56] In any case, it is estimated that since 1950 American military assistance under the MAP, the training program, sales, and commercial trade has amounted to nearly $200 billion, and these figures do not take into account the outright gifts of obsolete military equipment to foreign countries.[57]

In recent years the largest single recipient of military aid has been Israel, although the United States has also vastly increased the availability of modern weapons to Saudi Arabia, Egypt, and other Middle East countries.[58] The numerous wars between Israel and the Arab states have been testing grounds for modern American weapons systems against those made by the Soviet Union and supplied to its allies in the region. In general, the performance of American weapons in the hands of the Israelis has been vastly superior to that of the Soviet weapons used by various Arab states.

It is clear that in the 1980s modern weapons systems are desired by many countries not only for security from external threat (in many cases there is none) but also for the maintenance of internal security and for prestige. For example, many observers believe that Pakistan is well on its way to building an atomic bomb primarily because its traditional enemy, India, has built one.[59]

Arms Control and Mutual Force Reductions

The willingness to negotiate arms control and mutual force reductions has, on occasion, produced some relaxation of tension between the United States and the Soviet Union as well as some relief in all other states. It may also lead to specific agreements, such as the ban of nuclear testing in the atmosphere, the nuclear non-proliferation treaty, the Strategic Arms Limitation Treaties I and II, although SALT II was never ratified in the United States. Intense criticism of SALT II in the United States was based on the view that it did not provide comparable force levels and that it was unverifiable. In addition, the Soviet intervention into Afghanistan made approval of the treaty by the U.S. Senate impossible. In the first years of the Reagan administration the president proposed that the United States and the Soviet Union proceed on new arms-control discussions to reduce strategic weapons and changed the name from SALT to START—Strategic Arms Reduction Talks.[60]

During 1983 negotiations proceeded in Geneva on reduction of intermediate range nuclear forces (INF) and continued on the subject of Mutual Balanced Force Reductions (MBFR) in Europe.[61] However, in early 1984 the Soviet Union walked out of the talks at all levels, and progress toward arms control came to a temporary halt.

A number of possible explanations have been given for the stalemate in arms control that has characterized the first half of the eighties. First, the hostility that has marked the relationship between the Reagan administration and the Soviet leadership has been more intense than in any period since the late 1940s. The mood has been affected by bitter rhetoric and by arms buildup policies on both sides. Second, in recent years, the Soviet leadership has been in state of transition. In the last years of the life of Leonid Brezhnev, his serious illness seemed to create doubts about who was in control. After Brezhnev's death, Yuri Andropov assumed the leadership of the Communist party and of the government, but he, too, became seriously ill and died in early 1984. His successor is Konstantin Chernenko whose health is also in question. Thus the transition of Soviet leadership has contributed to its unwillingness and inability to make concessions in arms control. A third factor relating to the stalemate has been the uncertainty over American political leadership as the 1984 election hovered over arms control talks.

Underlying the discussion of arms control is the real national interest of both superpowers in seeking an accord. Each side may use the issue to attempt to influence world opinion and to enhance its own foreign policy in other areas. Each side may also use the issue to pressure or persuade the other. Both would benefit from an agreement that would permit a reduction of expenditures for arms. In any case, arms control strategy remains an element of the military track and can be used as an effective tool of policy.

Military Leadership and Management

The dramatic and colorful film portraits of Generals George Patton, Douglas MacArthur, Dwight Eisenhower, and Omar Bradley and Admiral William "Bull" Halsey suggest the importance of effective commanders in wartime. Battlefield leadership is indispensible to effective military operations. However, there is another level at which military leadership is critical to the achievement of politico-military objectives—management and organization.[62] General Eisenhower was chosen as supreme commander of Allied forces in Europe in World War II not because of battlefield skills but because of his managerial and political skills, and his record of welding an effective alliance among strong-willed allies contributed immeasurably to an Allied victory.[63] Less well known to the present generation of Americans is General George Marshall who, as army chief of staff and major adviser to President Roosevelt during World War II, was regarded by Winston Churchill as the "organizer of victory."[64]

Military leadership shapes the tactics, effectiveness, and command structures of military units, and the United States exerts considerable effort to develop skilled leaders capable not only of courageous combat leadership but also of planning, research, and organizational supervision. The maintenance of the three service academies—West Point, Annapolis, and the Air Force Academy—has been augmented with the operation of war colleges by the services for advanced training. Advanced leadership schools and graduate training at the nation's leading private universities provide a broader social-humanistic-political background for career officers. The officer corps is also supplemented through the operation of officer candidate schools and reserve officer training programs.

Access to an available pool of broadly educated leaders, especially in a time when technological development affects preparedness so profoundly, is a major factor in military strength, and massive resources must be committed to the process.

CONCLUSION

In assessing the importance of the military track of foreign policy and the tools available within it, we need to confront a few very basic political questions about the existence and use of military power. For example, is a military capability necessary, and if so, why? Under what conditions can and should war or military operations be used? Can war be limited, or is it important to achieve victory?

These questions are immensely important, and the answers are very complex. The pacifist-idealist view suggests that neither war nor the existence of military force is required or necessary in human relations and that war has been a cancer on human history. In recent years intensive studies of the causes of war have probed a number of possible explanations: human instinct to violence and aggression, the nature of the state system, individual personality, economic needs and desires, arms races, the human fascination with the drama of war, and the absence of a world order, to name just a few. Peace research has become a major intellectual project in the twentieth century as scholars, statesmen, and philosophers have sought theoretical answers to the prevention of war.

Those arguing against war confront a human history filled with war and violence in virtually every culture in every part of the world. The use of military force as an instrument of other drives does not obscure the use of military force from its own impulses—the use of force for its own sake. But whatever the cause or causes, war is ubiquitous in history and in the contemporary world, each state believing that it needs a minimum of force to protect itself from other states and to maintain internal order.

Thus there appears to be little conviction among the governments of the world in the possibility of total and complete disarmament and demilitarization.

Given this interpretation of the past, leaders tend to define contemporary reality partly in military terms, that is, that other countries possess weapons and may use them. Thus most states in the world in the 1980s possess military capabilities of one sort or another.

For the United States there is a further complication. Left by the events of World War II as the most powerful country on earth, the United

States assumed the leadership role in world affairs and the general responsibility for the order and stability of the Western world and the global system. This, it came to be believed, required a sizeable military establishment and the use of military force, if necessary, to obstruct the expansion of the Soviet Union and world communism.

But are perceptions of the necessity for the existence and possible use of military force valid? Is an alternative world possible? Conceptually, one can envision an ideal world in which force is no longer a factor in relations among states, or indeed, a necessity to maintain internal order. But in a world where social organization is desired, both among and within states, the need for force is inescapable. The authoritative use of force by the state is required to maintain internal law and order. Within a global system in which no central authority exists, military force is required to protect the security of one state against another.

If this suggests an answer to the questions of whether and why military force is required in a world of states, Americans need to ponder the second perplexing question: Under what conditions can and should military force be used?

Short of the consensus on the right to respond to a direct attack in self-defense with military means, American leaders and the American people have been much less clear about criteria for deciding when to use force, what level of force to use, or the comparative benefits of other tools of policy. President Truman decided that the North Korean aggression against South Korea required an American and United Nations response. President Johnson concluded that for a number of reasons vital to American interests it was necessary to intervene militarily on a massive scale in Vietnam. In both cases debate has never ceased about the wisdom of the military commitments. In the Korean case the final settlement left matters essentially where they were before the war began. The Vietnam War, however, led to a total victory by the North Vietnamese.

Aside from the clear right of self-defense, it is not at all clear that any coherent doctrine or criteria exist for determining when direct use of military tools is required. The belief that such matters should not be spelled out too specifically in order to keep an enemy guessing about American intentions has some validity. However, this means that the American people, who must pay the price of military commitment, are also to be kept guessing. Is this good enough in the dangerous world in which we live?

Thus far it has been suggested that the existence of military capabilities is unavoidable and that increased clarity and definition is required to determine when military tools are to be used. A further perplexing question then confronts policy makers and citizens alike.

General Douglas MacArthur argued that in war "there is no substitute for victory."[65] If this is so, what does it say about the concept of limited war? How limited can and should it be? Are limited wars such as Korea and Vietnam effective means for serving the national interest? Does it mean that if a commitment to war is made, it should be vigorously pursued to victory even if the commitment is later regarded as a mistake? Or should a mistaken commitment be canceled out and the policy changed? What do we mean by "limited war" anyway?

These are perplexing, painful, and unavoidable questions for Americans responsible for the maintenance of a peaceful and stable global system.

The determination of the limits on the wars in which the United States has been engaged since 1945 depends upon many factors other than the immediate and direct military challenge. Assuming that except in the circumstances of direct attack by the Soviet Union on the United States and its allies, nuclear weapons will not be used, we might define limited war as anything else beneath the nuclear threshhold. However, the Korean and Vietnamese experiences suggest that war can be limited even further. In each case the United States brought to bear far less than its total non-nuclear capability. In the Korean case, the Soviet threat in Western Europe constrained the United States from an escalation of war beyond the commitments made by mid-1951. In the Vietnam experience, domestic constraints—the economy, public opinion, politics—imposed limitations on expansion of the size and tactics of the commitment.

Both experiences have taught that the United States should avoid war if at all possible but that if the commitment must be made, it should be pursued in a way adequate to achieve a victory in the shortest possible time, since this minimizes the costs and maximizes the benefits, if any. Most important, if a military commitment cannot be justified convincingly in terms of American vital interests, it should be avoided, since successful military operations require massive public support.

Underlying the choice of the military option is the issue of separation of anti-Soviet from anti-Communist expansion. American policy makers confront the development of Marxist regimes in other countries of the world. In those cases where countries may develop Marxist regimes but remain legitimately unaligned, American interference may be unproductive in the service of the American national interest. In countries where the rise of Marxist regimes produce a base of operations for the Soviet Union a different set of responses may be required.

At bottom, it is conceivable that American military capabilities may be required in some circumstances in the contemporary world. American resistance to Soviet expansion of influence and Soviet resistance to American actions may produce circumstances where use of force is required. In these cases the American national interest must be clearly defined, articulated, and maintained, for American forces cannot be committed when public support is absent.

In chapter 4 we examined the role of the military in the political process within the United States. In this chapter we have attempted to relate the political effects of the military track to global politics. In each case it was suggested that there are dangers involved in the potential dominance of the political process by the military track. On the other hand, American public attitudes, and indeed the attitudes of most professional military leaders, affirm prevailing constraints on military thinking and military behavior. Nonetheless, the political impact of military capabilities on the behavior of other states in the global system persists in a world that often relates political power to military strength. To constrain the military track and to use it constructively to promote peaceful political change remains a major political challenge of the United States.

NOTES

[1] Karl von Clausewitz, *On War*, trans. O. J. Matthijs Jolles (New York: Modern Library, 1943), pp. 595-99.

[2] "A World at War—1983," report of Center for Defense Information, Washington, D.C., March 1983, *New Haven Register*, March 19, 1983, p. 1.

[3] Charles W. Kegley and Eugene R. Wittkopf, *American Foreign Policy: Pattern and Process*, 2nd ed. (New York: St. Martin's Press, 1982), pp. 99-101; Henry T. Nash, *American Foreign Policy: Changing Perspectives on National Security*, rev. ed. (Homewood, Ill.: Dorsey Press, 1978), pp. 60-62.

[4] Henry Kissinger, *White House Years* (Boston: Little, Brown & Company, 1979), p. 195.

[5] Cecil V. Crabb, Jr., *American Foreign Policy in the Nuclear Age*, 4th ed. (New York: Harper & Row, Publishers, 1983), pp. 82-84.

[6] See footnote 11, chapter 13.

[7] Robert J. Donovan, *Tumultuous Years* (New York: W. W. Norton & Company, 1982), pp. 199-203; James A. Nathan and James K. Oliver, *United States Foreign Policy and the World Order*, 2nd ed. (Boston: Little, Brown & Company, 1981), pp. 125-26.

[8] William Manchester, *One Brief Shining Moment: Remembering Kennedy* (Boston: Little, Brown & Company, 1983), pp. 224-25; Kenneth P. O'Donnell and David F. Powers with Joe McCarthy, *Johnny We Hardly Knew Ye: Memories of John Fitzgerald Kennedy* (Boston: Little, Brown & Company, 1972), pp. 13, 16-18.

A different view from that of Manchester, O'Donnell, and Powers is expressed by Peter Collier and David Horowitz in their book, *The Kennedys: An American Drama* (New York: Summit Books, 1984), p. 335. The authors cite an oral history interview with Robert Kennedy in which he answers "no" to a question of whether administration consideration had ever been given to pulling out of Vietnam.

[9] Steven R. Weisman, "Reagan Proposes U.S. Seek New Way to Block Missiles," *New York Times*, March 24, 1983, p. 1; and Weisman, "Reagan Says Plan on Missile Defense Will Prevent War," *New York Times*, March 26, 1983, p. 1.

[10] Charles Mohr, "Army Test Missile Is Said To Destroy a Dummy Warhead," *New York Times*, June 12, 1984, p. 1; Serge Schmemann, "Soviet, Urging Talks, Insists Space Arms Can Be Verified," *New York Times*, June 12, 1984, p. 18. Also, in late July 1983 the Air Force announced its first successful experiment using high-energy laser beams to knock out missiles traveling at nearly 2,000 miles per hour. "Missile Stopped By Laser Ray," *New York Times*, July 27, 1983, p. 11.

[11] Robert J. Art and Kenneth N. Waltz, "Technology, Strategy, and the Use of Force," in Art and Waltz, eds., *The Use of Force* (Boston: Little, Brown & Company, 1971), pp. 1-25; Glen Snyder, "Deterrence and Defense," in Art and Waltz, *Use of Force*, pp. 56-76.

[12] See chapter 11, pp. 155-60.

[13] Nathan and Oliver, *United States Foreign Policy*, pp. 57-58.

[14] Nash, *American Foreign Policy*, pp. 83-87.

[15] Kegley and Wittkopf, *American Foreign Policy*, pp. 80, 136, 146.

[16] Zbigniew Brzezinski, *Power and Principle* (New York: Farrar, Straus & Giroux, 1983), p. 56; Jimmy Carter, *Keeping Faith* (New York: Bantam Books, 1982), pp. 144-50.

[17] Crabb, *American Foreign Policy*, pp. 125-26.

[18] See footnotes 9 and 10 above.

[19] See chapter 11, pp. 155-60.

[20] Thomas C. Schelling, *Arms and Influence* (New Haven: Yale University Press, 1966), pp. 1-10, 12-34.

[21] Henry Kissinger, *Years of Upheaval* (Boston: Little, Brown & Company, 1982), pp. 575-99.

[22] Kegley and Wittkopf, *American Foreign Policy*, pp. 113-14.

[23] Steven Weisman, "Reagan Denies Aim is Bigger Presence in Latin America," *New York Times*, July 27, 1983, p. 1; Rogal and others, "Reagan's Gunboat Diplomacy," pp. 12-17.

[24] Crabb, *American Foreign Policy*, p. 374.

[25] Kegley and Wittkopf, *American Foreign Policy*, p. 106.

[26] Crabb, *American Foreign Policy*, pp. 340-42.

[27] Leslie H. Gelb, "As a Bargaining Chip, MX May Be No Bargain for the Soviets," *New York Times*, April 24, 1983, p. 4:1; "Hard Sell: Closing Windows, Opening Doors on Missile Debate," *New York Times*, April 24, 1983, p. 4:1; Jonathan Alter with John L. Lindsay, "The MX: One Step Closer," *Newsweek*, August 1, 1983, p. 25.

[28] Crabb, *American Foreign Policy*, p. 341.

[29] Ibid., pp. 130, 342-43.

[30] Kegley and Wittkopf, *American Foreign Policy*, pp. 425, 563.

[31] Ibid., p. 265.

[32] "Strategic Nuclear Arms: Where Each Side Stands," *New York Times*, June 8, 1983, p. 12.

[33] Judith Miller, "New Generation of Nuclear Arms with Controlled Effects Foreseen," *New York Times*, October 27, 1982, p. 1.

[34] Kegley and Wittkopf, *American Foreign Policy*, p. 400.

[35] Richard Halloran, "Reagan Extending Trident Program," *New York Times*, February 6, 1983, p. 17.

[36] Melinda Beck and others, "Unclear Sailing," *Newsweek*, March 16, 1981, p. 24; Kim Rogal and others, "Reagan's Gunboat Diplomacy," *Newsweek*, August 1, 1983, pp. 14-15.

[37] "Penatagon Analyst Proposing a Submersible Navy," *New York Times*, September 11, 1983, p. 32.

[38] Beck and others, "Unclear Sailing," p. 25.

[39] Deborah Shapley, "The Army's New Fighting Doctrine," *New York Times Magazine*, November 28, 1982, pp. 37-56.

[40] Ibid.

[41] Richard Halloran, "Chief of Army Assails Industry on Arms Flaws," *New York Times*, August 9, 1983, p. 1.

[42] See footnote 10, this chapter.

[43] See footnote 10, this chapter.

[44] William Stockton and John Noble Wilford, *Spaceliner* (New York: Times Books, 1981), pp. 41-42, 62-63, 124-27.

[45] Hans Morgenthau, *Politics Among Nations*, 5th ed., rev. (New York: Alfred A. Knopf, 1973), pp. 188-204; Bruce Russett and Harvey Starr, *World Politics: The Menu for Choice* (San Francisco: W. H. Freeman and Co., 1981), pp. 91-99.

[46] Bruce Bueno de Mesquita, *The War Trap* (New Haven: Yale University Press, 1981), pp. 115, 162-63; Russett and Starr, *World Politics*, p. 96; J. David Singer and Melvin Small, "Alliance Aggregation and the Onset of War, 1815-1945," in J. David Singer, ed., *Quantitative International Politics: Insights and Evidence* (New York: Free Press, 1968), pp. 247-86.

[47] Crabb, *American Foreign Policy*, p. 567.

[48] "Manila to Get $900 Million in Accord on Bases," *New York Times*, June 1, 1983, p. 6.

[49] Donald Rothchild and John Ravenhill, "From Carter to Reagan: The Global Perspective on Africa Becomes Ascendant," in Kenneth A. Oye, Robert J. Lieber, and Donald Rothchild, eds., *Eagle Defiant: United States Foreign Policy in the 1980s* (Boston: Little, Brown & Company, 1983), p. 352.

[50] Kegley and Wittkopf, *American Foreign Policy*, p. 101.

[51] Ibid., pp. 119-20.

[52] Ibid., p. 119.

[53] Ibid., p. 120.

[54] Ibid., pp. 122-23.

[55] Ibid., p. 123.

[56] Ibid., p. 126.

[57] Ibid., p. 119.

[58] Ibid., p. 120.

[59] Crabb, *American Foreign Policy*, p. 555.

[60] "Security and Arms Control: The Search for a More Stable Peace," Washington, D.C., U.S. Department of State, 1983, pp. 23-27.

[61] Victor Lusinchi, "U.S.-Soviet Arms Talks Adjourn," *New York Times*, August 5, 1983, p. 2.

[62] Morris Janowitz, "Organizing Multiple Goals: War Making and Arms Control," in Morris Janowitz, ed., *The New Military: Changing Patterns of Organization* (New York: Russell Sage Foundation, 1964), pp. 16-31; Kurt Lang, "Technology and Career Management," in Janowitz, *New Military*, pp. 39-80.

[63] Leonard Mosley, *Marshall: Hero for Our Times* (New York: Hearst Books, 1982), pp. 210, 254, 264-67.

[64] Ibid., p. xvii.

[65] William Manchester, *American Caesar* (Boston: Little, Brown & Company, 1978), pp. 629-30, 659.

CHAPTER SEVENTEEN
THE CULTURAL TRACK

When Red Chinese officials warned young people of the cultural corruption resulting from enjoying American cola, and when Soviet leaders railed against the "decadence" of rock music and blue jeans,[1] they were responding to what they perceived to be serious challenges to their culture implicit in the use of Western products. By connecting the enjoyment of cola, rock, and jeans to a potential threat to governmental control, officials in these countries are expressing an understanding of the underlying human attitudes they believe these products represent: desire for independence, freedom, and pleasure, hardly the characteristics of a dedicated Communist society according to orthodox Communist ideology. Whether such cultural artifacts can produce profound cultural and political change is doubtful, but some Soviet and Chinese leaders apparently believe that they can. These examples of political reaction to cultural change highlight the importance of the cultural track in foreign policy.

For many centuries people of the world have mingled with each other across seas and borders, exchanging bits and pieces of each other's unique cultures. Indeed, a sizeable portion of human history includes efforts of religious, governmental, and ideological institutions to impose their "truth" upon other peoples and to shape their cultures.

In the modern state system, the United States is one of the many countries that have made the effort to shape, change, and direct cultural formation in many parts of the world. Undoubtedly, this impulse has had many roots, not the least of which have been the "Christianizing" mission to "civilize" others and the good intentions to induce others to accept the liberalizing ideas of democracy.[2] President Woodrow Wilson's view that World War I was fought to "make the world safe for democracy" expressed the view succinctly.

One scholar has argued that "cultural relations can be viewed as no less than the totality of relations between cultures."[3] As we have seen, relations among differing cultures in the last half of the twentieth century have expanded enormously across a wide spectrum of activity: political, economic, military, social, organizational, and individual. Transportation and communications have made the global community a far more open one than it was just a hundred years ago. Thus cultures are interacting more frequently and more intensely than ever before in human history. The study of the effects of this interaction, the depth of cultural changes produced by it, and the political results of cultural evolution is far beyond the scope of this chapter or this book. We can imagine that the process, wherever it is taking us, will have ultimate effects on the global community and upon the United States.

Indeed, there has long been a controversy in the United States among those aware of the possible effects of cultural change among states. One school of thought has supported American cultural activities that would express a "faith in the universal scope of rationality and an unimpeded flow of ideas accompanied by the conviction that the spread of rationality, knowledge, and understanding provide the basis for an ecumenical world community."[4] This impulse toward development of a universality of ideas has been characterized as "not cultural at all, but *supra*cultural."[5] A more narrow and nationalistic perspective comes from those who argue that American cultural relations should be designed and pursued with the purpose of promoting American national interests and support of American foreign policy.

World War II and the cold war that followed it lent considerable weight to the more nationalistic purpose of using cultural activities to promote American interests and policy. As the United States became a global power operating in scores of foreign countries and cultures, it was essential to recognize the need to understand and be sensitive to the cultures in which Americans functioned in order to make American policies more effective. Robert Blum argues:

> An understanding of the cultural and social environment in which we have to carry out national policies is indispensable to the effectiveness of those policies. Moreover, that environment is one of the elements we have to influence in order to make policies effective.[6]

Since the end of World War II, American cultural contacts with the rest of the world have been extensive. One author has noted:

> Students are only one element, though a very important one, in an expanded cultural trade. The book and magazine, the film and musical recording, radio, television, and now Telstar, the visiting professor and specialist, the tourist and merchant, the soldier, the seaman, the performing artist and visiting athlete, the

adaptation of American institutions, science, and technology to foreign needs, all these are purveyors of cultural influences . . .

For better or worse, it is permeating and influencing virtually every other society in the world. . . . It is clear that they do constitute a powerful force which is reshaping old cultures and the daily lives of peoples, and molding their attitudes toward the United States and its policies.[7]

To some, the spread of American culture may constitute what Morgenthau has called cultural imperialism, which he says "aims not at the conquest of territory or at the control of economic life, but at the conquest and control of the minds of men as an instrument for changing the power relations between the nations."[8]

Consideration of the cultural impact of the United States on other countries, whatever its intent, must take into account the important distinction between the general culture and the political culture, the relationships between them, and the kinds of changes that may be produced in both.

WHAT IS A CULTURE?

Throughout history peoples have adapted to their physical environment and to their relations with other people in specific ways: social organization (family, kinship group, tribe, nation), economic activity, religion, political institutions, law, the arts, dress, language, philosophy, folkways, myths. The total pattern of such common and interconnected activities among a group constitutes a culture. Cultures may differ from each other for a number of reasons: geography, history, and religion, among others.[9] Thus in the present global system several distinct cultures coexist: the West, Asia, and Africa, each containing many subcultures.

Despite their distinctiveness, cultures change, some more slowly than others, even where there is little contact with the external world. In history, few cultures have been completely isolated, and cultural traits have long been exchanged.[10] Although the exchange of traits is not the same as the transformation of one culture by another, the exchange of traits has been a primary instrument of cultural change.

When one attempts to assess the effects of cultural change, especially in those cases where one country consciously tries to impress its views of desired change on others, the picture is not very clear. First of all, throughout history many cultures have been remarkably impervious to change.[11] Countries such as China have absorbed and adapted many cultural innovations imposed by outsiders, but the Chinese have changed the outsiders as much as or more than the outsiders have changed them. Inevitably, however, direct and indirect contacts among cultures, multiplied enormously by the technological capabilities of the twentieth century, have produced changes of varying depth and intensity. In many new states of Africa, for example, societies reflect seemingly contradictory combinations of traditional tribal forms, Western-style political structures, and Soviet-inspired economies. The cultural strains resulting from the coexistence of several levels of culture may lead to painful personal and societal pressures and severe doubts about individual and national identity.[12]

Although there is no known case of the extinction of any specific culture in the world in the last four decades, profound changes have been observed in those countries where the Western model of nationalism has forged national communities from smaller groupings and where the model of industrialism has led to the creation of new economic forms. In a country such as Japan, for example, cultural adaptation to Western models has been extensive in the political and economic spheres, while more deeply rooted psychological, religious, and social beliefs have remained relatively constant. In Africa modern national state systems have superseded fragmented tribal societies, the long-term effects of which cannot be known.

THE POLITICAL CULTURE

Although many observers believe that the increased cultural relationships developed in the twentieth century will eventually lead to profound changes in the general culture—social organization, folkways, and the like—the more direct target of American cultural programming is the political culture. Defined as "the set of attitudes, beliefs, and feelings about politics current in a nation at a given time," the political culture "affects the conduct of individuals in their political roles, the content of their political demands, and their responses to laws." Further, the political culture will be shaped by the existing political structures.[13]

The proportion of a population mobilized into the political culture may differ widely among nation-states, but in each country an active political structure and political elite are vital elements in determining the country's policies. It is most often to these parts of the culture that American efforts are directed.

In its most narrow sense the cultural track of American foreign policy has come to reflect the effort to foster in other countries the formation of values, attitudes, images, perceptions, policies, and structures capable of supporting and promoting the foreign-policy goals of the United States. In the past fifty years an expanding number of tools and techniques have been developed to communicate with other peoples.

Cultural policy has evolved on the basis of a number of major assumptions:

1. All cultures are subject to change as a result of intense contacts with external forces.
2. Through the use of certain tools, one nation can induce changes in other cultures.
3. Cultural change can lead to desired political change.
4. Favorable world opinion is necessary to achieve American goals.
5. It is the right and responsibility of the United States to exercise cultural influence in the service of American foreign policy.

Each of these assumptions is open to considerable dispute. While all cultures may be subject to change as a result of contacts with the external world, many cultures have been resistant to fundamental changes in cultural values. Exposure to American "pop" culture or the adaptation to American production techniques may produce little more than superficial changes in foreign cultures. Although many of the tools of cultural policy may induce certain changes in foreign cultures, the effects are either impossible to determine or are unpredictable. Even granting that one state can induce cultural change in another culture, it is by no means certain that this will lead to changes in political behavior, let alone to changes favorable to the state exercising the influence.

The power of world opinion to shape the policies of either super-power is open to doubt. Although approval by the international com-munity may be desirable and condemnation by the community unwelcome, the superpowers have occasionally ignored world opinion or have survived its disapproval with minimum costs. In recent years Soviet interventions in Afghanistan and Czechoslovakia and American involvements in Vietnam and Grenada have been roundly criticized by "world opinion" in votes in the United Nations and other organizations, in public attacks by allies or unaligned countries, and by bitter criticisms from adversaries.

World opinion neither deterred these actions nor diverted the super-powers from acting according to their perceptions of their national inter-ests. Since approval is preferable to disapproval, however, cultural tools are employed to create the most favorable reactions possible throughout the world.

Finally, the political right and responsibility of any state to attempt to change other cultures is debatable, yet such attempts have been a common practice of states for much of history.

Despite these reservations, two basic facts of contemporary life make cultural influence inevitable. First, in a world of modern communications and interdependence, massive cross-cultural contacts are inevitable with or without the conscious policies of governments. Second, in a system of com-petitive states, the use of cultural tools to promote national interests throughout the world is unavoidable. The effort by the United States to consciously use the cultural tools available to it to promote American inter-ests is an outgrowth of the broader political competition with the Soviet Union and with communism.

The effort has come to involve programs targeting not just the politi-cal leaders and other governing elites of foreign countries but also the masses and their value systems. The development of American capabilities in the cultural field reveals some of the issues involved in the creation of effective cultural policy.

THE AMERICAN EFFORT

The earliest American efforts at cultural influence involved various Chris-tian sects sending missionaries abroad.[14] In the twentieth century this effort was joined by private philanthropies, foundations, and civic organi-zations. The Carnegie Endowment, the Rockefeller Foundation, and the American Council of Learned Societies (ACLS) became part of a "private institutional system for the conduct of cultural relations" by the 1920s and reflected an antigovernment bias in cultural relations.[15] By 1935 the Roosevelt administration recognized the foreign-policy importance of cultural relations. Assistant Secretary of State Sumner Welles became the first government officer to define that importance publicly. In response to fears of the success of Nazi propaganda in Latin America in the late 1930s, the State Department announced in May 1938 plans to create a new Division of Cultural Relations. It went into operation in July under Ben Cherrington, a former university administrator. His view was that the new agency would be "definitely educational in character and would not be a diplomatic arm or a propaganda agency." In 1940 another new agency was developed—the Office of Coordinator of Inter-American Affairs, headed by Nelson A. Rockefeller. It was directed by President Roosevelt to include cultural affairs in its responsibilities. Rockefeller urged that the orientation of cultural affairs be attuned to the nation's immediate security needs. This was an important departure from previous attempts to keep American cultural efforts above promotion of specific foreign policies. In any case, Rockefeller intended to work through existing philanthropies and foundations, promoting Pan-Americanism through workshops, school programs, institutes, seminars, civic programs, subsidies to museums, and mobilization of the academic community. By 1942, the State Department's Division of Near Eastern Affairs had also increased its activity, and cultural efforts in China had been intensified.

In the early 1940s Professor Ralph Turner of Yale was hired to head a new research program in the Division of Cultural Relations and quickly took the position that cultural relations "should support concretely the foreign policy of the United States," a view that differed sharply from the more internationalist concepts that had existed among many in the field of cultural relations. He argued that cultural programs could be successful "only if they were based on a detailed knowledge of foreign cultures and if closely coordinated with diplomatic, political, and economic action." Of course, the context was World War II, and the need to promote specific national interests was obvious, but Turner's views drew sharp fire from within the State Department. These old arguments of 1943 about the purpose of cultural policy are stated because of their persistence at present. With the creation of the United Nations and of the United Nations Educational, Scientific, and Cultural Organization (UNESCO) many of those engaged in cultural relations concluded that the new U.N. agencies were ideal for promoting the internationalist cultural perspective, and participation by private citizens was provided. When American officials came to the conclusion that UNESCO was highly ideological and political, proposals were made to integrate American UNESCO policy into the operations of the State Department. As the Cold War developed, a conviction that a more directed cultural policy was needed and that government should take charge prevailed.

Another element involved in the development of American cultural policy was the wartime operation of the Office of War Information (OWI), which adopted many programs of a cultural nature. Cooperation between OWI and the State Department made a system of cultural programming possible on a global basis. In August 1945 OWI and a number of other units were placed into a new Interim Information Service, the precursor of the United States Information Agency. Arguments over the nature and organization of America's cultural activities led to the passage of the Smith-Mundt Bill in January 1948, which provided for the establishment of separate policy tracks dividing informational and educational functions. Given Soviet pressures in this period, the operational focus of cultural affairs within the State Department came to be regarded as part of American national defense. Nonetheless, the educational efforts of the United States produced a rapid expansion in the number of foreign students studying in the United States. In August 1946 the Fulbright Act established the mechanisms for the mutual exchange of students, scholars, and teachers, and its operation for almost forty years has been regarded as one of the most successful efforts in American cultural policy.

By the 1950s government agencies dominated the cultural programming of the United States, and cultural policy was aligned with national political and foreign-policy purposes.

The gradual commitment of the United States to the conscious use of cultural relations in the service of foreign policy has produced several major theoretical debates over their purposes and methods. The argument over the emphasis on national or international purposes has been cited. The second issue focused on whether cultural efforts should be concentrated only on elites or whether they should be directed at the masses. A third debate revolved around the question of whether education or propaganda should be predominant in American efforts, and finally, a fourth issue concerned the clash between private interests and government for primary control of cultural relations.

On the first issue, it has been noted that since the mid-1940s, the nationalist approach has come to predominate, that is, cultural policy was designed to serve the immediate foreign-policy interests of the United States. Communications technology has made the second issue moot, since direct communication with the masses is now inescapable. The separation of education and propaganda has gradually been eroded as techniques have evolved in both fields. Finally, since World War II, government has become the predominant agency for cultural relations, although private activity remains widespread.

American cultural activities abroad, whether governmental or private, often accompany political, economic, and military actions. Indeed, it is often hard to separate the tracks. One assessment of the success of American efforts was offered by Kenneth Thompson in 1968:

> We have assisted friendly nations in building more stable economies, meeting severe problems of food deficits, training indigenous leadership, staffing public services and scientific establishments, building stronger educational institutions, stabilizing population growth, and facing a broad range of social and economic problems .... Twenty years of foreign assistance which have brought notable success, of course produced few miracles.[16]

Consideration of the cultural track of foreign policy must also take into account the general culture and the domestic political culture of the United States, for these inform and shape the definition of the national interest and the kinds of cultural policies Americans are willing to support. From the beginning the United States has been a culture dedicated to diversity and pluralism in virtually every aspect of social life: religion, ethnicity, and class. Max Lerner has written:

> These—the expanse of space, the mixture of race, the pluralism of region and religion, the fresh start, the release of energies, the access to opportunity, the optimism and pragmatism of a society in motion, the passion for equality—were the crucial shaping forces of the American heritage.[17]

Thus dynamism, according to Lerner, is central to the American tradition.

With these cultural traits an American political culture developed, based on what might be called Lockean liberalism.

From national documents, statements of leaders, and respected political writing, the following political principles can be identified: government based on the consent of the governed, limited government, individual liberty, due process of law, self-determination, capitalism and free enterprise, inalienable rights, equality before the law, majority rule, minority rights, federalism, separation of powers, and legalism.[18] In relation to foreign policy, these domestic principles support the doctrines of free trade, the rule of law, and support of self-determination and equality of other states. Because of these principles and America's geographic isolation, isolationism was long an element in the American political culture, and little in it supported an active leadership role in the world community until the events of the twentieth century persuaded Americans of the need to play an activist role in the world community.[19] Policies were then developed reflecting the American political culture: anticommunism, anti-Soviet containment, promotion of capitalism. Indeed, some would argue that the American role in the world after 1945 was the result of efforts to protect and to expand American capitalism.[20]

In any case, the American culture and the American political culture are reflected in the ways in which the United States has developed the cultural track of foreign policy and in the tools that have been used in the process.

TOOLS OF POLICY

In the foregoing outline of the cultural track it was suggested that the policy has been to promote support throughout the world for American interests and also to advocate general cultural ideas.

In the process the United States has developed a wide range of tools for exercising cultural influence. In the previous sections I have identified some of the organizational evolution within the government and the development of agencies responsible for devising and implementing cultural policies.

It would be a mistake, however, to think of the range of tools in too narrow a focus, for as has been suggested, cultural change arises from changes in many spheres: economic, political, military, religious, ideological. In chapter 2 we noted the massive sweep of ideas and ideologies in the twentieth century and the rapid changes in technology (communication and transportation) which have made the spread of ideas inevitable, despite the efforts of superpowers to shape the world in desired ways. Nationalism and industrialism are outgrowths of the history of the West, but their appeal is not dependent solely upon the efforts of the United States and the Soviet Union. Further, the ambition of all states to modernize their economies is a major cause of cultural change in the opinion of non-Marxists and Marxists alike. Changing modes of production, agriculture, and trade lead to extensive social changes. Identifying some of the major forces for change operating in the world, as we did in chapter 2, we find that the efforts of the United States are just one force involved in the process.

To exercise this force the United States has attempted to exploit its ideals and achievements, promote emulation of the American system by emphasizing the prestige that arises from power and wealth, and persuade others to learn from the model effects of American institutions and practices. The maintenance of governmental and nongovernmental structures abroad is a direct form of contact and communication with other states. Diplomatic missions, military bases, the Peace Corps and AID units, multinational corporations, and expatriates are among the more or less permanent manifestations of the United States abroad. The contacts of people and elites through programs in education, arts, humanities, science, and tourism add another dimension to the American capability to communicate with other cultures.

Government propaganda efforts under the United States Information Agency provide the capability for communicating the perspectives of American foreign policy.

Finally, among the most powerful tools for cultural influence are the mass media of communication: journalism, radio, television, films, and popular music.

The process by which government attempts to coordinate all of these capabilities and to fashion a policy is sometimes called psychological warfare.

Psychological "Warfare"

In chapter 14 we discussed the concepts of "psychological warfare" as part of the effort by policy makers to shape the political attitudes of other governments and peoples.[21] As a part of the cultural track, the intended effects include the molding, changing, or creation of thoughts and feelings in other states and in other cultures in order to produce admiration, respect, fear, compliance, and even the desire for emulation.

Psychological strategy can encompass broad general goals directed toward the entire globe or specific initiatives aimed at particular countries.

In general, the rhetoric of American leaders has been aimed at defining the supposedly universal ideals that appeal to all peoples and demonstrating that the United States has been a model society for the attainment of these ideals and one worth emulating. Among the ideals espoused repeatedly by American leaders are such qualities as democracy, freedom, equality, rule of law, human rights, economic opportunity, individual dignity, self-determination of all peoples, free enterprise, and compassion. In addition, many American policies and actions have been carried out over the years to demonstrate the commitment of the American people to the achievement of these ideals and to the wish to see them extended to all people. From the standpoint of world politics, the United States has attempted since 1945 to project an image as a country of ideals: strength, opposition to tyranny, resistance to Communist and Soviet expansion, reasonableness in seeking peace and negotiating differences, and generosity in sharing abundance with others.

Two recent examples will illustrate the point. In the Carter administration the United States placed heavy emphasis on the theme of human rights and attempted to apply it to specific foreign-policy situations.[22] The administration withheld aid, for example, to some friends and allies because their record on human rights was less than admirable from the American point of view. Advocating human rights was seen as an effective method to communicate American ideals to the masses of people throughout the world subjected to limitations on freedom.

With the start of the Reagan administration, less emphasis was placed on human rights, and a major thrust of American policy became the effort to deter the Soviet leaders from achieving military superiority.[23] President Reagan took a highly critical line against the Soviets, charging that they were the source of all evil in the global system and threatening to expand American arms to regain military superiority over the Soviet Union. One of the reasons for this approach was to threaten the Soviet Union with a costly arms race in order to gain greater Soviet flexibility in arms-control negotiations. In addition, for several months both sides made intense efforts to persuade the public in Western Europe that they were flexible on arms control and a nuclear freeze. One of the direct objectives of this maneuvering in 1983 was to influence the upcoming West German elections. The election of the American-backed candidate for chancellor, Helmut Kohl, suggests that the United States prevailed on this specific issue.

Thus there is power in psychological warfare, and it remains an effective tool of leaders and policy makers who know how to use it.

Propaganda

According to Cecil Crabb, propaganda is "the effort of one group or nation to influence the actions of another group or nation by primary reliance upon methods of systematic persuasion, including methods of verbal coercion and inducement."[24] It is distinguished from other methods of psychological warfare by its use of the written and spoken word. I would add that it also includes the use of the visual image, in the print media as well as in television and films.

Governmental propaganda activities can be traced back to the World War I period.[25] In World War II the Office of Strategic Services and the Office of War Information were built upon foundations developed during the 1930s. In 1953 the Eisenhower administration created the United States Information Agency under the overall direction of the State Department.[26] Through the Voice of America, a global radio network broadcasting in thirty-nine languages, and also through motion pictures, television programs, various print materials, maintenance of libraries abroad, sponsorship of exchange programs, and numerous other services, USIA promotes American foreign-policy interests abroad.[27]

In addition to the communications facilities in USIA, the Armed Forces Press, Radio, and TV service under the jurisdiction of the Defense Department also disseminates a considerable amount of information about the United States, its society, and its government. Although it is not a propaganda agency, its output in foreign countries is widely disseminated and is believed to have some influence on foreigners' ideas about the United States.

It would be a mistake, however, to think of propaganda as exclusively a governmental operation. It must be made clear here that the government may seek to create and disperse propaganda through many nongovernmental outlets as well as through its own instruments. Indeed, the information disseminated through the nongovernmental media may be somewhat more credible, less overtly propagandistic, and therefore more effective in creating images of the United States (both favorable and unfavorable). Of considerable interest is the fact that the Soviet Union has begun to effectively utilize access to the American media through the availability of Soviet spokespersons, highly articulate in English, expressing the viewpoint of the Soviet Union. However, the Soviet Union does not permit similar access to Soviet citizens by Americans.

In brief, there is no lack of means by which the United States can explain its ideals, goals, and policies to much of the rest of the world. Whether it is always done effectively to promote support of American policies may be questioned, but the communication process is a powerful tool available to policy makers who recognize its value and can utilize it effectively.

Cultural Exchange

One of the most recognized forms of international influence making is cultural exchange, which involves a wide variety of individuals and groups. Scholars, scientists, athletes, artists, and other specialized groups play a subtle but effective role in promoting the interests of their countries by traveling, working, and touring in other countries.

Perhaps the most dramatic example of this in recent years was the opening of relations with the People's Republic of China through "ping-pong diplomacy," the exchange of ping-pong teams from the two countries in 1971.

A major showcase of national prestige through athletic competition, the Olympic Games have been the instrument of controversy between the superpowers in 1980 and 1984. The Carter administration cancelled American participation in the 1980 summer Olympics scheduled in Moscow. The action was in retaliation for the Soviet invasion of Afghanistan. In 1984 the Soviet Union cancelled its participation in the summer Olympics in Los Angeles. Although the games continued in both cases, the competition had lost some of its lustre. Of course, international sports events continue throughout the world every year. World championship events, tours of national teams, and competition among national teams provide increasing opportunities for contacts among people.

International conferences of scholars, artists, scientists, legislators, and many others provide opportunities for influential groups from the United States to meet with counterparts from other places. The exchange of scholars through fellowship programs, foundation grants, and the Fulbright scholarship programs is another type of opportunity to expand international understanding.

The aim of the United States in such efforts is to demonstrate the capabilities of the United States in many fields, underscore American accomplishments, and emphasize the opportunities for business development in the United States. It is more than just another form of propaganda, however. It is also designed to create groups in other countries whose personal and professional interests may impel them to influence their governments in ways that would promote common interests.

Tourism

A special form of cultural exchange is tourism—the interchange of private citizens traveling in each other's countries.[28] Two-way travel between the United States and the rest of the world approached the fifty-million mark during 1984, at least twenty-two million of them foreign travelers to the United States. Although American tourists do not always create a favorable impression of the United States when they travel abroad, and many Americans do not have the opportunity to meet foreign tourists when they visit the United States, tourism provides the opportunity for favorable cultural exchange.

Beyond the general improved understanding that tourism can produce, a more tangible benefit of tourism is the foreign exchange often badly needed by the host country. In many countries of the world, tourism is either the largest industry or very nearly the largest. Thus it is also a form of business that is of great importance to recipient countries, and friendly foreign relations between governments makes a tourist trade possible.

In this regard foreign-policy makers can either encourage or discourage tourism, according to current needs.

The Mass Media

We know that advertising in the mass media sells soap, deodorants, perfume, beer, and a wide range of other products and services. Yet it is not clear precisely how the media and their messages affect deeper cultural values, attitudes, and opinions. If it is only to disperse information about policies and personalities more broadly, the mass media have added a new dimension to foreign policy in the twentieth century. In several chapters we have suggested the outlines of the role of the mass media in communicating with the American public. Here we are concerned with the ways in which they relate to the publics and the leaders in other countries.

One scholar notes:

> Governments today talk not so much to each other as at each other through the media . . . . The use of the media to preempt governments may often

delay normal diplomatic relations or create foreign policy crisis largely unanticipated by governments, misleading both domestic publics and foreign publics and governments. . . . The use of public diplomacy may be directed at a particular audience to promote support for or antagonism against a particular policy or action of a foreign government. . . . Both the target and nontargeted populations become subject to the same battery of fire. . .

. . . Media diplomacy is conditioning the formulation and execution of policy and the public's understanding of international affairs.[29]

One notable example of this phenomenon was the role played by the media, especially television newsman Walter Cronkite, in arranging the trip by the late Egyptian president Anwar Sadat to Israel in 1977. In interviews with Sadat and with Israeli Prime Minister Menachem Begin, Cronkite elicited the information that Sadat wanted to go to Jerusalem and the commitment by Begin that he would invite Sadat.[30]

As we know, however, the mass media encompass more than television. The media include all the channels of communication that carry messages to the general public: newspapers, radio, television, film, records, magazines and periodicals, and books.[31]

In addition, the major wire services of the world constitute a prime source of information for all journalistic enterprises reporting on world affairs.

In considering the mass media in this context, we focus primarily upon the American media and the ways in which they relate to other countries, although the ways in which foreign media disseminate the content of American media are also of considerable importance.

1. **Print Media** Although the United States government has no control over the material printed in foreign newspapers (foreign governments often control their own press), many foreign newspapers report in considerable detail on the activities and the policies of the American government, on leading personalities, and on relevant internal events. This provides the American government a forum from which to communicate with the rest of the world, notwithstanding editorial decisions and/or censorship in other countries. Major policy statements and foreign-policy actions are likely to be fully reported in many countries, and foreign news media assign an increasing number of reporters to cover events in Washington. In fact, no country accredits more foreign journalists than the United States does.

American news magazines and periodicals may not reach as broad a foreign audience as other media do, but they are widely circulated abroad. Like American newspapers, they reflect a range of political views about American society and government policies.

The major wire services—Associated Press, United Press International, and Reuters—are sources of basic news and information for news media all over the world. Since many of the stories they transmit originate with American newspapers, the wire services are a means to distribute the material supplied by the American and Western press.

In addition, some forty thousand books are published in the United States each year, and many circulate and are sold abroad.[32] Many are scholarly works that discuss foreign affairs, security policy, and political developments.

2. **The Electronic Media** The impact of *television* abroad is considerably different

from that of the print media because TV offers entertainment as well as information. Consequently, the impact, if any, results from the images of American life conveyed by television programming at least as much from the news and information reported about the United States. Political messages arising from the television programs sold abroad are likely to involve subtle messages about the roles of women and minorities, economic status, and personal life styles. The image of American middle-class life depicted in American programming—well-groomed homes with many rooms, gadgets, and two-car garages—conveys at least one impression of the United States as a country of economic abundance.

The 1983 agreement between CBS and the People's Republic of China for the provision of sixty-four hours of programming and advertising in China marked the first regular scheduling of commercial network shows in China.[33] Programs are dubbed in Mandarin Chinese. Since between 200 million and 400 million Chinese have access to television sets, the American programming, although it will not include "Dallas," will provide an invaluable cultural contact.

The global transmission of television is facilitated not only through direct sales of taped programs but through the instantaneous programming made possible by communications satellites.

Another technological innovation that has made the spread of television possible is the video recorder for personal use. The effects may not always be welcomed abroad. In the spring of 1983 a Soviet newspaper warned readers not to watch black-market cassettes of forbidden Western pornographic and horror movies. Video-cassette players, originally confined to elites, are filtering into the country, enabling many Russians to have private access to movies.[34]

Radio has yet a different impact from television and film. Most of the people of the world have access to radios, and many countries, including the United States, maintain ambitious overseas broadcasting facilities. In many countries radio facilities are owned and operated by governments, unlike in the United States, where the bulk of the broadcasting facilities are owned and operated by private companies whose productions are independent of government control. The U.S. government operates the Voice of America and supports such other radio outlets as Radio Free Europe and Radio Liberty.[35] It also operates the Armed Forces Press, Radio and TV Service, which includes several hundred radio outlets serving American military personnel abroad. Among the staples of radio broadcasting are news and music, and when they are not jammed, American radio broadcasts are one of the most direct sources of information for millions of people abroad. In addition, the programming of music—classical, jazz, rock and roll—has introduced modern developments in music throughout the world. While there is little agreement on the precise effects of this programming on attitudes about the United States, some analysts think that the broadcasts have brought about some common cultural tastes even in very different cultures.

As suggested, a large portion of American broadcasting consists of the playing of records and tapes,[36] but recordings in and of themselves are a separate medium of communications. In addition to being played on radio stations, records of internationally known American performers sell well in many countries. The extent to which this affects the tastes, attitudes, and opinions of foreign listeners may be impossible to evaluate, but clearly American recording artists—classical, jazz, and popular—are regarded as among the best in the world and establish the standards of professional excellence and contemporary taste to a considerable degree.

3.   *Films*   Films provide another type of cultural message.[37] Like television programming, many of the movies shown abroad are produced by private companies independent of the control or influence of government and are usually not related to specific issues or policies, with rare exceptions. Yet American motion pictures

have been shown throughout the world during most of the twentieth century and surely have contributed to the impressions of the United States and its people held by millions of people elsewhere. Relatively little is known about the political reactions that movies have produced in other cultures toward the government and toward the American culture depicted, although a broad sampling of all American movies in the last seven decades would reasonably have presented a fairly comprehensive view of the best and worst in American society. In any case, the impressions created by movies, whatever they may be, are instruments that may make the implementation of American policy easier or harder, depending on the attitudes that a people may have acquired about the United States.

In addition to the commercial product, films produced by or in behalf of the government are also circulated abroad. This indeed is part of the job of the USIA. Designed with a specific propaganda purpose, these films reach millions of people and point out some of the virtues of American life.

Multinational Corporations

The role of American multinational corporations operating throughout the world has been a controversial one from a number of perspectives. Political, economic, and social effects have been mentioned in other parts of this book, but in this section some exploration of their cultural effects is in order.

First, by transmitting to other countries examples of modern American management, technology, and production techniques, American multinationals have contributed to extensive changes in the methods, ethics, values, and objectives of the business process. The effect has been the creation of more productive and profitable national models and the influx of new investment in many countries where it is essential for development.

Second, the multinationals have contributed to some cultural change. In a study of Mexican executives working for American multinational corporations, it was found that association with American firms is a notable factor in the change of values from narrow nationalism to an identification with internationalism.[38] At the very least, the association aroused the desire of some executives to work in the United States.

Such a finding should not be surprising when it is realized that recent Japanese industrial success has prompted many Americans to study Japanese production methods and the cultural relationships that underlie them.

In any case, American firms abroad, no matter how independent of control by the American government, represent American society in the eyes of foreign nationals, and their behavior can have meaningful cultural effects.

Business

Beyond the sharing of knowledge, American business has had a cultural impact in many countries through the products it sells, its methods of marketing and merchandising, and the advertising techniques used in developing a demand.[39]

Coca-Cola, blue jeans, and McDonald's hamburgers are examples of the internationalization of products, which reflects the changing of tastes in other cultures. To be sure, this is a two-way street, as Americans have become familiar with Japanese cars, French wine, Russian vodka, and Polish ham. Aside from the economic linkages such exchange represents, the cultural change that it can produce may be an important factor in relations between and among governments. Whether any culture is necessarily better off for the exchange may be debated, but that such exchange takes place is undeniable.

The Military

The American armed forces maintain some 350 installations in twenty-one countries.[40] However, the cry of "Yankee Go Home" is increasingly heard in some of them. According to State Department figures, there were 385 terrorist attacks against American targets in 1982, many of them military locations in countries of the NATO alliance.[41]

Despite some attacks by radical groups in West Germany, *Newsweek* reporters concluded that "there are places in the world where the GI is still a welcome sight."[42]

THE CULTURAL TRACK:
SUCCESS OR FAILURE?

There is no easy way to determine whether American efforts in the cultural track since 1945 have been successful. Much depends on the criteria we use to measure the impact of American efforts. If support of specific American foreign policies is used as a measurement of success, then the record is mixed. If the objective of establishing a global culture is used, again the record is mixed. The American culture has not supplanted, nor was it necessarily the intention of American policy makers to supplant, the unique folkways, traditions, and religions of various cultures. Yet it is apparent that American political, social, and economic models have contributed to massive change in some societies.

In Germany and Japan, for example, the establishment of democratic political forms and the emulation of American economic methods accompanied a change of national attitudes from authoritarianism to democratic-egalitarian commitment. In the less developed countries many of the political models introduced by the European colonizers have been retained, but economic structures have as often been modeled along socialist lines as along capitalist ones. On the other hand, the American model, so productive in creating abundance, has underscored the emphasis on industrialism, science and technology, and advanced education even in the poorest countries. The Western political model has produced more than structures to be copied. It has led to the vigorous practice of politics, as any observer of United Nations operations will note. Countries in all parts of the globe, with diverse national histories, have learned to play the game of politics—forming and utilizing blocs and consensus; bringing pressure; wheeling and dealing; debating and compromising.

Two sets of studies, conducted almost a generation apart, reveal some important findings about the effects of parts of the American cultural impact.

A number of follow-up studies performed in the 1950s on the effects of American-West German exchange programs are revealing. Without question, the exchange experience must be assessed in the context of overall American policy toward West Germany in the late 1940s. With the onset of the Cold War, the American policy to reindustrialize West Germany, restore its political independence, and make it a partner in Western opposition to Soviet expansion created close political and psychological bonds between the two countries. Thus measurement of the cultural effects of the relationship and of the American exchange programs is a complex matter. In a recent study of the experience and review of the government studies of the pre-1960 period Henry Kellerman found that "substantial numbers of the Germans changed their views of the United States and some of them took specific actions that confirmed this change upon their return to Germany."[43] However, the exchange programs were not uniformly successful in changing attitudes. A survey in 1955 indicated that some 25 percent of students studying in the United States, and a smaller percentage of specialists, had revised their opinion of the United States downward after short visits to the United States. In general, however, the attitudes of German visitors showed a marked change from authoritarian ones to more democratic ones. Attitudes toward American cultural life were favorable, and as the Cold War intensified, German support of American foreign policy became more pronounced. Kellerman found that Germans returning home actively communicated their favorable impressions within German society, and many benefited from the exchange experience in building professional careers.

A more recent study investigated a broader perspective. In July 1983 *Newsweek* magazine published results of a poll it had commissioned by the Gallup organization in six countries: France, West Germany, Great Britain, Japan, Brazil, and Mexico. Basically, it found deep support for the American people, American products, and American popular culture but less support for American foreign policy.[44] Nonetheless, in all six countries those polled believed that American influence in the world is growing. In addition, the United States remains far more popular among these groups than does the Soviet Union.

Especially noteworthy in the study was the impact of American television on foreign cultures. The authors of the *Newsweek* story note:

> Africans tune in "The Jeffersons" to view white American producers' fantasies of black American life; European connoisseurs of duplicity can choose between "Dallas" and "Dynasty"; the earnest Chinese can learn much from what one comrade from Szechuan Province referred to as that "great scientific and educational program from America: The Man From Atlantis."

Indeed, in all six countries people polled believed that American influence on local television exceeded the influence on science and business. At the same time, the American influence on the fine arts was regarded as slight.

The *Newsweek* reporters note: "Imitation, however, does not necessarily translate into political influence." In five of the six countries polled in the *Newsweek* survey most of the respondents believed that a strong American military presence throughout the world increased the chance of war. Only in Germany was the reverse true.

Further, what most Americans would regard as strengths of the American system, may be perceived quite differently abroad. For example, the openness of debate within the United States is sometimes interpreted not as a virtue but as a sign of weakness. The *Newsweek* authors cite a study by the USIA that found that "the Chinese are inclined to underestimate American resolve and strength because of the multiplicity of voices and currents in American life, which, in their eyes, signifies weakness and lack of unity." It was also found in the USIA survey that Europeans think the United States should do more to insure ethnic and minority rights, while in Israel, American race relations are regarded as a model.

The *Newsweek* authors argue, America has spawned two clear cultural patterns in the twentieth century: the blue-jeans culture, representing casualness, independence, adventure, and self-reliance; and the white-collar culture, representing modern management, technological proficiency, and industrial organization. Both are emulated abroad.

Finally, as David Potter has written, the United States' real revolutionary message to the world was not freedom but economic abundance, which ever since has kept Americans under a "curse of chronic envy."

The *Newsweek* and USIA studies suggest that the American cultural impact abroad has been mixed; some outstanding successes in promoting American goals, some failures, some misperceptions, and some mistakes.

CONCLUSION

Just as American presidents must "sell" their policies to Congress and the public, as we noted in chapter 3, they must also "sell" American policies abroad. The effort to accomplish this falls into the framework of cultural relations. However, it would be a mistake to suppose that "selling" American policies is only a matter of spreading propaganda, unless the term *propaganda* is defined so broadly as to destroy its more precise meaning.

The vast and complex process of cultural change in the world of the twentieth century is a fascinating and important feature of global life, and the fragmentary elements of a truly global community have emerged by the 1980s. Some American leaders have eagerly sought to spread the virtues and values of the American culture in the belief that it is an ideal model for the global system. Wilson argued for democracy, Jimmy Carter for human rights, and Ronald Reagan for capitalism. Most of the time, though, the efforts of American leaders in the cultural field have been more modest—achievement of understanding and support of particular American foreign policies abroad.

On the assumption that cultural policies directed at key elites and the masses can produce enough cultural change to provide political support of

American policies, the government has utilized a variety of tools since 1945 to persuade people that American actions are right.

As some of the evidence cited in this chapter indicates, these efforts have not been universally successful. While people in many countries admire the American people, they and their governments frequently doubt the wisdom of American policy. In public-opinion polls, in votes in the United Nations, in criticism of the United States and its policies in various forums, the evidence is clear that American policy is not always well understood or supported.

A high point in negative reaction came during the Vietnam War period during which allies as well as adversaries and nonaligned countries opposed American policy. In many places the United States is regarded as a neoimperialist power intent on expanding American influence and control by military means or by multinational corporations. At the same time the maintenance of a classical empire in Europe by the Soviet Union often appears to be accepted without question, and Soviet actions seem to provoke much less criticism in many countries.

It would be comforting and easy to attribute this fact to a more effective Soviet capability to wage cultural warfare or to argue, quite validly, that the United States government is less skilled at utilizing the cultural track in support of its foreign policy. However, the basic explanation lies much deeper. As a dominant power exercising global leadership, the United States is sometimes resented by allies and others, and its policies are often viewed as self-serving. As leader of the Western world, the United States is often regarded as the successor to the European colonial empires, which subjected other peoples to conquest, humiliation, and control. Further, as a predominantly white Christian people, Americans may provoke some natural suspicion in a world of many other races, colors, and religions. Some considerable envy of American and Western affluence is coupled with the impression that exploitation of non-Western peoples is the source of American wealth. American corporations and American tourists sometimes aggravate these impressions with a display of insensitive attitudes of cultural superiority. Thus the cultural obstacles to creating support for American foreign policies are formidable.

Nonetheless, the evidence suggests that throughout the world people have found much about the United States to admire or to envy. The achievements of material wealth in the United States, communicated throughout the world, have contributed to rising expectations for a better life everywhere. Ironically, such expectations have led to revolutions in many countries, and these revolutions have posed serious political challenges to the American view of world order and stability. In the process, the United States has developed policy that often seems opposed to revolutionary change and has instead supported authoritarian regimes dedicated to maintenance of the status quo. In this context the signals of American policy seem contradictory. The implication is that American cultural policy designed to produce support for specific policies is dependent upon American policies in other tracks: the political, the economic, and the military. Where other policies are sensitive and creative, cultural policy may have a better chance of producing desired effects.

Beyond the links among the various tracks of policy, the tools of cultural policy encounter other obstacles, which may limit their effectiveness. Contrary to the situation in many countries, the United States government does not control all of the information disseminated about American society. Private film makers, writers, artists, clergy, and others circulate images and information abroad that may or may not lead to a favorable impression of the United States. When information is transmitted, whether from official or from private sources, how it affects recipients is most difficult to determine. Indeed, important information may not reach some leaders or some publics at all. For example, American efforts to communicate with the people of the Soviet Union are limited by official Soviet policy and its own form of governmental control of information. Even when American information reaches Soviet or other foreign audiences, there is no assurance that those audiences will find it more credible than the messages provided by their own governments.

Why then is cultural policy useful? First of all, it conveys what an open society is, warts and all. It communicates its strengths and weaknesses. That all peoples and all governments may not wish to emulate an open society may be true, but they cannot be unaware that it provides the mechanisms for genuine public protest of unpopular policies. Protests in the United States and in Western Europe over the deployment of nuclear missiles in Europe or over a nuclear freeze by the superpowers may represent challenges to the politico-military policies of the United States and NATO, but they demonstrate that in an open society people have a chance to be heard.

But while the American model emphasizes the values of democracy, hungry people may be more interested in any system that provides food and establishes a sense of equality.

An effective cultural policy, systematically organized and operated, has other virtues. The power of ideas has been examined in this book, both in internal American politics and in the global politics of diplomacy. That ideas and values are as powerful an influence in politics as military power or economic tools of policy is accepted by many analysts. Second, the wise utilization of cultural policy sensitizes policy makers to the deep and important differences among peoples and to an appreciation of the value of these differences. The United States, long the leading example of a successful multiculture society, should be well equipped to apply its experience on a global basis to exhibit the respect for other cultures that is their right, even when (perhaps especially when) those cultures differ sharply from the American culture and their governments oppose American policy.

However, the United States has sometimes been less effective than it might have been in operating and conducting a sound cultural policy. Fewer resources are provided to operate USIA than the Soviets spend jamming it. Policy makers have usually demonstrated greater skill at using TV to get elected than in using it and other media to promote American goals and interests abroad. The recent memoirs of leading statesmen provide only scanty evidence of an awareness of the value of cultural policy in the deliberations of major policy decisions. The head of the USIA is rarely a participant in *major* policy considerations in the National Security Council, in informal policy breakfasts, or in cabinet meetings. Review of the cultural possibilities and implications of policy decisions is rarely cited.

Cancellation of American participation in the 1980 Olympics stands out as the only major cultural policy decided upon at the highest levels in recent years. Cultural policy and its effective uses are not primary subjects in the study of foreign policy.

At bottom, American values and practices, however imperfect, have proved to be successful and effective ways to organize society, produce and distribute wealth and opportunity, and provide a chance for individuals to achieve self-fulfillment and dignity. These are powerful ideas. They need to be communicated more effectively and integrated more fully into the foreign-policy process of the United States.

NOTES

[1] Jerry Adler and others, "What the World Thinks of America," *Newsweek*, July 11, 1983, pp. 44–53.

[2] Charles W. Kegley and Eugene R. Wittkopf, *American Foreign Policy: Pattern and Process*, 2nd ed. (New York: St. Martin's Press, 1982), pp. 245-46.

[3] Frank A. Ninkovich, *The Diplomacy of Ideas: U.S. Foreign Policy and Cultural Relations, 1938–1950* (New York: Cambridge University Press, 1981), p. 2.

[4] Ibid., p. 182.

[5] Ibid.

[6] Robert Blum, "Introduction: The Flow of People and Ideas," in Blum, ed., *Cultural Affairs and Foreign Relations* (Englewood Cliffs, N.J.: Prentice-Hall, 1963), p. 3.

[7] Philip H. Coombs, "The Past and Future in Perspective," in Blum, *Cultural Affairs*, pp. 141–42.

[8] Hans Morgenthau, *Politics Among Nations*, 5th ed., rev. (New York: Alfred A. Knopf, 1973), p. 64.

[9] T. Walter Wallbank and Alastair M. Taylor, *Civilization Past and Present* (New York: Scott, Foresman and Co., 1949), pp. 10–11.

[10] Ibid., pp. 11-14.

[11] Adda B. Bozeman, *Politics and Culture in International History* (Princeton, N.J.: Princeton University Press, 1960), pp. 6–7.

[12] Ibid., pp. 8–9.

[13] Gabriel A. Almond and G. Bingham Powell, Jr., *Comparative Politics* (Boston: Little, Brown & Company, 1978), p. 25.

[14] George N. Schuster, "The Nature and Development of United States Cultural Relations," in Paul J. Braisted, ed., *Cultural Affairs and Foreign Relations* (Washington, D.C.: Columbia Books, Publishers, 1968), p. 1.

[15] The material relating to the history of the development of American cultural policy and the governmental role is based on Ninkovich, *Diplomacy of Ideas*, pp. 22–168.

[16] Kenneth W. Thompson, "Beyond the Present," in Braisted, *Cultural Affairs*, p. 201.

[17] Max Lerner, *America as a Civilization* (New York: Simon & Schuster, 1957), p. 48.

[18] Morell Heald and Lawrence S. Kaplan, *Culture and Diplomacy* (Westport, Conn.: Greenwood Press, 1979), pp. 340–49; Kegley and Wittkopf, *American Foreign Policy*, p. 244.

[19] Heald and Kaplan, *Culture and Diplomacy*, pp. 348–49.

[20] Ralph Miliband, *The State in a Capitalist Society* (New York: Basic Books, 1969), pp. 83–87.

[21] See chapter 14, pp. 216–18.

[22] Jimmy Carter, *Keeping Faith* (New York: Bantam Books, 1982), pp. 141–45.

[23] Cecil V. Crabb, Jr., *American Foreign Policy in the Nuclear Age*, 4th ed. (New York: Harper & Row, Publishers, 1983), pp. 125–31.

[24] Ibid., p. 151.

[25] John H. Esterline and Robert B. Black, *Inside Foreign Policy* (Palo Alto, Calif.: Mayfield Publishing Co., 1975), pp. 108–9.

[26] Henry T. Nash, *American Foreign Policy: Changing Perspectives on National Security* (Homewood, Ill.: Dorsey Press, 1978), pp. 117–18.

[27] Crabb, *American Foreign Policy*, p. 154.

[28] Michael Demarest and others, "Americans Everywhere," *Time*, July 25, 1983, pp. 40–49.

[29] Patricia A. Karl, "Media Diplomacy," in Gerald Benjamin, ed., *The Communications Revolution in Politics* (New York: Academy of Political Science, 1982), pp. 149–50, 152.

[30] Kathleen Hall Jamieson and Karlyn Kohrs Campbell, *The Interplay of Influence: Mass Media and Their Publics in News, Advertising, Politics* (Belmont, Calif.: Wadsworth Publishing Co., 1983), pp. 70-73.

[31] Thomas R. Dye and L. Harmon Zeigler, *American Politics in the Media Age* (Monterey, Calif.: Brooks/Cole Publishing Co., 1983), p. 122.

[32] Ibid.

[33] Sandra Salmans, "CBS-China TV Pact Announced," *New York Times*, June 1, 1983, p. D20.

[34] *Sovietskaya Rossiya*, Moscow, USSR, April 3, 1983.

[35] Esterline and Black, *Inside Foreign Policy*, pp. 107–8; Anne Semmes Groo, "Radio Free Europe from Connecticut," *New York Times*, September 11, 1980, Connecticut section, pp. 4–5. The story is about Connecticut residents who occupy major positions with Radio Free Europe. It notes that RFE broadcasts to Eastern Europe, and Radio Liberty is beamed to the Soviet Union. James L. Buckley, the head of the broadcast operations under the Board of International Broadcasting, alleges that the Soviet Union spends $150 million a year jamming Western broadcasts and points out that the entire RFE/RL budget for the fiscal year 1983 was just over $90 million.

[36] Adler and others, "What the World Thinks of America," p. 46.

[37] Ibid.

[38] James Dull, "The Effects of American Multinational Corporations on the Attitudes of Mexican Executives," unpublished Ph.D. dissertation, Department of Political Science, Graduate School of Arts and Sciences, Columbia University, 1981.

[39] Adler and others, "What the World Thinks of America," pp. 44, 47.

[40] William J. Holstein, "U.S. Overseas Bases Unpopular," United Press International, in *New Haven Register*, March 27, 1983, p. 30.

[41] Ibid.

[42] Adler and others, "What the World Thinks of America," p. 51.

[43] Henry J. Kellerman, *Cultural Relations as an Instrument of U.S. Foreign Policy* (Washington, D.C.: Department of State, 1982), pp. 211–42.

[44] Data and quotes from the *Newsweek* study in Adler and others, "What the World Thinks of America."

CHAPTER EIGHTEEN
CHOICES

Decisions emerge from a combination of personal convictions, bureaucratic self-interest, administrative trade-offs, and Congressional and public pressures, with the dividing line between those elements often blurred in the discussion and even in the minds of the participants.

Henry Kissinger

Clearly, if a scholar-statesman of Kissinger's experience is uncertain about how all of the pieces fit together, the student may wonder if there is any hope for the rest of us.

Our uncertainty is confirmed by another scholar, who notes:

Perhaps we will never be in a position to explain and understand all foreign policies. Some policies may be irrational; some may be affected by so many variables that it becomes difficult, if not impossible, to separate out the impact of each factor; and some may be shrouded in considerable secrecy, making a full understanding difficult. Nevertheless, it is important that we try to understand why states act as they do . . . . [1]

How foreign policy is made is an important matter, and we have devoted a considerable part of this text to examining the strengths and pitfalls of the American process. Perhaps even more important are *what* policies are made and what tools are chosen to implement them.

It is easy to hypothesize connections among the process, the policies, and the tools of foreign policy. For example, some argue that a small power elite controls the economic base of the United States, dominates the policy process, and shapes foreign policy to protect its own economic interests. It is also possible to hypothesize that because policy is a result of consensus building and compromise required to create public support sufficient to sustain policy, policy choices reflect less than ideal responses to events. However, in the nuclear age, foreign policy serves purposes far broader than mere protection of economic interests. It seeks to assure human survival in the United States and throughout the world. Further, while the search for consensus may take the sharp edges off policy proposals, it also avoids more radical and dangerous choices. In the American policy process ample opportunity exists to afford consideration of a wide range of perceptions, interpretations, and images of reality and of the national interest. The system exposes decision makers to a broad range of demands, pressures, theories, and alternatives concerning American interests, Soviet intentions, European or Japanese concerns, and Third World problems. Elections provide the means of asserting public attitudes about the postures, priorities, and types of policies that most Americans are willing to support at a given time. Congress, mass media, opposition political parties, and special interests can be powerful means of questioning existing premises and the policy emphasis of a given administration. Within administrations vigorous differences among advisers, departments, and agencies can be debated.

In the United States informed and knowledgeable differences of opinion abound about the definition of the national interest and how best to pursue it. For example, in the Reagan administration the decision in October 1983 to use American military forces to intervene in Grenada as a means to serve American national interests had its detractors both within the administration and throughout the country, many of whom would have preferred nonmilitary means to deal with a complex geopolitical problem. Yet the policy also had considerable support.

Basically, in practice the national interest at any given time is defined to be what the incumbent administration says it is. A sitting president may adjust his own definition on the basis of internal administrative disagreement among trusted advisers or new conditions in the world or pressures within the country. Until another election produces a new set of leaders with a different definition of the national interest, however, the views of the incumbent president prevail. This fact emphasizes again that in the American system power is at the top.

POWER AT THE TOP

In the American system of government the power to make foreign policy is concentrated at the top—in the president and the presidency. Whether the number of people engaged in the making of foreign policy is very small—a select few of the power elite—or the two to three thousand suggested by former President Richard Nixon or the 7,400 identified by Thomas Dye, the fact remains that a relatively small number of Americans, out of a population of some 230 million, make or influence foreign policy. In addition to the president and his first team, Congress possesses real power to affect decisions, but its exercise of that power has been inconsistent. Otherwise, in terms of high policy, others exercise influence, not power. In public opinion there is latent power, capable of being exercised in elections or in mass outpourings of emotion. Mass media influence is strong, but journalists are powerless to make decisions. For special interests the opportunity for influence abounds, and their persuasive capabilities are substantial, but they too cannot make the decisions about public policy. Thus the power to decide policy lies at the top.

Persuaded that policy leadership should rest with Congress, the framers of the Constitution nonetheless created a system in which powers would be divided and shared among the three branches of government. It was a political system requiring the use of political mechanisms to produce agreement, and in the process the president accumulated broad powers in foreign policy. Through the vigorous exercise of presidential leadership from George Washington onward and a broad interpretation by presidents and by the courts of the foreign-policy powers granted to the president in the Constitution, the executive branch quickly became dominant in the foreign-policy process.

By the twentieth century, most Americans accepted the view that the president has the constitutional and legal authority to make decisions in foreign policy. As head of the government, the president has the political authority to provide leadership. As leader of his political party and as a symbol of the United States, the president has acquired the personal authority, founded in public acceptance and expectations, to act in behalf of the United States and to be responsible for its security.

The primary counterforce to presidential leadership is the Congress, when it chooses to exercise its power. Congressional initiative in the foreign-policy process has been erratic for almost two hundred years, waxing and waning from time to time. At the end of World War I, Congress blocked President Woodrow Wilson's effort to join the League of Nations and in the interwar period steadfastly rejected any presidential effort to increase American strength or to reverse an isolationist foreign policy. With the start of World War II, however, Congress went into a period of acquiescence to presidential leadership, which lasted until the late 1960s and the post-Vietnam War era. Once again, Congress reasserted its independent authority, and its automatic cooperation with presidents diminished. The era of bipartisanship between 1941 and 1968 was, nonetheless, a long stretch of presidential dominance.

Underlying the more prickly aspects of executive-legislative relations is the question of whether the type of bipartisanship so evident in the 1941–68 period can ever be restored and whether it is desirable. The nature and complexity of the world system, of weapons systems, and of policy options is such in the 1980s that it can be argued that vigorous debate between a president and the Congress is indispensable to the formation of wise policy. The desirability of this debate is evident in the recent clashes between President Reagan and many in Congress over Central American policy, over the MX missile, and over arms control. A more incisive challenge to presidential proposals by Congress in 1964 might well have limited the damages caused by Vietnam War policy. Still, Congress is not always willing or able to use its foreign-policy powers and its control of the purse to challenge presidential initiatives.

Upon examination of the system, we might conclude that it is highly stratified in terms of influence but highly centralized in terms of power. It is a hybrid political system in which a president is the center of power but in which the president must "sell" the decisions of his administration to the Congress, to the people, to other governments, to the media, and to parts of his own administration.

The fact that a president must "sell" his policies is an indication that while decision-making power may be centralized, it is severely constrained.

Below the level of high policy, decision-making authority may be legally, politically, or practically delegated to departments, agencies, or advisers. Entirely different groups of individuals, interests, coalitions, and levels of government may be activated in determining and implementing lower-level policies.

Finding that the structure of the American system is a hybrid one—containing both centralization and decentralization of influence—should not divert us from the fact that at the core of high policy, power is very much centralized in the president.

Providing for a vigorous interplay of the many forces that make up American society, the system is not a neat one where formal lines of power are crystal clear under all circumstances. One expert who has observed it closely from within the government as well as outside it, Zbigniew Brzezinski, called it "a chaotic nonsystem."[2] Yet it seems to work most of the time.

THE DECISION-MAKING PROCESS

In a system of such diversification and openness, the process by which policy options are decided can appear incomprehensible. Leaders' images of reality, partisan political interests, intellectual and philosophical convictions, the peculiarities of group behavior, and the competition among bureaucracies complicate even further the decision makers' exposure to pressures from Congress, the media, public opinion, and special interests.

The absence of orderliness seems to be the major characteristic of the process and is thought by some observers to be a weakness in the system.

On the other hand, is it possible that the absence of rigid, well-defined procedures constitutes a major strength of the system and is not a weakness at all? In a world in which change is rapid, issues are complex, and weapons are technologically baffling and dangerous, the loose and open structure of the system permits a fuller examination of a broader range of facts, options, and ramifications than would a more tightly structured system. Even as things are, decision-making groups have enough trouble absorbing new information and devising new and imaginative policies. "Muddling through" to decisions and relying on small incremental changes of policy have their virtues, although constraining boldness and creativity.

Scholars have just begun to explore and understand the dynamics of the decision-making process and to identify the types of factors that are dominant in different circumstances. However when a president who knows precisely what he wants to do occupies the White House, the complexities of the process may diminish.

LEADERSHIP

In any political system effective political leadership is essential to the development of rational policy. This is especially true in the type of democratic system described in this book. At its best, political leadership reasonably reflects the needs, hopes, and ambitions of the people it serves. In the American system the electoral system sets the acceptable boundaries of leadership behavior, and a free press, public-opinion polls, and public protests provide further guidelines to the limits of leadership discretion. In turn, the leadership helps to shape the values and attitudes of the system.

Thus in one sense, elected representatives and the people share responsibility for leadership.

In the last five decades the United States has experienced more or less strong presidential leadership most of the time. And when strong presidential leadership and direction of foreign policy have been in place, some of the apparent chaos in the system seems much less important.

In all presidencies since the start of World War II, policy direction has been sharply centered in the White House. The president and a few key advisers have produced clear policy direction, although decisions about methods have been much more open to disagreement and debate. In the presidencies of Franklin Roosevelt, Harry Truman, John Kennedy, Lyndon Johnson, and Richard Nixon there was little doubt that high policy was decided at the top by the president and a very few key advisers. Recent studies have also suggested that President Eisenhower was more decisive on foreign policy than it appeared at the time.[3]

In some cases highly centralized control of the process has produced innovative and dynamic new programs. The major policies of the Truman administration can hardly be regarded as incremental. John Kennedy attempted some broad new initiatives, and Richard Nixon attempted massive innovations in foreign policy. On the other hand, the close direction of policy by Lyndon Johnson led to the Vietnam War. Conversely, in the Eisenhower administration tight direction by the White House produced no major innovations and reflected the incremental approach as much as any administration in the past fifty years.

Strong presidents are able to influence the perceptions, values, and opinions of the public and to persuade it to accept their views of current reality, either maintaining established attitudes or changing them. Harry Truman's creation of public support for anti-Soviet and anti-Communist beliefs in 1945–47, Richard Nixon's success in changing public attitudes toward Communist China in the 1970s, and Ronald Reagan's ability to persuade Americans to support his military policies despite the Vietnam syndrome are three major examples of the effectiveness of presidents in defining American interests and acquiring public support. One major problem facing American democracy, however, is the limited countervailing power to a strong-willed president skilled in molding elite and public support. When Lyndon Johnson, one of the nation's most strong-willed presidents, committed the United States to a major military involvement in Vietnam, few voices were raised in objection to the policy. When Ronald Reagan committed American forces to Lebanon and to an invasion of Grenada in 1983, he obtained widespread public support. In short, strong presidential leadership is a two-edged sword in foreign policy. It cuts through the jumble of debate and political argument, but it may also pierce the mantle of prudence and wisdom. The emergence of an increased sense of skepticism over basic premises of American policy, observed in the public and in the Congress in the past decade, is a healthy sign that respect for presidential leadership does not require unquestioning obedience. In spite of this, the amount of consensus developed among Americans over the last four decades remains impressive, and the process, however chaotic it often appears, functions more or less effectively most of the time.

FIVE LEVELS OF CHOICE

American policy makers and the American people struggle with a bewildering range of choices as they create foreign policy and engage in foreign relations. These choices and the methods by which they are resolved constitute the raw materials of politics: defining problems, goals, and options and choosing the tools with which to carry them out in a world of other states. The choices encompass serious intellectual, moral, theoretical, philosophical, and practical dilemmas that confront all human beings in the twentieth century. In any case, five major levels of choice are engaged in the political process by which foreign policy is designed.

    1. *The kind of world we live in.* Convictions about the nature of human behavior and about the way states have behaved in the past form a powerful basis for making policy decisions. Realists and idealists offer conflicting interpretations of human nature and behavior and strong convictions about the desirable forms of world political order. At this level it is decided whether the world system contains friends, adversaries, enemies, or neutrals, and the decision suggests the ways in which one state should relate to another. If it is assumed that there are no enemies or competitors, one set of responses is possible. If it is assumed that there are major enemies and/or competitors, another set of responses is needed. In any case, distinguishing among enemies, competitors, allies, and neutrals flows from these convictions.

    2. *Theoretical frameworks.* Conclusions about the nature of states lead to consideration of the theoretical frameworks that facilitate the organization of policy. Realism, idealism, interdependence, and other theories concerning the political relationships of states provide other choices to policy makers. Whether to base American policy on power, law and negotiation, mutual interests, or some combination of all of these confronts decision makers with additional choices of some

complexity. Deciding which combination provides the best chance for assuring American security and well-being, for achieving world peace, and for seeking other desirable objectives engages the American political system in painful choices.

3. *Geographical priorities.* Given its current status in the world, the United States confronts problems at several geographic levels: global, hemispheric, cross-hemispheric, regional, continental, and domestic. Competition with the Soviet Union in every part of the globe imposes a global perspective on policy makers, while events in the Western Hemisphere (North and South America), in the different regions (North America, Central America, South America, Southeast Asia, Middle East, Europe), and on the North American continent involve different numbers and kinds of other countries. Domestic American concerns relating to foreign policy add yet another dimension to the agenda. Finally, American relations with individual states function quite apart from their regional or hemispheric context. Although the importance of particular regions or states may vary from time to time in the perspective of American policy makers, the following list would seem to suggest the priorities of the 1980s:

1. The Soviet Union
2. Western Europe and Japan
3. The Middle East
4. Asia (China, the western Pacific, Southwest Asia)
5. Latin America (Central America, South America)
6. Africa
7. Eastern Europe
8. Individual countries (West Germany, Japan, Great Britain, and others)
9. The global community

Each area and each country in it contains its own unique problems, needs, and demands. Further, the global system as a whole, apart from specific American interests in it, has increasingly been recognized as a unit with its common problems and dangers.

Thus the geographical focus that policy makers choose to consider at any given moment can be a critical factor in the creation of policy.

4. *The Tracks and Tools of Policy.* As we saw in part IV, consideration of four tracks of policy and the tools that go with them is a formidable job and a controversial one. Deciding which types of policies are required in given circumstances and which tools will most productively serve to make the policy successful provokes a good deal of the political controversy within the United States. In a world faced by many problems that are relatively new, many Americans find few certain guideposts to productive policy and may tend to rely too heavily on experiences of the past rather than on imaginative departures from it.

No set of choices is more difficult than those involving the military track and the use of military tools. This point was reemphasized in October 1983 during the commitment of American military forces to Lebanon and Grenada.

Moreover, the problem of how to orchestrate and coordinate all of the tools and tracks of policy remains troublesome. When can economic and cultural policy be more effective than military policy in obtaining the cooperation of a particular country or bloc? When is military policy or the use of force the only alternative? When is covert political warfare necessary?

These are the kinds of questions that continue to produce political disagreement among Americans and their leaders.

5.   *The American Role in the World.* For the past four decades the United States
has played a role of world leadership and in that role has led opposition to the
behavior of the Soviet Union. Yet serious questions persist about the desirability
and the capability of the United States to bear the burdens of leadership. Other
questions have been raised about the right and necessity of the United States to play
a leadership role in the pluralist world in which other states also possess political
and economic power. Clearly, the decision about the American role reflects the
continuing assessment of the Soviet Union as an expanding, hostile power, but
some Americans reject that view or argue that the global interests of the Soviet
Union are as legitimate as those of the United States. Since the Vietnam War many
Americans have adopted the view that the United States should intervene in the
affairs of other countries as little as possible, while others maintain that the United
States must continue to act as a world policeman of sorts.

The answers to these five levels of choice distinguish the hawks from
the doves in the United States. They reflect very different conceptions
about the nature of the world in which we live, the ways states behave, the
nature of the Soviet Union and its government, the role of the United
States, the ways in which the United States should utilize its great resources
to serve the national interest, and indeed, the national interest itself.

Each citizen, each expert, each public official and leader must decide
individually how to answer such issues.

There is little certainty about how such choices will—or should—be
made in the future. Avoidance of nuclear war, indeed, avoiding war or
violence in any form seems a fundamental choice. Yet what would American leaders actually do if the Soviet Union decided to invade and occupy
West Berlin, West Germany, or Western Europe? Would the United States
risk nuclear annihilation to retaliate? What would be the American
response—what should it be—if the Vietnamese government sought to
overrun Thailand, a long-time American ally in Asia? What can and should
the United States do to assure the Soviet Union that it does not intend to
attack, and what can be done either to help transform the Soviet system
into a more open and cooperative one or to reach agreement upon rules of
mutual behavior? On what basis should any or all of the decisions in these
hypothetical situations be made? What role should the American citizen
play in making such choices, and how can the citizen play any role if he or
she is uninterested, uninformed, and unwilling to be heard? Do history and
our leaders' interpretation of history and of the ways states behave limit the
imagination of those leaders to deal with unprecedented situations and
threats? Are we bound by an incrementalism that fails to free the mind to
deal intelligently and creatively with new realities?

Proposals to break the political logjam in relations with the Soviet
Union abound. One scholar suggests that the United States offer Moscow a

> . . . world wide nuclear deal—no first use, a comprehensive test ban, a missile
> test ban, deep cuts in nuclear inventories in exchange for a substantial reduc-
> tion in the readiness and offensive capabilities of Warsaw Pact conventional
> forces. This would involve nuclear free zones, substantial thinning out of
> forces and a demilitarized zone on both sides of the Elbe. Washington should

encourage trade and cultural relations between the two halves of the divided continent as it increases its own trade with the East.[4]

Another proposal that might be offered to reduce East-West competition is a nonaggression pact with the Soviet Union in which each side agrees not to attack each other or its allies. It can be argued that the superpowers already have a nonaggression pact—the United Nations Charter—and that it seems to reassure neither side. According to this view, a formal nonaggression pact would be extraneous, subject to cancellation, and no more reassuring than any other agreement. Further, it can be argued that such a pact would not produce deeper political agreement and understanding between the superpowers and that if that cooperation existed in the first place, no nonaggression pact would be necessary. In addition, many Americans would surely argue that the Soviets could not be trusted to abide by an agreement. Aside from these reservations about a nonaggression pact, some would argue that unless it also covers the Third World, countless opportunities for conflict and misunderstanding would continue to exist outside Europe. Besides, the strong belief persists that the most effective way to deal with the Soviet Union is not through accommodation and diplomacy but by the threat of countervailing and superior force. Also unless a nonaggression pact either explicitly or implictly contained a body of agreed-upon rules and limits of the behavior of its signatories, it would mean little; it would have to include a mutual agreement over the permissible boundaries of each other's interests, rights, and activities. Short of such an understanding, a pact would do little to prevent further clashes.

These examples of choices available to policy makers suggest that not all policies are solely dependent upon the wishes or judgments of American leaders. They are also dependent upon the judgments and actions of leaders of other countries. One available policy choice, however, is the commitment to vigorously pursue any opportunity to reconcile differences. This is the essence of diplomacy. It is also the essence of wisdom in the nuclear age, when possible catastrophe lies beyond the next demonstration of brinksmanship by either side.

John Kennedy said in his inaugural speech in 1961: "Let us never negotiate out of fear, but let us never fear to negotiate."[5] On another occasion, at the University of Washington in 1961, Kennedy also offered this advice to policy makers:

> We must face up to the chance of war, if we are to maintain the peace . . . . Diplomacy and defense are not substitutes for one another . . . a willingness to resist force, unaccompanied by a willingness to talk, could provoke belligerence—while a willingness to talk, unaccompanied by a willingness to resist force, could invite disaster.[6]

There is much to suggest that power and strength are essential elements in American foreign policy, and like it or not, they will occasionally have to be used or threatened. However, beyond balance of power and deterrence lies the opportunity for diplomacy, flexibility, and reconciliation of interests. American foreign policy and foreign relations based in this reality is the inescapable choice for the future.

A BALANCE SHEET
OF AMERICAN FOREIGN POLICY

On the whole, American foreign policy since 1945 has succeeded in achieving and maintaining American security and survival, in contributing to American prosperity, and in strengthening American prestige. It has managed to avoid nuclear catastrophe and has helped to create a new international system in which less developed nations have been able to acquire political and economic capabilities.

On the negative side, American foreign policy has been unable to produce more acceptable relations with the Soviet Union, a fact that is due as much to the nature of the Soviet Union and its government as to American actions. The capability of transformation is extremely limited. Nonetheless, the inability to find and develop a broader range of mutual interests and to more effectively minimize the number of conflicting interests remains, in part, a failure of American policy.

American policies toward the industrialized world, while not a record of perfect success, have been, on the whole, effective in serving the mutual interests of members of the Western alliance. In the Third and Fourth Worlds, the record is more mixed. American policy has not always been effective in responding to the national and social revolutions occurring throughout the world.

In this polycentric world, American power is said to have declined and American hegemony eroded. On this question three points need to be made. First, it is not at all clear that precise measurements of power are possible, and our evaluations must be impressionistic and subject to numerous reservations. In spite of this, we may generalize about two additional points. In the immediate post-World War II period, when American power relative to all other countries seemed to be at its maximum, the United States was not able to impose either the Marshall Plan or the North Atlantic Treaty on Western Europe—the countries involved had to agree—nor would it have been able to reshape the Japanese political and economic systems without Japan's agreement and participation. Short of war, it was not able to expel the Soviet Union from Eastern Europe or to influence the form of government the Soviets installed in the countries it occupied during the war. Thus American power and influence in the 1945-55 period was substantial but not unlimited. Then the very success of American policies during this period—the reinvigoration of Western Europe and Japan and the containment of Soviet expansion into these areas—inevitably led to a rise of new political and economic centers. A final point: In the 1980s, it can be argued, American power has not diminished but in fact has increased, although other states have also acquired additional power relative to American power. Thus by the start of this decade, several centers of power other than the United States had evolved within the global system.

In any case, the net result has been a reordering of the nature of the global political system in which the United States remains preeminent but not dominant. The rules and procedures by which states relate to each other have changed, and if anything, the change has elevated the importance of politics among nations. American preferences must be negotiated more vigorously than in the past, but it is a matter of degree, not of substance.

From a moral, political, psychological, and practical point of view, the system of 1945-50 with its disproportionate distribution of power and capabilities was undesirable, and with or without American policies, its evolution was inevitable. The need to understand the changing political shape of the world and to adapt American foreign policy to it is the major challenge facing American policy makers in the future.

AN AMERICAN VISION

In a pluralist world the United States is still in a position to influence the course of events throughout the system. But do we have a vision of the kind of world we would like to see, one that might be persuasive to the majority of countries in the world system? Do we know what we think about the kinds of structures, rules, and solutions necessary to produce an ideal model of an ideal world system? First, if we assume that for the foreseeable future, the state system will exist, we must conclude that the primary function of American foreign policy is to serve the national interests of the United States.

Second, we must also acknowledge that the power of any state to direct the shape of change is limited. Not that American influence is inconsequential, but even if Americans had a clear vision of an ideal world, our capacity to impose that vision on everyone else is limited. American policy may help to channel the tide of change in desired directions. It cannot control its power, the shape of its waves, or the force of its undertow.

Clearly, most Americans would prefer a global model that included the ideals of personal and political freedom, democratic governments based on the consent of the governed, the end of political and economic inequality and the suppression of the poor, the eradication of hunger and poverty, and unlimited opportunities to develop the human personality to its fullest. Presumably, most Americans would prefer a model that reflected a belief in free enterprise and free trade and a world in which the elements of military power were minimized in the effort to produce peace. However, the need for instruments capable of producing peaceful change for those who have legitimate economic, social, and political goals offers a challenge to strengthen international machinery through which all states can make legitimate demands and receive redress of grievances.

In a world of pluralism, politics is a primary instrument in forging a new order, and Americans are as experienced in the practice of politics as anyone.

What are the alternatives to the incremental shaping of a system in a world of diversity? One alternative involves the withdrawal of the United

States into its own isolated, independent world. Another is the creation of an American empire in which the American model is imposed upon others by conquest and power. Neither is practically possible or morally desirable, and both entail costs that far exceed potential benefits.

Thus an open, democratic global system in which all states are free to make demands, compromises, and adjustments and in which the United States relies upon persuasion in its nonviolent forms seems to be a workable model. Indeed, it may be an inevitable one.

The American experience has much to teach the world system about creation of wealth, political competition, and the capacity to change and to learn. The lessons may not be universally admired or welcomed, but American foreign policy serves American national interests best that responds to the desire for change.

NOTES

¹ Lloyd Jensen, *Explaining Foreign Policy* (Englewood Cliffs, N.J.: Prentice-Hall, 1982), pp. 267-68.
² Zbigniew Brzezinski, "Deciding Who Makes Foreign Policy," *New York Times Magazine*, September 18, 1983, p. 58.
³ Fred Greenstein, *The Hidden-Hand Presidency: Eisenhower as Leader* (New York: Basic Books, 1982), pp. 228-48.
⁴ Richard Barnet, "Needed: A New Western Political Strategy," *New York Times*, November 29, 1983, p. 31.
⁵ John F. Kennedy, cited in Theodore Sorenson, *Kennedy* (New York: Harper & Row, Publishers, 1965), p. 511.
⁶ Ibid.

SELECTED
BIBLIOGRAPHY

Books

ABLE, ELIE, ed., *What's New: The Media in American Society*. San Francisco: Institute for Contemporary Studies, 1981.

ABRAHAMSEN, DAVID, *Nixon vs. Nixon: An Emotional Tragedy*. New York: Farrar, Straus & Giroux, 1977.

ALLISON, GRAHAM, *Essence of Decision: Explaining the Cuban Missile Crisis*. Boston: Little, Brown & Company, 1971.

ALMOND, GABRIEL A., *The American People and Foreign Policy*. New York: Praeger Publishers, 1960.

ALMOND, GABRIEL A., AND G. BINGHAM POWELL, JR., *Comparative Politics*. Boston: Little, Brown & Company, 1978.

ALMOND, GABRIEL A., AND SIDNEY VERBA, *The Civic Culture*. Princeton, N.J.: Princeton University Press, 1963.

ARON, RAYMOND, *Peace and War: A Theory of International Relations*. New York: Praeger Publishers, 1967.

ART, ROBERT J., AND KENNETH N. WALTZ, eds., *The Use of Force*. Boston: Little, Brown & Company, 1971.

BAMFORD, JAMES, *The Puzzle Palace*. Boston: Houghton Mifflin Company, 1982.

BARBER, JAMES DAVID, *The Presidential Character*. Englewood Cliffs, N.J.: Prentice-Hall, 1977.

BARNETT, RICHARD, AND RONALD E. MULLER, *Global Reach: The Power of the Multinational Corporations*. New York: Simon & Schuster, 1974.

BELL, DANIEL, *The Coming of Post-Industrial Society: A Venture in Social Forecasting*. New York: Basic Books, 1973.

BENJAMIN, GERALD, ed., *The Communications Revolution in Politics*. New York: Academy of Political Science, 1982.

BLAKE, DAVID H., AND ROBERT S. WALTERS, *The Politics of Global Economic Relations*, 2nd ed. Englewood Cliffs, N.J.: Prentice-Hall, 1983.

BLUM, ROBERT, ed., *Cultural Affairs and Foreign Relations*. Englewood Cliffs, N.J.: Prentice-Hall, 1963.

BOWLES, CHESTER, *Promises To Keep*. New York: Harper & Row, Publishers, 1971.

BOZEMAN, ADDA B., *Politics and Culture in International History*. Princeton, N.J.: Princeton University Press, 1960.

BRADLEY, OMAR N., AND CLAY BLAIR, *A General's Life: An Autobiography*. New York: Simon & Schuster, 1983.

BRAISTED, PAUL J., ed., *Cultural Affairs and Foreign Relations*. Washington, D.C.: Columbia Books, Publishers, 1968.

BRAYBROOKE, DAVID, AND CHARLES LINDBLOM, *A Strategy of Decision: Policy Evaluation as a Social Process*. New York: Free Press of Glencoe, 1963.

BRIERLY, J. L., *The Law of Nations*, 5th ed. London: Oxford University Press, 1955.

BRZEZINSKI, ZBIGNIEW, *Between Two Ages: America's Role in the Technetronic Era*. New York: Penguin Books, 1976.

————, *Power and Principle*. New York: Farrar, Straus & Giroux, 1983.

CARTER, JIMMY, *Keeping Faith*. New York: Bantam Books, 1982.

CHARLESWORTH, JAMES C., ed. *Contemporary Political Analysis*. New York: Free Press, 1967.

CLAUDE, INIS, JR., *Power and International Relations*. New York: Random House, 1962.

CLAUSEWITZ, KARL VON, *On War*, trans. O. J. Matthiajs Jolles. New York: Modern Library, 1943.

COLLIER, PETER AND DAVID HOROWITZ, *The Kennedys: An American Drama*, New York: Summit Books, 1984.

CONSIDINE, BOB, *The Remarkable Life of Armand Hammer*. New York: Harper & Row, Publishers, 1975.

COOPER, RICHARD, *The Economics of Interdependence: Economic Policy in the Atlantic Community*. New York: McGraw-Hill Book Company, 1968.

COULOUMBIS, THEODORE A., AND JAMES H. WOLFE, *Introduction to International Relations: Power and Justice*, 2nd ed. Englewood Cliffs, N. J.: Prentice-Hall, 1982.

CRABB, CECIL V., JR., *American Foreign Policy in the Nuclear Age*, 4th ed. New York: Harper & Row, Publishers, 1983.

CRABB, CECIL V., JR., AND PAT M. HOLT, *Invitation to Struggle: Congress, the President, and Foreign Policy*. Washington, D.C.: Congressional Quarterly Press, 1980.

CUSHMAN, ROBERT E., AND ROBERT F. CUSHMAN, *Cases in Constitutional Law*, 3rd ed. New York: Appleton-Century-Crofts, 1968.

DAHL, ROBERT A., *Democracy in the United States: Promises and Performance*, 3rd ed. Chicago: Rand McNally, 1976.

————, *Polyarchy*. New Haven: Yale University Press, 1971.

————, *Who Governs: Democracy and Power in an American City*. New Haven: Yale University Press, 1961.

DEUTSCH, KARL W., *The Analysis of International Relations*. Englewood Cliffs, N.J.: Prentice-Hall, 1968.

————, *The Nerves of Government*. New York: Free Press, 1966.

DEUTSCH, KARL W., ET AL., *Political Community and the North Atlantic Area*. Cambridge, Mass., Harvard University Press, 1972.

DE MESQUITA, BRUCE BUENO, *The War Trap*. New Haven: Yale University Press, 1981.

DeRivera, Joseph, *The Psychological Dimensions of Foreign Policy.* Columbus, Ohio: Charles E. Merrill Publishing Co., 1968.

DiRenzo, Gordon, ed., *Personality and Politics.* Garden City, N.Y.: Doubleday-Anchor, 1974.

Donovan, Robert J., *Tumultuous Years: The Presidency of Harry S. Truman.* New York: W. W. Norton & Company, 1982.

Doob, Leonard, *Patriotism and Nationalism: Their Psychological Foundations.* New Haven: Yale University Press, 1964.

Dougherty, James E., and Robert L. Pfaltzgraff, *Contending Theories of International Relations.* Philadelphia: J. B. Lippincott Company, 1971.

Dull, James, "The Effects of American Multinational Corporations on the Attitudes of Mexican Executives," unpublished Ph.D. dissertation, Department of Political Science, Graduate School of Arts and Sciences, Columbia University, 1981.

Dye, Thomas R., *Who's Running America?* 3rd ed., Englewood Cliffs, N.J.: Prentice-Hall, 1983.

Dye, Thomas R., and L. Harmon Zeigler, *American Politics in the Media Age.* Monterey, Calif.: Brooks/Cole Publishing Company, 1983.

Easton, David, *A Framework for Political Analysis,* Englewood Cliffs, N.J.: Prentice-Hall, 1965.

Edwards, David, *The American Political Experience,* 2nd ed. Englewood Cliffs, N.J.: Prentice-Hall, 1982.

Emerson, Rupert, *From Empire to Nation: The Rise to Self-Assertion of Asian and African Peoples.* Boston: Beacon Press, 1962.

Enthoven, Alain, and K. Wayne Smith, *How Much is Enough?* New York, Harper & Row, Publishers, 1971.

Esterline, John H., and Robert B. Black, *Inside Foreign Policy.* Palo Alto, Calif.: Mayfield Publishing Company, 1975.

Farrell, R. Barry, ed., *Approaches to Comparative and International Politics,* Evanston, Ill.: Northwestern University Press, 1966.

Frank, Jerome, *Sanity or Survival: Psychological Aspects of War and Peace.* New York: Random House, 1967.

Friedmann, Wolfgang, *The Changing Structure of International Law.* New York: Columbia University Press, 1964.

Fulbright, J. William, *Arrogance of Power.* New York: Random House, 1966.

Galbraith, John Kenneth, *Economics and the Public Purpose.* Boston: Houghton Mifflin Company, 1973.

Gardner, Lloyd C., *American Foreign Policy: Present to Past.* New York: Free Press, 1977.

Geelhold, E. Bruce, *Charles E. Wilson and Controversy at the Pentagon, 1953 to 1975.* Detroit: Wayne State University Press, 1979.

George, Alexander and Juliet, *Woodrow Wilson and Colonel House: A Personality Study.* New York: Dover Publications, 1964.

Goldman, Sheldon, *Constitutional Law and Supreme Court Decision-Making.* New York: Harper & Row, Publishers, 1982.

Greenstein, Fred, *The Hidden-Hand Presidency: Eisenhower as Leader.* New York: Basic Books, 1982.

Gunther, Gerald, *Cases and Materials on Constitutional Law,* 10th ed. Mineola, N.Y.: Foundation Press, 1980.

Haas, Ernst B., *Beyond the Nation-State.* Stanford, Calif.: Stanford University Press, 1958.

Haig, Alexander M. Jr., *Caveat: Realism, Reagan, and Foreign Policy,* New York: Macmillan Publishing Company, 1984.

Halberstam, David, *The Powers That Be.* New York: Alfred A. Knopf, 1979.

HALPERIN, MORTON, AND ARNOLD KANTER, *Readings in American Foreign Policy: A Bureaucratic Perspective.* Boston: Little, Brown, & Company, 1973.

HANREIDER, WOLFRAM, ed., *Comparative Foreign Policy: Theoretical Essays.* New York: David McKay Co., 1971.

HARTMANN, FREDERICK, H., *The Relations of Nations,* 6th ed. New York: Macmillan Company, 1983.

HEALD, MORELL, AND LAWRENCE S. KAPLAN, *Culture and Diplomacy.* Westport, Conn.: Greenwood Press, 1979.

HENKIN, LOUIS, *Foreign Affairs and the Constitution.* Mineola, N.Y.: Foundation Press, 1972.

HERMANN, MARGARET G., *A Psychological Examination of Political Leaders.* New York: Free Press, 1976.

HICKS, JOHN D., *The Federal Union: A History of the United States to 1865,* 2nd ed. Cambridge, Mass.: Riverside Press, Houghton Mifflin Company, 1952.

HILSMAN, ROGER, *The Crouching Future.* Garden City, N.Y.: Doubleday and Company, 1975.

————, *The Politics of Policy Making in Defense and Foreign Affairs.* New York: Harper & Row, Publishers, 1977.

————, *To Govern America.* New York: Harper & Row, Publishers, 1979.

————, *To Move A Nation.* New York: Doubleday and Company, 1967.

HOFFMANN, STANLEY, *Primacy or World Order: American Foreign Policy Since the Cold War.* New York: McGraw-Hill Book Company, 1978.

HOLSTI, K. J., *International Politics: A Framework for Analysis,* 3rd ed. Englewood Cliffs, N.J.: Prentice-Hall, 1977.

HOUGH, JERRY, *Soviet Leadership in Transition.* Washington, D.C.: Brookings Institution, 1980.

JAMIESON, KATHLEEN HALL, AND KARLYN KOHRS CAMPBELL, *The Interplay Of Influence: Mass Media and Their Publics in News, Advertising, Politics.* Belmont, Calif.: Wadsworth Publishing Company, 1983.

JANIS, IRVING, L., *Groupthink.* Boston: Houghton Mifflin Company, 1982.

JANOWITZ, MORRIS, ed., *The New Military: Changing Patterns of Organization.* New York: Russell Sage Foundation, 1964.

JENSEN, LLOYD, *Explaining Foreign Policy.* Englewood Cliffs, N.J.: Prentice-Hall, 1982.

JERVIS, ROBERT, *Perception and Misperception.* Princeton, N.J.: Princeton University Press, 1976.

JOHNSON, LYNDON B., *From the Vantage Point.* New York: Holt, Rinehart and Winston, 1971.

JORDAN, HAMILTON, *Crisis: The Last Year of the Carter Presidency.* New York: G. P. Putnam's Sons, 1982.

KAPLAN, MORTON, *Systems and Process in International Politics.* New York: John Wiley and Sons, 1962.

KEGLEY, CHARLES W., AND EUGENE R. WITTKOPF, *American Foreign Policy: Pattern and Process,* 2nd ed. New York: St. Martin's Press, 1982.

————, eds., *Perspectives on American Foreign Policy.* New York: St. Martin's Press, 1983.

————, *World Politics: Trend and Transformation.* New York: St. Martin's Press, 1981.

KELLERMAN, HENRY J., *Cultural Relations As an Instrument of U.S. Foreign Policy.* Washington, D.C.: Department of State Publication, 1982.

KEOHANE, ROBERT O., AND JOSEPH S. NYE, *Power and Interdependence: World Politics in Transition.* Boston: Little, Brown & Company, 1977.

————, eds., *Transnational Relations and World Politics.* Cambridge, Mass.: Harvard University Press, 1972.

KISSINGER, HENRY, *American Foreign Policy*, 3rd ed. New York: W. W. Norton & Company, 1977.

————, *White House Years*. Boston: Little, Brown & Company, 1979.

————, *Years of Upheaval*. Boston: Little, Brown & Company, 1982.

KOLKO, GABRIEL, *The Roots of American Foreign Policy*. Boston: Beacon Press, 1969.

LAPALOMBARA, JOSEPH, AND STEPHEN BLANK, *Multinational Corporations In Comparative Perspective*. New York: Conference Board, 1977.

LASH, JOSEPH, *Eleanor, The Years Alone*. New York: W. W. Norton & Company, 1972.

LASSWELL, HAROLD D., *Power and Personality*. New York: W. W. Norton & Company, 1948.

————, *World Politics and Personal Insecurity*. New York: Free Press, 1965.

LERNER, MAX, *America as a Civilization*. New York: Simon & Schuster, 1957.

L'ETANG, HUGH, *The Pathology of Leadership*. New York: Hawthorne Books, 1970.

LEYTON-BROWN, DAVID, "Governments of Developed Countries as Hosts to Multinational Corporations: The Canadian, British, and French Policy Experiences," unpublished Ph.D. dissertation, Department of Government, Harvard University, 1975.

LINDBLOM, CHARLES, *Power and Markets*. New York, Basic Books, 1977.

————, *The Policy-Making Process*. Englewood Cliffs, N.J.: Prentice-Hall, 1968.

LUARD, EVAN, *The International Protection of Human Rights*. New York: Praeger Publishers, 1967.

MAHAN, ALFRED THAYER, *The Influence of Seapower Upon History*. Boston: Little, Brown & Company, 1897.

MANCHESTER, WILLIAM, *American Caesar: Douglas MacArthur 1880–1964*. Boston: Little, Brown & Company, 1978.

————, *The Glory and the Dream: A Narrative History of America, 1932–72*. New York: Bantam Books, 1975.

————, *One Brief Shining Moment: Remembering Kennedy*. Boston: Little, Brown & Company, 1983.

MANSBACH, RICHARD W., AND JOHN A. VASQUEZ, *In Search of Theory: A Paradigm for Global Politics*. New York: Columbia University Press, 1981.

MILBRATH, LESTER, *Political Participation*. Skokie, Ill.: Rand McNally, 1965.

MILIBAND, RALPH, *The State in a Capitalist Society*. New York: Basic Books, 1969.

MILLS, C. WRIGHT, *The Power Elite*. New York: Oxford University Press, 1956.

MORGENTHAU, HANS, *Politics Among Nations: The Struggle for Power and Peace*, 4th ed. New York: Alfred A. Knopf, 1967.

MOSLEY, LEONARD, *Marshall: Hero for Our Times*. New York: Hearst Books, 1982.

NASH, HENRY T., *American Foreign Policy: Changing Perspectives on National Security*, rev. ed. Homewood, Ill.: Dorsey Press, 1978.

NATHAN, JAMES A., AND JAMES K. OLIVER, *United States Foreign Policy and World Order*, 2nd ed. Boston: Little, Brown & Company, 1983.

NEUSTADT, RICHARD, *Presidential Power*. New York: John Wiley and Sons, 1980.

NINKOVICH, FRANK A., *The Diplomacy of Ideas: U.S. Foreign Policy and Cultural Relations, 1938–1950*. New York: Cambridge University Press, 1981.

O'CONNOR, JAMES, *The Fiscal Crisis of the State*. New York: St. Martin's Press, 1973.

O'DONNELL, KENNETH P., AND DAVID F. POWERS, *Johnny We Hardly Knew Ye: Memories of John Fitzgerald Kennedy*. Boston: Little, Brown & Company, 1972.

OYE, KENNETH A., ROBERT J. LIEBER, AND DONALD ROTHCHILD, EDS., *Eagle Defiant: United States Foreign Policy in the 1980s*. Boston: Little, Brown & Company, 1983.

PALETZ, DAVID L., AND ROBERT M. ENTMAN, *Media Power Politics*. New York: Free

Press, 1981.

PARENTI, MICHAEL,   *Democracy for the Few*, 4th ed. New York: St. Martin's Press, 1983.

PATERSON, THOMAS G., J. GARRY CLIFFORD, AND KENNETH L. HAGEN,   *American Foreign Policy, a History.* Lexington, Mass.: D. C. Heath & Company, 1977.

PETTMAN, RALPH,   *Human Behavior and World Politics*, 2nd ed. Englewood Cliffs, N.J.: Prentice-Hall, 1965.

REEVES, RICHARD,   *American Journey.* New York: Simon & Schuster, 1982.

RICHARDSON, LEWIS,   *Statistics of Deadly Quarrels.* Chicago: Quadrangle, 1960.

ROGOW, ARNOLD A.,   *James Forrestal: A Study in Personality, Politics, and Policy.* New York: Macmillan Company, 1963.

ROSENAU, JAMES, ed.,   *Comparing Foreign Policies.* New York: Sage/Halstead Press, 1974.

ROSENAU, JAMES, VINCENT DAVIS, AND MAURICE EAST, eds.,   *The Analysis of International Politics.* New York: Free Press, 1972.

ROSENAU, JAMES, KENNETH W. THOMPSON, AND GAVIN BOYD, eds.,   *World Politics: An Introduction.* New York: Free Press, 1976.

ROSENCRANCE, RICHARD,   *Action and Reaction in World Politics.* Boston: Little, Brown & Company, 1963.

RUBENSTEIN, ALVIN Z.,   *Soviet Foreign Policy Since World War II: Imperial and Global.* Cambridge, Mass.: Winthrop Publishers, 1981.

RUBIN, LESLIE, AND BRIAN WEINSTEIN,   *Introduction to African Politics*, 2nd ed. New York: Praeger Publishers, 1977.

RUMMEL, RUDOLPH,   *Dimensions of Nations.* Beverly Hills, Calif.: Sage Publications, 1972.

RUSSETT, BRUCE M.,   *What Price Vigilance?* New Haven: Yale University Press, 1970.

RUSSETT, BRUCE M., AND ELIZABETH C. HANSON,   *Interest and Ideology: The Foreign Policy Beliefs of American Businessmen.* San Francisco: W. H. Freeman and Co., 1975.

RUSSETT, BRUCE M., AND HARVEY STARR,   *World Politics: The Menu for Choice.* San Francisco: W. H. Freeman and Co., 1981.

SCHELLING, THOMAS C.,   *Arms and Influence.* New Haven: Yale University Press, 1966.

SCHLESINGER, ARTHUR M., JR.,   *A Thousand Days.* Greenwich, Conn.: Fawcett Publications, 1965.

————,   *The Politics of Upheaval.* Boston: Houghton Mifflin Company, 1960.

SINGER, J. DAVID, ed.,   *Quantitative International Politics: Insights and Evidence.* New York: Free Press, 1968.

SINGER, J. DAVID, AND MELVIN SMALL,   *The Wages of War 1816–1965: A Statistical Handbook.* New York: John Wiley and Sons, 1972.

SMITH, ADAM,   *The Wealth of Nations*, ed. Edwin Cannan. New York: Modern Library, 1937.

SNYDER, LOUIS,   *The Meaning of Nationalism.* New York: Greenwood Press, 1968.

SORENSON, THEODORE C.,   *Kennedy.* New York: Harper & Row, Publishers, 1965.

SPANIER, JOHN,   *American Foreign Policy Since World War II*, 8th ed. New York: Holt, Rinehart and Winston, 1980.

SPANIER, JOHN, AND JOSEPH L. NOGEE,   *Congress, the Presidency, and American Foreign Policy.* New York: Pergamon Press, 1981.

SPANIER, JOHN, AND ERIC M. USLANER,   *Foreign Policy and the Democratic Dilemmas*, 3rd ed. New York: Holt, Rinehart and Winston, 1982.

SPERO, JOAN EDELMAN,   *The Politics of International Economic Relations*, 2nd ed. New York: St. Martin's Press, 1981.

SPRAGENS, WILLIAM C. WITH CAROLE ANN TERWOORD, *From Spokesman to Press Secretary: White House Media Operations.* Lanham, Md.: University Press of America, 1980.

SPROUT, HAROLD AND MARGARET, *The Context of Environmental Politics: Unfinished Business for America's Third Century.* Lexington: University Press of Kentucky, 1978.

————, *the Ecological Perspective on Human Affairs with Special Reference to International Politics.* Princeton, N.J.: Princeton University Press, 1965.

SPYKMAN, NICHOLAS, J., *American Strategy in World Politics: The United States and the Balance of Power.* New York: Harcourt, Brace and Company, 1942.

STEEL, RONALD, *Walter Lippmann and the American Century.* Boston: Little, Brown & Company, 1980.

STEINBRUNER, JOHN D., *The Cybernetic Theory of Decision.* Princeton, N.J.: Princeton University Press, 1974.

STERLING, RICHARD W., *Macropolitics: International Relations in a Global Society.* New York: Alfred A. Knopf, 1974.

STIMSON, HENRY L., AND MCGEORGE BUNDY, *On Active Service in Peace and War.* New York: Harper and Brothers, 1947.

STOESSINGER, JOHN, *Crusaders and Pragmatists: Movers of Modern American Foreign Policy.* New York: W. W. Norton & Company, 1973.

————, *Why Nations Go to War.* New York: St. Martin's Press, 1974.

STRAUSZ-HUPE, ROBERT, WILLIAM R. KINTNER, JAMES E. DOUGHERTY, AND ALVIN J. COTTRELL, *Protracted Conflict.* New York: Harper and Brothers, 1959.

SWANBERG, W. A., *Citizen Hearst: A Biography of William Randolph Hearst.* New York: Charles Scribner's Sons, 1961.

THOMPSON, KENNETH W., ed., *Ten Presidents and the Press.* Washington, D.C.: University Press of America, 1980.

TRUMAN, MARGARET, *Harry S. Truman.* New York: Pocket Books, 1974.

ULAM, ADAM B., *Expansion and Coexistence: Soviet Foreign Policy 1917–73,* 2nd ed. New York: Praeger Publishers, 1974.

VANCE, CYRUS, *Hard Choices: Critical Years in America's Foreign Policy.* New York: Simon & Schuster, 1983.

VERNON, RAYMOND, *Sovereignty at Bay.* New York: Basic Books, 1971.

VOGLER, DAVID J., *The Politics of Congress,* 4th ed. Boston: Allyn & Bacon, 1983.

WALLBANK, T. WALTER, AND ALASTAIR M. TAYLOR, *Civilization Past and Present.* Glenview, Ill.: Scott, Foresman and Company, 1949.

WALTZ, KENNETH N., *Theory of International Politics.* Reading, Mass.: Addison-Wesley Publishing Co., 1979.

WHITE ELLIOT, ed., *Sociobiology and Human Politics.* Lexington, Mass.: Lexington Books, 1981.

WHITE, RALPH K., *Nobody Wanted War: Misperception in Vietnam and Other Wars.* New York: Doubleday & Company, 1970.

WILLIAMS, WILLIAM APPLEMAN, *The Tragedy of American Diplomacy,* 2nd ed. New York: Delta, 1972.

WILSON, EDWARD, *Sociobiology: The New Synthesis.* Cambridge, Mass.: Belknap Press of Harvard University Press, 1975.

WOLL, PETER, *Constitutional Law.* Englewood Cliffs, N.J.: Prentice-Hall, 1982.

WOODWARD, BOB, AND SCOTT ARMSTRONG, *The Brethren.* New York: Avon Books, 1979.

WRIGHT, QUINCY, *The Study of War,* 2nd ed. Chicago: University of Chicago Press, 1965.

YERGIN, DANIEL, *Shattered Peace: The Origins of the Cold War and the National Security State.* Boston: Houghton Mifflin Company, 1978.

ARTICLES

Books/Periodicals

ART, ROBERT J., AND KENNETH N. WALTZ,   "Technology, Strategy, and the Use of Force," in Robert J. Art and Kenneth N. Waltz, *The Use of Force.* Boston: Little, Brown & Company, 1971, pp. 1–25.

BLUM, ROBERT,   "Introduction: The Flow of People and Ideas," in Robert Blum, ed., *Cultural Affairs and Foreign Relations.* Englewood Cliffs, N.J.: Prentice-Hall, 1963, pp. 1–7.

BRONFENBRENNER, URI,   "The Mirror-Image in Soviet-American Relations," *Journal of Social Issues* 17 (1961), 45–56.

COHEN, BENJAMIN J.,   "An Explosion in the Kitchen? Economic Relations with Other Advanced Industrial States," in Kenneth Oye et al., *Eagle Defiant: United States Foreign Policy in the 1980s.* Boston: Little, Brown & Company, 1983, pp. 105–30.

COHEN, BERNARD C.,   "The Influence of Special Interests Groups and Mass Media on Security Policy in the United States," in Charles W. Kegley and Eugene R. Wittkopf, *Perspectives on American Foreign Policy.* New York: St. Martin's Press, 1983, pp. 222–41.

COOMBS, PHILIP,   "The Past and Future in Perspective," in Robert Blum, ed., *Cultural Affairs and Foreign Relations.* Englewood Cliffs, N.J.: Prentice-Hall, 1963, pp. 139–71.

COOPER, RICHARD,   "Economic Interdependence and Foreign Policy in the Seventies," *World Politics* 24 (January 1972), 159–81.

CRONIN, THOMAS E.,   "A Resurgent Congress and the Imperial Presidency," in Charles W. Kegley and Eugene R. Wittkopf, *Perspectives on American Foreign Policy.* New York: St. Martin's Press, 1983, pp. 320–45.

DAHL, ROBERT A.,   "A Critique of the Ruling Elite Model," *American Political Science Review,* June 1958, pp. 463–69.

————,   "The Concept of Power," *Behavioral Science* 2 (1957), 201–15.

DALLIN, ALEXANDER, AND GAIL W. LAPIDUS,   "Reagan and the Russians: United States Policy Toward the Soviet Union and Eastern Europe," in Kenneth A. Oye et al., *Eagle Defiant: United States Foreign Policy in the 1980s.* Boston: Little, Brown & Company, 1983, pp. 191–236.

DESTLER, I. M.,   "The Rise of the National Security Assistant 1961–81," in Charles W. Kegley and Eugene R. Wittkopf, *Perspectives on American Foreign Policy.* New York: St. Martin's Press, 1983, pp. 260–80.

DEUTSCH, KARL W., AND J. DAVID SINGER,   "Multipolar Power Systems and International Stability," *World Politics* 16 (1964), 390–406.

DULL, JAMES W.,   "Philippine Politics and American Strategy in the 1980s," seminar paper, delivered at U.S. Naval War College, Newport, R.I., October, 1982.

EAST, MAURICE, AND CHARLES HERMANN,   "Do Nation-Types Account for Foreign Policy Behavior?" in James Rosenau, ed., *Comparing Foreign Policies.* New York: Sage/Halstead Press, 1974, pp.

EPSTEIN, EDWARD JAY,   "The Selection of Reality," in Elie Abel, ed., *Whats News: The Media in American Society.* San Francisco: Institute for Contemporary Studies, 1981, pp. 119–32.

ETHERIDGE, LLOYD,   "Personality and Foreign Policy: Bullies in the State Department," *Psychology Today,* March 1975, p. 38.

GLADSTONE, ARTHUR,   "The Concept of the Enemy," *Journal of Conflict Resolution* 3 (1959), 132–37.

HERMANN, MARGARET G., "Leader Personality and Foreign Policy Behavior," in James Rosenau, ed., *Comparing Foreign Policies.* New York: Sage/Halstead Press, 1974, pp. 201–33.

HOLSTI, OLE, "The Belief System and National Images: A Case Study," *Journal of Conflict Resolution* 6 (1962), 244–52.

JANOWITZ, MORRIS, "Organizing Multiple Goals: War Making and Arms Control," in Morris Janowitz, ed., *The New Military: Changing Patterns of Organization.* New York: Russell Sage Foundation, 1964, pp. 9–37.

KARL, PATRICIA A., "Media Diplomacy," in Gerald Benjamin, ed., *The Communications Revolution in Politics.* New York: Academy of Political Science, 1982, pp. 143–52.

KEOHANE, ROBERT O., AND JOSEPH S. NYE, "Transnational Relations: An Introduction," in Robert O. Keohane and Joseph S. Nye, eds., *Transnational Relations and World Politics.* Cambridge, Mass.: Harvard University Press, 1972, pp. ix–xxix.

LANDE, CARL, "Authoritarian Rule in the Philippines: Some Critical Views," *Pacific Affairs* 55 (1982), 80–93.

LANG, KURT, "Technology and Career Management," in Morris Janowitz, ed., *The New Military: Changing Patterns of Organization.* New York: Russell Sage Foundation, 1964, pp. 39–81.

LINDBLOM, CHARLES, "The Science of Muddling Through," *Public Administration Review* 19 (spring 1959), 79–88.

LOWENTHAL, ABRAHAM F., "Ronald Reagan and Latin America: Coping With Hegemony in Decline," in Kenneth A. Oye et al., *Eagle Defiant: United States Foreign Policy in the 1980s.* Boston: Little, Brown & Company, 1983, pp. 311–35.

MONGAR, THOMAS M., "Personality and Decision-Making: John F. Kennedy in Four Crisis Decisions," in Gordon DiRenzo, ed. *Personality and Politics,* Garden City, N.Y.: Doubleday-Anchor, 1973, pp. 334–72.

NATIONS, RICHARD, "New U.S. Defense Role for Japan and ASEAN," *Far Eastern Economic Review,* June 18–24, 1982, pp. 10–11.

NEHER, CLARK, "The Philippines in the 1980s: The Gathering Storm,"*Asian Survey* xxi (February 1981), 261–73.

NOGEE, JOSEPH, "Congress and the Presidency: The Dilemmas of Policy-Making in a Democracy," in John Spanier and Joseph L. Nogee, *Congress, the Presidency and American Foreign Policy.* New York: Pergamon Press, 1981, pp. 189–200.

OSGOOD, ROBERT, "The Expansion of Force," in Robert J. Art and Kenneth N. Waltz, eds., *The Use of Force.* Boston: Little, Brown & Company, 1971, pp. 29–55.

PILLER, GEOFFREY, "DOD's Office of International Security Affairs: The Brief Ascendancy of an Advising System," *Political Science Quarterly,* spring 1983, pp. 59–78.

RANSOM, HARRY HOWE, "Strategic Intelligence and Intermestic Politics," in Charles W. Kegley and Eugene R. Wittkopf, *Perspectives on American Foreign Policy.* New York: St. Martin's Press, 1983, pp. 298–319.

RIDING, ALLAN, "The Central American Quagmire," *Foreign Affairs* 61 (1983), 641–59.

ROBINSON, MICHAEL J., AND KEVIN R. APPEL, "Network News Coverage of Congress," *Political Science Quarterly,* fall 1979, pp. 409–15.

ROSENAU, JAMES, "Pre-Theories and Theories of Foreign Policy," in R. Barry Farrell, ed., *Approaches to Comparative and International Politics.* Evanston, Ill.: Northwestern University Press, 1966, pp. 27–92.

————, "The Premises and Promises of Decision-Making Analysis," in James C. Charlesworth, ed., *Contemporary Political Analysis*. New York: Free Press, 1967, pp. 189–211.

————, "The Study of Foreign Policy," in James Rosenau et al., eds., *World Politics: An Introduction*. New York: Free Press, 1976, pp. 15–35.

ROSENCRANCE, RICHARD, "Bipolarity, Multipolarity, and the Future,"*Journal of Conflict Resolution* 10 (1966), pp. 314–27.

ROTHCHILD, DONALD, AND JOHN RAVENHILL, "From Carter to Reagan: The Global Perspective on Africa Becomes Ascendant," in Kenneth A. Oye et al., eds., *Eagle Defiant: United States Foreign Policy in the 1980s*. Boston: Little, Brown & Company, 1983, pp. 337–65.

RUBIN, BARRY, "The Reagan Administration and the Middle East," in Kenneth A. Oye et al., eds., *Eagle Defiant: United States Foreign Policy in the 1980s*. Boston: Little, Brown & Company, 1983, pp. 367–89.

RUMMEL, RUDOLPH, "The Relation Between National Attributes and Foreign Conflict Behavior," in J. David Singer, *Quantitative International Politics: Insights and Evidence*. New York: Free Press, 1968, pp. 187–214.

SANDMAN, JOSHUA, "A Prescriptive Model for Handling Nuclear Age Crisis in the Executive Office," *Presidential Studies Quarterly* 13 (winter 1983), pp. 121–28.

SCHAMBRA, WILLIAM, "More Buck for the Bang: New Public Attitudes Toward Foreign Policy," *Public Opinion*, January/February 1973, pp. 47–48.

SCHUSTER, GEORGE N., "The Nature and Development of United States Cultural Relations," in Paul J. Braisted, ed., *Cultural Affairs and Foreign Relations*. Washington, D.C.: Columbia Books, Publishers, 1968, pp. 1–44.

SINGER, J. DAVID, AND MELVIN SMALL, "Alliance Aggregation and the Onset of War, 1815–1845," in J. David Singer, ed., *Quantitative International Politics: Insights and Evidence*. New York: Free Press, 1968, pp. 247–86.

SMALL, MELVIN, AND J. DAVID SINGER, "The Diplomatic Importance of States, 1816–1970: An Extension and Refinement of the Indicator," *World Politics* 25 (1973), 577–99.

SNYDER, GLEN, "Deterrence and Defense," in Robert J. Art and Kenneth N. Watlz, eds., *The Use of Force*. Boston: Little, Brown & Company, 1971, pp. 56–76.

STARR, HARVEY, "The Kissinger Years: Studying Individuals and Foreign Policy," *International Studies Quarterly* 24 (December 1980), 465–95.

TANTER, RAYMOND, "Dimensions of Conflict Behavior Within and Between Nations, 1958–60," *Journal of Conflict Resolution* 10 (1966), 41–64.

THOMPSON, KENNETH W., "Beyond the Present," in Paul J. Braisted, ed., *Cultural Affairs and Foreign Relations*. Washington, D.C.: Columbia Books, Publishers, 1968, pp. 172–202.

TRAVERS, ROBERT, "Sociobiology and Politics," in Elliot White, ed., *Sociobiology and Human Politics*. Cambridge, Mass.: Lexington Books, 1981, pp. 1–43.

WILKENFELD, JONATHAN, "Domestic and Foreign Conflict Behavior of Nations," *Journal of Peace Research* 1 (1961), 56–69.

ZINNES, DINA, AND JONATHAN WILKENFELD, "'n Analysis of Foreign Conflict Behavior," in Wolfram Hanreider, ed., *Comparative Foreign Policy: Theoretical Essays*. New York: David McKay Co., 1971, pp. 167–213.

ARTICLES

NEW YORK TIMES

AYRES, B. DRUMMOND, "A New Breed of Diplomat," *Magazine*, September 18, 1983, p. 66.

BARNET, RICHARD, "Needed: A New Written Political Strategy," November 29, 1983, p. 31.

BEECHER, WILLIAM, "Foreign Policy: Pentagon Also Suffering Rebuffs," January 21, 1971, p. 1.

BENNETT, ROBERT A., "Stock Prices Fall Sharply Abroad, but New York Shows Strong Rally," September 29, 1981, p. 1.

BRZEZINSKI, ZBIGNIEW, "Deciding Who Makes Foreign Policy," *Magazine*, September 18, 1983, p. 56.

BURNHAM, DAVID, "The Silent Power of the N.S.A.," *Magazine*, March 23, 1983, p. 60.

BURNS, JOHN F., "Grain Pact Signed: U.S. Assures Soviet of Steady Supply," August 26, 1983, p. 1.

————, "Moscow Will Try Again to Widen the Powers of Factory Managers," August 6, 1983, p. 1.

FARNSWORTH, CLYDE H., "Trade Department Plan Issued by Reagan," June 2, 1983, p. D6.

————, "U.S. Lifts Its Curbs on Sale to Soviet of Pipeline Gear," August 21, 1983, p. 1.

————, "Wealthy Nations Agree to More Aid for Poorer Lands," September 5, 1982, p. 1.

FEDER, BARNABY, "The World Banking Crisis, Phase Two," March 27, 1983, p. F1.

FREEDMAN, SAMUEL G., "Local Disputes with Foreign Missions Call for Diplomacy," January 23, 1983, p. E7.

FRIEDMAN, THOMAS L., "West Bank Puts Disputes Aside to Rally to Arafat," July 31, 1983, p. 3.

FUERBRINGER, JONATHAN, "IMF Bill Advances in House," July 30, 1983, p. 33.

GARGAN, EDWARD A., "Chinese Says Taiwan Is Still Main Issue," September 27, 1983, p. 3.

GELB, LESLIE, "As Bargaining Chip, MX May Be No Bargain for the Soviets," April 24, 1983, p. 4:1.

————, "Poll Finds Doubt on U.S. Strategy on the Russians," April 15, 1983, p. 1.

————, "Shultz, Pushing A Hard Line, Becomes A Key Voice In Crisis," November 7, 1983, p. 1.

GILPIN, KENNETH N., "Parts of IMF Bill Assailed," August 6, 1983, p. 43.

————, "Talking Business: Third World's Debt Burden," July 19, 1983, p. D2.

"Glen Cove Affair," May 22, 1983, p. 4.

GLYNN, LEONARD M., "Have Currencies Floated Too Long?" May 8, 1983, p. F1.

GREENHOUSE, LINDA, "Supreme Court, 7–2, Restricts Congress' Right to Overrule Action by Executive Branch," June 24, 1983, p. 1.

GROO, ANNE SOMMES, "Radio Free Europe From Connecticut, "September 11, 1983, Conn. Sec., pp. 4–5.

GWERTZMAN, BERNARD, "Damascus Appears to Rebuff Shultz on Pullout Plan," May 8, 1983, p. 1.

————, "Habib Replaced as U.S. Envoy to Middle East," July 23, 1983, p. 1.

————, "Under Shultz, A Shift to a Less Personalized Role," October 28, 1982, p. B12.

————, "U.S. Sees Chad as a Protest of Qaddafi's Ambition," August 19, 1983, p. 1.

HALLORAN, RICHARD, "Chief of Army Assails Industry on Arms Flaws,"August 9, 1983, p. 1.

————, "Reagan Extending Trident Program," February 6, 1983, p. 17.

"Hard Sell: Closing Windows, Opening Doors on Missile Debates," April 24, 1983, p. 4:1.

HEINEMANN, H. ERICH,   "Dollar High Despite Support," August 6, 1983, p. 33.
————, "Trying to Avoid Another Versailles," May 15, 1983, p. F1.
"House Approves Overriding Reagan's Veto on Spending," September 10, 1982, p. 1.
HOWE, MARVINE,   "Papandreou Renewing Greece's Ties to West," August 21, 1983, p. 7.
KAMM, HENRY,   "In Perpetual Political Standoff, Italy Elects a 44th Government," June 26, 1983, p. 4:3.
KILBORN, PETER T.,   "The Testing of Martin Feldstein," September 18, 1983, p. F1.
KING, SETH S.,   "July Jobless Rate Dropped to 9.5% in a Rapid Decline, August 6, 1983, p. 1.
"Lending Restrictions on IMF Legislation," August 6, 1983, p. 43.
LUSINCHI, VICTOR,   "U.S.-Soviet Arms Talks Adjourn," August 5, 1983, p. 2.
"Major Laws with Veto Provisions," June 24, 1983, p. B5.
"Marcos Gets Boost in Washington," September 19, 1982, p. E2.
"Marcos to Get $900 Million in Accord on Bases," June 8, 1983, p. 6.
MARCUS, STEVEN J.,   "Corporate Push for Space Lasers," April 24, 1983, p. F4.
MILLER, JUDITH,   "New Generation of Nuclear Arms with Controlled Effects Foreseen," October 27, 1982, p. 1.
"Missile Stopped by Laser Ray," July 27, 1983, p. 11.
NOSSITER, BERNARD D.,   "Sea Law Signed by 117 Nations: U.S. Opposes It," December 11, 1982, p. 1.
————, "What's the Bottom Line on World Debt?" May 15, 1983, p. E3.
"1,900 U.S. Troops, with Caribbean Allies, Invade Grenada and Fight with Leftist Units," October 27, 1983, p. 1.
"Pentagon Analyst Proposing a Submersible Navy," September 11, 1983, p. 32.
"President's Speech on Military Spending and a New Defense," March 24, 1983, p. 20.
"Reagan Is Replacing Top Official on Latin Policy at the State Department," May 28, 1983, p. 1.
"Reagan Orders Refugees Halted on High Seas," September 30, 1981, p. 1.
ROBERTS, STEVEN V.,   "Congress Adopts Measures Allowing Marines in Beirut," September 20, 1983, p. 1.
————, "Vote on Aid Cut-Off: A House Divided and Confused," July 30, 1983, p. D3.
SALMANS, SANDRA,   "CBS-China TV Pact Announced," June 1, 1983, p. D20.
SCHMIDT, WILLIAM E.,   "Poll Shows Lessening of Fear That U.S. Military Is Lagging," February 6, 1983, p. 1.
SHABECOFF, PHILIP,   "EPA Report Says Earth Will Heat Up Beginning in 1990's," October 18, 1983, p. 1.
SHAPLEY, DEBORAH,   "The Army's New Fighting Doctrine," *Magazine*, November 28, 1982, p. 36.
SILK, LEONARD,   "American Plan for the IMF," September 3, 1982, p. D2.
————, "Avalanche of Debt Threatens Global Economy," September 12, 1983, p. E3.
SMITH, HEDRICK,   "Would a Space-Age Defense Ease Tensions or Create Them?" March 27, 1983, p. 4:1.
"Strategic Nuclear Arms: Where Each Side Stands," June 8, 1983, p. 12.
TAUBMAN, PHILIP,   "Shultz, in Manila, Affirms Support of U.S. For Marcos," June 26, 1983, p. 1.
TOLCHIN, MARTIN,   "House Bars Cut in Funds to MX and B-1 Plane," November 2, 1983, p. 1.

WEISMAN, STEVEN R., "Reagan Denies Aim Is Bigger Presence in Latin Countries," May 28, 1983, p. 1.

————, "Reagan Proposes U.S. Seek New Way to Block Missiles," March 24, 1983, p. 1.

————, "Reagan Says Plan on Missile Defense Will Prevent War," March 26, 1983, p. 1.

WHITE, THEODORE H., "Weinberger on the Ramparts," *Magazine*, February 6, 1983, p. 14.

"World's People Total 4.7 Billion," September 4, 1983, p. 9.

WREN, CHRISTOPHER S., "Weinberger Hopeful on Arms for China," September 29, 1983, p. 3.

INDEX